THE NEW DEAL
AND THE PROBLEM
OF MONOPOLY

THE

NEW DEAL

AND THE PROBLEM

OF MONOPOLY

A STUDY IN ECONOMIC AMBIVALENCE

ELLIS W. HAWLEY

PRINCETON, NEW JERSEY

PRINCETON UNIVERSITY PRESS

1966

and does not attempt to deal in any detail with agricultural, labor, or financial policies.

My chief debt is to the late Howard K. Beale of the University of Wisconsin, under whose direction this study was originally undertaken. His suggestions, criticisms, and support were invaluable. In addition, I should like to express my gratitude to the following: Professor Robert A. Lively, whose stimulating teaching provided many insights and suggested the topic of research; Professor Paul F. Sharp, for his criticisms, suggestions, and encouragement on portions of the study; and Professor James C. Malin, who first aroused my interest in this general subject. I am also deeply indebted to a number of devoted and competent librarians and archivists, particularly to Meyer H. Fishbein and his assistants at the National Archives, to Herman Kahn and his staff at the Roosevelt Memorial Library, and to Gene M. Gressley and his staff at the University of Wyoming.

ELLIS W. HAWLEY

North Texas State University

CONTENTS

CONTENTS

PART IV · NEW DEAL POLICY AND THE RECESSION OF 1937

To the Memory of
Howard K. Beale

PREFACE

ONE of the central problems of twentieth-century America has revolved about the difficulty of reconciling a modern industrial order, necessarily based upon a high degree of collective organization, with democratic postulates, competitive ideals, and liberal individualistic traditions inherited from the nineteenth century. This industrial order has created in America a vision of material abundance, a dream of abolishing poverty and achieving economic security for all; and the great majority of Americans have not been willing to destroy it lest that dream be lost. Yet at the same time it has involved, probably necessarily, a concentration of economic power, a development of monopolistic arrangements, and a loss of individual freedom and initiative, all of which run counter to inherited traditions and ideals. Americans, moreover, have never really decided what to do about this industrial order. Periodically they have debated the merits of "regulated competition" and "regulated monopoly," of trustbusting and economic planning; and periodically they have embarked upon reform programs that would remake the economic system. Yet the resulting reforms have been inconsistent and contradictory. Policies that would promote competition have been interspersed with those that would limit or destroy it. And American economists as a whole have never reached any real consensus in regard to the origins and nature of monopoly, its effects, or the methods of dealing with it.

During the period covered by this study, the six-year span from 1933 to 1939, this conflict over economic policy was particularly acute. The industrial machine, for all its productivity, was seemingly unable to fulfill the dream of abundance and security, and its failure to do so led to demands for political action. Yet there was little agreement on the course that this action should take. Did the situation call for centralized planning and detailed regulation? Did it call for a restoration of competition? Or did it call for government-sponsored cartels that could rationalize the competitive process and weather deflationary forces? In practice, there were a variety of pressures and forces pushing the government in all of these directions. The result was an amalgam of conflicting policies and programs, one that might make some sense to the politician, but little to a rational economist.

Historians, of course, have long been aware of these conflicting crosscurrents in the New Deal's business policies. Arthur M. Schlesinger, Jr., for example, has dealt extensively with the conflict between the economic planners and the neo-Brandeisians, and Eric Goldman, in his *Rendezvous with Destiny*, described the New Deal as an amalgam of the New Nationalism, the New Freedom, and the Associational Activities of the nineteen twenties. So far as I know, however, no one has yet focused upon this conflict as a central theme or attempted to trace out, describe, and analyze its implications in detail.

The present study makes an effort to fill this gap. It attempts, first of all, to trace the pattern of conflict and compromise between various schools of thought, between those which desired a type of rationalized, government-sponsored business commonwealth, those that hoped to restore and preserve a competitive system, and those that envisioned a form of democratic collectivism in which the monopoly power of businessmen would be transferred to the state or to other economic groups. Secondly, it attempts to relate these various schools of thought to the interplay of pressure groups and popular symbols, to trace the major shifts and innovations in policy, and to explain these policy changes. Throughout the study, in fact, the emphasis is on policy-making, on the men, beliefs, pressures, and symbols that resulted in policy decisions, not on the validity or economic merit of the policies involved. The study is also limited primarily to the field of business and does not attempt to deal in any detail with agricultural, labor, or financial policies.

My chief debt is to the late Howard K. Beale of the University of Wisconsin, under whose direction this study was originally undertaken. His suggestions, criticisms, and support were invaluable. In addition, I should like to express my gratitude to the following: Professor Robert A. Lively, whose stimulating teaching provided many insights and suggested the topic of research; Professor Paul F. Sharp, for his criticisms, suggestions, and encouragement on portions of the study; and Professor James C. Malin, who first aroused my interest in this general subject. I am also deeply indebted to a number of devoted and competent librarians and archivists, particularly to Meyer H. Fishbein and his assistants at the National Archives, to Herman Kahn and his staff at the Roosevelt Memorial Library, and to Gene M. Gressley and his staff at the University of Wyoming.

ELLIS W. HAWLEY

North Texas State University

CONTENTS

PART IV · NEW DEAL POLICY AND THE RECESSION OF 1937

ABBREVIATIONS

In addition to standard abbreviations, the following are used throughout:

AAA–Agricultural Adjustment Administration
AC–Advisory Council (NRA)
AEA–American Economic Association
AER–American Economic Review
AHR–American Historical Review
Annals Am. Acad.–Annals of the American Academy of
   Political and Social Science
BAC–Business Advisory Council
BAPC–Business Advisory and Planning Council
CAB–Consumers' Advisory Board (NRA)
CAF–Consolidated Administrative File (NRA Records)
CCF–Central Correspondence File (NRPB Records)
CCH–Commerce Clearing House
CGF–Classified General File (NRA Records)
CHF–Code Histories File (NRA Records)
CIA–Committee of Industrial Analysis
CIC–Coordinator for Industrial Cooperation
CIP–Council for Industrial Progress
CTS–Consolidated Typescript Studies (NRA Records)
DIE–Division of Industrial Economics
FDR–Franklin D. Roosevelt
FPC–Federal Power Commission
FTC–Federal Trade Commission
GPO–Government Printing Office
IAB–Industrial Advisory Board (NRA)
ICC–Interstate Commerce Commission
LAB–Labor Advisory Board (NRA)
MR&D–Miscellaneous Records and Documents (NRA
   Records)
MVHR–Mississippi Valley Historical Review
NAM–National Association of Manufacturers
NBCC–National Bituminous Coal Commission

NEC–National Emergency Council
NIRA–National Industrial Recovery Act
NIRB–National Industrial Recovery Board
NPB–National Planning Board
NPPC–National Power Policy Committee
NRA–National Recovery Administration
NRB–National Resources Board
NRC–National Resources Committee
NRPB–National Resources Planning Board
NRRB–National Recovery Review Board
OF–Official File(s) (Roosevelt Papers)
PPF–President's Personal File(s) (Roosevelt Papers)
PR–Press Release
PSF–President's Secretary's File (Roosevelt Papers)
PWA–Public Works Administration
QJE–Quarterly Journal of Economics
R&P Div.–Research and Planning Division (NRA)
SEC–Securities and Exchange Commission
SIRB–Special Industrial Recovery Board
SR&P–Special Research and Planning Reports (NRA
   Records)
TNEC–Temporary National Economic Committee
TVA–Tennessee Valley Authority
WPA–Works Progress Administration

NOTE ON SOURCES

In order to avoid an excessively large number of notes, I have followed the practice of collecting the references necessary for a particular passage in a single note at the end of the passage. The full citation to each title is given on the first mention in each chapter. Of the manuscript and archival collections cited, the Franklin D. Roosevelt and Harry L. Hopkins papers are in the Roosevelt Library at Hyde Park, New York; the Harold L. Ickes and William Borah papers are in the Library of Congress; the Thurman W. Arnold and Joseph C. O'Mahoney papers are in the University of Wyoming Library at Laramie, Wyoming; and the records of the National Recovery Administration, the Temporary National Economic Committee, the National Resources Planning Board, the National Emergency Council, the National Bituminous Coal Commission, the National Power Policy Committee, and the Works Progress Administration are in the National Archives. Special mention should also be made of two collections of source materials on the NRA. One is the Division of Industrial Economics' Staff Studies (cited as DIE, Staff Studies) available in mimeographed form at the National Archives. The other is the NRA Work Materials, which were mimeographed and distributed to depositories of government documents in 1935 and 1936.

THE NEW DEAL
AND THE PROBLEM
OF MONOPOLY

INTRODUCTION. THE PROBLEM
AND ITS SETTING

THE term "monopoly," as commonly used in American parlance, has a variety of meanings and connotations. To the man in the street it usually carries an implication of evil and appears as a vague synonym for such emotionally charged concepts as "big business," the "interests," or the "trusts." To lawyers and academic economists its meaning is far from precise. Some use the word in its generic sense to mean a condition where a single seller controls the entire supply of a "commodity," a term that is itself hard to define. Some use it to designate a situation in which a seller dominates an industry and enjoys protection against potential competition from the outside. Some use it to describe almost any deviation from the abstract model of pure and perfect competition. Some, probably a majority, use it as a synonym for market power, for the ability of a seller or group of sellers acting in concert to control or influence the price and output of what they have for sale.

Charges of "monopoly," then, almost always need further clarification; and the same holds true of any discussion of the "monopoly problem," a term that has also been employed in a variety of ways and with a variety of different meanings. Some have used it to describe the classic evils of monopoly, the alleged tendency, in other words, of market controls to result in economic inefficiency, misallocation of resources, technical stagnation, and the exploitation of unorganized groups. Others have used it as a convenient synonym for the whole gamut of business-government relations. Still others have associated it with the general effects of industrialization and urbanization, with the increasing impersonality of corporate relationships, the decline of a self-employed middle class, the growth of absentee controls, the lack of a corporate moral code, or some other aspect of the general shift from an agrarian to an industrial society.

For the most part, however, those who have used the term have been concerned with questions of power, with the development, in particular, of private concentrations of economic power and with the implications of this development for a democratic society. The "problem," when viewed from this angle, has been one of democratizing "big business," of finding some way to reconcile the tightly organized, stratified, and authoritarian institutions of modern industrialism with the democratic, individualistic, and libertarian ideals of an earlier era. And the hope has been that some "solution" could be found, that Americans could discover some formula that would enable them to enjoy the material benefits of industrialization and economic planning without sacrificing the democratic goals that they had inherited from the past.[1]

It is in this latter sense that the present study deals with the "problem of monopoly"; and in this sense, the problem has been common to most of Western civilization. As Gustav Stolper once noted, "The trend of modern industrialism has been determined in all countries by two conflicting tendencies: the one toward liberation of the individual from ties and codes inherited from the Middle Ages and the mercantilistic era; the other toward integration on a more or less monopolistic basis." [2] In the United States, a land that had long cherished its frontier tradi-

---

[1] The various meanings attached to "monopoly" and the "monopoly problem" are discussed in Clair Wilcox, *Competition and Monopoly in American Industry* (TNEC Monograph 21, 1940), 9–11; Fritz Machlup, *The Political Economy of Monopoly* (Baltimore: Johns Hopkins Press, 1952), 3–45; John P. Miller, in Earl Latham, ed., *The Philosophy and Policies of Woodrow Wilson* (Chicago: U. of Chicago Press, 1958), 134–36; and Mark S. Massel, *Competition and Monopoly* (Washington: Brookings, 1962), 186–91, 337–39.

[2] Gustav Stolper, *German Economy* (N.Y.: Reynal & Hitchcock, 1940), 83.

tions and democratic postulates, the rise of giant business combinations presented this clash of values in a particularly acute form. Yet curiously, the efforts to do something about it made little progress during the initial stages of industrialization. Material conditions, after all, were better in America than in Europe, and even if they had not been, the ideological climate and power structure made political action difficult. The critics, generally speaking, were lacking in political strength and cohesion. Their long devotion to a philosophy of laissez faire, local rights, and individual liberty made them reluctant to use the federal government as a positive instrument of reform. Even those who favored governmental intervention tended to think in terms of some simple, usually impractical solution, some master coup that would restore the economic and social system to the pristine purity of the pre-industrial era.

The lack of political action was also due in part to the wide appeal of ideological doctrines that justified the status quo and masked the gap between ideal and reality. In the language of contemporary lawyers, politicians, and scholars the giant corporations of the late nineteenth century became "individuals" and the new corporate system became the desirable end product of "rugged individualism" and "free enterprise." Opportunity, so the defenders of the system argued, was still open. Competition, actual or potential, still protected the public and stimulated economic expansion; and even if social evils did exist, nothing could be done about them, at least not in the short run. Human society, like the animal kingdom, was a product of the "survival of the fittest." Poverty was the result of immorality, shiftlessness, and fundamental defects in character. Any interference with "natural law" was bound to penalize the industrious, produce an inferior society, and make things worse instead of better.

In view of these political and ideological obstacles, it is

not surprising that the early attempts to deal with the "monopoly problem" enjoyed little success. Prior to 1900, in spite of considerable agitation on the part of the populists and other protest groups, the only federal measures of any consequence were the Interstate Commerce and Sherman Antitrust Acts, neither of which proved very effective in practice. The Interstate Commerce Commission, in fact, found it virtually impossible to win a case in the federal courts. And the Sherman Act, while it forbade all monopolies and all attempts to monopolize, was laxly enforced, narrowly interpreted, and effective only against loose combines, not against such tight combinations as holding companies and mergers. Ironically, the great era of business consolidation, the years from 1897 to 1904, came after the Sherman Act and not before.[3]

It was not until the progressive era in the early twentieth century that major changes in the political and ideological climate began to take place. Then gradually, as economic independence declined and new and larger consolidations appeared, more and more middle-class Americans became convinced that the new industrial and financial empires amounted to a gross perversion of the American dream. They were increasingly dubious, moreover, about the doctrines of laissez faire and Social Darwinism. Man, so they were told by a new generation of intellectuals, could shape his own destiny. He could reform and improve his social and economic institutions, and the place to start was with the "trusts" and the social evils for which they were responsible. When it came to formulating a program, how-

[3] See Samuel P. Hays, *The Response to Industrialism* (Chicago: U. of Chicago Press, 1957), 24–47; Richard Hofstadter, *Social Darwinism in American Thought* (Boston: Beacon Press, 1955 ed.), 44–50, 201; Hans B. Thorelli, *The Federal Antitrust Policy* (Baltimore: Johns Hopkins Press, 1955), 66–85, 109–17, 143–59, 221–32, 254–72, 306–11, 343–58, 371–410, 560–72; Edward C. Kirkland, *Industry Comes of Age* (N.Y.: Rinehart & Winston, 1961), 126–36, 310–24.

ever, there was little agreement. Some reformers, impressed by the productivity of the new corporate institutions, would keep them and then rely upon a strong central government to achieve a more equitable, more humane, and more democratic system. Others, still wary of governmental intervention, hoped that business could reform itself or that non-business groups could develop their own market power. Still others, intent upon returning to a decentralized and automatic economy, favored a program that would limit size, penalize bigness, break up the "trusts," remove the unfair advantages of big business, and enforce competitive behavior.

This divergence in reform philosophies was particularly apparent in 1912 in the clash between Woodrow Wilson's New Freedom and Theodore Roosevelt's New Nationalism. As Louis Brandeis and other advocates of the New Freedom saw it, the "trusts" had grown strong because they enjoyed special privileges or because they used unfair practices to crush their rivals, not because of their greater efficiency or productivity. And the solution was to remove these causes of "monopoly," wipe out special privileges, liberate the credit system from Wall Street control, and pass new legislation that would eliminate unfair practices and restore the reign of free competition. In the New Nationalist view, on the other hand, concentration of economic power was the inevitable result of mass production and an advancing technology. In many areas, competition resulted in a gross waste of natural resources, human life, and human energy. And the real solution was to forget about competition and concentrate upon developing national controls, upon establishing a government that could protect underprivileged groups, engage in purposeful planning, supervise the big corporations, and insure that the benefits of modern industrialism were more evenly distributed. The government, so the New Nationalists insisted, could be used to democratize big business. Jeffersonian ends could be achieved through Hamiltonian means.[4]

Some aspects of the New Nationalism also appealed to business leaders. Industrialists like George Perkins and Frank Munsey, for example, would agree that large corporations were both desirable and inevitable, that excessive competition was mainly responsible for child labor, sweatshop conditions, and other social problems, and that the situation called for some type of regulation and planning. They had their own views, however, about the nature, degree, and type of regulation. Enlightened businessmen, they insisted, were developing a social conscience, a growing awareness of social problems and the need for remedial action; and since these people knew more about the business system than anyone else, business groups should be allowed to govern and discipline themselves with a minimum of government supervision. Along the same line, too, were the theories of the "new competition" expounded by Arthur Jerome Eddy or the idea of government-approved business agreements sponsored by a number of business organizations. Gradually, from these various sources, a third approach to the "monopoly problem" took shape, one that would repeal the Sherman Act, encourage business organization, and allow self-governing

[4] See Hays, *Response to Industrialism*, 73–74, 84–89, 138–39; Eric F. Goldman, *Rendezvous with Destiny* (N.Y.: Knopf, 1952), 93–96, 193–96, 214–15; George E. Mowry, *The Era of Theodore Roosevelt* (N.Y.: Harper, 1954), 18–21; John D. Clark, *The Federal Antitrust Policy* (Baltimore: Johns Hopkins Press, 1931), 109–87; Richard Hofstadter, *The Age of Reform* (N.Y.: Knopf, 1955), 225–54. For contemporary solutions see Herbert Croly, *The Promise of American Life* (N.Y.: Macmillan, 1909), 358–59, 362–63, 369–81; Charles R. Van Hise, *Concentration and Control* (N.Y.: Macmillan, 1912), 248–66, 277–78; Osmond Fraenkel, ed., *The Curse of Bigness: Miscellaneous Papers of Louis D. Brandeis* (N.Y.: Viking Press, 1934), 104–24, 129–36; Woodrow Wilson, *The New Freedom* (N.Y.: Doubleday, Page, 1913), 163–222; J. B. and J. M. Clark, *The Control of Trusts* (N.Y.: Macmillan, 1914 ed.), 187–202; J. B. Clark, Bruce Wyman, E. S. Meade, Allen Foote, and Harry Seager, in *Annals Am. Acad.*, July 1912, pp. 63–73, 83–88, 108–15, 238–45.

trade associations, loosely supervised by federal authorities, to rationalize competition, improve business ethics, and handle the nation's social problems.[5]

By 1912, then, three broad approaches to the "monopoly problem" had emerged, each with its own methods and value configurations, and yet each claiming that it could implement the American dream, narrow the gap between ideal and reality, and achieve an abundant, dynamic, and equitable system. Each approach, moreover, had some influence on progressive reform. Such measures as the Clayton, Federal Trade Commission, Federal Reserve, and Underwood Tariff Acts, for example, were essentially products of the New Freedom. Their sponsors hoped to do away with the causes of monopoly, with unfair practices, special privileges, a rigged credit system, and the various devices by which monopolistic combines were put together and perpetuated; and by doing this, they hoped to restore, strengthen, and preserve a competitive system. Yet alongside these measures came a variety of laws and activities that were basically inconsistent with the New Freedom. The railroads, for example, came under direct regulation. Farm and labor groups received special aid and protection. Action against tight combinations was tempered by the "rule of reason." The job of controlling unfair competitive practices was eventually entrusted to a special trade commission, an agency that resembled the one proposed by the New Nationalists and one that might conceivably sanction cooperative business agreements and carry out the ideas associated with business self-government and the "new competition." [6]

[5] See Goldman, *Rendezvous*, 205–7; Mowry, *Era of Roosevelt*, 55–56; Arthur S. Link, *Wilson: The New Freedom* (Princeton: Princeton U. Press, 1956), 434–35; Arthur J. Eddy, *The New Competition* (Chicago: McClurg, 1920 ed.), 347–57; Robert H. Wiebe, *Businessmen and Reform* (Cambridge: Harvard U. Press, 1962), 80–85, 186–90.

[6] See Link, *Wilson and Progressive Era*, 66–75, 225–29; Miller, in

National planning and industrial self-government also moved to the fore during World War I. The emphasis, once the United States became involved in hostilities, shifted from economic reform to maximum war production; and the latter, it seemed, could best be attained under a form of war socialism, a system under which federal agencies directed and controlled broad areas of the economy, business and labor organizations received official encouragement, and industrial leaders cooperated with government officials to plan production, eliminate waste, and organize the nation's resources and energies. The wartime system, moreover, left some permanent marks. The newly organized trade associations remained as a prominent feature of the postwar economy. Business leaders, especially those who had worked in Washington, had caught a new vision of what could be done by economic planning and business-government cooperation. A new breed of public administrators, skilled in the techniques of wartime control, were more prone to reject competitive values and stress the goal of a planned economy. In the crisis of the nineteen thirties a number of business and governmental leaders would remember the war experience and call for action along similar lines.[7]

It was not surprising that the wartime program of industrial self-government should blossom into the Associational Activities of the nineteen twenties. Once again, public officials were equating business interests with the

Latham, ed., *Policies of Wilson*, 137–38; Edward D. Durand, *The Trust Problem* (Cambridge: Harvard U. Press, 1920), 86–112; Charles C. Chapman, *The Development of American Business and Banking Thought, 1913–1936* (N.Y.: Longmans, Green, 1936), 6–12; Henry R. Seager and Charles A. Gulick, Jr., *Trust and Corporation Problems* (N.Y.: Harper, 1929), 413–26; Wiebe, *Businessmen and Reform*, 137–41.

[7] See Goldman, *Rendezvous*, 293–94; William E. Leuchtenberg, *The Perils of Prosperity* (Chicago: U. of Chicago Press, 1958), 39–42; Wiebe, *Businessmen and Reform*, 221–22; Grosvenor B. Clarkson, *Industrial America in the World War* (Boston: Houghton Mifflin, 1923), 45–64, 299–314, 477–88; Frederic L. Paxson, in *AHR*, Oct. 1920, pp. 54–76.

national interest; and in this atmosphere the vision of a business commonwealth, of a benevolent capitalism under which everyone would be happy and prosperous, took on a new and wider appeal. The kind of thinking once characteristic of George Perkins, Frank Munsey, and a few other Eastern businessmen began to seep through the chambers of commerce all over the country. The result was a rapid burgeoning of trade associations, a rationale that justified their anticompetitive activities, and a public policy under which such agencies as the Department of Commerce and the Federal Trade Commission helped these associations to standardize their products, expand their functions, and formulate codes of proper practices, codes that generally regarded a price cutter as a "chiseler" and price competition as immoral. If the official propaganda of these business organizations could be believed, the nation had entered a new era of cooperative activities, an era in which poverty and class conflict would disappear, business would discipline itself, and everyone would benefit from the joint action of enlightened business leaders.

Eventually, the policies and attitudes of the nineteen twenties ended in economic disaster. They concentrated economic and political power in the hands of a business-financial elite that was less altruistic and far less prescient than was generally assumed; and the result was not utopia but economic breakdown, a system that accentuated maldistribution, encouraged speculation, piled up excessive savings, destroyed its own markets, and plunged the nation into the worst depression in its history. Yet so long as prosperity continued, there was little awareness of these underlying defects and little concern about the decline of competition or the growing concentration of wealth and power. The great majority seemed to agree that what was good for business, or at least what businessmen thought was good for them, was by definition good for everyone. If there were troubled consciences left, they could take comfort from the retention of the antitrust laws, the con-

stant praise of "free enterprise," and the fact that the
cartels and supercorporations usually masked their activities behind a veil of competitive terminology.[8]

The Great Depression, however, with its mass unemployment and declining incomes, brought a new and acute
awareness of the monopoly problem, a new consciousness
of the gap between ideal and reality. Along with the concern over centralization, injustice, and loss of individual
freedom, came a new concern, a growing belief that the
misuse of business power was responsible for the economic
breakdown and the persistence of depression conditions.
Reorganization and reform of the business system, so
many Americans felt, had now become an imperative
necessity; as one might expect, the approaches to the
problem tended to follow the patterns established earlier.
Once again, opinion divided along lines that were roughly
similar to those which had divided the New Freedom,
the New Nationalism, and the "new competition."

Like the advocates of the New Freedom, for example,
the antitrusters or neo-Brandeisians favored a policy of
decentralizing the business structure and enforcing competitive behavior. They did so both with the idea of
implementing democratic and individualistic ideals and
with a growing conviction that enforced competition
was the best way to achieve sustained prosperity. The
depression, as they saw it, was a product of monopolistic
rigidities. The businessmen, because of their market
power, had been able to maintain prices even though
their costs of production were falling. This had resulted
in excessive profits, oversavings, and a failure of consumer
purchasing power. And the only real solution, they felt,

---

[8] See Goldman, *Rendezvous*, 286–87, 306–9; Leuchtenberg, *Perils
of Prosperity*, 9, 199–203; Arthur R. Burns, *The Decline of Competition* (N.Y.: McGraw-Hill, 1936), 45–75; Chapman, *American
Business Thought*, 68–97; Clark, *Federal Antitrust Policy*, 227–42;
George Roberts, Gilbert Montague, Wilson Compton, and Hugh
Baker, in *Proceedings of the Academy of Political Science*, Jan.
1926, pp. 5–18, 27–39, 77–91.

if such crises were to be averted in the future, was a program that would restore flexible prices and allow competitive forces to keep the economy in balance. They believed, moreover, that these goals were attainable. They could be attained by rigorous antitrust prosecution, by limits on size, by a tax on bigness, by controls over business financing and competitive practices, and by other measures that would encourage more reliance on free markets.

The economic planners, on the other hand, like the New Nationalists of an earlier period, felt that antitrust action was a hopeless anachronism. In a modern economy, they maintained, concentrations of economic power were inevitable. They were necessary for efficient mass production, technical progress, and reasonable security; and while the abuse of this power was largely responsible for the depression, the idea that it could be dispersed was both impractical and dangerous. The only real answer lay in systematic organization and planning, in conscious and rational administrative control of economic processes so as to restore economic balance and prevent future breakdowns.

Again, however, there was strong disagreement as to who should do the planning and the degree and type that would be necessary. On the political left were national economic planners who would deprive businessmen of their power and transfer much of it to the state or to organized non-business groups. In the center were those who felt that some scheme of business-government cooperation could be effective. On the right were industrialists and pro-business planners, men who drew their ideas from the war experience or the Associational Activities of the nineteen twenties, and who felt that an enlightened business leadership, operating through self-governing trade associations, should make most of the decisions. The depression, so some of these business planners argued, was due mostly to irresponsible "chiseling" and "cutthroat competition";

and the government, if it wanted to bring about recovery, should help "responsible and enlightened businessmen" to force the "chiselers" into line.

Under depression conditions, this clash of values and policies became particularly acute. On the one hand, the depression produced insistent demands for planning, rationalization, and the erection of market controls that could stem the forces of deflation and prevent economic ruin. On the other, it intensified antimonopoly sentiment, destroyed confidence in business leadership, and produced equally insistent demands that big business be punished and competitive ideals be made good. The dilemma of the New Deal reform movement lay in the political necessity of meeting both sets of these demands, in the necessity of creating organizations and controls that could check deflationary forces and provide a measure of order and security while at the same time preserving democratic values, providing the necessary incentives, and making the proper concessions to competitive symbols. From a political standpoint, the Roosevelt Administration could ignore neither of these conflicting currents of pressure and opinion; and under the circumstances, it could hardly be expected to come up with an intellectually coherent and logically consistent set of business policies.[9]

The present study is the story of the New Deal's efforts to resolve this political dilemma, both in terms of the conflicts and compromises between various schools of thought and in terms of achieving a balance between the pressure groups and popular symbols that affected policy decisions. Part I deals with the NRA program, the accompanying conflicts between planners, antitrusters, and business rationalizers, and the resulting inconsistency be-

[9] This conflict among New Dealers is described in detail in Chapter 2. See also Arthur M. Schlesinger, Jr., *The Coming of the New Deal* (Boston: Houghton Mifflin, 1959), 179–84; and *The Politics of Upheaval* (Boston: Houghton Mifflin, 1960), 385–408; Goldman, *Rendezvous*, 326–28, 333–42, 361–67; William Hale, in *Common Sense*, July 1938, pp. 16–20.

tween the competitive goals set forth in formal policy pronouncements and the anticompetitive provisions that remained in the codes. Part II deals with economic planning after the NRA and notes, in particular, the waning influence of the national planners and business rationalizers, the growth of the idea of counterorganization, and the circumstances that led to government-supported cartelization in such areas as transportation, natural resource industries, and retail trade. Part III deals with the antitrusters, with their ideas and programs, the sources of their support, their activities prior to 1938, and their limited success in such fields as financial policy, electrical power, and the control of unfair practices. Finally, in Part IV, the study deals with the reaction of the Roosevelt Administration to the recession of 1937, the resulting monopoly investigation, the new antitrust campaign, and the growing tendency to avoid broad programs of reform and concentrate on compensatory spending as the way out.

From the viewpoint of a logical economist, about the only term that could adequately describe these conflicting policies and gyrations would be "economic confusion." The New Deal began with government sponsorship of cartels and business planning; it ended with the antitrust campaign and the attack on rigid prices; and along the way, it engaged in minor excursions into socialism, public utility regulation, and the establishment of "government yardsticks." Certainly, there was little in the way of economic consistency. Nor was there much success in terms of restoring prosperity and full employment. Neither the planning approach nor antitrust action nor any of the compromises in between ever contributed much to economic recovery, although they did lead to increased governmental activities of each sort. Recovery, when it came, was largely a product of large-scale government spending, and not of any major reorganization of the business system.

From a political standpoint, however, there was a certain amount of consistency and logic to the New Deal programs. In dealing with business, Roosevelt faced a political dilemma. On the one hand he was confronted with strong pressures for punitive action against big business and with the necessity of making proper obeisance to the antitrust tradition. On the other was the growing pressure for some sort of planning, control, and rationalization. As a practical matter, his Administration did a fairly respectable job of satisfying both sets of demands. The denunciations of "monopoly" and the attack on unpopular groups like Wall Street, the Power Trust, and the Sixty Families kept the antitrusters happy, while at the same time organized industrial pressure groups were being allowed to write their programs of market control into law, particularly in areas where they could come up with the necessary lobbies and symbols. Politically speaking, New Deal business policy was a going concern, and one of the basic tasks of this book is to explain why this was so and how this policy developed and changed.

PART I

THE NRA EXPERIENCE

Many good men voted this new charter with misgivings. I do not share these doubts. I had part in the great cooperation of 1917 and 1918 and it is my faith that we can count on our industry once more to join in our general purpose to lift this new threat and to do it without taking any advantage of the public trust which has this day been reposed without stint in the good faith and high purpose of American business.—*Franklin Roosevelt*

CHAPTER 1. THE BIRTH
OF AN ECONOMIC CHARTER

FOR the group of congressmen standing behind the President's desk on the morning of June 16, 1933, the occasion was obviously a momentous one. With a few strokes of the pen, Franklin Roosevelt had just affixed his signature to the National Industrial Recovery Act, a measure that in the President's own estimation represented "the most important and far-reaching legislation ever enacted by the American Congress." And in the summer of 1933 it was difficult to find anyone that would challenge the President's statement. Senator Robert Wagner, the man chiefly responsible for piloting the bill through Congress, was convinced that the new measure would "bring this country out of the depression." Henry I. Harriman, president of the United States Chamber of Commerce, felt that it marked the beginning of a "new business dispensation," a new rule of "constructive co-operation," under which fair-minded business leaders might rid themselves of the "industrial buccaneer," the "exploiter of labor," and the "unscrupulous price-cutter." Hugh Johnson, the man who would administer the law, hailed it as "the charter of a new industrial self-government." William Green, president of the American Federation of Labor, saw it as an opportunity for the resuscitation of trade unionism, as final recognition of labor's contention that prosperity depended upon the development of strong labor unions.[1]

From the act alone, however, it was difficult to tell just what was intended. In essence, the National Industrial Recovery Act was a piece of enabling legislation, a law that

[1] Franklin D. Roosevelt, *Public Papers and Addresses*, II (N.Y.: Random House, 1938), 246; *Time*, June 26, 1933, p. 12; *American Federationist*, June 1933, pp. 565–69; *Literary Digest*, June 24, 1933, pp. 3–4; *New York Times*, June 8, 14, 17, 25, 1933.

gave the President unprecedented peacetime powers to reorganize and regulate an obviously ailing and defective business system. There was no definite prescription as to just what course this reorganization and regulation would take. As Hugh Johnson said, the law provided an economic charter, not a prescribed course of action. There was a good deal of validity in Senator William Borah's contention that the act prescribed no standards at all, that it laid down no rules and gave no indication of what codes of "fair competition" should include. Such codes, apparently, might include anything "which industry agrees upon and can get approved."

In practice, the content of the law was likely to depend upon the ideas and preconceptions of its administrators. And in this very fact, in the widespread confusion over the meaning of the act, lay the explanation of much of its popularity. To some it represented an attempt to elevate, humanize, and purify the competitive struggle, to stop the type of "cut-throat competition" that resulted in drastic wage reductions, declining quality, reckless waste of natural resources, and predatory price cutting. To a second group it appeared primarily as a labor measure, as a means of raising wage rates, spreading work, abolishing child labor, and promoting trade unions. To others its major objective was the promotion of a cartelized, risk-free economic order, a system in which the government would help organized business groups to fix prices, restrict production, control entry, protect capital investments, and eliminate the "chiselers." To still others it offered an escape from the "anarchy of the competitive system," a promise of both the organization and control that were necessary for the development of a centrally planned, collectivist democracy. Within a single piece of legislation, the authors of the measure had made room for the aspirations and programs of a variety of economic and political groups; but in a phraseology that could be used to implement any of several policies, they had laid the basis for future confusion and controversy.[2]

II

A part of the ambiguity stemmed from the necessity for speed and improvisation, coupled with a willingness to use broad, vaguely worded language that would mask internal conflicts and allow a maximum of experimentation and flexibility. In a sense the National Industrial Recovery Act was a product of rapid, impromptu consideration. When Congress convened in March 1933 the new Administration had no plans for broad changes in the business structure. The current discussions of economic planning and reorganization, Roosevelt felt, had not "jelled" sufficiently to justify action; and accordingly, his Administration showed little official interest. It was not until other developments had made some action imperative that he changed his mind.[3]

The train of events that led to the writing of the Na-

[2] C. L. Dearing et al., *The ABC of the NRA* (Washington: Brookings, 1934), 7–9, 23; Leverett S. Lyon et al., *The National Recovery Administration* (Washington: Brookings, 1935), 4–7, 14, 19–26, 751–52; Charles F. Roos, *NRA Economic Planning* (Bloomington: Principia, 1937), 43–44; John P. Miller, *Unfair Competition* (Cambridge: Harvard U. Press, 1941), 312–14; Rexford G. Tugwell, *The Battle for Democracy* (N.Y.: Columbia U. Press, 1935), 6–9, 14, 18–20, 56; Charles A. Beard and G. H. E. Smith, *The Future Comes* (N.Y.: Macmillan, 1933), VIII, 43; Saul Nelson, *NRA Work Materials 56* (*Minimum Price Regulation under Codes of Fair Competition*), 17–19, 23; CIA, *The National Recovery Administration* (House Doc. 158, 75 Cong., 1 Sess., 1937), 2; *Congressional Record*, 73 Cong., 1 Sess., LXXVII, 5166; L. S. Lyon and C. L. Dearing, in *American Journal of Sociology*, May 1934, p. 760; R. E. Flanders, in *Atlantic Monthly*, Nov. 1933, pp. 626–27; *New York Times*, June 17, 1933.

[3] Raymond Moley, *After Seven Years* (N.Y.: Harper, 1939), 185–86; Hugh S. Johnson, *The Blue Eagle from Egg to Earth* (Garden City: Doubleday, Doran, 1935), 201–3; Arthur M. Schlesinger, Jr., *The Coming of the New Deal* (Boston: Houghton Mifflin, 1959), 8, 87–89; Lyon et al., *NRA*, 563–65, 883.

tional Industrial Recovery Act began on April 6, when the Senate passed Senator Hugo Black's thirty-hour-week bill, a measure that would prohibit the shipment in interstate commerce of any goods produced by men working more than a six-hour day or a five-day week. The bill reflected the popular notion that available work should be shared; it enjoyed the support of organized labor; and in the atmosphere of the time, it seemed likely to win the approval of the House as well as the Senate. Roosevelt, moreover, was reluctant to embarrass the Democratic senators who had voted for the bill; yet, from his point of view, it was seriously defective. It was far too rigid, likely to be held unconstitutional, and said nothing about minimum wages. Under the circumstances, he asked Secretary of Labor Frances Perkins to develop a "workable" substitute; and on April 17 Miss Perkins submitted a number of proposed amendments to the House Labor Committee. Drawing upon her experience with the New York minimum wage law, she proposed, first of all, to establish minimum wage levels based upon the recommendations of special industrial boards, agencies upon which labor, management, and the government would each have representatives. A similar board, she suggested, might grant limited exemptions from the requirement of a thirty-hour week; and in certain cases, the Secretary of Labor might impose and enforce machine-hour limitations.

The Perkins proposal produced a flood of protests from business leaders. Such an "inelastic measure," they claimed, was "inequitable and grossly impractical." It would substitute "the judgment of a Federal officer for that of experienced and responsible management"; and if ever put into operation, it was likely to dislocate industry, increase production costs, and aggravate the unemployment problem. Constructive wage-and-hour legislation, said Henry Harriman, should be based upon the principles of "industrial self-government" that had been recommended by such organizations as the Chamber of Commerce, the National Association of Manufacturers, and the American Bar Association. The antitrust laws should be relaxed so as to allow employers to enter into voluntary trade association agreements covering such things as hours, wages, and "destructive competition." Such agreements should then be approved by an appropriate government agency; and, once approved, they should be forced upon recalcitrant industrial minorities.[4]

Efforts to devise a measure more acceptable to industry were also underway in other quarters. Ever since March, the office of Raymond Moley, Assistant Secretary of State and one of the key figures in the President's so-called Brains Trust, had served as a sort of clearinghouse for industrial recovery plans. Following the Senate's approval of the Black bill, Moley undertook a serious investigation of the proposals emanating from the Chamber of Commerce and the Brookings Institution, and, during the course of his inquiry, he enlisted the aid of General Hugh Johnson and decided that he was just the man to draw up an industrial bill. Johnson, after all, was familiar with the operations of the War Industries Board, the only comparable project that could serve as a precedent. The depression had strengthened his conviction that unregulated competition led to disaster. Long conversations with such individuals as Bernard Baruch and Alexander Sachs had convinced him that he knew exactly what should be done. With a minimum of delay, he wrote out his first

[4] Moley, *After Seven Years*, 186–87; Schlesinger, *Coming of New Deal*, 91–92, 95; Charlotte Williams, *Hugo L. Black* (Baltimore: Johns Hopkins Press, 1950), 47–48; John P. Frank, *Mr. Justice Black* (N.Y.: Knopf, 1949), 89–91; Frances Perkins, *The Roosevelt I Knew* (N.Y.: Viking, 1946), 192–96; House Labor Committee, *Thirty-Hour-Week Bill* (73 Cong., 1 Sess., 1933); *Congressional Record*, 73 Cong., 1 Sess., LXXVII, 1350; John T. Flynn, in *Harper's*, Sept. 1934, pp. 388–91; *Nation*, April 19, 1933, p. 432; *Business Week*, April 19, 1933, pp. 4–5; April 26, 1933, p. 4; May 3, 1933, p. 9; *Congressional Digest*, May 1933, pp. 157–58; *New York Times*, April 2, 7, 13, 19–21, 26–30, 1933.

draft on a couple of sheets of legal-size foolscap. It would suspend the antitrust laws, empower the President to sanction business agreements dealing with competitive and labor practices, and then allow federal licensing to secure compliance.

The conflicting testimony of participants makes it difficult to reconstruct the drafting process, but Moley and Johnson soon discovered that they were not the only ones working on an industrial recovery measure. Another group centered in the office of Senator Robert Wagner, although the initiative here seems to have come originally from Meyer Jacobstein, a former congressman from New York. Jacobstein, with the assistance of Harold Moulton, a Brookings Institution economist, had persuaded Wagner to broaden his public works bill to include a program of industrial loans; and later, at the suggestion of President Roosevelt, Wagner began exploring the whole matter of industrial recovery. Eventually, he drew upon the advice of a wide assortment of business, labor, and governmental planners. Included were prominent trade association lawyers, like David Podell and Gilbert Montague; advocates of a government guarantee against losses, like Fred Kent; progressive business executives, like Malcolm Rorty and James Rand; labor economists, like W. Jett Lauck; and interested congressmen, like Clyde Kelley and Robert M. LaFollette, Jr. The work of the group continued to emphasize public works, but plans were also made for direct loans to industry and for governmental sanction of trade association agreements.

Still another version of industrial recovery was being developed in the office of John Dickinson, the Undersecretary of Commerce. Since his position constantly exposed him to the current agitation against the antitrust laws, Dickinson had early become interested in the possibilities of economic planning, and his interest had led him into long conversations with the economic planners of the Department of Agriculture, particularly with such individuals as Jerome Frank and Rexford G. Tugwell. Frances Perkins had later joined the group; and with the aid of such advisers, Dickinson had drafted a measure that would make use of the trade associations as instruments of national planning. From the beginning, too, he had established contact with the Wagner group; eventually, the two groups got together and went to work on a common draft.

By early May there were two major drafts, and consultations with business and labor leaders were underway. The Wagner-Dickinson version combined a program of public works and government loans with a plan for industrial self-government through trade associations. The Johnson version laid more stress on federal licensing, an approach that had the support of Raymond Moley, Budget Director Lewis Douglas, and Donald Richberg, a prominent labor lawyer whom Johnson had brought in to represent the unions. On May 10 the principal drafters met at the White House, where the President, after listening to arguments for each of the rival versions, suggested that they lock themselves in a room until an agreement could be reached. As Johnson put it, "We met in Lew Douglas's office—Lew, Senator Wagner, John Dickinson, Mr. Richberg and myself, with a few 'horners-in' from time to time." In the process of compromise, the provision for industrial loans disappeared; but most of the other provisions survived, and the final version contained something for nearly all of its principal authors. The authority to formulate codes of fair competition satisfied the business planners. Section 7a, with its promise of collective bargaining and minimum labor standards, made the measure attractive to the trade unions and social workers. The provision for federal licensing gave some hope for national economic planning. And a $3,300,000,000 public works program appealed to the spenders and pump-primers.

On May 17 the President sent the bill to Congress,

along with a message recommending immediate action. Congress, he said, should provide the necessary machinery for "a great cooperative movement throughout all industry in order to obtain wide reemployment, to shorten the working week, to pay a decent wage for the shorter week and to prevent unfair competition and disastrous over-production." [5]

III

For a time it seemed that the President's plea for co-operation had fallen on fertile ground. Business, labor, and political spokesmen united in a chorus of approval. The Chamber of Commerce hailed the new bill as a "Magna Charta of industry and labor"; and the National Association of Manufacturers, while it had some reservations about the licensing and labor provisions, regarded the proposal as a great step forward. After all, noted *Business Week*, the measure was substantially what industry had been asking for "ever since Senator Black first confronted it with the threat of rigid control from above."

Nor was there much doubt about the goals that business leaders had in mind. The Administration might stress the idea that recovery would come through an increase in mass purchasing power, that cooperative business groups would hire more workers, pay higher wages, defer price increases, and return to profitable operations by expanding their volume. But business spokesmen were quick to combine the idea of chiseling on wages with that of chisel-

[5] Moley, *After Seven Years*, 184–89; Johnson, *Blue Eagle*, 101, 160–63, 193, 196–204; Perkins, *Roosevelt*, 197–200; Roos, *NRA Planning*, 37–41; Schlesinger, *Coming of New Deal*, 87–88, 93–99; FDR, *Public Papers*, II, 163, 202; Flynn, in *Harper's*, Sept. 1934, pp. 390–94; Johnson, in *Saturday Evening Post*, June 30, 1934, pp. 5–7, 87; *Business Week*, May 24, 1933, p. 3; *New York Times*, April 14, 19, May 3–8, 10–14, 17–18, 1933.

ing on prices. "We must take out of competition," said Henry Harriman of the Chamber of Commerce, "the right to cut wages to a point which will not give an American standard of living, and we must recognize that capital is entitled to a fair and reasonable return, . . . that . . . goods must be sold at a price which will enable the manufacturer to pay a fair price for his raw material, to pay fair wages to his men, and to pay a fair dividend on his investment." The real difficulty, as business leaders saw it, was that excessive competition had destroyed profitable operations, undermined business confidence, and reduced the rate of investment. The solution, they maintained, lay in devices that would stop competitive price cutting and insure a reasonable profit, in price fixing, production controls, and extensive regulation of trade practices. The model code issued by the National Association of Manufacturers on May 31 bristled with provisions for controlling prices and output, and a number of trade association spokesmen made it plain that they hoped to imitate the practices of European cartels.

In some industries, moreover, the argument for publicly sanctioned cartels had a particularly strong appeal. In the oil industry, for example, the opening of new pools during the period 1926 to 1931 had produced a condition of excess capacity; and after voluntary arrangements and state laws had failed to solve the problem, industry leaders and conservationists had begun to plead for federal controls, both to check the fall in prices and to prevent the immense waste involved in competitive development. Many lines of retail trade were also greatly overexpanded in terms of existing demand, and the associations of independent retailers had long been pushing for legislation that would peg prices and remove the competitive advantages of the chain stores. Similar conditions existed in the garment trades and in such industries as cotton textiles and bituminous coal. In all of these peculiarly depressed industries, the phenomena of glutted markets, chronic losses, and drastic wage cutting constituted real problems. In all of them, there was a long history of proposals for antitrust exemption. And in all of them, the new industrial recovery bill was hailed as the way out. The leaders of these industries felt that industrial codes offered a better solution than special legislation. They would presumably be more flexible, would offer less chance of governmental dictation, and would leave the initiative and controls in the hands of the industry itself.

Labor spokesmen, too, were jubilant over the prospect of industrial stabilization. Leaders like John L. Lewis of the United Mine Workers and Sidney Hillman of the Amalgamated Clothing Workers had long advocated a planning approach and a measure of industrial self-government. It was illogical, they argued, to expect a chaotic and overly competitive industry, one that was almost chronically depressed, to pay decent wages. The labor theory of recovery, however, differed considerably from that being expounded in business circles. "The essential factor in this new order," declared the American Federation of Labor, "is a guarantee to labor of the right to organize and bargain collectively. . . . Strong union organization in each industry can keep workers' income constantly moving upward as their producing power increases. Without this constant check, we shall again find billions of dollars diverted into million-dollar incomes while mass buying power falls behind."

Finally, the proposed legislation had a strong appeal for social workers and national economic planners. Frances Perkins, for example, stressed the prospect of eliminating child labor and sweatshop conditions. Adolf Berle thought the measure was indispensable, both as a means of restoring economic order and a method of forcing business leaders to recognize their social responsibilities. For Rex Tugwell, the bill represented a growing recognition that "cooperation and not conflict" was the better "organizing principle," that "the old sentiment of fear of big business" had now become unnecessary.[6]

In spite of Tugwell's reassurances, however, most of the opposition to the proposal came from antitrusters and small business liberals, men who stressed the evils of monopoly and were reluctant to abandon the competitive tradition. A good deal of the congressional debate, in fact, centered about the efforts of Administration spokesmen to convince such old-line progressives as Senator William Borah that the measure would strengthen the competitive system rather than destroy it. In reality, said Senator Wagner, the bill was designed "to protect the small business man," to prevent the use of "rebates, discrimination, and selling below the cost of production in order to destroy some little business man." Actually, Wagner argued, the antitrust laws had never prevented the growth of monopoly. They had been used chiefly against labor and small business; and the proposed bill, by providing a method of rationalizing small business, would remove the existing incentive for further mergers and consolidations. The real intention was not to abolish competition, but to purify and strengthen it.

[6] Roos, NRA Planning, 43–44; Perkins, Roosevelt, 200; Schlesinger, Coming of New Deal, 89, 122–23; Tugwell, Battle for Democracy, 56–58; Dearing et al., ABC of NRA, 30–32; Schuyler C. Wallace, New Deal in Action (N.Y.: Harper, 1934), 160–66; Edward Chamberlin, in Douglass V. Brown et al., Economics of the Recovery Program (N. Y.: McGraw-Hill, 1934), 30–37; Myron W. Watkins, Oil: Stabilization or Conservation? (N.Y.: Harper, 1937), 43–54; H. E. Michl, The Textile Industries (Washington: Textile Foundation, 1938), 103–5, 260–62, 271–72; W. E. Fisher and C. M. James, Minimum Price Fixing in the Bituminous Coal Industry (Princeton: Princeton U. Press, 1955), 9–27; Ruth P. Mack, Controlling Retailers (N.Y.: Columbia U. Press, 1936), 71–74, 128–32; DIE, Staff Studies, 45; Harry Mulkey, NRA Work Materials 36 (The So-Called Model Code), 3–5; FDR, Public Papers, II, 255; House Ways and Means Committee, National Industrial Recovery (73 Cong., 1 Sess., 1933), 1–7, 117–20, 132–38, 192; Congressional Digest, June 1931, pp. 165–68; June 1933, p. 176; Business Week, May 24, 1933, p. 1; May 31, 1933, pp. 3–4; New York Times, May 3, 14, 18, 20, 21, 26, 28–30, June 3, 4, 11, 1933.

In the lower chamber, the protests of a few conservatives and antitrusters were easily ignored; and on May 26 the House passed the measure by the overwhelming majority of 325 to 76. In the Senate, however, the bill ran into greater difficulties. Efforts to strike out the licensing provisions, emasculate Section 7a, and add a manufacturers' sales tax were defeated; but amendments were adopted limiting the duration of the licensing powers to one year, authorizing the establishment of import controls, and revamping the new taxes that were to help finance the public works program. The senators also inserted a brief section empowering the President to stop interstate shipments of oil produced in violation of state laws. And they seemed more inclined to listen to the criticisms of the antitrusters, to Senator Borah's contention that the measure would create a system of gigantic trusts under which competition would disappear and the monopolies would "regulate the regulators." In the end, Borah succeeded in adding an amendment providing that no code should "permit combinations in restraint of trade, price fixing, or other monopolistic practices"; and with this gesture toward the competitive tradition, the Senate passed the measure by a vote of 58 to 24.

The victory of the antitrusters, however, proved to be short-lived. Business protests made it clear that Borah was striking at the heart of the measure, that businessmen were set upon establishing "fair, just, and reasonable price levels, in consideration of decreased working hours and increased wages." If the bill did not permit price fixing, wired one industrialist, then it became "nothing more than an unsatisfactory labor measure." Upon second thought, too, Senator Wagner became convinced that the Borah amendment might interfere with cooperative agreements in the public interest. "Monopolistic price fixing," he thought, was obviously wrong, but some form of price control might be necessary to protect small enterprises, halt destructive price wars, and prevent senseless and harmful price fluctuations. Accordingly, the conference committee decided to remove the specific prohibition of price fixing, to forbid only "monopolies or monopolistic practices." The Senate, in spite of strong protests from Borah and other old-line progressives, went along with the conference report.[7]

IV

In its final form, the National Industrial Recovery Act contained three titles, two of which dealt with public works and the taxes that would help to finance them. Under Title II, a total of $3,300,000,000 might be spent on a variety of projects ranging from highways to public housing; and in order to increase revenue, chief reliance was placed upon a new system of capital stock and excess profits taxes. The plan, as finally adopted, called for a levy of one-tenth of one percent on the declared value of a company's stock, and, to encourage fair valuation, all profits over twelve and one-half percent of the declared value were to be taxed at the rate of five percent.

The act's most widely publicized provisions, however, were contained in Title I, the portion that dealt with the formulation of industrial codes. In the first two sections, the authors of the measure set forth its general purposes, limited its application to a period of two years, and authorized the President to designate or create appropriate administrative agencies. Then, in subsequent sections, they proceeded to lay down rules for the making of codes. The President, under Section 3, might approve codes drawn up by trade or industrial groups providing that he found such codes to be equitable, truly representa-

[7] *Congressional Record*, 73 Cong., 1 Sess., LXXVII, 4373, 5152–53, 5162–66, 5238, 5247, 5257, 5275, 5279–84, 5293–99, 5404–5, 5411–16, 5424–25, 5620, 5701, 5834–46, 5861; Roos, *NRA Planning*, 45–52; Schlesinger, *Coming of New Deal*, 99–102; *Congressional Digest*, June 1933, pp. 172, 175, 177; *New York Times*, May 10, 11, 27, June 2–4, 6, 8–11, 14, 1933.

tive, and not designed to promote monopolies or monopolistic practices. He might also make any necessary additions or deletions; and in an industry where no agreement could be reached, he might impose a code.

The act, however, said little about the type of provisions that should be included in the codes. The only specific instructions, in fact, were those dealing with labor standards. Each code, according to Section 7, had to contain an acceptable provision for maximum hours, minimum wages, and desirable working conditions. In addition, it had to include a prescribed Section 7a, which outlawed yellow dog contracts and guaranteed the right of laborers to organize and bargain collectively through representatives of their own choosing. Aside from these labor clauses, the only other guide was the declaration of policy contained in Section 1, a declaration that was couched in terms of broad, general goals rather than specific instructions. The act, it stated, was designed to promote cooperative action, eliminate unfair practices, increase purchasing power, expand production, reduce unemployment, and conserve natural resources; but there was little to indicate the type of code provisions that might be used to achieve these laudable objectives.

The act also contained several other important provisions. Section 5 exempted the codes from the antitrust laws; Section 8 provided that they should not conflict with the provisions of the Agricultural Adjustment Act; and Section 3e allowed the President to control imports that might have an adverse effect upon code operations. There was, in addition, the controversial licensing power, under which the President, for a period of one year, might resort to licensing particular industries in order to prevent destructive wage and price cutting. Other powers, too, were conferred upon the President. He could prescribe the necessary rules, regulations, and fees; he could require the filing of necessary information; he could enter into voluntary agreements with business firms; he could approve and give the force of law to collective bargaining agreements between business and labor; and finally, under Section 9, he could regulate pipeline companies and prohibit the interstate shipment of oil produced in excess of the limit prescribed by state law.

Within the confines of a single measure, then, the formulators of the National Industrial Recovery Act had appealed to the hopes of a number of conflicting pressure groups. Included were the hopes of labor for mass organization and collective bargaining, the hopes of businessmen for price and production controls, the hopes of competitive industries to imitate their more monopolistic brethren, the hopes of dying industries to save themselves from technological advance, and the hopes of small merchants to halt the inroads of mass distributors. Overlying these more selfish economic purposes was a veneer of ideals and conflicting ideologies, conflicting beliefs as to what the act would do and the ultimate form that the business system should take. Finally, added to the superstructure, were conflicting theories of economic recovery, a belief, on one hand, that by raising wages, spreading work, and holding down prices, total purchasing power could be expanded; a belief, on the other, that by checking destructive competition and insuring profits, business confidence could be restored and new investment spending stimulated.

For the time being, the numerous conflicts had been glossed over by a resort to vagueness, ambiguity, and procrastination. Congress, in effect, had refused to formulate a definite economic policy or to decide in favor of specific economic groups. It had simply written an enabling act, an economic charter, and had then passed the buck to the Administration. The very nature of the act made internal dissensions among its administrators virtually inevitable. In practice, the NRA became a mechanism that conflicting groups sought to use for their own ends, an agency that was unable to define and enforce a consistent line of policy; and in this welter of conflict and confusion, it was scarcely surprising that the result turned out to be what Ernest Lindley called an "administrative, economic, and political mess." [8]

[8] 48 *U.S. Statutes* 195, Public, No. 67, 73 Cong.; Dearing et al., *ABC of NRA*, 23, 30–32; Lyon et al., *NRA*, 751–52, 756–58; Ernest K. Lindley, *Halfway with Roosevelt* (N.Y.: Viking, 1937), 156; Miller, *Unfair Competition*, 314–17; Memo. re Interview of Corwin Edwards, Nov. 16, 1933, Lorwin File, NRPB Records.

CHAPTER 2. THE CONFLICT
OF GOALS

To many people in 1933 the National Industrial Recovery Act represented something new and unique, a bold and original plan that would lift the blight of depression from a stricken country. Yet appearances were deceptive. In reality the act was a product of trends, objectives, and ideals that were deeply rooted in American history. The attempt to administer it produced a running debate over these historic goals, over the best way to organize, motivate, and operate an industrial system. In order to understand the conflict, one must look briefly at the nature and background of the goals involved.

The policy struggle of the NRA period, insofar as it related to the business structure, was a three-cornered affair. At one corner was the vision of a business commonwealth, of a rational, cartelized business order in which the industrialists would plan and direct the economy, profits would be insured, and the government would take care of recalcitrant "chiselers." At the second was the concept of a cooperative, collectivist democracy, a system under which organized economic groups would join to plan their activities, rationalize their behavior, and achieve the good life for all. At the third corner was the competitive ideal, the old vision of an atomistic economy in which basic decisions were made in an impersonal market and the pursuit of self-interest produced the greatest social good. As written, the National Industrial Recovery Act could be used to move in any of these directions, to cartelize the economy, establish overhead planning, or attempt to eliminate the market riggers and enforce competition. There were those who would move in each of them, and it was not surprising that a conflict resulted.

It would be an oversimplification to represent the policy struggle as merely a conflict between three schools of thought. It was much more complex. Individuals simply refused to accept ideological systems intact and then stick to a given position. They changed their minds, made exceptions, accepted intellectually inconsistent ideas, yielded to political and personal loyalties or pressures, and tried to stake out positions that were somewhere between the three points of orientation. Pressure groups, too, used ideological symbols for selfish ends, sometimes to mask operations that were completely at variance with the professed ideals. And non-ideological figures, men who regarded themselves as pragmatic realists, were inclined to skip from one approach to the other on the basis of what seemed to work at the moment or what was expedient from a political standpoint. Such complexities made it difficult to follow the struggle, define positions, and identify the participants. Yet for purposes of analysis, the concept of a three-cornered ideological clash is useful, particularly if one uses the ideological goals to identify policy directions rather than fixed positions. Once the conflict of goals is understood, the nature of the National Industrial Recovery Act and the administrative debates over its implementation become much more understandable.[1]

II

One possible goal, then, was the business commonwealth, the further elaboration of the "associational activities" that had been so prominent in the "New Era" of the nineteen twenties. In a sense this philosophy dated back to medieval civilization, and critics could point to striking parallels between the concepts of medieval ideology and

[1] William H. Hale, in *Common Sense*, July 1938, pp. 16–20; Arthur M. Schlesinger, Jr., *The Coming of the New Deal* (Boston: Houghton Mifflin, 1959), 18–19, 193–94; *The Politics of Upheaval* (Boston: Houghton Mifflin, 1960), 233–35, 393–94, 399–400, 650–51; J. F. Carter, *The New Dealers* (N.Y.: Literary Guild, 1934), 3–6, 25–27.

those contained in latter-day trade association literature. Both stressed a system of cooperative, associational activity. Both laid emphasis upon security and status. Both had visions of a "just price." And in each there was the idea of government-granted monopolies and the notion that governmental powers could be properly exercised by economic or vocational groups. More immediately, however, the proponents of the business commonwealth had drawn their ideas from the defenders of business combination, the critics of the antitrust laws, the advocates of cartelization in Europe, and the economic planners of World War I. The war had led to the creation of hundreds of trade associations; and following the war, the so-called "association idea" came into its own. Open price associations flourished under the benign auspices of the Department of Commerce. Formal codes of ethics "blossomed like spring flowers in every field." And the Federal Trade Commission gave official sanction through its trade practice conference procedure. In such an atmosphere, price-cutting became taboo. The price-cutter became a chiseler, a fellow closely akin to the "scab" in labor circles; and the competition that remained shifted from the field of price to the fields of quality, service, and advertising.[2]

[2] Louis M. Hacker, *Short History of the New Deal* (N.Y.: Crofts, 1934), 27, 43; Charles F. Roos, *NRA Economic Planning* (Bloomington: Principia, 1937), 1–5; Arthur R. Burns, *The Decline of Competition* (N.Y.: McGraw-Hill, 1936), 8–25, 40–45, 73–75; N. S. B. Gras, in M. P. McNair and H. T. Lewis, eds., *Business and Modern Society* (Cambridge: Harvard U. Press, 1938), 43–53; Emmet H. Naylor, in Dept. of Commerce, *Trade Association Activities* (1923), 301–4; Frank Hursey et al., *NRA Work Materials 61* (*Code Compliance Activities of NRA*), 56–58; *NRA Work Materials 46* (*Code Authorities and Their Part in the Administration of NIRA*), 161–62; DIE, Staff Studies, 61–68, 78–90; Richard H. Hippelheuser, ed., *American Industry in the War* (N.Y.: Prentice-Hall, 1941), 105; George Galloway, "Industrial Control in the U.S. before NRA," Feb. 1935, SR&P, NRA Records; Harry W. Laidler, *Concentration and Control in American Industry* (N.Y.: Crowell, 1931), 453–55; R. L. Wilbur and A. M. Hyde, *The Hoover Policies* (N.Y.: Scribner's, 1937), 303–4; Leon Henderson

Throughout the twenties, too, business apologists and trade association secretaries elaborated a rationale to justify their activities. At the center of their system was the concept of the industrial group, a body of individuals engaged in the same trade and united for the joint protection of their common interests. This group had legitimate group interests that transcended those of individual members. Where the competitive ideal called for the free action of the individual in his own interest, the "new competition" required that the individual conform to group standards and refrain from engaging in any form of competition that might be destructive to the group as a whole. Nor were such requirements inimical to the public interest. Price competition, after all, was essentially wasteful. And a higher degree of group control would mean less waste, more stability, steadier employment for labor, greater security for the investor, and more and better goods for the general public. Besides, business leaders knew more about economic processes and were better qualified to make economic decisions than anyone else. They had played a major role in the creation of American society; they were responsible for its continued well-being; they had taken and would take a paternalistic and fair-minded interest in the welfare of their workers, so it was only fair that they should be given a free hand to organize the system in the most efficient, rational, and productive manner.

The government was generally assigned a supervisory role, but if one assumed, as was usually done, that the interests of business were identical with those of society as a whole, it followed that the supervisors would not have a very difficult task. For the most part, they would limit their activities to advising and supporting business

---

and Theodore Kreps, "On the Necessity for a Broad Inquiry into the Present Status of Competition," Dec. 30, 1935, Blaisdell File, NRPB Records; Ellis W. Hawley, "The Relation of Hoover's Policies to the NIRA," M.A. Thesis, U. of Kans. (1951), 14–50.

leaders, enforcing business decisions, assisting in the organization of the more backward trades, and rounding up any stray chiselers that were not as yet convinced that what was good for their industry was also good for them. In business circles, such a system usually went by the name of "self-government in industry," a term first brought into currency by the guild socialists after World War I. Its originators had envisioned the participation of workers and consumers as well as managers and owners; but as the term found its way into the businessman's lexicon, it meant that business leaders should be entrusted with governmental powers and the making of economic decisions should be the exclusive prerogative of the managerial group.[3]

With the onset of the depression in 1929, this idea moved rapidly to the fore. Under depression conditions, the private controls and tacit understandings of the nineteen twenties were difficult to enforce; and to make matters worse, the FTC, at the insistence of John L. O'Brian, head of the Antitrust Division, began to revise the trade practice conference agreements and eliminate rules that were not strictly within the law. "Individualistic competition," noted Leon Henderson, was breaking out in 1931, "even in the stabilized steel industry"; and for the more competitive industries or the declining ones in which the depression had intensified the impact of tech-

[3] John P. Miller, *Unfair Competition* (Cambridge: Harvard U. Press, 1941), 283, 333–35; G. A. Dommisse, *Regulation of Retail Trade Competition* (N.Y.: Colonial, 1939), 50–52; Benjamin A. Javits, *Business and the Public Interest* (N.Y.: Macmillan, 1932), 185–90; Charles R. Stevenson, *The Way Out* (N.Y., 1932), 24–33; Philip Cabot, in *Yale Review*, Sept. 1931, pp. 38–55; Joseph Dorfman, *The Economic Mind in American Civilization*, IV (N.Y.: Viking, 1959), 185; G. D. H. Cole, *Self-Government in Industry* (London: Bell, 1917), 106–23, 281–302; Charles A. Pearce et al., *Trade Association Survey* (TNEC Monograph 18, 1941), 346–53; Clair Wilcox, *Competition and Monopoly in American Industry* (TNEC Monograph 21, 1941), 15; Walton Hamilton, *A Prologue to Prices* (NRA Consumer Report 1, 1935), 55–56; "Business Self-Government," Executive Secretary's File, TNEC Records.

nological changes, the results were little short of disastrous. Under the circumstances, businessmen turned increasingly to the idea of government-supported cartels. Increasingly, they advocated the use of production quotas, price agreements, entry controls, and cost-accounting formulas for calculating the "economic right price," the "universal use" of which, through federal regulation, "would wholly and permanently eliminate unfair price-cutting" and "promote an unequalled degree of stability in all phases of industrial and economic affairs." If only they could achieve the necessary organization, thought many hard-pressed businessmen, and if only some means were provided to force the chiselers into line, then prices might be fixed at profitable levels to all, and production, employment, and wages might be maintained at satisfactory levels.[4]

These aspirations of the business community were soon embodied in numerous demands for the repeal or modification of the antitrust laws. Fairly typical were those made by Charles R. Stevenson, head of a prominent trade association management firm and a strong believer in the notion that business was "being crucified on the cross of competition." "Excessive competition," he declared, was forcing prices below cost, producing excess capacity, and reducing wages to a bare subsistence level. It was the villain responsible for "shoddy, badly made, poor quality articles," for the drastic decline in dividends, and for the inability of industry to reduce hours and

[4] George B. Galloway et al., *Industrial Planning under Codes* (N.Y.: Harper, 1935), 23; Basil Rauch, *History of the New Deal* (N.Y.: Creative Age, 1944), 73; William L. Churchill, *Pricing for Profit* (N.Y.: Macmillan, 1932), 4, 99–100; Saul Nelson, *NRA Work Materials 56* (*Minimum Price Regulation under Codes of Fair Competition*), 7–8, 13–17; DIE, Staff Studies, 94, 1437–45; Edwin George, *NRA Code Revision Memorandum No. 1* (1935); Henderson and Kreps, "Status of Competition," Blaisdell File, NRPB Records; Hawley, "Hoover and NIRA," 56–65; Ludlow Smith to A. Sachs, Aug. 31, 1933, Price Agreements File—CAF, NRA Records; K. E. Boulding, in *QJE*, Aug. 1945, pp. 529–32; *Business Week*, Oct. 8, 1930, pp. 13–14; April 29, 1931, p. 7.

employ everyone. "Not only must business be given the right to combine and operate our various industries as a unit," he insisted, "but also the majority in an industry must be given the right of compulsion over the minority." Industry, properly organized, should schedule and regulate production, allot quotas to individual plants and marketing territories, determine and enforce a "fair price," and issue certificates of convenience and necessity to new entrants.

Such proposals were symptomatic of a type of thinking that was becoming increasingly acceptable in business circles. Both the Chamber of Commerce and the American Bar Association had endorsed similar proposals; and the same sort of planning was being discussed and advocated by numerous business spokesmen and trade association apologists, by lawyers like Benjamin Javits and David Podell, economists like Edgar Heermance and Philip Cabot, former members of the War Industries Board like Bernard Baruch and Hugh Johnson, and prominent business leaders like James Harvey Williams, Charles Abbot, Henry S. Dennison, Malcolm Rorty, Fred Kent, Albert Deane, and Gerard Swope. Swope, in particular, had attracted wide attention with his vision of a cartelized economy run by the trade associations; and his plan was soon receiving general acclaim, not only in business circles, but in academic and governmental circles as well.[5]

[5] Stevenson, *Way Out*, 3–4, 25–33; J. G. Frederick, *Readings in Economic Planning* (N.Y.: Business Bourse, 1932), 295–97, 304–8, 313–32; Dorfman, *Economic Mind*, v, 632–35; Roos, NRA Planning, 18, 36–37; Miller, *Unfair Competition*, 290–305; Javits, *Business and Public Interest*, 52–90; Gerard Swope, *The Swope Plan* (N.Y.: Business Bourse, 1931), 25–45; Charles A. Beard, ed., *America Faces the Future* (N.Y.: Houghton Mifflin, 1932), 160–216; Edgar L. Heermance, *Can Business Govern Itself?* (N.Y.: Harper, 1933), 6–13, 106–7, 231–37; Wallace B. Donham, *Business Adrift* (N.Y.: McGraw-Hill, 1931), 126–29, 141–42; David Podell, in Milton Handler, *The Federal Anti-Trust Laws* (N.Y.: CCH, 1932), 72–73; Raymond Moley, *After Seven Years* (N.Y.: Harper, 1939), 185–86; Albert L. Deane and H. K. Norton, *Investing in Wages* (N.Y.: Macmillan, 1932), 66–78; Senate Com-

Gradually, the attack on the antitrust laws found its way into Congress, into bills that would prohibit sales below cost, establish resale price maintenance, create economic councils, and give legal sanction to the FTC's trade practice conference procedure. President Hoover, however, declared that the Swope Plan was "the most gigantic proposal of monopoly ever made in history," and he refused point blank to have anything to do with the proposals of the Chamber of Commerce and similar schemes for business rationalization. In the past he had been a leading spokesman for the trade association movement, but the notion of a rationalized order run by business cartels was carrying his idea of voluntary cooperation much too far. Consequently, it was not until the Administration had changed hands and Roosevelt was casting about for a substitute to stave off the rigid thirty-hour-week bill that the prophets of the business commonwealth were able to write some of their ideas into the National Industrial Recovery Act. They were, in fact, highly influential in shaping the final product. Men like Fred Kent, Malcolm Rorty, David Podell, and Henry I. Harriman participated in the drafting process; and men with only slightly less inclination toward governmental control, men like Hugh Johnson, Donald Richberg, and Lewis Douglas, whipped the bill into final shape. From their handiwork emerged the central idea of self-governing trade associations that would write their own codes

---

mittee on Manufacturers, *Establishment of a National Economic Council* (72 Cong., 1 Sess., 1931), 182–210; Hawley, "Hoover and NIRA," 65–86, 91–92; G. Working, "Statements in Support of Theories upon Which NIRA Is Based," Nov. 20, 1934, MR&D, NRA Records; Cabot, in *Yale Review*, Sept. 1931, pp. 48–53; James H. Williams, in *Atlantic Monthly*, June 1931, pp. 787–96; M. C. Rorty, in *Harvard Business Review Supplement*, April 1932, pp. 389–91; *Business Week*, Sept. 30, 1931, p. 15; Nov. 4, 1931, p. 8; *New York Times*, Feb. 7, March 25, 1931; Jan. 22, Feb. 12, April 14, 1932.

of law and enforce them through public power with a minimum of governmental supervision.[6]

III

A second vision that found its way into the National Industrial Recovery Act was that of a collectivist democracy engaged in purposeful national planning. The spectacle of poverty in the midst of plenty, of millions of workers idle while the community lacked goods, had led many intellectuals to question the very assumptions of a private enterprise system. And in their quest for a solution, they turned to the old dream of a planned economy, the vision of cooperative production that had once been preached only by socialists and utopians.

A few drew inspiration from foreign precedents, particularly from the newly inaugurated Soviet Five Year Plan. But the great majority elaborated a planning ideology that was indigenous to America. One line of inspiration here came from the discipline of scientific management, from the system of ideas developed by such men as Frederick W. Taylor and Henry L. Gantt and applied to the economy as a whole by writers influenced by Thorstein Veblen. From Veblen these men drew such concepts as the technological imperative, the work-a-day, matter-of-fact discipline of the machine process, and the

[6] William S. Myers and W. H. Newton, *The Hoover Administration* (N.Y.: Scribner's, 1936), 119, 155–56, 245–46, 488; Moley, *After Seven Years*, 186–89; Lewis L. Lorwin and A. Ford Hinrichs, *National Economic and Social Planning* (Washington: GPO, 1935), 38, 54–56; Hugh S. Johnson, *The Blue Eagle from Egg to Earth* (Garden City: Doubleday, Doran, 1934), 196–204; Roos, *NRA Planning*, 16–17; Dorfman, *Economic Mind*, v, 634; C. L. Dearing et al., *The ABC of NRA* (Washington: Brookings, 1934), 11; Ruth P. Mack, *Controlling Retailers* (N.Y.: Columbia U. Press, 1936), 138–44; *Congressional Record*, 72 Cong., 1 Sess., LXXV, 87, 99, 490, 1287–89; Hawley, "Hoover and NIRA," 77–81; J. H. Williams to FDR, Feb. 24, 1933, OF 277, Roosevelt Papers; John T. Flynn, in *Harper's*, Sept. 1934, pp. 385–94.

distinction between the business interest and the industrial interest. The most spectacular result was Technocracy, the proposal to abolish the price system and establish an administrative dictatorship of the engineers; but most of the planners did not apply the concepts so rigorously. A second line of inspiration came from the works of such men as Herbert Croly and Charles Van Hise and from the philosophy of the New Nationalism as it had been developed in the campaign of 1912. Concentration, cooperation, and control had been the key words in the Van Hise system, and these same objectives were now advanced as the proper policies for a collectivist democracy. Through concentration a more efficient system could be established; through cooperation waste could be eliminated; and through control one could assure fair wages, full employment, reasonable prices, conservation of resources, and fair trade practices.

Accordingly, alongside the plans of such men as Charles Stevenson and Gerard Swope, there soon appeared the plans of numerous intellectuals, economists like Rexford Tugwell, George Soule, and Stuart Chase, historians like Charles A. Beard and Will Durant, philosophers like John Dewey, and clergymen like Father John Ryan. Like the proponents of the business commonwealth, the intellectual planners were convinced that economic concentration was inevitable, that it was the product of technological change and economies of scale, and that the antitrust laws were outmoded and generally useless. As Tugwell put it, the attempt to abolish business combination was "a good deal like trying to forbid the use of electricity or modern accounting." Unlike the business planners, however, the intellectuals were suspicious of businessmen, wary of a rationale that stressed scarcity profits, and reluctant to entrust business leaders with the operation of the economic controls. Such leaders, they felt, because of their background and past experience, were bound to make decisions that would lead to economic stagnation rather than maximum production, decisions that would aggravate the problems of maldistribution, oversavings, and inadequate purchasing power, the factors responsible for the depression in the first place. Consequently, it became necessary to bring in other economic groups, to foster the participation of organized workers, farmers, and consumers; and it might be necessary for the state itself to make the key decisions.

Typically, then, the national economic planners envisioned a process in which planning was carried on by joint participation of business, labor, and consumer groups. The typical proposal called for the detailed planning itself to be undertaken by a system of industrial councils, composed of representatives of each of the special interests involved; and once formulated, the plans would then be perfected, coordinated, and enforced by a central board of technicians, economists, engineers, and other "qualified experts." Real planning, in the view of men like Tugwell, would involve more than simply limiting production to amounts that could be sold profitably. It would involve controls over profits and investments as well as prices and production; and, in the last analysis, it would imply the operation of an integrated group of enterprises for its consumers rather than its owners.

The end product, of course, depended largely upon who would do the planning, how much of it would be done, and for whose benefit. Since the National Industrial Recovery Act left these questions substantially unanswered, they soon became the subject of a major policy conflict. On the political right were those who believed that businessmen should do most of the planning, that the long-range business interest was substantially identical with the public interest, and that business leaders possessed sufficient social vision to pursue their long-range interests. Somewhat to the left were those who doubted that the era of industrial statesmanship had already arrived, but still hoped that it might, that if the government provided the necessary degree of inspiration, supervision, and control, business leaders might develop the necessary social vision. Still further to the left were those who felt that business leaders would never operate as industrial statesmen, that the only solution was to transfer business power to other economic groups or to the government itself. Ultimately, if the NRA was to pursue a consistent line of policy, it would have to make some decision as to who was right. And around this issue of controls, around such matters as the power and composition of the code authorities, the basis of group representation, and the degree of governmental supervision, there developed one of the major controversies that split NRA administrators into rival groups.[7]

[7] Planning concepts and antecedents are discussed in Lorwin and Hinrichs, *National Planning*, 52–54; Carter, *New Dealers*, 30; Adolf A. Berle, Jr., and Gardiner Means, *The Modern Corporation and Private Property* (N.Y.: Macmillan, 1932), 350–57; Moley, *After Seven Years*, 184, 189; Rexford G. Tugwell and Howard Hill, *Our Economic Society and Its Problems* (N.Y.: Harcourt, Brace, 1934), 532–44; Tugwell, *The Industrial Discipline and the Governmental Arts* (N.Y.: Columbia U. Press, 1933), 129–30, 193–96, 203–19; Tugwell, in *AER Supplement*, March 1932, pp. 75–92; Schlesinger, *Coming of New Deal*, 87–88, 92–94, 179–84; and *Politics of Upheaval*, 212, 215–19; Dorfman, *Economic Mind*, IV, 97–100; V, 509–10, 636–37, 641, 644–45, 648–49, 758–61, 765–66; J. G. Frederick, ed., *For and Against Technocracy* (N.Y.: Business Bourse, 1933), 221–29; Frederick, *Economic Planning*, 136–38, 142, 297, 301–3, 306–7, 310–11; Lewis L. Lorwin, "Planning and Business Enterprise," Lorwin File, NRPB Records; Lorwin, in *AER Supplement*, March 1932, 93–104; and in *Survey Graphic*, March 1932, pp. 569–70; Donald Richberg, Address, May 14, 1935, Speeches File —MR&D, NRA Records; Tugwell, Proposed Address, Sept. 28, 1934, OF 1, Roosevelt Papers; *Literary Digest*, Dec. 5, 1931, pp. 38–40. Specific proposals are set forth in Stuart Chase, *A New Deal* (N.Y.: Macmillan, 1932), 213–41; Chase, in *Harper's*, June 1931, pp. 1–10; George Soule, *A Planned Society* (N.Y.: Macmillan, 1932), 234–63; Charles A. Beard, in *Forum*, July 1931, pp. 1–11. Earlier versions of the planning orientation are found in Herbert Croly, *The Promise of American Life* (N.Y.: Macmillan, 1909), 358–67; Charles Van Hise, *Concentration and Control* (N.Y.: Macmillan, 1912), 8–20, 88–100, 248–66, 277; Thorstein Veblen, *The Engineers and the Price System* (N.Y.: Huebsch, 1921), 28–45, 52–58, 141–69.

IV

Directly opposed to the planning concept, regardless of who did the planning, was the competitive model of classical economics, the ideological system developed by Adam Smith, John Stuart Mill, Alfred Marshall, John Bates Clark, and other economists of the classical tradition. In the United States this competitive ideal was reinforced by the frontier process, and eventually became deeply embedded in American folklore. Economists taught it to their students; politicians paid homage to it; businessmen gave it lip service when they engaged in oratory for public consumption; and federal statutes, beginning with the Sherman Act in 1890, reflected the popular desire to incorporate it into law. Individualistic competition, according to the tenets of the faith, would bring the best possible society. It would call resources into use and allocate them so as to maximize their productivity. It would adjust all claims upon the joint product equitably, insure fair prices and high quality, and make for progress and experimentation, new blood and new ideas.

It followed, then, that the most desirable policy was one that encouraged a maximum of free competition, one that brought about as close an approximation to the competitive model as possible. The proposals for business rationalization and economic planning, said the antitrusters, were based on false premises. If individual firms were allowed to combine or to eliminate their rivals, they would create power concentrates directly opposed to the public interest, combinations that would gouge the consumer, exploit the worker, corrupt the political process, discourage technological innovation, and preserve inefficient concerns. Such a policy could never bring recovery because the whole analysis behind it was wrong. It was not competition that caused depressions, but rather the lack of it, the system of private monopolies that created violent inequalities in the distribution of income and destroyed the purchasing power of the masses.

Nor would governmental supervision be sufficient to protect the public interest. In fact, judged from past performance in the field of public utilities, the results of a policy of regulated monopoly were likely to be extremely sad. Too often the regulatory commissions simply reflected the underlying structure of special privilege. Too often the regulated industry came to control the regulators, and while it enjoyed the benefits of state protection, acted like a private monopoly. If one went beyond public utility regulation, the problems became insurmountable. How, in a capitalist democracy, could one implement the expert planners' concept of a program for the general welfare? How could he achieve the quick decisions and adjustments, the rapid and continuous coordination, necessary to carry the plans into effect? And where would the expert plans come from? How could one assemble the necessary information and enlist public servants that were possessed of the necessary imagination, knowledge, and skills without turning the whole system into a sterile bureaucracy, enmeshed in red tape and subject to the whims of political favoritism or economic privilege? The answer, said the antitrusters, was that it simply could not be done.

Most of the advocates of enforced competition also rejected the view that economic concentration was the inevitable result of a changing technology and the economies of large-scale units. Large organizations, they argued, were handicapped by fixed overhead charges, overcapitalization, overcautiousness, and lack of flexibility, disadvantages that usually made them less efficient than their smaller rivals. Consequently, with the exception of a few areas of "natural monopoly," it was safe to assume that firms reached the size of optimum efficiency at a relatively early stage, at least at a stage before they had acquired much in the way of monopoly power. Further

growth was the result of financial manipulations, buc-
caneering practices, special governmental privileges, and
the use of brute bargaining strength. Instead of encouraging such a trend, the government should be bending
every effort toward clearing the channels of trade and
restoring the flexibility that the competitive system required.[8]

Traditionally, the policy of enforcing competition had
been one of preventing the competitive process from
breeding its antithesis, monopoly, a policy of drawing the
line between practices in pursuit of competition and those
in restraint of trade, and of eliminating those methods
that made no contribution to increased efficiency. One of
the basic tenets of Woodrow Wilson's New Freedom had
been its denial of the size-efficiency dilemma, its assumption that the size of greatest efficiency was reached at a
relatively early stage and that further growth resulted
from the employment of unfair competitive practices. It
followed that if the government could keep competition
fair, then a competitive economy could be preserved; and
this philosophy underlay such measures as the Clayton
Act and the Federal Trade Commission Act. In a sense,
too, it lay behind the FTC's sponsorship of trade practice

[8] DIE, Staff Studies, 53–57; Miller, *Unfair Competition*, 5–7, 12–
13; Wilcox, *Competition and Monopoly*, 13; Charles S. Tippetts
and Shaw Livermore, *Business Organization and Public Control*
(N.Y.: Van Nostrand, 1941), 1–4; Horace M. Gray, in AEA,
Readings in the Social Control of Industry (Philadelphia: Blakiston,
1942), 281–84, 294–95; Gerhard Colm, in Max Ascoli and Fritz
Lehman, eds., *Political and Economic Democracy* (N.Y.: Norton,
1937), 32–39; Warren Bishop, in *Nation's Business*, Aug. 1931,
pp. 35–36, 102–3; Edward Mason, in Douglass V. Brown et al.,
The Economics of the Recovery Program (N.Y.: McGraw-Hill,
1934), 52–54, 59–61. For general statements of competitive theory
and philosophy, see Louis D. Brandeis, *The Curse of Bigness* (N.Y.:
Viking, 1934), 114–22; J. B. and J. M. Clark, *The Control of
Trusts* (N.Y.: Macmillan, 1912), 25–36, 96–104, 187–202; Woodrow Wilson, *The New Freedom* (Garden City: Doubleday, Page,
1913), 163–222; Frank A. Fetter, *The Masquerade of Monopoly*
(N.Y.: Harcourt, Brace, 1931), 400–29; W. H. S. Stevens, *Unfair
Competition* (Chicago: U. of Chicago Press, 1917), 217–44.

conference agreements in the nineteen twenties, although in practice the rules written into these agreements often tended to facilitate monopolistic collusion rather than strengthen competition.

Consequently, to men who still believed in an antitrust approach, the National Industrial Recovery Act was represented simply as a logical extension of the New Freedom. After all, was not predatory price-cutting one of the chief breeders of monopoly? Why, then, should not sales below cost be outlawed as an unfair practice? Was not price discrimination one of those predatory tactics whereby small competitors were driven from the field? Why, then, should not all businessmen be required to post their prices and adhere to them? The same logic was applied to other competitive practices. Sometimes the preservation of competition was confused with the preservation of small entrepreneurs; but even the latter objective could reasonably be justified as a logical extension of traditional antitrust policy.

Because of the strength of this competitive ideal and the necessity of making some gestures towards it, the National Industrial Recovery Act was a contradiction in terms from the beginning. Its proponents wanted to permit agreements that would violate the Sherman Act, yet they could not admit that they would permit monopolies or monopolistic practices; and the solution had been a clause exempting the proposed codes from the antitrust laws and another providing that no code should be so applied as "to permit monopolies or monopolistic practices, or to eliminate, oppress, or discriminate against small enterprises." The incompatibility between the goals of the planners and those of the antitrusters was thus glossed over and the buck passed to the administrators. It was not surprising that a second major policy conflict should develop around the "monopoly" issue, around such matters as the content of the trade practice provisions, their contribution to collusive arrangements, their effect on small business, and the extent to which they promoted or destroyed a free market.[9]

v

In the background of the National Industrial Recovery Act, then, were three visions of the ideal business structure, three analyses of the depression, three lines of policy recommendations, and three sets of policy prescribers, each convinced that the other two were basically wrong. The policy of enforcing competition, said the planners and business rationalizers, was outmoded, intellectually bankrupt, and a proven failure. The vision of a business commonwealth, said the antitrusters and national planners, was only a mask for the proven evils of private monopoly. And the idea of democratic planning, said the antitrusters and business planners, was a contradiction in terms, a policy that could only result in the eventual destruction of political democracy, property rights, individual liberty, and the capitalist system.

Such conflicting counsels were hardly conducive to logically consistent administration, particularly when they were backed by rival economic pressure groups, subordinated to the demand for action, and set in the midst of the worst depression in American history. The administrators of the National Industrial Recovery Act had to take into account not only conflicting ideologies, but also the more basic economic conflicts within business, between business and labor, and between producer and consumer. They had to move swiftly, to take some sort of action.

[9] Miller, *Unfair Competition*, 7–11, 71–72, 312–14; Russell Hardy, *Relation of the Industrial Recovery Act and the Antitrust Laws* (1934), 2, 6–8; DIE, Staff Studies, 95; Jack Levin, "Status of the Antitrust Laws under NIRA," SR&P, NRA Records; *Congressional Record*, 73 Cong., 1 Sess., LXVII, 5158; Karl A. Boedecker, "A Critical Appraisal of the Antitrust Policy of the United States Government from 1933 to 1945," Ph.D. Dissertation, U. of Wis. (1947), 107–9, 130–34; G. Cullom Davis, in MVHR, Dec. 1962, pp. 438, 449–54; Schlesinger, *Politics of Upheaval*, 388.

And they had to maintain a political base, a constituency that would insure their survival. Under the circumstances, it was not surprising that policy decisions rarely followed any consistent pattern. Only one thing seemed certain: laissez faire as a respectable policy was dead. The state would be used as a positive instrument of economic intervention; whether to restore and maintain a competitive system, to aid industrial groups in suppressing competition, or to plan a new industrial order was not clear.

CHAPTER 3. THE TRIUMPH OF INDUSTRIAL SELF-GOVERNMENT

WHEN President Roosevelt signed the National Industrial Recovery Act on June 16, 1933, the demand for some sort of governmental action was overwhelming; and gruff, tough General Hugh Johnson, with his picturesque vocabulary and flair for invective, was just the man to provide it. Whatever else he might be doing, it was action, action with color, drama, movement, and a wartime sense of crisis.

This was particularly true of the mid-summer drive to put over the President's Reemployment Agreement. Johnson, in the hope of placing all industries on an equal footing and stimulating the submission of formal codes, launched a campaign to secure voluntary agreements, arrangements under which individual firms would pledge themselves to eliminate child labor, pay a minimum wage of twelve or thirteen dollars a week for forty hours work, and display a Blue Eagle emblem as a symbol of compliance. Securing such pledges seemed to call for a great patriotic crusade, for something similar to the Liberty Loan campaigns of World War I. And accordingly, with the assistance of Charles S. Horner, the man who had directed the war bond drives, Johnson proceeded to treat the nation to the greatest outpouring of ballyhoo and patriotic appeal since the war. From the radio, the press, the pulpits, and the rostrums of thousands of four-minute speakers came the exhortation to join the President in his war against depression. There was no longer any room for "shirkers and slackers." Everyone must do his part! [1] Every-

[1] Frank Hursey et al., NRA Work Materials 61 (Code Compliance Activities of NRA), 56–57; H. C. Hoover, NRA Work Materials 82 (The President's Reemployment Agreement), 4–6; J. F. Carter, The New Dealers (N.Y.: Simon & Schuster, 1934), 31; Arthur M. Schlesinger, Jr., The Coming of the New Deal (Boston: Houghton Mifflin, 1959), 112–15; Raymond Clapper, in Review of

one, in the words of one songwriter, should:

Join the good old N.R.A., Boys, and we will end this aw-
ful strife.
Join it with the spirit that will give the Eagle life.
Join it, folks, then push and pull, many millions strong,
While we go marching to Prosperity.

How the Nation shouted when they heard the joyful news!
We're going back to work again, and that means bread
and shoes.
Folks begin to smile again. They are happy and at ease,
While we go marching to Prosperity.[2]

For a short period, too, New Deal and business spokesmen wrought a virtual revolution in popular symbolism.
"Competition" became "economic cannibalism," and
"rugged individualists" became "industrial pirates." Conservative industrialists, veteran antitrusters, and classical
economists were all lumped together and branded "social
Neanderthalers," "Old Dealers," and "corporals of disaster." The time-honored practice of reducing prices to
gain a larger share of the market became "cut-throat and
monopolistic price slashing," and those that engaged in
this dastardly activity became "chiselers." Conversely,
monopolistic collusion, price agreements, proration, and
cartelization became "cooperative" or "associational" activities; and devices that were chiefly designed to eliminate
competition bore the euphemistic title, "codes of fair
competition." A whole set of favorable collectivist symbols emerged to describe what American law and the

---

Reviews, Aug. 1933, pp. 20–21; E. F. Brown, in Current History,
Oct. 1933, pp. 78, 83; NRA, Handbook for Speakers (1933);
Pointed Paragraphs for Speakers (1933); SIRB, "Abstract of Editorial
Comment on the National Industrial Recovery Program," June 1933,
OF 466, Roosevelt Papers; SIRB Minutes, June 26, 1933; M. F.
Boyd, "History of PRA," 47–49; M. Creditor to Alvin Brown, Oct.
2, 1933, all in NRA Records (MR&D, Histories Unit File, and
Policy Decisions File—CAF).
   [2] "The NRA Prosperity March," in Misc. File, Ickes Papers.

courts had previously, under other names, regarded as harmful to society.[3]

The glorious crusade tapered off only slightly in the late summer of 1933, when General Johnson's code-making machine began to grind out codes by the dozen, and 250,000 people paraded down the streets of New York from 1:30 p.m. until midnight. Not since World War I had businessmen descended on Washington in such multitudes; and never, not even in the days of Herbert Hoover, had the Commerce Building witnessed such business-government cooperation. "Washington was up to its nervous neck," wrote one observer, "in codifiers, coordinators and all the great assemblage of other seekers after light and lucre."[4]

II

Behind the facade of propaganda and histrionics the code-making process moved steadily ahead. Prior to the launching of the NRA campaign, only the cotton textile industry had been codified; but as the campaign gathered momentum, the logjam was broken. The codes for the shipbuilding and wool textile industries were promulgated in late July. Electrical manufacturing and the coat and suit trades joined the procession during the first week of August; and by the end of August, the President had

[3] See Leverett S. Lyon et al., *The National Recovery Administration* (Washington: Brookings, 1935), 94; Karl A. Boedecker, "A Critical Appraisal of the Antitrust Policy of the United States Government from 1933 to 1945," Ph.D. Dissertation, U. of Wis. (1947), 132–34; Eugene W. Burr et al., "Memorandum on the Steel Code," Dec. 29, 1933, PPF 1820, Roosevelt Papers. The specific phrases are from Hugh Johnson, in *American Magazine*, Aug. 1934, p. 21; Johnson, *The Blue Eagle from Egg to Earth* (Garden City: Doubleday, Doran, 1935), 169, 177, 262; and the NRA's *Handbook for Speakers*, *Pointed Paragraphs for Speakers*, and *Helpful Hints for Speakers* (1933).

[4] Brown, in *Current History*, Oct. 1933, pp. 78–81; Samuel G. Blythe, in *Saturday Evening Post*, Dec. 2, 1933, p. 10; *New York Times*, Sept. 14, 1933.

signed the codes for the steel, petroleum, lumber, and automobile industries. On September 18 the promulgation of the Bituminous Coal Code completed the codification of most of the major industries, although months of code writing for minor industries still lay ahead.

Essentially, the writing of the codes was a bargaining process; and those that bargained for the government had no set policy to follow. In the early days, as one commentator put it, policy enunciations were "like the folk lore of the ancients, . . . transmitted, for the most part, orally and based on the sometime cryptic recommendations of the Administrator." Actual policy depended largely upon the judgments and sympathies of individual deputy administrators; and these judgments and sympathies naturally varied from man to man, depending upon the deputy's background, the way in which issues were presented, and the political pressures inherent in the underlying power structure.[5]

Under the circumstances, business domination of the code-writing process was virtually inevitable. Business leaders could muster the necessary economic and political power; and more important, they could count on a friendly administration. General Johnson himself sympathized with their aspirations. The deputy administrators were drawn almost invariably from the ranks of business. And most of Johnson's key subordinates, men like Alvin Brown, Robert Lea, Kenneth Simpson, Arthur D. Whiteside, Clarence Williams, and Malcolm Muir, came from industrial or military backgrounds and tended to share business views. The result, noted one observer, was

[5] CIA, *The National Recovery Administration* (House Doc. 158, 75 Cong., 1 Sess., 1937), 19–21, 36, 129–31; Schlesinger, *Coming of New Deal*, 112, 116–19; Lyon et al., *NRA*, 84–88, 104–13, 132–40, 562–65; Donald Richberg, *The Rainbow* (Garden City: Doubleday, Doran, 1936), 31, 124; NRA, *Work Materials 19* (*History of the Review Division*), 2–3; Harry Mulkey, *NRA Work Materials 36* (*The So-called Model Code*), 10–12. The codes mentioned, together with their dates of promulgation, are available in NRA, *Codes of Fair Competition*, Vol. 1.

little more than a "bargain between business leaders on the one hand and businessmen in the guise of government officials on the other." [6]

In many instances, the codes did not go so far as some businessmen desired. Even in the surcharged atmosphere of 1933, concessions had to be made to competitive symbols; and in a few areas, like the clothing and sewing trades, the labor unions were strong enough to play an active role. Generally speaking, however, the wage-and-hour provisions were riddled with exceptions and loopholes, labor representation on the code authorities was held to a minimum, and the demand for "constructive relief from the antitrust laws" was substantially satisfied. As code making proceeded, industrialists succeeded in incorporating a whole series of provisions that were designed essentially to eliminate competition and establish business cartels.[7]

One set of these provisions was designed to establish minimum prices, sometimes directly, sometimes indirectly. A few codes, like those for the lumber, cleaning and dyeing, and coal industries, contained authority for direct price fixing, although as a general rule, such grants of au-

[6] Lewis L. Lorwin and A. Ford Hinrichs, *National Economic and Social Planning* (Washington: GPO, 1935), 71, 85; NRA, *Employees of the National Recovery Administration* (Senate Doc. 164, 73 Cong., 2 Sess., 1934), 1–38; Carter, *New Dealers*, 31–50; Lyon et al., *NRA*, 129–31, 136–37, 566–67, 706; *Who's Who in America?* (1934–5). Johnson's attitude was probably also affected by doubts concerning the constitutionality of the National Industrial Recovery Act. If he could win the uncoerced assent of major industries, he might bypass the constitutional issue. See Schlesinger, *Coming of New Deal*, 108–9.

[7] Students of the code-writing process are almost unanimous in noting the weakness of the labor provisions and the triumph of the business point of view. See Lyon et al., *NRA*, 93, 120–23, 346, 427–44, 458–61, 568–77; Lorwin and Hinrichs, *National Planning*, 71, 85–86; CIA, *NRA*, 14, 33–34, 38–40; Schlesinger, *Coming of New Deal*, 125–26; Mulkey, *Work Materials 36*, 12; Saul Nelson, *NRA Work Materials 56* (*Minimum Price Regulation under Codes of Fair Competition*), 23–24; Herbert F. Taggart, *Minimum Prices under the NRA* (Ann Arbor: U. of Mich. Press, 1936), 22.

thority were limited to exceptional areas like natural resources, transportation, or the service trades, areas where such alternative appeals as conservation, the public utility concept, or the desire to save the "little fellow" could be used to justify a direct break with competitive standards.[8] In the great majority of cases, NRA officials suggested a milder price provision prohibiting sales below cost, a provision that violated competitive standards to a lesser extent, since it was ostensibly designed to prevent the monopolistic abuse of predatory price cutting and was usually qualified by allowing firms to meet the price of lower-cost competitors. Eventually, this type of provision appeared in approximately four hundred codes and supplements, although the specific wording varied from code to code and cost was variously defined as "individual cost," "average cost," "lowest reasonable cost," "reasonable cost," and "lowest representative cost." Whatever the definition, industries tended to use the word "cost" when they meant "price" in an effort to fix minimum prices sufficiently high to enable the majority of their members to make a profit. And to facilitate administration and enforcement, they secured added provisions for the development of uniform cost-accounting formulas. By the time these were worked out, however, the NRA had become much more skeptical about arbitrary definitions of "cost," and consequently, only a small fraction of them ever became effective.

The minimum price provisions also took a special form

[8] The codes usually listed in this category are iron and steel, lumber, bituminous coal, cleaning and dyeing, domestic freight forwarding, motor bus, motor vehicle retailing, laundry, bowling and billiard, barber shop, shoe rebuilding, petroleum, and wood-cased lead pencil. For the last six of these, the provision never became effective. The count differs among various authorities because minimum price fixing shaded imperceptibly into other devices designed to achieve this end by a more indirect route. R&P Div., *Post-Code Analysis Series*, No. 40-D; Taggart, *Minimum Prices*, 20–22, 111–38; C. A. Pearce, NRA *Trade Practice Programs* (N.Y.: Columbia U. Press, 1939), 59–60; Nelson, *Work Materials* 56, xi, 47.

in the retail codes. Here the typical provision prohibited sales below invoice cost plus a percentage mark-up, a requirement commonly known as loss limitation. Ostensibly, this was designed to eliminate the loss leader, a marketing practice that small retailers regarded as deceptive, unfair, and conducive to monopoly; but more generally, its purpose was to maintain traditional methods of distribution and thus aid independent retailers and wholesalers in their struggle against the chain stores, mail-order houses, and vertically integrated manufacturers. Closely related, too, both in purpose and effect, were the provisions for resale price maintenance, an arrangement under which distributors were required or expected to maintain prices established by the manufacturer. Such provisions appeared in approximately eighty codes and supplements, although the amount of compulsion behind them differed considerably from code to code.

A second set of provisions legalized and regulated the use of open-price systems, arrangements under which businessmen were required to file prices and engage in the open exchange of price statistics. These were sold to the public as a means of strengthening competition, as devices that would increase knowledge among competitors and prevent hidden price discrimination. More generally, however, they were designed to stabilize prices, reveal "chiselers," and facilitate the enforcement of other price provisions. In all, some 444 of these price-filing plans were eventually adopted, most of which went far beyond previous legal limits. They called for the filing of current and future prices, not just statistics on past transactions; they required the identification of individual sellers; they allowed the disseminating agency to reinforce the statistical materials with interpretative comments and suggestions; they prohibited deviation from filed prices without notification of the code authority; they penalized those who failed to comply; and they required "waiting periods" before a filed price became effective, periods during which pressure could be applied to prevent a price cut.[9]

A third major group of trade practice provisions related primarily to the terms of a sale and were designed generally to reinforce the minimum-price provisions by standardizing costs, sales practices, and non-price competition. Some of these, like the restrictions on combination sales, trade-in allowances, credit terms, and premiums, were intended to prevent indirect concessions that might influence a sale. Some, like the requirements for customer classification or the restrictions on quantity discounts, advertising allowances, and brokerage fees, were designed to preserve existing channels of distribution. Others, like the requirements for basing-point or zone pricing, attempted to preserve existing geographical relationships. And still others tried to regulate bidding and awarding practices, obstruct competition in quality and type, or modify advantages arising out of specialization. In all, they represented a bewildering variety of restraints on competitive freedom.

Still another group of provisions approached the control of price indirectly through the control of production. Limitations on machine or plant hours, for example, appeared in sixty-one codes, authority to establish production quotas appeared in eight, and provisions for inventory control in four. Over thirty industries, too, succeeded in winning approval for restrictions on productive capacity, either by limiting the construction of new capacity, preventing the opening of closed plants, or controlling the

[9] Taggart, *Minimum Prices,* 17–20, 34–35, 71–88, 140–50, 290–91; Charles F. Roos, NRA *Economic Planning* (Bloomington: Principia, 1937), 249–50, 277–79; Lyon et al., *NRA,* 224, 585–89, 599–601, 610–11; Pearce, *Trade Practices,* 46, 65–66; DIE, Staff Studies, 1499–1500, 1980; Appendix A, 7–8, 10; Exhibit 1, 1–2; Nelson, *Work Materials* 56, xi, 102–7, 183; CIA, NRA, 132–35, 144–45, 152–56; R&P Div., *Post-Code Analysis Series,* No. 40-D; Enid Baird, NRA *Work Materials* 76 (*Price Filing under NRA Codes*), 21, 445–47.

transfer of existing facilities to other types of production or other localities.[10]

Finally, there were the provisions establishing code authorities and setting up administrative and enforcement machinery. And generally speaking, these reflected a willingness to entrust businessmen with broad governmental powers and a marked reluctance on the part of the businessmen to share the privileges of control with other groups. Most of the early code authorities enjoyed a high degree of autonomy, including the power to interpret code provisions, grant code exemptions, and exercise a wide variety of other quasi-legislative and judicial functions. Nor was there much in the way of a check over these powers. Code authorities could handle statistical reporting to suit themselves; clauses giving the government access to corporate books were few and far between; and provisions for maximum prices, limited salaries, or profit controls were nonexistent. Most code authorities, too, were made up almost exclusively of businessmen, since typically they were either selected by trade associations or chosen in association-dominated elections. Only fifty-one authorities, less than ten percent of the total, ever had labor members, and only ten had consumer representatives.

Practically all authorities included governmental members; yet often the value of such members was more ceremonial than real. Usually, they were selected by the NRA's Industrial Advisory Board, appointed on a part-time, non-paid basis, and given very little power, either to vote or to act on their own initiative. Initially, in fact, many of them were deputy administrators, whose duties elsewhere did not allow them much time to attend code

[10] Lyon et al., NRA, 623–37, 653–69, 689–94; Pearce, *Trade Practices*, 78–79, 91, 121, 124, 201–8; CIA, NRA, 139, 152–55; Schlesinger, *Coming of New Deal*, 126; DIE, Staff Studies, 1637–38, 2064; Appendix A, 7; NRA, *Work Materials 2 (Summary of Analysis of Trade Practice Provisions in NRA Codes)*, II–III.

authority meetings. Almost invariably, too, they came from the ranks of business and were convinced that business leaders could be counted on to do "the right thing." The idea, said Johnson, was to promote "self government," as distinguished from "political government" of industry; and the practical result was government by the larger concerns or by the older, larger, and more strongly established trade associations.[11]

As one considered the whole gamut of code provisions, the drift of events became fairly apparent. Businessmen had not received all they desired, but they had clearly emerged as the stronger of the contending forces and were able to win a good deal, both in terms of code provisions and in terms of the agencies that were to administer them. The codes, although they did contain the mandatory labor clauses and some concessions to competitive ideals, tended essentially to reflect the "association idea" of "industrial self-government." In the initial phase, at least, the philosophy of government-supported cartels was clearly outdistancing the concepts of enforcing competition or of creating a centrally planned economy.

III

Gradually, Johnson and his deputies were developing a formal policy, a set of statements, precedents, and policy pronouncements that would justify their activities, guide the code-making process, and spell out the extent to which industries might govern themselves and the extent to which they might depart from competitive standards.

[11] Lorwin and Hinrichs, *National Planning*, 86; Lyon et al., *NRA*, 166, 212, 267, 275, 280; CIA, *NRA*, 68; Richberg, *Rainbow*, 120–24; DIE, Staff Studies, 509, 610; NRA, *Work Materials 46 (Code Authorities and Their Part in the Administration of NIRA)*, 69, 120, 132–37, 161–63; NRA, "History of the Industrial Advisory Board," II, 188–90; Industrial Advisers' Handbook, Pt. E-6(m); "Origin of the Code Authority"; NRA PR1847, Nov. 22, 1933, all in NRA Records (Finding Aids File, MR&D, Histories Unit File, CAB File—CAF).

These rules, however, were rarely the result of much thinking about broad goals and underlying issues. On the contrary, Johnson deliberately discouraged such an approach. It was "important to the concept of industrial self-government," he told the Special Industrial Recovery Board, "not to have general rules of what should and what should not be in codes," and "resolutions requiring the Administrator to include or not to include this or that thing" were "very embarassing to the Administration." Consequently, policy was made largely by improvisations, by day-to-day responses to contested proposals, business disputes, and emerging problems.

One area of controversy, for example, in which deputy administrators had to make constant decisions, was that relating to the shape and form of the minimum price provisions. Yet it was not until October 25 that a formal policy memorandum attempted to provide a standardized guide and give some idea of what the NRA would accept. In line with the Administration's early announcements, the memorandum stated, the NRA would allow provisions prohibiting sales below cost, with cost preferably defined as "individual cost" and with the exclusion of such inflationary items as return on capital. Such provisions, however, should permit an individual firm to meet the price of a lower-cost competitor, and while they might encourage the formulation of cost-accounting systems, they should not, except in rare cases, compel firms to adopt any particular system. The memorandum also gave official approval to other methods of price stabilization, including loss-limitation clauses, rules against destructive price cutting, resale price maintenance in "exceptional" cases, the prohibition of premiums and other indirect concessions, and the establishment of open-price plans provided they contained certain necessary safeguards. An acceptable plan, for instance, should allow the seller to withdraw a filed price, should make the price information available to both buyers and sellers, should not allow the code authority to veto or modify a filed price, and should not require a waiting period longer than five to ten days.

Another important though less publicized area of controversy was that relating to the nature and form of production controls. Here there was no governing memorandum at all. Johnson had merely stated that production quotas should be discouraged, but that they should not be ruled out completely, that there were cases where the use of them might be justified. As a result, the formulation of a detailed policy was left to the deputy administrators; and in practice, they were officially encouraging inventory control, accepting machine and plant hour limitations without much argument, and allowing controls over physical output in such natural resource industries as oil, copper, and lumber. On some proposals, however, they drew the line. They rejected almost all attempts to limit entry. They turned down most of the elaborate schemes for individual production quotas. And they resisted efforts to restrict new construction or the installation of new equipment, largely because of protests from the manufacturers of such equipment.[12]

A third area of controversy in which policy decisions were necessary was that relating to the make-up, powers, and supervision of code authorities, an area in which the early decisions of Johnson and his deputies leaned distinctly to the side of industrial self-government. Not until late October was there any formally announced policy in regard to code authority organization and procedure.

[12] DIE, Staff Studies, 189, 262, 267, 324–26, 330–31, 1469, 1478–1524, 1637–38, 1810–58; Lorwin and Hinrichs, *National Planning*, 84, 94; Lyon et al., *NRA*, 213–14, 272–74, 603–5, 624–37; NRA, "History of IAB," II, 187–88; SIRB Minutes, Sept. 11, Nov. 27, 1933; Policy Memorandum, Oct. 25, 1933; Notes on Staff Meetings, July 13, 22, 1933, all in NRA Records (Finding Aids File, MR&D, O'Connell File); NRA Progress Report to SIRB, Sept. 9, 1933, OF 466, Roosevelt Papers; Roos, *NRA Planning*, 259, 266; Baird, *Work Materials* 76, 446, 450–51; Pearce, *Trade Practices*, 91, 109–10, 130; Arthur R. Burns, *The Decline of Competition* (N.Y.: McGraw-Hill, 1936), 465–66, 509–10.

Then, beginning on October 24, a series of policy memoranda and announcements laid down a few basic rules. The code authority, they declared, must represent all interests within a particular industry, and if it was identical with or selected by a trade association, the latter must be properly representative. It should also include from one to three non-voting governmental members, one of whom should have a background, but no present interest, in the industry concerned. And it might enforce the provisions for mandatory assessment through the use of labels and insignia. No effort was made, however, to define code authority powers in detail. Instead, said the Administration, it was preferable "to provide that the duty of the Code Authority shall be to execute the provisions of the code and the act, subject to disapproval by the Administrator."

Not much was done either to establish machinery for governmental supervision; yet steps were being taken to encourage and supplement code authority activities. On November 21 Johnson created a Code Authority Organization Committee to facilitate the establishment of code authorities and turn them into working organizations. And the next day, on November 22, he announced that the newly-organized NRA Compliance Division would be used to "fill the blanks in industrial self-government," to act where an industry was not yet organized to handle compliance or govern itself. This action, he felt, again illustrated the "fundamental theory underlying NIRA," a theory based on "industrial self-discipline" tempered by "governmental partnership."

In practice, then, the NRA showed a marked tendency not only to give businessmen the type of arrangements they wanted, but also to justify these arrangements in formal policy pronouncements. Men sympathetic with the business view dominated the NRA's Policy Board, an organization of staff officials that Johnson had created on September 16. It was these men who were chiefly responsible for the policy memorandum of October 25, the model

code of November 6, and the other formal policy pronouncements. And in shaping these pronouncements, they
seemed willing to go along with the rationale of trade association secretaries and business planners, to accept the
ideal of "industrial self-government" and to allow a substantial measure of cartelization.[13]

IV

For a time the real drift of code policy was hidden behind
a facade of propaganda, patriotism, and dramatic action.
Yet popular hysteria could not be maintained indefinitely,
particularly when the promised recovery failed to mate-
rialize. By the fall of 1933 the speculative summer boomlet was over, economic indices were falling again, and a
mood of disenchantment was settling over the country.
And with the change in mood, the realization began to
dawn that essentially the codes reflected the interests of
the larger and more highly organized businessmen, that
the NRA was busily promoting cartels in the interest of
scarcity profits.

The result was a barrage of criticism, a shower of the
"dead cats" that General Johnson had predicted from the

[13] DIE, Staff Studies, 228, 325, 327; NRA, *Work Materials* 46,
163–64; CIA, NRA, 64–68, 72; Lyon et al., NRA, 62–63, 215, 272–
74; Lorwin and Hinrichs, *National Planning*, 167–68; Code Authority Organization Committee, *Information for Code Authorities*
(1934); Mulkey, *Work Materials* 36, 14–29, 32, 159–68; NRA,
Work Materials 19, 3; *Business Week*, Nov. 25, 1933, p. 6; "Origin
of the Code Authority"; Walker Duvall, "Code Administration";
Policy Memorandum, Oct. 25, 1933; Office Order 38, Oct. 24,
1933, in Industrial Advisers' Handbook; SIRB Minutes, Nov. 27,
1933; NRA, "History of IAB," II, 188; Johnson Press Conferences,
Dec. 29, 1933; Report of NRA-Commerce Committee, Oct. 1, 1933;
Alvin Brown to Blackwell Smith, March 8, 1934; Code Standardiza-
tion Group to Smith, Oct. 25, 1933; W. H. Rastall, "NRA and
Relations with Other Government Agencies," 16–17; NRA PR1847,
Nov. 22, 1933, all in NRA Records (Histories Unit File, MR&D,
Finding Aids File, Coles File, Brown File, Hughes File, CTS, CAB
File—CAF).

first. Economists charged that the drive to create mass purchasing power was working in reverse, that prices were rising more rapidly than wages. Farm spokesmen complained vociferously about the rising industrial prices that were cancelling out the effects of the farm program. And labor leaders, too, were sorely disappointed, particularly after the massive organizing campaign launched by the American Federation of Labor ground to a halt and employers began circumventing Section 7a by herding their workers into company unions. The NRA, in the view of some labor spokesmen, was either a fraud or the advance guard of fascism, and the "Congressional theory of a real partnership in industry" had been "ruthlessly and illegally set aside by General Hugh Johnson and his biased deputy administrators." The whole situation, moreover, was made to order for Roosevelt's political enemies. Alfred E. Smith talked about the "heavy, cold, clammy hand of bureaucracy"; William Randolph Hearst spoke of "No Recovery Allowed"; and Virgil Jordan of the National Industrial Conference Board inveighed against a program that was paralyzing "the economic initiative and constructive enterprise of American citizens."

The general public, too, was becoming increasingly disillusioned; and, as a result, the NRA was soon swamped with protests. Workers wanted to know "why the costs of the necessaries of life, such as flour and fuel, are allowed to increase as they are." A university instructor was convinced that the merchants were using "the N.R.A. banner to sail under so as to reap benefits by unfair means," and as a Texas dentist saw "the whole thing, from a local standpoint," it was resolving itself into "a 'price-fixing' combination, without increasing employment in any way." "NRA! That's all I hear!" was a typical reaction. "Why don't you people wait until folks are back to work before you start raising prices?" The change in attitude was also apparent in the reports from district offices. The New York office reported "a noticeable trend toward apathy on the part of the public," the Charleston office noted an "indifferent attitude," the Dallas office, "a perceptible turn to questioning and dissatisfaction," and the Boston office, "a decided intensity in the critical attitude towards the Blue Eagle." All across the country the story was much the same. The millions that had once cheered the NRA parades were lapsing into indifference or hostility.

A spectacular demonstration of the reversal in public sentiment came in October when General Johnson launched a new "Buy Now" campaign, a fresh outburst of propaganda that tried to wring from the consumer what was left of his savings. The campaign, however, was a resounding fiasco, a clear-cut illustration of public exasperation with a recovery program that brought higher prices instead of jobs. An Illinois farmer probably reflected the sentiments of millions when he wrote: "Over the radio you shout, 'Buy, buy, buy now!' In reply, we farmers of the Middle West would like to ask you one question—'What with?' " [14]

[14] Lyon et al., NRA, 97, 489–90, 535–37; Schlesinger, Coming of New Deal, 118–21, 144–46; Hursey et al., Work Materials 61, 56–57; Nation, Nov. 1, 1933, p. 498; New York Times, Aug. 7, 28, Oct. 9, 29, Nov. 7–14, 16, 1933; Johnson, Blue Eagle, 290–91; Literary Digest, Nov. 11, 1933, p. 7; New Republic, Nov. 8, 1933, p. 349; Nov. 22, 1933, p. 36; Time, Nov. 13, 1933, pp. 10–11; Raymond S. Rubinow, NRA Work Materials 45-E-1 (Section 7-a), 1, 55–56, 64–66; William H. Spencer, Collective Bargaining under Section 7-a of the National Industrial Recovery Act (Chicago: U. of Chicago Press, 1935), 7–8; DIE, Staff Studies, 1392–97; Anna Page, NRA Work Materials 45-B-1 (Employment and Unemployment, 1929–35), 36; Federal Reserve Bulletin, Dec. 1933, p. 752; Ruth P. Mack, Controlling Retailers (N.Y.: Columbia U. Press, 1936), 436–39; Business Week, Sept. 23, 1933, pp. 3–4; Chester Gray, "NRA from the Farm Viewpoint"; SIRB Minutes, Oct. 2, 16, 1933; M. Creditor to A. Brown, Oct. 2, 1933; Blue Eagle Letter 13, Oct. 11, 1933; E. J. Evans to Johnson, Dec. 4, 1933; M. H. Filson to Johnson, Aug. 9, 1933; J. D. Ellington to FDR, Aug. 2, 1933; G. A. Anderson to Johnson, Aug. 24, 1933; NRA Public Attitude Reports, N.Y. (Oct. 21, 1933), Dallas (Oct. 21, 1933), Ohio (Oct. 7, 1933); "Comments of District Compliance Directors," Oct. 19, Nov. 22, 1933, all in NRA Records (MR&D, Policy Decisions File

In view of the farm, labor, and consumer complaints, one might expect that businessmen would be jubilant over the outcome. Yet this was hardly the case. Once the sense of panic had passed, some business leaders began to have serious misgivings; and there was a noticeable decline in their willingness to cooperate, either with the government, the unions, or their business colleagues. Some felt that the NRA was paving the way for "labor domination," particularly after it squelched the efforts to write "open shop" clauses into the codes. Others were afraid that the whole program was the first step toward "bureaucratic socialism," that it was setting up "more or less permanent machinery for the future government control of industry." And still others were irked by the red tape involved, the rejection of their pet plans, and the administrative complexities that stemmed from an unplanned and increasingly complex code structure. In the beginning, for example, almost any group of businessmen that saw fit to call itself an "industry" was treated as such, and the result was an amalgam of overlapping jurisdictions. There were codes that cut vertically through the distributive trades, codes that cut segments out of a larger industry, codes with overlapping definitions, and codes of all degrees of prominence. Caught in this tangle of multiple code coverage, many businessmen found themselves subject to conflicting orders, multiple assessments, and overlapping interpretations, an experience that was at best irritating and at worst downright disillusioning.

Many of the business complaints, too, stemmed from the welter of conflicts within industries or between industries, conflicts between large units and small ones, integrated firms and non-integrated, chain stores and independents, manufacturers and distributors, new industries and declining ones, and so on ad infinitum. These conflicts had

---

—CAF, Coles File, Price Lifting File—CGF, Buy Now File— CGF, Public Attitude Reports File, Galvin File); Corwin Edwards to Ben W. Lewis, June 3, 1935, Blaisdell File, NRPB Records.

once been left to the marketplace, but now they were to be settled politically. And many business groups, it seemed, while they sought to enhance their own economic power, were determined to break down the power of their rivals or suppliers. In an atmosphere of this type, where businessmen sat in judgment on their competitors and where aid to one group frequently resulted in harm to another, strong differences inevitably arose, and charges of persecution became rife. The losers in the process were quick to protest and seek redress through political means, quick to discover that their rivals were "monopolistic combinations" and that the code authorities were only legalized agencies of discrimination through which their competitors were trying to put them out of business. The Administration, moreover, was often caught in the middle. It was blamed by one side for not enforcing the codes and by the other for not correcting what seemed to it to be wrongful discrimination.[15]

From almost every angle, then, complaints were increasing; and with the waning of support came demands for basic changes in the direction that the NRA was taking. Antitrusters, who had been temporarily lured by the idea that the NRA would help small business and strengthen competition, were now convinced that the

[15] Rubinow, *Work Materials 45-E-1,* 57–63; *Time,* Nov. 13, 1933, p. 10; Taggart, *Minimum Prices,* 18; Lyon et al., *NRA,* 100, 142–61, 214, 221, 229–31, 240–41, 260–61; CIA, *NRA,* 21, 24–26; Hursey et al., *Work Materials 61,* 50–51, 57–58; Mack, *Controlling Retailers,* 144; Paul C. Aiken, *NRA Work Materials 81* (*Administrative Law and Procedure under NIRA*), 97–98, 120; Clair Wilcox, in TNEC, *Investigation of Concentration of Economic Power,* Pt. 25 (1941), 13323–25; Ely C. Hutchinson, *NRA Work Materials 39* (*Problems of Administration in the Overlapping of Codes*), 16–30; Lorwin and Hinrichs, *National Planning,* 72, 93; DIE, Staff Studies, 2080–81; John P. Miller, *Unfair Competition* (Cambridge: Harvard U. Press, 1941), 352–53; Rexford G. Tugwell, *The Battle for Democracy* (N.Y.: Columbia U. Press, 1935), 263; *Business Week,* Dec. 30, 1933, p. 11; "Comments of District Compliance Directors," Nov. 1933; IAB Minutes, Sept. 7, Oct. 5, Nov. 9, 1933, all in NRA Records (Galvin File, MR&D); FDR to Johnson, Oct. 19, 1933, OF 466, Roosevelt Papers.

program was fostering monopoly everywhere, that it was not a New Deal at all, but rather the "Old Deal in high gear." And economic planners, although they were not opposed to conscious economic controls, disliked intensely the idea of such controls being exercised by business cartels. All they could see so far was "good old capitalist planning," which was subordinating not only the "socialistic implications in the original Roosevelt program, but the remnants of self-adjusting laissez-faire" as well. To both of these groups it seemed that business, in spite of its continued complaints, was getting away with "murder"; and consequently, they had soon joined forces in an attempt to change the course of NRA policy.[16] At first they would have little success, but as the rising stream of protest swelled into an angry torrent, the Administration was forced to make some concessions to their points of view.

[16] Lyon et al., NRA, 705–9; George Soule, in New Republic, Oct. 18, 1933, pp. 269–71; Soule, The Coming American Revolution (N.Y.: Macmillan, 1934), 261; Frank A. Fetter, in Survey Graphic, Nov. 1933, pp. 546–48; John T. Flynn, in Forum, Jan. 1934, p. 7; New York Times, Nov. 6, 1933; April 15, 1934; Dexter Keezer to Paul Homan, Oct. 24, 1934, Blaisdell File, NRPB Records.

CHAPTER 4. THE ASSOCIATION
IDEA IN RETREAT

As the antitrusters and economic planners viewed the drift of NRA policy in late 1933, they found little that was to their liking. Although they disagreed strongly about ultimate goals, they could agree that certain changes were in order. The planners would still rather see the basic economic decisions left to what competition there was than to see them turned over to business cartels; and the antitrusters, once they conceded the necessity for controls, wanted to be sure that they were exercised in the public interest. Consequently, those who advocated policy changes tended to stress two major objectives. One was the promotion of freer markets through the elimination of price and production controls. The other was the development of more responsible code authorities through broader representation and closer governmental supervision.[1]

At first most of these demands for change seemed to come from rival agencies and Administration leaders who found it difficult to get along with Johnson. The Department of Labor was strongly critical of the way statistical reporting was being turned over to the code authorities. The Department of Agriculture was deeply concerned about the effects of rising industrial prices. And the Federal Trade Commission regarded the codes as a perversion of the whole concept of regulated competition. Johnson was quarreling, too, with Harry Hopkins over the wage scales of the Civil Works Administration; and there was almost constant friction between the General and the Secretary of the Interior, Harold Ickes, the man

[1] Dexter Keezer to Paul Homan, Oct. 24, 1934, Blaisdell File, NRPB Records; George Soule, in *New Republic*, Oct. 18, 1933, p. 271; Leverett S. Lyon et al., *The National Recovery Administration* (Washington: Brookings, 1935), 705–6, 712–14.

in charge of the Public Works Administration and the Petroleum Administration. In Johnson's view, the PWA was taking much too long to get into operation, and the oil program resembled a "dictatorship" instead of a "plan of industrial self-government." Ickes, on the other hand, felt that the NRA codes were deliberately promoting monopoly and were responsible for the increased number of identical bids on public works contracts.[2]

The early focal point for much of this criticism was the Special Industrial Recovery Board, the interdepartmental agency that was supposed to coordinate the NRA with the rest of the recovery program. At meeting after meeting, such critics as Rexford Tugwell and Henry A. Wallace objected strenuously to the establishment of price and production controls unless they were accompanied by "adequate positive government regulation," by provisions for quality standards, access to corporate books, and adequate consumer representation. To Johnson, however, price stabilization was a necessary weapon, a means of halting destructive price wars and maintaining labor standards. Consequently, he ignored the Board, refused to submit codes to it, and finally demanded its dismissal. The President, moreover, was inclined to agree with Johnson. In December 1933 he abolished the Board and transferred its functions to the National Recovery Council, a remote coordinating agency unlikely to give Johnson much difficulty.

[2] Lewis L. Lorwin and A. Ford Hinrichs, *National Economic and Social Planning* (Washington: GPO, 1935), 164–69; Hugh S. Johnson, *The Blue Eagle from Egg to Earth* (Garden City: Doubleday, Doran, 1935), 210–11; J. F. Carter, *The New Dealers* (N.Y.: Simon & Schuster, 1934), 182; W. H. Rastall, "NRA and Relations with Other Government Agencies," 5–6; SIRB Minutes, July 18, Aug. 28, Sept. 6, 1933; Johnson's Press Conferences, Dec. 22, 1933; S. C. Oppenheim, Report on Relation of NRA to FTC, Aug. 2, 1934, all in NRA Records (CTS, MR&D, Coles File, Reorganization of NRA File—CAF); Johnson to FDR, Sept. 7, 1933; Turner Battle to Marvin McIntyre, Sept. 8, 1933, both in Roosevelt Papers (OF 15C).

As the SIRB faded out, the spotlight shifted to Johnson's quarrel with the Department of Agriculture and the similar policy conflict there. In negotiating the trade practice provisions of the food-processing codes, for which the Department of Agriculture was initially responsible, Agricultural Adjustment Administrator George Peek seemed willing to give the processors almost any type of controls they wanted, provided they would agree to raise prices paid to farmers. The leftist economic planners in the Department, however, led by Undersecretary Tugwell and General Counsel Jerome Frank, did not share Peek's view. The processors, they felt, owed the government something in exchange for antitrust immunity, and that something should be a check over excessive prices and unreasonable profits, preferably in the form of clauses providing for quality standards and full access by the government to corporate books and records. To Peek such talk was un-American nonsense. To Johnson it was all "part of Mr. Frank's general sabotage of N.I.R.A." It had needlessly frightened the food-processing industries and had left them little incentive to accept the decent labor provisions proposed by the NRA. By the end of 1933, this quarrel had reached a boiling point, and the President was finally forced to intervene. The result was a partial victory for each side. George Peek left the Department of Agriculture, but all food codes, except those for "first processors" of raw products, were transferred to the NRA, where, as everyone knew, book-inspection and quality standard clauses were not necessary.[3]

[3] George Peek and Samuel Crowther, *Why Quit Our Own* (N.Y.: Van Nostrand, 1936), 107–119; Gilbert C. Fite, *George N. Peek and the Fight for Farm Parity* (Norman: U. of Okla. Press, 1954), 259–62; Arthur M. Schlesinger, Jr., *The Coming of the New Deal* (Boston: Houghton Mifflin, 1959), 50–52, 55–57, 123–24, 127–28; Persia Campbell, *Consumer Representation in the New Deal* (N.Y.: Columbia U. Press, 1940), 210–19; *Literary Digest*, Dec. 23, 1933, p. 7; Rastall, "NRA and Other Agencies," 36–40; SIRB Minutes, July 18, 19, Aug. 28, Nov. 13, 27, 29, 1933; Johnson to Donald Richberg, Dec. 26, 1933; Rexford Tugwell to Johnson, June 29,

Initially, then, Johnson had succeeded in squelching the attempts of his critics to bring about a general reorientation in trade practice policy. His victories, however, did not prevent the gradual emergence of an opposing point of view within his own organization, particularly on the part of the liberal, consumer-minded economists and sociologists who manned such agencies as the Consumers' Advisory Board and the Research and Planning Division. The former agency was inclined to take its job of protecting consumers much more seriously than its creators had intended. It was headed by Johnson's old friend, Mary Rumsey, daughter of E. H. Harriman, the railroad king; and according to Dexter Keezer, the second executive director, its members could be classified into three general schools of thought, all of which were strongly opposed to the type of price and production controls that Johnson was allowing in the codes. Some members, said Keezer, were semi-collectivist in outlook; others favored rules that would elevate the plane of competition; and still others retained considerable faith in the philosophy of laissez faire.[4]

During the early phases of the NRA, though, the views of the Consumers' Advisory Board counted for little.

1933, all in NRA Records (CTS, MR&D, Johnson File—CAF, Agriculture File—CGF); Henry Wallace to FDR, Aug. 22, Sept. 7, Oct. 2, 1933; Johnson to FDR, Sept. 7, 1933; Johnson to Marvin McIntyre, Nov. 17, 1933, all in Roosevelt Papers (OF 1, 466).

[4] Campbell, *Consumer Representation*, 11, 28, 38–44; Lyon et al., *NRA*, 706; Carter, *New Dealers*, 66–72; NEC Consumers' Division, *Bulletin* 2 (1934); Keezer to Homan, Oct. 24, 1934, Blaisdell File, NRPB Records. Included on the board at one time or another were Robert S. Lynd, co-author of the *Middletown* series; Paul H. Douglas of the University of Chicago; William T. Foster of the famous underconsumptionist team of Foster and Catchings; Frank Graham, president of the University of North Carolina; George Stocking of the University of Texas; Walton Hamilton of Yale Law School; Stacy May, an economist for the Rockefeller Foundation; Frederic C. Howe, Consumers' Council for the AAA; Gardiner Means and Louis H. Bean, economists for the Department of Agriculture; and Thomas Blaisdell, professor of economics at Columbia.

Johnson concluded that the intellectual "theorizing" of the agency was troublesome and useless nonsense. The deputy administrators paid little attention to the Board's protests. Its first director, William Ogburn, had finally resigned in exasperation after his suggestions for consumer representation, book-inspection clauses, quality standards, and purchasing power indices were consistently ignored. Still the Board did not resign itself to inaction. It brought Corwin Edwards down from New York University to take charge of a new section dealing with price complaints. It kept issuing memoranda and policy statements criticizing the use of price and production controls without adequate safeguards. And it tried, without much success, to develop a consumer constituency that would back a change in policy. By enlisting the aid of Henry Wallace and Frances Perkins, Mrs. Rumsey persuaded Johnson to acquiesce in the establishment of a Bureau of Economic Education headed by Paul Douglas of the University of Chicago and responsible for a limited experiment in the organization of county consumer councils. Approximately 150 of these councils were eventually established, but they never developed into the effective pressure group that their creators had in mind.[5]

The Consumers' Board also kept calling for a public

[5] Campbell, *Consumer Representation*, 31, 35–36, 46–51, 56–58, 64–66, 70, 109, 117–19; Johnson, *Blue Eagle*, 179–80; Lyon et al., *NRA*, 126–28, 706; Schlesinger, *Coming of New Deal*, 129–30; Robert S. Lynd, in *New Republic*, Jan. 3, 1934, p. 221; William F. Ogburn, in *Nation*, Sept. 20, 1933, pp. 318–20; NEC Consumers' Division, *Bulletin* 1 (1934); *New York Times*, Aug. 15, 1933; Keezer to Homan, Oct. 24, 1934; Corwin Edwards to Ben Lewis, June 3, 1935; Memo. re Interview of Corwin Edwards, Nov. 16, 1933, all in NRPB Records (Blaisdell File, Lorwin File); Ogburn to Deputy Administrators and Staff, Aug. 1, 1933; Ogburn to Johnson, Aug. 14, 1933; SIRB Minutes, Aug. 7, 14, 1933; "Suggested Policies in Handling Codes," Oct. 22, 1933; NRA PR's 669, 684, Sept. 8, 1933; NRA PR1759, Nov. 16, 1933; NEC PR, April 7, 1934; Sue S. White, "The County Consumers' Councils," March 8, 1935; Paul Douglas, "The Functions and Organization of Consumer County Councils," Jan. 5, 1934, all in NRA Records (CAB File—CGF, MR&D, CAB File—MR&D).

hearing on the price question; and in November 1933 Johnson did schedule one for December 12. A few days later, however, he changed his mind and postponed the hearing until January, largely, it seems, because merchants were afraid that the publicity would injure their holiday business. His decision brought a vigorous protest from a group of New York consumer organizations. Mrs. Rumsey then invited these groups to a consumers' conference in Washington. And following the conference, on December 17, she took fourteen consumer spokesmen, headed by Leon Henderson of the Russell Sage Foundation, to see General Johnson. The result was the famous "shouting interview." Johnson was soon pounding his desk and shouting about "unjustified complaints." Then, much to his surprise, Henderson began shouting back. He told the General in strong language that the consumer was being pushed around and that he had better do something about it. "If you're so goddamned smart," Johnson roared, "why don't you come down here and be my assistant on consumer problems?" Probably to the General's consternation, Henderson took the job. The time of the Consumers' Board, Johnson informed his press conference later, had finally arrived, and he had "told them if they wanted to name somebody it was all right—especially the fellow doing the most of the kicking." [6]

As consumer representative, Leon Henderson soon emerged as a leading critic of the NRA's business-oriented price and production policies. Eventually, in February 1934, he took over the direction of the Research and Planning Division, an agency that was staffed largely by

[6] Campbell, *Consumer Representation*, 60–61, 66–67; Ruth P. Mack, *Controlling Retailers* (N.Y.: Columbia U. Press, 1936), 463; Schlesinger, *Coming of New Deal*, 130–31; Samuel Lubell, in *Saturday Evening Post*, Sept. 13, 1941, p. 13; *New York Times*, Dec. 16–17, 1933; Edwards to Lewis, June 3, 1935, Blaisdell File, NRPB Records; Johnson's Press Conferences, Dec. 17, 1933; NRA PR's 1720, 2140, 2209, Nov. 16, Dec. 8, 11, 1933; Gardiner Means, Report on the Consumers' Conference, Dec. 17, 1933, all in NRA Records (Coles File, CAB File—MR&D).

academic economists who tended to share the views of their colleagues on the Consumers' Advisory Board.[7] Like the members of the CAB, however, the Research and Planning economists had not had much of a voice in early policy decisions. In Johnson's view, the Division was not designed for long-range planning and policy formulation, as some of its staff seemed to think. It was simply a statistical bureau; and even in this field, its role was limited since Johnson had no intention of turning "a bunch of statisticians loose on American industry." Under Stephen DuBrul, a former General Motors sales manager who replaced Alexander Sachs as head of the agency in October 1933, the Division had become particularly inactive. According to one official, DuBrul "first sabotaged and then suspended" the whole effort to centralize statistical reporting, standardize procedures, and come up with meaningful and useful data and recommendations.[8]

During the early period, then, the Consumers' Advisory Board and the Research and Planning Division were largely ignored. Yet they had challenged existing policy, set forth alternative goals, and aroused misgivings and fears in business circles, fears that if the "intolerant and dictatorial attitude" of the "Advisory Divisions" should prevail, it would result in "putting Government into business," undermining the whole theory of industrial "self-government," and imposing "untried and impractical ideas upon experienced business men." Perhaps, suggested Gerard Swope in November 1933, it would be best if the NRA could be supplanted by a National

[7] The more prominent figures in the agency were Charles F. Roos, Victor S. Von Szeliski, George Galloway, Andrew Court, Albert J. Hettinger, and James Hughes.

[8] Lyon et al., NRA, 131, 564–65; Lorwin and Hinrichs, National Planning, 93, 164–69; Charles F. Roos, NRA Economic Planning (Bloomington: Principia, 1937), 94–97; George H. Soule, The Coming American Revolution (N.Y.: Macmillan, 1934), 230–31; New York Times, Feb. 25, 27, 1934; SIRB Minutes, Sept. 11, 1933; MR&D, NRA Records.

Chamber of Commerce and Industry, which would then take over the job of supervising the code authorities and securing compliance. Johnson agreed that this was "a kind of a goal to shoot at," but President Roosevelt expressed doubt that business could run itself. For Johnson's critics, the Swope proposal was only one more indication that the NRA was paving the way for fascism and the corporate state. They were more convinced than ever that a basic reorientation in policy was needed; and their hope was that the price hearings scheduled for January 1934 could provide sufficient evidence and generate enough support to bring about the necessary changes.[9]

II

At the Commerce Building on January 9, 1934, General Johnson opened his long-heralded price hearing, an event that his opponents later regarded as a crucial turning point, as the beginning of a transitional period that would culminate in the revival of the competitive ideal, an attempt to restore freer markets, and the ouster of the General himself. At last the critics of the NRA were to be given a chance to present their case, accumulate evidence, analyze complaints, and initiate studies and debates that would lead to policy changes. And generally speaking, they tried their best to take advantage of the opportunity.

The complaints at the hearing came chiefly from governmental purchasing agents, large retailers, farm organi-

[9] *Business Week*, Nov. 4, 1933, p. 11; *New York Times*, Nov. 2–4, 1933; Trade Association Executives' Advisory Committee on NRA, "Policy Questions," Dec. 14, 1933; and "Suggestions for Improvement of the NRA," Feb. 6, 1934; IAB Minutes, Sept. 15, Oct. 10, 1933; E. A. Chavennes to Sol Rosenblatt, Jan. 26, 1934; Johnson's Press Conferences, Nov. 1, 1933; all in NRA Records (Montgomery File, MR&D, Rosenblatt File, Coles File); Gerard Swope, Statement to BAPC, Nov. 1, 1933, OF 3, Roosevelt Papers.

zations, and consumers' groups. In all, the complaints covered some thirty-four codes, but most of them were concentrated against such industries as lumber, textiles, paper, printing, steel, cement, bituminous coal, and scientific apparatus. In these areas, so the complainants charged, the codes had resulted in uniformity of bids and unjustified price increases. Such devices as price filing, prohibition of sales below cost, uniform surcharges, and limited discounts had been used to standardize prices, facilitate collusion, and eliminate competitive safeguards.[10]

The real fireworks, however, were provided by the Consumers' Advisory Board. For more than a month its price section under Corwin Edwards had been piecing together individual complaints and weaving them into running accounts of the situations in particular industries. "Morale ran high," Edwards recalled, since "we felt ourselves an isolated fighting group in a hostile environment." After completing its reports, the section had sent brief summaries to the industries concerned. But because of resulting protests from business leaders, Arthur D. Whiteside, the presiding officer at the price hearing, ruled that the reports were inadmissible as evidence. This, in turn, brought vigorous protests from the CAB. Although Whiteside later relented and allowed the Board to present summary statements of its findings, the damage was already done. The press quickly picked up the story that the Consumers' Board had been gagged; it featured the story in bold headlines; and veteran antitrusters, like William

[10] Lyon et al., NRA, 706–9; Herbert F. Taggart, *Minimum Prices under the NRA* (Ann Arbor: U. of Mich. Press, 1936), 27–28; *New York Times*, Jan. 10, 11, 13, 1934; R&P Div., "Summary of Complaints at Price Hearing," Jan. 25, 1934; Gertrude Working et al., "Report on Character and Disposition of Complaints Made at Price Hearing," May 4, 1934; Memo. re Complaints by Commodities, Feb. 6, 1934; NRA PR 2706, Jan. 12, 1934, all in NRA Records (SR&P, Price Hearing File—CAF); Edwards to Lewis, June 3, 1935; Keezer to Homan, Oct. 24, 1934, both in Blaisdell File, NRPB Records.

E. Borah and Gerald P. Nye, promptly took advantage of the unfavorable publicity to begin blasting away at the NRA from the Senate floor.[11]

On January 18 Senator Nye opened the Senate debate with a charge that the NRA was a breeder of monopoly. The price hearing, he said, demonstrated clearly that trade associations dominated by large firms were fixing prices, gouging consumers, eliminating small businessmen, and intimidating hesitant association members. If present policy continued, he concluded, the "plunderers" might as well adopt "The Last Round-up" as their theme song and "trample under heel" whatever remained of independent business. Nye's blast was followed by a similar one from Senator Borah. Already, he claimed, his office had received over nine thousand complaints from small businessmen; and it was now high time that the antitrust laws were revived and enforced.

On the evening of January 18, in an address before a convention of the National Retail Dry Goods Association, Johnson struck back at his critics. These men, he declared, knew about as much about industry as he knew about "the queer ichthyology of the great Pacific Deep." In reality, the codes were highly beneficial to small enterprises because they had helped to stabilize prices and check "a downward spiral into an economic hell." The people that were complaining were the "chiselers," and "chiselers" had to go, "whether they be big or little." Johnson, though, did end his speech with a desperate plea: "If I had only nine words with which to address you . . . I would rise here and say: 'Keep prices down. For God's sake, keep prices down.'"

Whether or not they knew anything about industry,

[11] Campbell, *Consumer Representation*, 48, 70–73; Lyon et al., *NRA*, 706–9; *New York Times*, Jan. 11, 1934; Edwards to Lewis, June 3, 4, 1935; Keezer to Homan, Oct. 24, 1934, both in Blaisdell File, NRPB Records.

Borah and Nye knew they had hit upon one of the NRA's sore spots. Letters from small businessmen poured in, praising them for the "great service" they were rendering. And heartened by the response, they stepped up their offensive. When he learned that the FTC had produced a memorandum criticizing the steel code, Borah promptly pushed a resolution through Congress calling upon the Commission to investigate price fixing in the steel and oil industries. A few days later, Nye introduced another resolution calling upon the NRA to furnish the Senate with the names and business affiliations of all its employees. And on February 7 Borah discussed the sad plight of the small businessman in a major radio address. "When these conditions are pointed out," he declared, "someone goes into a trance and begins to ejaculate about how we cannot go back to rugged individualism; that we have arrived at a new era, the era of planned industrialism." He was of the opinion, however, that whatever one called it, domination by "combines, trusts, and monopolies" was a "travesty upon justice" and "brutal indefensible system." [12]

For political reasons, if for no other, it was clear that something would have to be done about the protests of such men as Borah and Nye. They were prominent progressive Republicans, a group that Roosevelt was trying to weld into the New Deal coalition; and the charges they were leveling at the NRA appealed strongly to the antimonopoly tradition, a tradition that still had a powerful grip on the American public. "You can always get sym-

[12] *Congressional Record*, 73 Cong., 2 Sess., LXXVIII, 866, 871–77, 1075–86, 1442–44, 1824–25, 1992, 2156–58, 2845, 2945–46; *New York Times*, Jan. 19, 20, Feb. 3, 7, 8, 21, 22, 1934; *Time*, Jan. 29, 1934, p. 14; J. E. Cannady to William Borah, Jan. 20, 1934; J. A. Whelan to Borah, Jan. 20, 1934; F. W. Prentice to Borah, Jan. 20, 1934, all in Repeal of Antitrust Laws File, Borah Papers. For the FTC memorandum see Eugene Burr et al., "Memorandum on the Steel Code," Dec. 29, 1933, PPF 1820, Roosevelt Papers.

pathy by using the word small," remarked Frances Perkins. "With little industries you feel as you do about a little puppy."

Such charges, moreover, were not without some basis. Johnson could and did point to such areas as retail trade, bituminous coal, cotton textiles, and the needle trades, areas where code provisions did tend to favor the small units and where there was some justification for the official theory that a reduction of competition would help to maintain labor standards. Such areas, however, were exceptional. A study of the codes as a whole could only conclude that most of the price clauses were directed against price cutting by "little fellows." In numerous industries the advantage of large firms lay not so much in the area of price as it did in non-price fields, in such matters as advertising, access to credit, ability to conduct research, control of patents, and attraction of the best managerial talent. Small firms often existed only because they offered lower prices to offset consumer preference for advertised brands, prices sometimes made possible by lower wage rates, sometimes by more favorable location, sometimes by other advantages arising out of specialization or recapitalization. It was in the interest of larger firms, therefore, to eliminate price and wage differentials and wipe out the special advantages that made them possible. In general, the majority of the codes did move in this direction.

To the small businessman the destruction of these differentials seemed like an effort to legislate him out of existence. He protested that he was unable to pay the same wages and charge the same prices as larger firms, that he could not possibly find his way through all the reports and red tape that were meant for larger companies, that he was being strangled by code authority bureaucrats and greedy monopolists. And for a government largely dedicated to improving the plight of the "little fellow," the emotional appeal and political dynamite inherent in such charges were impossible to ignore.[13]

The Administration, in fact, was already moving to placate the champions of small business. In January 1934 the President issued an executive order under which a small businessman could appeal directly to the Federal Trade Commission if he were dissatisfied with the disposition that the NRA had made of his case. And as early as December 1933 Johnson had begun discussing the establishment of a board to receive and investigate small business complaints. The details of this proposal were worked out in conferences with Senator Nye; and in what the General later regarded as a "moment of total aberration," he himself suggested that it be headed by the famed criminal trial lawyer, Clarence Darrow. Other members included William R. Neal, a North Carolina hoisery manufacturer, Fred P. Mann, a retail merchant from North Dakota, John F. Sinclair, a New York banker, Samuel C. Henry, head of a druggists' association, and William O. Thompson, Darrow's former law partner.

Once the Board was organized, according to Lowell B. Mason, its general counsel, the members went to call on Johnson. He told them they "could stay around and do some investigating and let him know if the codes were all right." "But supposing we find out the codes are not all right?" Darrow asked him. "Then you report to me," said Johnson. "I am the big cheese here." Darrow, not at all satisfied with this arrangement, decided he would

[13] Claudius O. Johnson, *Borah of Idaho* (N.Y.: Longmans, Green, 1936), 479–81, 484–85; John P. Miller, *Unfair Competition* (Cambridge: Harvard U. Press, 1941), 353–54; Schlesinger, *Coming of New Deal*, 168–69; Taggart, *Minimum Prices*, 236–37, 249–51; DIE, Staff Studies, 1533–36; Lyon et al., *NRA*, 745; Raymond Willoughby, in *Nation's Business*, May 1934, pp. 80, 82–84; NEC Proceedings, March 20, 1934, pp. 8–15; April 17, 1934, p. 17; R&P Div., "Effect of Codes on Small Enterprise," Aug. 1934; R. H. Lansburgh to Leon Henderson, March 26, 1935; Reports of Small Companies Committee of BAPC, Jan. 1, March 8, 1934, all in NRA Records (SR&P, Small Industries File—CAF).

rather report directly to the President. Accordingly, on March 7, 1934, Executive Order 6632 created a National Recovery Review Board, charged with the task of investigating the effect of the codes on small business and recommending any changes that might be necessary. The Board established its headquarters in the Willard Hotel, and the Darrow Board report was on its way.[14]

III

While the Darrow Board was being established, Johnson's critics within the NRA were analyzing the complaints presented at the price hearing, suggesting changes in policy, and winning some minor concessions to their point of view. By late January the Consumers' Advisory Board, the Research and Planning Division, the Legal Division, and a committee appointed by Arthur D. Whiteside were all studying the alleged abuses of open-price plans, particularly the effect of "waiting periods" that could be used to bring prospective price-cutters into line. Men like Corwin Edwards and Leon Henderson were demanding a change; and in view of the congressional debates, the unfavorable publicity, and the growing disillusionment of the public, Johnson seemed willing to take some sort of corrective action. He began by ruling that further provisions for "open price associations" were to be eliminated or suspended, at least until the studies in progress could be completed. But this ruling brought immediate protests from deputy administrators and trade association exccutives, protests that the Administrator was yielding to "political expediency" and being drawn into a "very dan-

---

[14] Johnson, *Blue Eagle*, 272; Lowell B. Mason, in *North American Review*, Dec. 1934, p. 525; *Business Week*, Jan. 27, 1934, p. 22; *New York Times*, Jan. 21, 25, Feb. 20, 1934; SIRB Minutes, Dec. 12, 1933; NRA Office Manual, V-C, 20–21, 25, both in MR&D, NRA Records; Johnson to FDR, Dec. 13, 1933; FDR to Johnson, Dec. 18, 1933; FDR to Homer Cummings, Jan. 4, 1934; Garland Ferguson to FDR, Jan. 19, 1934, all in OF 466, Roosevelt Papers.

gerous deviation" from established policy. Johnson then retreated and modified the order so that it applied only to provisions for "waiting periods." Systems under which a revised price became effective immediately upon filing were still acceptable.

The Consumers' Advisory Board still hoped for more. On February 19 Corwin Edwards and Dexter Keezer sent a report to Johnson, which, along with other suggestions for code revision, stressed particularly the undesirability of the open-price provisions. To back up their argument, they had compiled extensive appendices citing examples of uniform bids and of the pressure being applied to concerns that quoted lower than standard prices. The General, however, was in no mood to listen. Across the face of the report he scribbled such remarks as "Anonymous, indefinite, and not fit for publication," "Appendix A is not evidence," "Nothing of the kind," "No general formula," "Read the Act," and "Balls—just the name." After some delay, he did agree that the report might be published, but it brought no further changes in the policy toward open prices.[15]

In the meantime, the focus of internal controversy had

[15] Campbell, *Consumer Representation*, 74; *New York Times*, March 5, 1934; Enid Baird, NRA *Work Materials 76* (*Price Filing under NRA Codes*), 453–58; DIE, Staff Studies, 336, 341–44; Walter Mitchell to A. D. Whiteside, Jan. 24, 1934; Leon Henderson, Address, Feb. 16, 1934; Office Orders 63, 63-A, 63-B, in Policy Group Proceedings, a, 6–8; M. J. Harron to Blackwell Smith, Jan. 24, 1934; Harron to Jack Levin, Jan. 22, 1934; Whiteside to Johnson, Feb. 1, 1934; Levin to Harron and T. I. Emerson, Jan. 29, 1934; C. W. Smith, "Open Prices vs. Political Expediency"; Edwards to Keezer, Jan. 23, 1934; Alvin Brown to Johnson, Jan. 29, 1934; C. W. Smith to Blackwell Smith, Feb. 3, 1934; Henderson to Johnson, March 2, 1934; Henderson to Keezer, March 2, 1934; CAB, "Suggestions for Code Revision," Feb. 19, 1934; and "Experience with Open Price Provisions," May 4, 1934; Simon Whitney, "Open Prices," April 3, 1934, all in NRA Records (SR&P, MR&D, Price Hearing File—CAF, Keezer File—CAF, Policy File —CAF, Henderson File, CAB File—MR&D, Open Prices File— CAF); Edwards to Lewis, June 4, 1935, Blaisdell File, NRPB Records.

shifted more to the minimum-price provisions, the production controls, and the methods of computing costs. Again, the price hearings had provided the critics with ammunition; and in the weeks that followed, they stepped up their protests against a set of policies that were allegedly inflating the cost structure, gouging the consumer, protecting inefficient concerns, preventing expansion, and perpetuating unemployment. The NRA would do well, they insisted, to abandon all production controls and all attempts at cost-of-production pricing. And if the latter was to continue at all, "cost" must be strictly defined and all debatable items excluded. As yet, though, costing policy still tended to reflect business views. The NRA sanctioned the use of current replacement cost, a figure generally higher than original cost, as the proper basis for evaluating raw materials. It allowed the inclusion of "reasonable" depreciation charges, and in some industries, the addition of research and selling expenses. And it declared that "principles of cost finding" could be made mandatory, although code authorities were not supposed to enforce an accounting system in detail. Key NRA officials also continued to defend the production controls. In the view of Johnson's assistant, Alvin Brown, they were the best means of stabilizing the economy, and if properly enforced, they could prevent "market gluts, prices below cost, and resulting unemployment."

The one major innovation to emerge from the controversy over costing provisions was the device of the "emergency minimum price," a concept that was designed to placate critics, simplify administration, get around the difficulties of determining "individual cost," and reduce the need for accepting and defending complicated cost-accounting systems. Under the new procedure a code authority might determine when "destructive price cutting" was of such intensity as to constitute an "emergency," whereupon it might determine the industry's "lowest reasonable cost" and submit this figure to the Administrator. Then, if approval were given, the Administrator would declare an emergency, and it would become an unfair practice to sell below the figure found to constitute the "lowest reasonable cost."

The new device was largely the brainchild of Robert H. Montgomery, a professional accountant who headed the Research and Planning Division for a brief period in early 1934. It was recommended to deputy administrators as a "desirable" provision in February 1934, was eventually written into approximately two hundred codes, and became the subject of mixed reaction, both among the NRA's critics and among its business supporters. Some critics regarded it as a distinct improvement over the previous price provisions; others were afraid that "industrial emergencies" would now "flourish as the bay tree" and would soon degenerate into rackets. And while some businessmen were critical of the government controls implied in the new procedure, others regarded it as the "best news we have had since the inception of the NRA." Prices, said one code authority executive, could now be established on "a statistical basis," which could only result "in greater profit to all concerned." The actual effect, of course, was going to depend largely upon the willingness of the Administration to declare an "emergency" and the way in which it defined the term "lowest reasonable cost." [16]

[16] Taggart, *Minimum Prices*, 29–31; C. C. Linnenberg, Jr., NRA *Price Study* 10 (1935), 2–3; C. A. Pearce, NRA *Trade Practice Programs* (N.Y.: Columbia U. Press, 1939), 47–48; DIE, Staff Studies, 1478, 1482, 1511–24, 1548–50; V. S. Von Szeliski to Montgomery, Jan. 25, 1934; Brown to Montgomery, Jan. 29, Feb. 2, 1934; L. D. Tompkins to Brown, Jan. 30, 1934; Taggart to Montgomery, Feb. 10, 1934; Brown to Policy Board, Jan. 29, 1934; A. J. Hettinger to Henderson, May 10, 1934; Henderson to Johnson, May 14, 1934; B. E. Babbit to J. W. Barton, Feb. 7, 1934, in "Excerpts from Hearing on the Mop Stick Industry"; R&P Advisory Committee Minutes, Jan. 26, Feb. 3, 1934; James Hughes to Blackwell Smith, Aug. 21, 1934; Office Memoranda, Jan. 29, Feb. 3, 1934, in Policy Group Proceedings, a, 9, 11; G. B. Galloway to Von Szeliski, Feb. 8, 1934; Minutes of a Meeting with Alvin Brown,

Still another area of controversy in which changes were underway was that relating to code authority organization and supervision. Here, too, the price hearings and congressional debates had focused attention on abuses; and, as a result, the NRA moved slowly in the direction of more governmental control. Under a new definition of the powers and functions of code authorities, they could no longer modify code provisions, exempt code members, exercise judicial functions, or engage in actual code enforcement. On the contrary, they were to stick primarily to such areas as research, fact-finding, education, adjustment, arbitration, and the collection of statistical data. And even in these areas, their role was growing more limited. In January 1934 a new system of state compliance offices relieved them of many activities in this field, and in March the Bureau of Labor Statistics finally won the right to collect employment data directly from code members. Johnson, moreover, had reasserted his power to approve, review, suspend, or veto code authority actions; and in March he agreed that the government members of code authorities should have labor and consumer advisers, who would have access to official records and the right to be heard. This latter policy, however, was never really implemented, partly because it was strongly opposed by industrial leaders and partly because the matter of remuneration and tenure for such advisory personnel was never settled.[17]

June 1, 1934; NRA PR2875, Jan. 22, 1934; Ben Lewis, "Emergency Price Experience," Jan. 9, 1935; Brown to Johnson, Jan. 29, Feb. 13, 1934; Galloway and Y. S. Leong, "Control of Production and Productive Capacity," March 22, 1934; Keezer to Brown, Jan. 29, 1934; Brown to Keezer, Jan. 30, 1934, all in NRA Records (Montgomery File, Henderson File, Hughes File, MR&D, Bardsley File, Policy Meetings File—CAF, Small Industries File—CAF, CAB File—MR&D, Policy File—CAF, SR&P, CAB File—CGF).

[17] Lorwin and Hinrichs, National Planning, 164–65; Campbell, Consumer Representation, 36–7; Lyon et al., NRA, 212–15, 272–76; DIE, Staff Studies, 422, 509; NRA, Bulletin 7 (1934), 5–11, Exhibit I; "Origin of the Code Authority"; Myron Watkins to Henderson, Feb. 17, 1934; Manual re Mandatory Contributions to Code Authorities; Office Memoranda, Jan. 27, Feb. 5, 23, 1934, in R&P

Gradually, then, although business views were still in the ascendancy, policy changes were taking place. The mounting tide of criticism, particularly from small businessmen and their senatorial champions, had greatly strengthened the dissident forces within the NRA. The price hearings had furnished them with ammunition. And by March 1934 they were pushing strongly for the elimination of price and production controls, the restoration of freer markets, and the subjection of the code authorities to stricter public supervision. "Industrial self-government" and the "association idea" were definitely in retreat, and the time was rapidly approaching when the Administration would be forced to make further concessions to the competitive ideal.

Policy Digest; Office Memo. of Jan. 2, 1934, and Office Order 81, in Industrial Advisers' Handbook, E-4, G-7; Paul Douglas to CAB, Jan. 25, 1934; CAB to Johnson, Feb. 19, 1934; E. G. Stone to Johnson, Feb. 24, 1934; NRA PR4823, May 3, 1934; NRA, "History of the Industrial Advisory Board," II, 190–91; Henderson to C. W. Putnam, May 19, 1934; Brown to Blackwell Smith, March 8, 1934; Edwards to Keezer, May 4, 8, 1934, all in NRA Records (Histories Unit File, Henderson File, Galvin File, Hamm File, MR&D, CAB File—MR&D, Small Firms File—CAF, Policy File—CAF, Finding Aids File, Richberg File, Brown File, Keezer File—CAF).

CHAPTER 5. THE POLICY DEADLOCK

ADMINISTRATOR Hugh Johnson declared in a radio address on February 20, 1934, "NRA has a triple duty. It is to see that industry does not hornswoggle labor; that labor does not bullyrag industry; that neither separately, nor both in concert, shall exploit the consuming public." If there was any "hornswoggling" or "bullyragging" going on, he intended to find out about it at a public "field day of criticism" scheduled for February 27.

For some time Johnson had been searching for a way to recapture the initiative. Congress and the press were still hammering away at the iniquities of his program. The NRA's compliance machinery, particularly in retail and service fields, had come to a virtual standstill. Organized labor was growing more and more critical, particularly of the General's refusal to support the National Labor Board and accept the "majority rule," the principle that a union designated by the majority of employees in a free election should become the recognized bargaining representative for all workers in the plant. Under the circumstances, Johnson had decided upon another effort to win business cooperation. He had scheduled a grand conference of the code authorities for March 5, and prior to this meeting, there would be an open hearing at which his critics could let off steam.[1]

[1] Leverett S. Lyon et al., *The National Recovery Administration* (Washington: Brookings, 1935), 242, 462–67, 472–74, 491; William H. Spencer, *Collective Bargaining under Section 7-a of NIRA* (Chicago: U. of Chicago Press, 1935), 35–37; Arthur M. Schlesinger, Jr., *The Coming of the New Deal* (Boston: Houghton Mifflin, 1959), 146–50; Raymond S. Rubinow, *NRA Work Materials 45-E-1 (Section 7-a)*, 64–73; *Business Week*, Feb. 24, 1934, p. 20; *Newsweek*, March 3, 1934, p. 24; *Time*, Feb. 26, 1934, p. 12; *New York Times*, Feb. 10, 14, 18, 21, 22, 1934; "Public Attitude toward NRA Program," 1 (Jan. 27–May 1, 1934); NRA PR3125, Feb. 4, 1935, both in NRA Records (MR&D, Policy File—CAF).

On February 27 Johnson opened the ceremonies by presenting a twelve-point program for the improvement of the NRA. Among other things, he called for a more equitable rule of price stabilization, further insurance that price increases would not outrun wage increases, higher wages and shorter hours, better protection of small enterprises, improved compliance procedures, and adequate labor and consumer representation in an advisory capacity. Following Johnson's address, his critics took their turn; and during the next four days, they loosed a barrage of protests. Large distributors, consumers' groups, and government purchasing agents charged that the costing, price-filing, and production provisions were being used to stifle competition, fix prices, discourage innovation, and produce uniform bids. Small businessmen charged that the code authorities were still dominated by large firms. Political leftists claimed that the NRA was a fascist organization. And labor leaders called strenuously for stricter enforcement, shorter hours, and labor representation on the code authorities. After the critics had finished, noted one observer, there was "left little that seemed desirable, or even decent, of the N.R.A." [2]

On March 5 the code authorities assembled to answer the criticisms, discuss Johnson's twelve points, and listen to the President's call for "immediate cooperation" to secure increased wages, shorter hours, and fuller employment. The specific proposal in mind was Johnson's Ten-and-Ten Plan, calling for a ten percent reduction in hours and a ten percent increase in wages. To the majority of businessmen, the plan was anything but welcome. In

[2] Lyon et al., NRA, 711–12; Hugh Johnson, *The Blue Eagle from Egg to Earth* (Garden City: Doubleday, Doran, 1935), 295; E. F. Brown, in *Current History*, April 1934, pp. 69–70; Jonathan Mitchell, in *New Republic*, March 21, 1934, p. 149; *Newsweek*, March 10, 1934, p. 4; *New York Times*, Feb. 28, March 1–3, 1934; NRA PR's 3509, 3511, 3512, Feb. 27–28, 1934; R&P Div., Abstracts of Statements at Public Hearings, Feb. 27–March 3, 1934, all in NRA Records (Public Conferences File—CAF, SR&P).

speech after speech, they claimed that implementation of it would produce disaster rather than recovery. They were also critical of the failure to deal with "chiselers," the shifts in policy, the overlapping of codes, and the trend toward "Bureaucracy." Yet most of them still felt that the trade practice provisions were desirable. Unrestricted competition, they insisted, was one of the principal causes of the depression, and some means of price stabilization was necessary to prevent "economic slaughter." At the end of the sessions, Johnson announced the establishment of three industrial study committees, from which he hoped to obtain meaningful recommendations. Their subsequent reports, however, did little more than rehash the earlier complaints. They were "typically Old Deal," said Leon Henderson, just "water over the dam, and no grist ground." [3]

II

The hearings and conferences, then, produced no easy solution for Johnson's problems. Yet they did provide new data and stimulate a new round of studies, debates, and conflicting counsels. On one side were the reports and recommendations of business-oriented administrators, men like A. D. Whiteside and Averell Harriman who

[3] Solomon Barkin, NRA Work Materials 45-B-2 (NRA Policies, Standards, and Code Provisions on Basic Weekly Hours of Work), 168–76; NRA, Hearings on General Conference of Code Authorities (1934), 11, 70–74; Newsweek, March 10, 1934, p. 3; March 17, 1934, p. 26; Business Week, March 17, 1934, p. 7; Time, March 19, 1934, p. 13; New York Times, March 6–9, 16, 29, 1934; R&P Div., Abstracts of Statements at Code Authority Conferences, March 5–7, 1934; W. A. Harriman and A. D. Whiteside, Reports on Code Authority and Group II Conferences; NRA PR3687, March 7, 1934, and Memo. re Industrial Committees, in Industrial Advisers' Handbook, B-4; Report of Durable Goods Committee, April 30, 1934; Henderson to Johnson, May 14, 1934, all in NRA Records (SR&P, MR&D, Williams File, Henderson File); Reports of Durable Goods and Consumer Goods Committees, March 15, May 14, 1934, OF 466, Roosevelt Papers.

stressed the evils of unrestricted competition, the necessity for price stability, and the desirability of retaining the open-price and costing provisions, at least until they could be given a thorough trial. On the other side were the reports and studies of the Consumers' Advisory Board, the Research and Planning Division, and the Compliance Division, studies that stressed the evils of cartelization, the necessity for expansion, the monopolistic implications of the open-price plans, and the practical difficulties of enforcement. "Prices," these critics insisted, "should be determined either by free competition or else by an independent agency . . . concerned with the welfare of consumers and employers as well as equity-holders." [4]

The critics within the NRA, moreover, were again receiving support from such rival agencies as the Federal Trade Commission, which had long felt that the term "codes of fair competition" was a gross misnomer. The steel code, it now charged, was only a cloak for monopoly, a means of fixing prices and evading the Commission's earlier order against the basing-point system. This, it felt, was a clear violation of the National Industrial Recovery Act, particularly of the section providing that no code should be used as a cloak for monopolistic practices or to oppress small enterprises. And it proposed to proceed against the steel industry on that basis. Johnson, who was in the process of negotiating an extension of the steel code, was immediately up in arms. Such action by the FTC, he felt, would be a "death blow to NRA." Again, the President was forced to intervene. The FTC took no action, but in the executive order extending the steel code,

[4] William H. Davis to FDR, May 31, 1934, NRA File—PSF, Roosevelt Papers; Minutes of R&P Office Meetings, March 20, 1934; Harriman and Whiteside, Report on Group 11 Conferences; CAB to Harriman and Whiteside, March 23, 1934; Simon Whitney to Charles Roos, March 27, 1934; G. B. Galloway and Y. S. Leong, Memo. re Production Control, March 22, 1934; CAB, Report on Open Price Provisions, May 4, 1934; Whitney, "Open Prices," April 3, 1934, all in NRA Records (Hamm File, SR&P, CAB File—MR&D, Open Prices File—CAF).

both it and the NRA were authorized to conduct a joint study of basing-point pricing and report their findings to the President.[5]

Similar clashes with the Department of Agriculture and the Public Works Administration were also reasserting themselves. The former agency was still complaining about the restrictionist policies of the NRA and the dire effects of rising industrial prices, while the latter was growing more and more concerned about the submission of identical bids on public works contracts. The cement industry, in particular, said Harold Ickes, had built up "one of the tightest little combinations in the whole United States." In early May, partly because of such protests, Roosevelt designated Frances Perkins as chairman of an interdepartmental committee on prices; and this agency had soon established an investigating subcommittee under the direction of Walton Hamilton to explore the whole problem of price policy.[6]

The atmosphere of late May, however, was hardly conducive to dispassionate study. On May 20 came the publication of the long-heralded Darrow Report, along with

[5] FTC, *Practices of the Steel Industry under the Code* (Senate Doc. 159, 73 Cong., 2 Sess., 1934), 49–50, 61–65; Paul Y. Anderson, in *Nation*, April 4, 1934, p. 383; *New York Times*, March 21–22, May 31, 1934; Ewin Davis to FDR, May 26, 1934; Memo. re phone call from Johnson, May 18, 1934, both in Roosevelt Papers (OF 100, 466); W. H. Rastall, "NRA and Relations with Other Government Agencies," 5–6; S. C. Oppenheim, Report on Relation of NRA to FTC, Aug. 2, 1934, both in NRA Records (CTS, Reorganization of NRA File—CAF). The joint investigation eventually produced two contrasting reports that took almost diametrically opposed positions in regard to the desirability of basing-point pricing. See NRA, *Report on the Operation of the Basing Point System in the Iron and Steel Industry* (1934); FTC, *Report with Respect to the Basing-Point System in the Iron and Steel Industry* (1935).

[6] Secretary of Agriculture, Report to NEC, April 25, 1934; Harold Ickes to FDR, April 23, 1934; Frances Perkins to FDR, Dec. 5, 1934, all in Roosevelt Papers (OF 788, 526, 327); Ickes to F. Marx, Feb. 8, 1934, Interviews File, Ickes Papers; Henderson to Frances Robinson, May 11, 1934; Johnson to Perkins, June 1, 1934, both in Henderson File, NRA Records.

replies by Johnson and Richberg; and for the next few days the air was filled with polemics and invective. The report covered eight codes and found a trend toward monopoly and oppression of small business in practically all of them. Particularly bad, in its view, was the situation in the steel and motion picture industries, where "monopolistic practices" were "bold and aggressive," code authorities had grossly abused their powers, and small enterprise was "cruelly oppressed." Only the cleaning and dyeing code, the Board said, was free of monopoly, and it was not being enforced. To correct the situation, the majority report recommended a basic reversal in policy, including the elimination of most price and production provisions and major changes in the composition of code authorities. Not all members, though, agreed with the conclusions or recommendations. John F. Sinclair filed a minority protest against "the kind of sloppy, one-sided, half information" upon which the report was allegedly based. And in a special supplementary report, Darrow and William Thompson declared that the real choice was between government-sustained monopoly and socialism, that the former would only make the situation worse, and that the latter was distinctly preferable.

In their replies Johnson and Richberg charged that the Darrow Board had "deliberately encouraged the presentation of incompetent, misleading, one-sided testimony," chiefly from chiselers and sweat-shop operators who refused to pay code wages and work code hours. The report, declared Johnson, was the most "superficial, intemperate and inaccurate document" he had ever seen. Far from oppressing the "little fellow," he claimed, the NRA had reversed a trend toward savage competition that had nearly wiped him out. Yet, as one editor pointed out, it was obvious that the Blue Eagle had "lost some feathers from the discharge of the Board of Review's shotgun." Johnson's critics had been greatly strengthened; and Senator Nye, who for weeks had been trying to call the President's attention to the monopolistic implications of the codes, naturally claimed that he had been fully vindicated. The report, he said, demonstrated clearly that the NRA was designed chiefly "to lend larger aid to monopoly." [7]

III

By the end of May the NRA was showing the effects of accumulated buffetings and setbacks. The whole organization seemed demoralized, on the verge of breaking down from overextension, sheer complexity, and internal conflict. "Without odds this is the damnedest mess it has ever been my misfortune to be connected with," wrote one disgusted deputy administrator. "The entire NRA is in a suspended state—crying for simplification of policy and routine—for broad simple policy determination—and getting nothing. The interstaff and interboard conflicts would be laughable were they not so serious."

Johnson, however, was still trying to ride out the storm. In the face of mounting criticism, he was granting exemptions, creating new agencies, and reshuffling the organizational structure. In late May he began granting exemptions from the trade practice provisions of the service codes and thus carried out a belated retreat from an area in which the NRA was clearly overextended and com-

[7] NRRB, *First Report to the President*, 2–23, 134; *Supplementary Report*, 2, 6; *Minority Report*, 4–5; NRA, *Report to the President in Answer to the First Darrow Report*, 1–19, all in MR&D, NRA Records; Johnson, *Blue Eagle*, 274, 279–80; *Business Week*, May 26, 1934, p. 9; *Literary Digest*, June 2, 1934, p. 8; *Congressional Record*, 73 Cong., 2 Sess., LXXVIII, 9235; *New York Times*, May 3, 5, 8, 10, 12, 21–24, 1934; Schlesinger, *Coming of New Deal*, 133–34; Statement by John F. Sinclair, May 7, 1934; NRA PR5292, May 23, 1934, both in NRA Records (Hamm File, General Counsel's File); Dexter Keezer to Paul Homan, Oct. 24, 1934, Blaisdell File, NRPB Records; Gerald P. Nye to FDR, May 16, 1934; Johnson to Marvin McIntyre, May 24, 1934; FDR to Nye, May 18, 1934, all in PPF 1614, Roosevelt Papers.

pliance among such groups as barbers, beauticians, and dry cleaners had broken down almost completely. The minimum-price provisions of the cleaning and dyeing code, in particular, had produced an enormous amount of unfavorable publicity, and the atomistic structure of the industry, its lack of industry consciousness, and the bitter conflict between the old-line elements and the newer cash-and-carry establishments made it almost impossible to develop a workable substitute. In this area at least, the NRA was ready to admit that conditions were not yet ripe for the cooperative order.

Steps were also being taken to reshape and revitalize the administrative system. The division administrators now took over the functions of the old Code Authorities Organization Committee. The compliance and enforcement activities were reorganized and strengthened. The central administration was revamped along military lines, with personal and administrative staffs. A new office was established to help simplify the codes and head off further proliferation. All of these moves, it was hoped, would help to improve compliance, prevent abuses, and simplify lines of authority.

Other moves gave promise at last of producing a more definite written policy. One was the creation on May 21 of the Advisory Council, an organization that was expected to reduce internal conflict, settle policy disputes, and provide a common meeting ground for representatives from each of the advisory boards. The second move was the abolition of the old Policy Board and the creation of a new Policy Group, made up of a single administrator for policy and three deputy administrators, one each for trade practices, labor provisions, and code authority administration. Both the Consumers' Board and the Research and Planning Division had long been pressing for the creation of such a group; and they hoped now to get a policy settlement favorable to their point of view, especially since the trade practices division was to be headed by Leverett

S. Lyon of the Brookings Institution, a former critic of NRA price and production policies.[8]

The first task, Lyon felt, was to determine the extent to which the NRA intended to modify price competition. And after he was assured that it had no intention of establishing a system of fascist cartels, he proceeded to devise a set of criteria by which he and his advisors could judge specific provisions. Desirable provisions, he decided, should aim at stimulating recovery, expanding production and employment, advancing "an intelligent basis for managerial action," preserving freedom of judgment in managerial decisions, and preventing monopolistic practices. Judged in terms of these goals, he concluded, many of the code provisions were undesirable; and he was soon submitting recommendations, fifteen in all over the next four months, that called for their elimination or modification. Open-price plans and cost education, he thought, might be permitted, but only with proper safeguards and without provisions for waiting periods. And prohibitions of sales below cost should be eliminated, except for genuine emergencies.[9]

[8] Herbert F. Taggart, *Minimum Prices under the* NRA (Ann Arbor: U. of Mich. Press, 1936), 129–32; Saul Nelson, *NRA Work Materials 56* (*Minimum Price Regulation under Codes of Fair Competition*), 57–59; Lyon et al., NRA, 56–67, 284–85, 448, 716–19, CIA, *The National Recovery Administration* (House Doc. 158, 75 Cong., 1 Sess., 1937), 27–28, 51–55, 72; DIE, Staff Studies, 228–30; *Business Week*, April 14, 1934, p. 22; *New York Times*, May 28, 29, June 16, 22, 30, 1934; Howard Colgan, "NRA Code History 101" (Cleaning and Dyeing), 81–82, 110, 158–64, Exhibits 27, 30, 35–37; Office Orders 74, 83, in Policy Group Proceedings, b, 1, 3–5; Exec. Order 6723, Adm. Orders X-37, X-50, X-54, in AC Decisions, v, 378–88; Robert Ayers, "History of the Advisory Council," 1–3; James Hughes to John Riggleman, March 20, 1934; Leverett Lyon to Leon Henderson, Feb. 16, 1934; CAB to Johnson, May 31, 1934, all in NRA Records (CHF, MR&D, AC File, Hughes File, Henderson File, CAB File—MR&D); E. T. Gushee to G. Hall Roosevelt, May 23, 1934, OF 466, Roosevelt Papers; Keezer to Homan, Oct. 24, 1934, Blaisdell File, NRPB Records.

[9] On other minor policy disputes, Lyon also generally sided with the market restorers. The use of premiums might be restricted, he

Lyon's recommendations provided the initial stimulus for what was probably the NRA's most important and most controversial declaration of policy, its famous Office Memorandum 228 of June 7, 1934. The memorandum was drafted by Blackwell Smith, the newly appointed deputy administrator for policy, and after it had been diluted somewhat to make allowances for "emergencies" and genuinely "destructive price cutting," it was issued as an official policy statement. Essentially, it meant the acceptance, at least on the level of policy principles, of the Lyon-Henderson-Edwards approach to price policy. It recognized that the goal was a free market and that code provisions should strengthen rather than eliminate competition. In the future, for example, open-price provisions were to include strict safeguards against price fixing and were not to require waiting periods or other practices that would facilitate collusion. Costing provisions, too, were to be used only for educational purposes. "Destructive price cutting" was to be an unfair practice only if it imperiled small enterprise, impaired labor standards, or tended to promote monopoly. And the fixing of minimum prices was to take place only in "emergencies," which should be declared only after full study by NRA econo-

---

suggested, but there should be no general prohibition of them. Provisions for customer classification should go no further than authorizing the code authority to maintain a list of the types of customers to be found in a given industry. Provisions for resale price maintenance, machine-hour limitations, and control of productive capacity should be excluded completely. Restrictions on brokerage fees, returned goods, and selling on consignment should be limited to a requirement of publicity. Provisions for the standardization of goods should have the approval of the Bureau of Standards or some other appropriate agency. Restrictions on advertising allowances should be limited to the requirement of a separate contract setting forth the services to be performed and the consideration to be paid. And loss limitation provisions, although permissible to protect small merchants, should not establish minimum prices higher than invoice cost plus transportation. Lyon et al., NRA, 702–3, 719–34; DIE, Staff Studies, 356–76; Abstracts of Policy Issued by Policy Group, 27–32, MR&D, NRA Records.

mists, for critical causes, and for periods limited to ninety days.

To Johnson's critics the new memorandum represented a signal victory; and in the press it was hailed as an abandonment of all price fixing. This interpretation, however, brought an immediate deluge of inquiry and objection from the business camp. In the face of this wave of protest, Johnson backed down. On the evening of June 8 he announced that there had been some "misunderstanding," that the new policy applied only to future codes, not to those already approved. This was soon confirmed by official orders, stating that Office Memorandum 228 would not affect approved codes so long as they were causing no difficulty, that it would not be used to "impose" changes, and that it might be waived for codes that were "near completion at the time of its issuance." Consequently, the practical effect was very slight. By June 7, 1934, some 459 codes, covering over ninety percent of the industries subject to the NRA and virtually all the major industries, had already been approved; and to this figure must be added about fifty other codes that were approved after June 7, but nevertheless contained provisions contrary to official policy. The result was a marked divergence between policy and practice; and the job of revising the codes to conform with declared policy, the market restorers soon discovered, was a very difficult one.[10]

The NRA had now backed itself into a position where

[10] Lyon et al., NRA, 677–78, 723–27, 734–39; Taggart, Minimum Prices, 36–42; Schlesinger, Coming of New Deal, 135; DIE, Staff Studies, 398–405; Enid Baird, NRA Work Materials 76 (Price Filing under NRA Codes), 467–69, 474–76; Newsweek, June 16, 1934, pp. 25–26; New York Times, June 8, 9, 10, 1934; Office Memorandum 228, 260, June 7, July 16, 1934, in Policy Group Proceedings, C, 1–7; Blackwell Smith to Johnson, May 22, June 2, 1934; Address by Johnson, June 8, 1934; Smith to Legal Staff, April 13, 1934; Brown to E. M. Jeffrey, June 28, 1934; M. Katz to W. Bardsley, Oct. 9, 1934; H. Mulford, "Price Provisions in Codes Approved Subsequent to June 7, 1934," April 6, 1935, all in NRA Records (MR&D, General Counsel's File, Prices File—CAF, Brown File, Marshall File, Evolution of Trade Practice Policy File—CAF).

it was difficult to take any action at all. Initially, it had yielded to the demands for planning, rationalization, and economic controls, although in doing so, it had masked the collective nature of such action behind a facade of individualistic terms. It had also tried to win business co-operation and had yielded to the power of organized business, with the result that the action taken had moved in the direction of government-supported cartelization. Then had come the reaction, the resurgence of the deeply rooted antimonopoly tradition and the appeal to this tradition by small businessmen, farmers, laborers, academic economists, and progressive politicians. Again the NRA had yielded, and the result was a formal policy statement that reaffirmed faith in the competitive ideal.

It was unlikely, however, that this policy could ever be implemented, particularly when implementation would have to come from an organization staffed by businessmen and oriented toward business views. Any serious attempt to do so would alienate business support, engender charges of bad faith on the part of the government, produce wholesale "resignations" from the NRA, and perhaps set off the whole process of deflation again. Under the circumstances, the market restorers could not even remove provisions that violated official policy, much less write provisions that would achieve the declared goal of strengthening competition. Yet they could force the business-oriented administrators to pay lip service to Office Memorandum 228, and this meant that the latter were extremely reluctant to engage in an open defense or active enforcement of provisions that ran counter to it. To do so would almost certainly produce a political storm that might sweep away the entire program. Nor was it ever really possible to turn the NRA into the agency for collectivist planning envisioned by some of its critics. Such an approach was simply not politically realistic. It had no organized political constituency behind it; it ran counter to America's traditional mythology of individualism;

and it would have aroused intense opposition, both from businessmen and from the defenders of the competitive model and individualistic values.

The stalemate, then, could not be easily broken, although Johnson's critics did keep pounding away at the inconsistency between policy and practice, and Johnson did react with further gestures toward the competitive ideal. In response to new Darrow Board reports, for example, he established an Industrial Appeals Board to handle small business complaints. In response to protests from the PWA and the Treasury Department about uniform bids, he agreed to a Presidential executive order permitting code members to quote prices to the government up to fifteen percent below their posted prices. And in response to the critics within his organization, he agreed to newer and stricter interpretations of "lowest reasonable cost," the methods of computing the cost of raw materials, and the extent to which code provisions might classify customers or ban the use of premiums. The trend on paper was unmistakably toward greater reliance on competition. Yet the policy directives, like Office Memorandum 228, applied only to new codes; the Industrial Appeals Board was to deal only with prima facie cases of individual hardship, not with matters of general policy or the validity of code provisions; and the new executive order dealing with government contracts seemed to have little effect upon tie bids one way or the other. Most of the action was still in the field of policy "principles" rather than actual code revision.[11]

[11] Lyon et al., NRA, 734–40; Edwin George, Code Revision Memorandum 1 (1935), 2, 11–13; NRRB, Second Report to the President (1934); and Third Report (1934); Rexford G. Tugwell, The Democratic Roosevelt (Garden City: Doubleday, 1957), 221, 326–28; Blue Eagle, July 23, 1934; Taggart, Minimum Prices, 43, 62–63; Senate Finance Committee, Investigation of the NRA (74 Cong., 1 Sess., 1935), 636–37, 2048–54; Jordan D. Hill, NRA Work Materials 49 (Relationship of NRA to Government Contracts), 46–47, 54, 115; Tugwell, "The Progressive Tradition," Western Political Quarterly, III (Sept. 1950), 392–93, 400–2, 405,

IV

It was perhaps natural that those who were frustrated and disappointed with the actions of the NRA should place much of the blame on General Johnson himself. A change in leadership, they seemed to think, would improve matters. And by the late summer of 1934, as Johnson alienated one group after another, such a change did seem likely. Organized labor, for example, had grown increasingly critical, particularly of the General's persistent refusal to accept the "majority rule," his unwelcome intervention in labor disputes and strikes, and his reluctance to co-operate with or support the rulings of the newly established National Labor Relations Board. The NRA, labor spokesmen declared, had become the "National Run Around," and the General had demonstrated his "utter unfitness to hold public office." Farm leaders, too, were still insisting that Johnson's policies would "encompass the farmer's ruin." Small businessmen and antitrusters were still claiming that the NRA was a big business racket. And even the leaders of organized business were becom-

420; William A. Orton, in *Current History*, Aug. 1934, pp. 532–34; *Christian Century*, Jan. 31, 1934, pp. 142–43; *New Republic*, June 27, 1934, pp. 168–69; *Business Week*, July 7, 1934, pp. 7–8; *New York Times*, June 29, 1934; President Roosevelt's Press Conferences, June 29, 1934, Roosevelt Papers; Herman Oliphant to FDR, June 28, 1934; Henderson to FDR, June 27, 1934, both in Roosevelt Papers (OF 526, NRA File—PSF); Office Memoranda 232, 265, 267, in Policy Group Proceedings, C, 6, 8–9; Smith to Johnson, July 6, 1934; NIRB, Report on Effects of Exec. Order 6767, April 8, 1935; Memo. re Procedure of Industrial Appeals Board, June 26, 1934; Hughes to Smith, Aug. 21, 1934; Whitney to Pearce, July 2, 1934; Roos to Pearce, July 2, 1934; Keezer to Edwards, June 15, 1934; Robert C. Ayers, "History of the Advisory Council," 33, 46; Gardiner C. Means, "NRA and AAA and the Reorganization of Industrial Policy Making," Oct. 15, 1934, all in NRA Records (MR&D, Hamm File, Richberg File, Industrial Appeals Board File —CGF, Hughes File, Keezer File—CAF, AC File, Bardsley File); Keezer to Homan, Oct. 24, 1934; Mordecai Ezekiel to Henry Wallace, Jan. 2, 1935, both in NRPB Records (Blaisdell File, Industrial Section File—CCF).

ing increasingly disillusioned, especially with the shifting policies, the lack of enforcement, the labor troubles, and the confusion over Section 7a. "The trouble," declared Willard M. Kiplinger in his monthly newsletter, "is and always has been due to the temperamental incompetence of the man at the top." [12]

Even within his own organization Johnson was having difficulty keeping the peace. Differences of opinion had become entangled in emotional clashes of personality, and these in turn were reflected in petty bickerings and contending factions. Many officials, for example, resented the influence and power of Johnson's confidential secretary, Miss Frances Robinson, or "Robbie" as she was generally known. And others resented the General's tendency to run a one-man show. "A team of horses can't be driven in harness with a wild bull," Donald Richberg told the President. "That sort of cooperation is impossible." Johnson, moreover, had grown increasingly irresponsible. His explosions became more frequent and more intemperate. He became convinced that Richberg, who as director of the National Emergency Council was being played up in the press as "Assistant President," was out to get his job. And when life seemed unbearable, he took refuge in drink. "Everyone is very much upset . . . ," Rexford Tugwell reported to the President. "The opinion is unanimous that Johnson can no longer be useful."

[12] Charles Michelson, *The Ghost Talks* (N.Y.: Putnam's, 1944), 194; Rubinow, *Work Materials 45-E-1*, 73–74; Johnson, *Blue Eagle*, 311, 318–25; Spencer, *Section 7-a*, 10–12; Frances Perkins, *The Roosevelt I Knew* (N.Y.: Viking, 1946), 240–43; Schesinger, *Coming of New Deal*, 150–52, 398; *Congressional Record*, 73 Cong., 2 Sess., LXXVIII, 9320; W. M. Kiplinger, in *Nation's Business*, Aug. 1934, p. 23; *Time*, June 18, 1934, p. 14; *Business Week*, Aug. 18, 1934, p. 36; Aug. 25, 1934, pp. 9–10; *New York Times*, March 26, 28, June 9, July 1, 15, 18–22, Aug. 22, Sept. 15–17, 1934; Fred Brenckman to Wallace, Aug. 1934, Price Fixing File—CGF, NRA Records; Lloyd Garrison to Johnson, Aug. 17, 1934; Johnson to Garrison, Aug. 18, 1934; Tugwell to FDR, Sept. 5, 1934; Kayce Blackburn, Memo. re Editorial Reaction to the Recovery Administration, Aug. 10, 1934; Henderson to FDR, June 27, 1934, all in Roosevelt Papers (OF 466, NRA File—PSF).

Under the circumstances, the President decided to ease Johnson out, preferably in a manner that would allow him to save face and would avoid an open break. Johnson, however, was deeply hurt by the suggestions that he should leave, and although he did offer to resign, Roosevelt, much to the dismay of other New Deal officials, sympathetically asked him to stay on. Again the General's critics protested. Finally, on August 21, 1934, Roosevelt summoned Johnson to the White House, and in the presence of Richberg and Miss Perkins, proposed that the General go abroad with a commission to study recovery in European countries. Johnson immediately submitted his resignation. An executive committee made up of George Lynch, Blackwell Smith, and Leon Henderson took over the NRA. And after some face-saving conferences, at which Johnson discussed his plans for reorganization, the President accepted his resignation.[13]

To replace Johnson and dramatize the end of one-man rule, the President's advisers recommended the establishment of an administrative board. And accordingly, on September 27, Roosevelt announced the appointment of a five-man National Industrial Recovery Board under the chairmanship of S. Clay Williams, former chief executive of the R. J. Reynolds Tobacco Company. Together with Arthur D. Whiteside, a former Division administrator, Williams would represent the industrial position. Sidney

[13] Lyon et al., NRA, 67–68; Schlesinger, Coming of New Deal, 152–57; Michelson, Ghost Talks, 122, 126; Harold L. Ickes, Secret Diary, 1 (N.Y.: Simon & Schuster, 1953), 173, 195, 197–98; J. F. Carter, The New Dealers (N.Y.: Simon & Schuster, 1934), 36; Donald Richberg, The Rainbow (Garden City: Doubleday, Doran, 1936), 182–83; Johnson, Blue Eagle, 385–400; New York Times, Sept. 11, 12, 16, 23, 26, 27, 1934; New Republic, Oct. 10, 1934, p. 20; Business Week, July 21, 1934, pp. 20–21; Literary Digest, Oct. 6, 1934, p. 8; Tugwell to FDR, Sept. 5, 7, 1934; "Outline of a Program," June 21, 1934; FDR to Johnson, July 2, Sept. 25, 1934; Richberg to Marvin McIntyre, Sept. 5, 1934; Richberg to FDR, Sept. 4, 1934; Johnson to FDR, Sept. 9, 24, 1934; McIntyre to FDR, Sept. 13, 1934; FDR to Lynch, Sept. 13, 1934, all in OF 466, Roosevelt Papers.

Hillman of the Amalgamated Clothing Workers would represent labor; two college professors, Walton Hamilton and Leon C. Marshall, would represent the public and consumers; and Blackwell Smith and Leon Henderson, as ex officio members, would take part in discussions but have no vote. There would also be a revised Industrial Emergency Committee directed by Richberg to formulate broad policy for all the recovery agencies.

The reorganization was generally regarded by the press as a victory for the professors and economists, for the so-called liberal experts as opposed to the conservative, practical men of affairs. In reality, the new board was little more than an institutionalization of the existing stalemate, a prime example of Roosevelt's practice of splitting agencies down the middle and playing the two factions against each other. It was designed to balance and conciliate opposing interests, not to take effective action. And subsequent efforts to change its basic nature and provide really effective leadership came to naught. The attempts of Harold Ickes, for example, to get Robert M. Hutchins of the University of Chicago appointed as operating head of the NRA ran into strong and effective opposition from Richberg and Williams. Hutchins, they claimed, had "no background industrially"; he was likely to be arrogant and dictatorial; and his appointment would almost certainly alienate business, upset the balance of the board, and bring about a "Brain Trust set up." [14]

[14] Richberg, *Rainbow*, 191–93; Schlesinger, *Coming of New Deal*, 157–58; Ickes, *Diary*, I, 198, 200–1, 209–11, 219–20, 235–36; *Newsweek*, Oct. 6, 1934, pp. 5–6; *Business Week*, Oct. 13, 1934, pp. 23–24; *New Republic*, Oct. 10, 1934, p. 230; *New York Times*, Sept. 28, Oct. 7, 1934; Raymond G. Swing, in *Nation*, Oct. 17, 1934, pp. 431–32; Richberg to FDR, Sept. 4, 14, 1934; Tugwell to FDR, Sept. 5, 7, 1934, OF 466, Roosevelt Papers; Henderson to Lynch, Sept. 24, Oct. 29, 1934; Leon C. Marshall, Notes on NIRB Meetings; Ayers, "History of AC," 33, 46; Blackwell Smith, Notes for Improvement of NRA, Aug. 4, 1934; Edwards, "Development of NRA Policy," March 8, 1935; Executive Orders 6859, 6860, in NRA Office Manual, v, C, 41–42, all in NRA Records (Hamm File, Bardsley File, AC File, Reorganization of NRA File—CAF, CAB

The considerations that ruled out the appointment of Hutchins also governed the board's decisions on other matters. It tended from the first to accept the existing stalemate, postpone all postponable decisions, and occupy its time with perplexing but minor problems. Consequently, in spite of constant criticism and pressure for code revision from such agencies as the Research and Planning Division, the Consumers' Advisory Board, the Advisory Council, and the Federal Trade Commission, the advocates of change could score only minor gains. They succeeded, for example, in preventing the activation of further cost-accounting formulas and the further extension of a number of "preparatory," "emergency," or "experimental" provisions. They secured new policy directives declaring that freedom of action in competitive tactics should be encouraged and that limitations on premiums, advertising allowances, and forward contracts to sell were contrary to sound policy. They held down the number of declared "emergencies." And they had some success in shifting the emphasis in compliance to the labor provisions and in bringing about the appointment of a new, more professional, and better informed set of governmental code authority members.

None of these moves, however, came very close to the general code revision that the market restorers kept demanding. As late as March 1935 Corwin Edwards could find only two major instances in which the NIRB had acted against business wishes and forced code provisions into line with declared policy. "Although a great many minor battles have been won," Edwards concluded, "and a number of valuable principles have been announced, very few changes in important codes have actually been made." Nor were the critics of the NRA successful in their efforts to split off key codes or functions and place

File—MR&D, MR&D); Robert Hutchins to FDR, Oct. 4, 1934; Stephen Early to FDR, Oct. 15, 1934, both in OF 466, Roosevelt Papers.

them under the supervision of more friendly agencies. In the end the NRA beat off all attempted raids by such agencies as the Federal Trade Commission, the Interstate Commerce Commission, the Federal Power Commission, and the Departments of Agriculture and the Interior.[15]

The new board, then, showed a marked tendency to maintain the status quo and to listen sympathetically to business complaints, to claims that the price provisions were still desperately needed and that a general code revision would violate the President's "partnership policy," do irreparable damage to business confidence, and force businessmen to give up their entire codes. Sporadically, some board members did suggest policy changes and withdrawals from untenable areas. Donald Richberg, for example, occasionally talked about a return to "good old competition," and S. Clay Williams suggested that if the labor provisions were fully enforced, there would be no real need for putting a floor under prices. Yet when these remarks produced new streams of business protest,

[15] Persia Campbell, *Consumer Representation in the New Deal* (N.Y.: Columbia U. Press, 1940), 79; NRA, *Work Materials 46 (Code Authorities and Their Part in the Administration of NIRA)*, 190; Senate Finance Committee, *Investigation of NRA*, 940–61; DIE, Staff Studies, 424–26, 509–12; *Blue Eagle*, Nov. 19, 26, 1934; *New York Times*, Nov. 23, 1934; George B. Galloway, in *Plan Age*, July 1935, pp. 16–17; Henderson to Lynch, Sept. 24, Oct. 29, 1934; Henderson to W. A. Harriman, Nov. 19, 1934; T. K. Urdahl to Whitney, Nov. 1934; Katz to Smith and Henderson, Oct. 9, 1934; Edwards to Blaisdell, Oct. 2, 1934; Pearce to Henderson, Dec. 21, 1934; Edwards, "Development of NRA Policy," March 8, 1935; Mary Rumsey to S. Clay Williams, Nov. 1, 1934; Byres Gitchell to NIRB, Oct. 18, 1934; Ayers, "History of AC," 3, 17, 33; AC to NIRB, Oct. 26, 1934; Marshall's Notes on NIRB Meetings; R. W. Shannon and B. T. Ansell to NIRB, Dec. 21, 1934; W. H. Davis, "Enforcing Codes of Fair Competition," Nov. 19, 1934; Office Memoranda 316, 322, 326, 327, in NRA Office Manual, I, 2000, II, 1746, 1756–57, all in NRA Records (Hamm File, Henderson File, Hughes File, Blaisdell File—CAF, Pearce File—CAF, CAB File—MR&D, Richberg File, AC File, AC Memoranda—MR&D, Bardsley File, Marshall File, MR&D); Lewis Lorwin, Memo. re Efforts to Keep Control within NRA; CAB Minutes, Oct. 25, 1934, both in NRPB Records (Lorwin File, Blaisdell File).

the NIRB, like Johnson before it, beat a hasty retreat and offered profuse assurances that there would be no "broad sweeping changes" without full consultation with the industries concerned, that the goal was still cooperation rather than dictation, and that reorganization was not for the purpose of reversing policy, but to "create a sense of security and confidence in the way in which the NRA is operating."

Thus the board had come to occupy a position very similar to that once occupied by Johnson. The only real difference was that the new leadership was somewhat more adept than Johnson in handling the divergence between policy and practice. In Williams, with his courtly ways and general lack of color, the NRA had found a soothing nominal head. And in Richberg, with his amiable, deceptively sluggish appearance, his background as a labor lawyer, his newly-formed connections with big business, and his line of speeches extolling the virtues of competitive capitalism, it had found a man who seemed admirably suited to preside over the stalemate that the NRA had become.[16]

[16] Richberg, *Rainbow*, 74–75; Schlesinger, *Coming of New Deal*, 158; Lewis Stark, in *Nation's Business*, Dec. 1934, pp. 15–16; Jonathan Mitchell, in *New Republic*, April 24, 1935, pp. 301–4; *Business Week*, Oct. 13, 1934, p. 36; Jan. 5, 1935, p. 11; *New York Times*, Oct. 1, 3, 5, 6, 9, 10, 12, 14, 22, Dec. 14, 18, 23, 1934; Jan. 15, 1935; IAB Minutes, Aug. 1, Oct. 24, 25, 1934; NIRB Minutes, Oct. 6, 9, 1934; NRA, "History of the Industrial Advisory Board," 1, 177–85; J. Santos to Henderson, Oct. 25, 1934; Ayers, "History of AC," 17, 33; Bourassa to Richberg, Oct. 5, 1934; Walter Johnson to FDR, Aug. 11, 1934; Edwards, "Development of NRA Policy," March 8, 1935; Report of Exec. Director of CAB, March 8, 1935; IAB, "Policy on Code Amendments," July 24, 1934; Neal Foster to George Brady, Sept. 29, 1934; Frank Purcell to Williams, Dec. 15, 1934; Bourassa to Williams, Dec. 17, 1934; Bernard Ginsberg to Williams, Jan. 21, 1935; Addresses by Donald Richberg, Oct. 4, 9, 15, Nov. 2, 1934, by S. Clay Williams, Dec. 13, 1934, and by A. D. Whiteside, Nov. 20, 1934, all in NRA Records (MR&D, Finding Aids File, Henderson File, AC File, Price Fixing File—CGF, CAB File—MR&D, Policy Recommendations—CAF, Policy Decisions—CAF, Williams File, Speeches File—MR&D).

CHAPTER 6. THE LAST DAYS
OF THE NRA

BY January 1935, as public officials began to discuss the desirability of extending the NRA, that agency was still locked in a frustrating stalemate. Official policy said one thing; most of the codes said something else; and the leaders of the agency were showing less and less inclination to define their goals and take effective action, particularly since the whole matter would soon come under congressional consideration. An organization that is simply marking time, however, must give the appearance of doing something; and this the NRA was doing. In December 1934 it had scheduled a new series of public hearings to begin on January 9. And once again men like Leon Henderson and Corwin Edwards had mustered a wide variety of memoranda, charts, and studies to show that the price and production controls were economically harmful and administratively unworkable. The code groups, they hoped, when confronted with the facts, might be persuaded to surrender their restrictionist provisions voluntarily.

At the hearings, though, the majority of businessmen quickly made it clear that what they wanted was more price control, not less. Without price protection, declared one code authority executive, "the whole Marine Corps would be unable to enforce the wage provisions." And most of the others agreed that Office Memorandum 228 was a bad and "disturbing" statement of policy, one that paralyzed "industry thinking" and offered no solution to the problem of "price demoralization." Industry, so its representatives insisted, still needed some way to rationalize competitive behavior, establish a "price floor," and halt destructive price wars. And it was really idle, misleading, and mischievous to talk about "monopoly" until an industry could at least pay the costs of production.[1]

[1] *New York Times*, Dec. 18, 1934; Jan. 10, 11, 1935; *Blue Eagle*, Jan. 16, 1935; *Nation's Business*, March 1935, pp. 31–32, 66–70;

The price hearing was followed by two other major hearings in early 1935, one on the labor provisions and a second on the distributive codes where attempts to force large-scale retailers to pay higher prices than wholesalers had stirred up a good deal of controversy. Neither hearing, however, produced any major changes in policy. Like the price hearings, they were essentially a means of marking time, excusing inactivity, and postponing real decisions. About all they provided was a fresh accumulation of data that led to new debates, new studies, and a further demonstration that the lines of conflict had not changed. On one side the industrial divisions and code authorities were complaining bitterly about "inelastic policies," undue interference by impractical and irresponsible theorizers, the tendency of "special pleaders" on the Advisory Council to block or delay industrial proposals, the failure of the government to live up to its agreements with industry, and the reluctance of the Administration to grant "emergencies" and thus provide a "prompt and efficacious remedy" for "destructive price cutting." On the other side, the Research and Planning economists, backed in general by the Advisory Council, the Legal Division, the Consumers' Advisory Board, and the Cabinet Committee on Prices, were urging freer markets as the basis for industrial expansion, listing the codes in "crying need of change," and trying to establish some definite procedure that would facilitate code revision. Their only substantial success, though, was the essentially meaningless one of writing new policy pronouncements that reasserted the

Edwin George, NRA *Code Revision Memorandum* 1 (1935), 12–13, 16; *Business Week*, Jan. 5, 1935, pp. 11–12; NIRB Minutes, Dec. 17, 1934; R&P Div., Analysis of Statements at the Price Hearing, Jan. 23, 1935; Leon C. Marshall, Notes on NIRB Meetings; Leon Henderson to NIRB, Jan. 2, 1935; CAB Memoranda, Jan. 9, 1935; R&P Div., Classification of Statements at the Price Hearing of Jan. 1935, all in NRA Records (MR&D, Bardsley File, Marshall File, CAB File—MR&D, Price Fixing File—CAF).

goals and principles embodied in Office Memorandum 228.

Again, in three long policy memoranda, the NRA declared that the objective was a "free and open market" and that wherever costing, open-price, and other trade practice provisions were used to destroy rather than strengthen competition, they were contrary to sound policy. Again, though, the memoranda did not apply to codes already approved, except for cases where provisions were in "direct conflict" with the public interest or the "justifiable interests of any group." In such cases the NRA would try to negotiate changes. In reality, said Thomas Blaisdell, the new directives were not statements of policy; they were simply statements of possibilities. "I . . . remain firmly convinced," he declared, "that until NRA policy is clarified by action of the Recovery Board, rather than by policy statements, or until Congress has specifically declared a policy, further statements of this type . . . have little significance." [2]

[2] *Business Week*, Feb. 9, 1935, p. 6; March 23, 1935, pp. 8–9; *Nation's Business*, April 1935, p. 22; R&P Div., *Abstracts of Speeches, Briefs, and Letters Presented at the Public Hearings on Employment Provisions* (1935); DIE, Staff Studies, 393–95, 1469; NRA PR10466, March 13, 1935; James Hughes to Henderson, Feb. 20, March 14, 1935; Horace Drury, Report on Production and Capacity Control, March 9, 1935; Walton Hamilton and Irene Till, Report on Cost Formula for Price, March 1, 1935; V. S. Von Szeliski, "Effect of Price Levels on Employment," Jan. 24, 1935; Corwin Edwards, "Development of NRA Policy," March 8, 1935; CAB Executive Director's Report, March 8, 1935; R. K. Straus to W. A. Harriman, March 13, 1935; Alvin Brown to Harriman, March 19, 1935; William Bardsley to Marshall, April 11, 1935; Kilbourne Johnston to Donald Nelson, March 30, 1935; Charles Edison to Hamilton, May 14, 1935; Blackwell Smith to NIRB, Feb. 20, 25, 1935; Armin Riley to Smith, March 2, 1935; A. H. Onthank to Nelson, March 18, 1935; Administrative Policy, New Series, Nos. 1, 2, 3, April 23, May 2, 21, 1935, in Policy Group Proceedings, Appendices A, B, C; NIRB Minutes, Jan. 9, Feb. 14, 28, March 4, 7, 1935, all in NRA Records (Distribution Differential Hearings —CAF, Henderson File, SR&P, Price Studies File, Von Szeliski File, CAB File—MR&D, Brown File, Marshall File, Richberg File,

II

NRA officials, however, were reluctant to enforce provisions that ran counter to the policy pronouncements; and in some of the more highly competitive industries, this lack of government support had led to the breakdown of controls and the voluntary abandonment of anti-competitive provisions. Generally speaking, the difficulties of maintaining and enforcing cartel arrangements were greatly enhanced in industries that were made up of a large number of units producing a variety of unstandardized products, particularly where limitations upon entry were slight. Securing cooperation was also difficult in industries with large and growing markets, relatively simple technologies, or problems of competing substitutes; and it was equally difficult in cases where one faction of an industry was using the code as an instrument of aggression against a second faction strong enough to put up active resistance. Under these conditions, the code provisions generally broke down; and since they had failed, only moderate resistance was offered to their deletion from the codes.[3]

The lumber industry was an excellent case in point. In practice the lumber code's complicated price schedules and production quotas proved unmanageable and unenforceable, especially in view of the Administration's refusal to sanction what it called "birth control." The prospect

Smith File, Reports to Nelson—CAF, MR&D); Jack Levin, "A New Deal for the NRA"; CAB to Smith, March 2, 1935; Blaisdell to Emily Blair, May 2, 1935, all in Blaisdell File, NRPB Records.

[3] Saul Nelson, NRA Work Materials 56 (Minimum Price Regulation under Codes of Fair Competition), xii; CIA, The National Recovery Administration (House Doc. 158, 75 Cong., 1 Sess., 1937), 164; DIE, Staff Studies, 2079–83; W. H. Davis, "Enforcing Codes of Fair Competition," Nov. 19, 1934; Edwards, "Development of NRA Policy," March 8, 1935, both in NRA Records (Marshall File, CAB File—MR&D).

of high code prices, coupled with relatively slight limitations on entry, attracted many new mills, generally small establishments that were almost entirely lacking in industry consciousness and solidarity. This, coupled with the determination of lumber consumers not to pay code prices, soon made compliance a bad joke. Mills that observed code prices found it difficult to sell any lumber at all. In October 1934 the West Coast Lumbermen's Association voted formally to discontinue minimum prices; and at the lumber price hearing in December, much of the industry was ready to call it quits. Accordingly, on December 22, 1934, the NRA suspended the price provisions.[4]

In some of the retail and service trades conditions were similar to those in the lumber industry; here, too, controls broke down and were abandoned. The cleaning and dyeing code, as noted previously, had foundered on the conflict between the newer cash-and-carry element and the old-line establishments; and in other service trades, code provisions were largely unenforceable, especially when public opinion favored the price cutter. Price schedules also broke down and were eventually abandoned in the retail tire industry and the fur dressing trade. The efforts of the plumbing fixtures industry to maintain traditional forms of distribution collapsed when the mail-order houses and small manufacturers openly defied the code. In the Atlantic mackerel industry, according to one observer, the "only ones to benefit" from the attempt to impose production quotas were "the mackerel themselves." In such industries the resurgence of competitive forces, coupled with withdrawal of government support, did bring about a

[4] Peter A. Stone et al., NRA Work Materials 79 (Economic Problems of the Lumber and Timber Products Industry), 103–10; Nelson, Work Materials 56, 49–54; Herbert F. Taggart, Minimum Prices under the NRA (Ann Arbor: U. of Mich. Press, 1936), 52–54; C. A. Pearce, NRA Trade Practice Programs (N.Y.: Columbia U. Press, 1939), 96–98; Senate Finance Committee, Investigation of the NRA (74 Cong., 1 Sess., 1935), 892–93; Business Week, Dec. 29, 1934, p. 12; A. C. Dixon et al., "NRA Code History 9" (Lumber), 229–31, 260, CHF, NRA Records.

certain amount of realignment between declared policy and approved codes.[5]

As one examines the list of actual code revisions during the period from June 1934 to March 1935, he is immediately struck by the highly atomistic or competitive nature of the industries involved or by their lack of significance in the total business picture. Machine hour limitations, for example, were stayed only in the celluloid buckle, button, and novelty industry. Minimum price schedules were deleted or suspended only in the lumber, mop, waste paper, and motor bus industries. Prohibitions of sales below cost were removed only from the codes of the shoe polish, gray iron foundry, twine, and scientific apparatus industries. The list of industries in which open-price plans, uniform cost-accounting formulas, and other similar provisions were eliminated, suspended, or revised reflected the same preoccupation with minor industries or with cases in which the provisions had lost all real meaning for the industries involved. Revision, it seemed, depended not upon the degree to which a code device violated official policy or subverted a free market, but rather upon how well the device could be enforced; and naturally enforcement was far easier in those industries where competition had largely disappeared. From the standpoint of the market restorers, the codes that were revised were those that needed it least.

This rule, though, was not without exceptions. In the first place, there were industries that insisted upon retaining obviously unenforceable provisions, either because

[5] Irwin Moise and George Haddock, NRA *Work Materials 62* (*Manufacturers' Control of Distribution*), 5, 64, 396; Taggart, *Minimum Prices*, 164–69; DIE, *Staff Studies*, 2079–80; Senate Finance Committee, *Investigation of NRA*, 883–89, 1422–23; Howard Colgan, "NRA Code History 101" (Cleaning and Dyeing), 158–64; Frederick Lipps, "NRA Code History 410" (Retail Trade), 16–23; D. G. Pilkington, "NRA Code History 204" (Plumbing Fixtures), 16–19, 25, 59–70; Ross Chamberlain, "NRA Code History 308D" (Atlantic Mackerel), 14–20, all in CHF, NRA Records.

of their value in "educating" code members or because someday they hoped to make the provisions work. In the second place, there were a few industries that could base their case on broader grounds than market control, slip inside the charges of monopoly, and secure a fair amount of governmental support. In the bituminous coal industry, for example, largely because of the conservation argument and the long concern over coal as a "sick" industry, the NRA reacted to non-compliance by moving in the direction of tighter controls rather than trying to dismantle those already in existence. In the third place, there were some industries that had once been highly competitive, but in which the trade associations had now developed enough industry consciousness to secure a fair degree of cooperation even without extensive governmental support. Such was probably the case in the cotton textile industry and among some retail groups, like the tobacconists, booksellers, and druggists. In the fourth place, some industries were successful in reducing competition because they discovered a particularly effective means of enforcement. The success of the garment codes was due largely to labor union support and the benefits that derived from use of the code label. Finally, there were some rare cases in which controls were dislodged over the violent protests of industrial groups. One of these was in the retail coal trade, where a storm of protests from large consumers during the summer of 1934 led the NRA to review and lower price schedules in spite of strong opposition from the trade group concerned. Another was in the rubber industry where the FTC presented proof of a bid-rigging conspiracy and thus forced the NRA to censure the offending code authority and stay all price provisions in the rubber manufacturing code.

These exceptions, however, were hardly enough to invalidate the general rule. On the whole, the codes in the more highly concentrated industries—steel, electrical manufacturing, copper, paper, and glass—were more fully implemented and produced fewer problems from a compliance standpoint. Consequently, even though the market restorers felt that these codes needed revision the most, they were the ones hardest to revise and were therefore revised the least. The over-all effect was to strengthen existing organizations, to confirm and reinforce private controls already in operation, not to create new controls in previously competitive industries. And this effect naturally led to continued protests from the market restorers, the advocates of national planning, and the disappointed spokesmen of the more competitive and more atomistic industries.[6]

III

The inability to break the policy deadlock, coupled with renewed protests from labor, led again in early 1935 to demands for a change in leadership. S. Clay Williams had become unpopular, both with the market restorers and the labor leaders. And both groups, too, had become

[6] J. W. Hathcock, NRA Work Materials 58 (The Men's Clothing Industry), 148–56, 161–68; F. E. Berquist et al., NRA Work Materials 69 (Economic Survey of the Bituminous Coal Industry), 76–77, 123–33, 518–27; Taggart, Minimum Prices, 118, 175–78; Pearce, Trade Practice Programs, 60–62, 175–80; W. H. Cross et al., NRA Work Materials 41 (The Rubber Industry Study), 139–41; Senate Finance Committee, Investigation of NRA, 661–68, 695–734, 946–62, 999–1004; DIE, Staff Studies, 2077–88; Business Week, Aug. 11, 1934, pp. 15–16; New York Times, April 2, May 4, 1935; George Soule, in AER Supplement, March 1935, pp. 21–30; George Dickson, "NRA Code History 1" (Cotton Textiles), 108; John Soell, "NRA Code History 34" (Cotton Garment), 49–50, 74–75; Carl H. Monsees et al., "NRA Code History 280" (Retail Solid Fuel), 63–69; Dean Edwards, "NRA Label Agency Activities," June 19, 1935; W. M. Galvin, "Fair Trade Practice Provisions in Light of Compliance Division Experience," June 25, 1935; Taggart and Boyd, "Selling Below Cost," Nov. 1934, pp. 26–27; Edwards, "Development of NRA Policy," March 8, 1935; CAB Executive Director's Report, March 8, 1935; Ruth Ayres and Enid Baird, "Private Price Control and Code Policy," Jan. 9, 1935, all in NRA Records (CHF, Galvin File, Richberg File, CAB File—MR&D); Raymond Kenney to Blaisdell, March 29, 1935, Blaisdell File, NRPB Records.

increasingly disenchanted with Donald Richberg, who, according to labor, had been using his influence to undermine the authority of the National Labor Relations Board and secure Presidential rulings that were in direct conflict with the NLRB's "majority rule." Richberg, so his critics charged, was a "traitor" to the liberal cause. He and Williams should resign, and the NIRB should be reconstituted to include equal representation for labor.

An opportunity for reorganization came in early March when Williams resigned, ostensibly because he wished to return to business duties. Richberg now recommended that the NIRB be enlarged to seven members, including two representatives each for industry, labor, and the public, plus an impartial chairman, a position he thought he could fill. Labor leaders were none too pleased with the proposal, but did agree to go along. Accordingly, on March 21, 1935, Roosevelt announced that William P. Witherow of the Witherow Steel Company would replace Williams as a representative of industry, Philip Murray of the United Mine Workers would be the new labor representative, Hamilton and Marshall would continue to represent the public, Richberg would be the new chairman, and Henderson and Smith would continue as advisers but would no longer be ex officio members. Shortly thereafter Whiteside also resigned and was replaced by Charles Edison of Edison Industries.[7]

The change in leadership, though, did not alter the basic nature of the NIRB, or break the existing deadlock.

[7] Harold L. Ickes, *Secret Diary*, I (N.Y.: Simon & Schuster, 1953), 210–11, 220–21, 242, 247–48, 289; Arthur M. Schlesinger, Jr., *The Coming of the New Deal* (Boston: Houghton Mifflin, 1959), 163–65; Sidney Fine, in *MVHR*, June 1958, pp. 42–48; Raymond G. Swing, in *Nation*, Feb. 6, 1935, pp. 156–57; Feb. 13, 1935, p. 181; *Newsweek*, Feb. 9, 1935, p. 10; *New York Times*, Jan. 23–24, Feb. 1, 3, 4, 7, March 6, 22, April 26, 1935; *Blue Eagle*, Feb. 15, 1935; Richberg to FDR, March 19, 1935; S. Clay Williams to FDR, March 5, 1935, both in OF 466, Roosevelt Papers; Marshall's Notes on NIRB Meetings; Exec. Order 6993, March 21, 1935, both in NRA Records (Bardsley File, NIRB File—CAF).

This would persist until new legislation established basic guidelines and provided a definition of goals. Consequently, as the date for the expiration of the NRA approached, its critics turned their attention to the type of agency that might replace it. The market restorers, for example, had visions of a combination Federal Trade Commission and Fair Labor Standards Administration, an agency that would establish minimum standards for labor, prevent monopolistic combinations, and limit future trade practice provisions to those that promoted knowledge, strengthened competition, or prevented the use of coercive and predatory tactics. The economic planners, on the other hand, still felt that an antitrust approach was an exercise in futility, at least for large and important areas of the American economy. The real answer, they insisted, lay in greater public supervision, stronger public representatives, more governmental planning, and the inclusion of organized workers and consumers on the agencies of control. Since free markets were unattainable, it was necessary to devise new institutions and controls that could accomplish the same balance and expansion that a free market was supposed to achieve.[8]

The proposals of the antitrusters and planners were also accompanied by new visions of the business commonwealth. The NRA's big mistake, according to business leaders, was its tendency to abandon "industrial self-government" and make unwarranted concessions to radicals,

[8] Senate Finance Committee, *Investigation of NRA*, 636–37, 660, 849–57; Edwin George, *Code Revision Memo. 1*, 16; Jack Levin, "A New Deal for the NRA"; Edwards to Walter Mangum, April 24, 1935; Mordecai Ezekiel to Henry Wallace, Jan. 2, 1935, all in NRPB Records (Blaisdell File, Industrial Section File—CCF); Gustav Seidler, "Monopoly, Perfect Competition, and Modified Monopolistic Competition," March 15, 1935; C. A. Pearce, "Revision of Trade Practice Provisions," May 11, 1935; Gardiner Means, "NRA and AAA and the Reorganization of Industrial Policy Making," Oct. 15, 1934; CAB Report on Revision of NIRA, Jan. 5, 1935; G. D. Larner to Code Planning Committee, April 24, 1935, all in NRA Records (SR&P, Henderson File, Bardsley File, Marshall File).

labor leaders, and anti-business demagogues. While some of the more satisfied industries and most of Roosevelt's business advisers favored a simple one or two year extension, the majority of businessmen, if polls and resolutions were any indication, did want some changes. Any new law, they felt, should allow each industry to formulate its own code without bargaining with either the government or other economic groups; and it should recognize the "open shop," specifically disallow the "majority rule," limit the government's power to impose or modify codes, and permit an industry to withdraw from the program if it desired to do so. The situation, S. Clay Williams had once remarked, was comparable to that of the desert community where an enterprising cowboy had provided food for his cattle by taking a blowtorch and burning the spines off the cactus plants. The "essentials" of the NRA were like that cactus. Businessmen wanted them and would thrive on them, but a set of spines had developed to the extent that the NRA had gone beyond the "essentials" and "undertaken to put business generally under the management of Government or of any other group than its owners and managers." The President, he suggested, should grab a blowtorch and burn off the spines.

A fairly large minority of businessmen and their political allies, however, were against the extension of the NRA in any form, and this group was now stressing the dangers of governmental "regimentation" and implying that the whole idea had been imported from Moscow, Rome, or Berlin. Some of them were thoroughly disillusioned now with the way the code system had worked or the way it had strengthened rival groups or rival industries. Others were convinced that a restrictionist approach was no longer desirable. And still others were afraid that the program would eventually breed an elaborate set of permanent controls operated in the interests of non-business groups, a possibility that seemed more and more likely as Roosevelt's New Deal shifted to the political left and paid less and less attention to business opinion. The organizational spokesman for the group was the National Committee for Elimination of Price Fixing and Production Control, organized in Washington on February 27, 1935. It was this organization that gathered up the numerous business dissenters, the furniture industry because of its unfavorable experience with the lumber code, heavy-duty industries that had no sweatshop problems and were worried about sharp rises in the costs of materials, the carpet industry because it felt oppressed by the provisions of the textile codes, the mass distributors who had long fought the efforts to restrict volume and prevent innovation, and fringe groups from various other industries, all of which were denouncing the NRA as an alien agency that was placing unbearable shackles on American business.[9]

IV

Roosevelt's task, then, as he addressed himself to the problem of renewing the NRA, was to arrive at a compromise between the various conflicting groups. The new

[9] George, *Code Revision Memo.* 1, 12–13; Senate Finance Committee, *Investigation of NRA*, 735, 1624, 1687, 1734, 1768, 1801, 1826–27, 1892–97, 1931, 2907–9; House Ways and Means Committee, *Extension of the National Industrial Recovery Act* (74 Cong., 1 Sess., 1935), 399; TNEC, *Investigation of the Concentration of Economic Power*, Pt. 25 (1941), 13323–25; *Nation's Business*, Feb. 1935, p. 60; May 1935, p. 16; *Business Week*, Oct. 20, 1934, p. 22; Nov. 3, 1934, p. 18; Nov. 17, 1934, pp. 22–23; Nov. 24, 1934, p. 7; March 30, 1935, p. 36; May 25, 1935, p. 18; *Newsweek*, May 11, 1935, p. 6; *New York Times*, March 28, April 21, 23, May 3, 16, 25, 1935; Whaley-Eaton Service, *American Letter*, April 6, 1935; *Congressional Record*, 74 Cong., 1 Sess., LXXIX, 2708–9, 3202–4, 6113–16; *Harland Allen Economic Letter*, Dec. 24, 1934; John T. Flynn, in *Scribner's*, Oct. 1934, pp. 201–6; Williams to Daniel Roper, Aug. 15, 1934; BAPC Report on Revision of NIRA, Jan. 17, 1935; H. I. Harriman to FDR, Dec. 28, 1934; Report of Special Committee on NRA, Chamber of Commerce, Sept. 22, 1934; Walter Teagle, Memo. re NRA Extension, Jan. 1935, all in Roosevelt Papers (OF 172, 3Q, 105, PPF 1820); Resolutions from Industry on Future of NRA, Bardsley File, NRA Records.

law would have to allow enough price and production control and enough "self-government in industry" to retain the support of a majority of businessmen; yet at the same time, if it was to get through Congress and especially through the Senate, it would have to take into account public hostility toward price fixing and the demand of the old-line progressives that the antitrust laws be revived. The task would be a difficult one, but Presidential advisers like Donald Richberg thought that it could be done, that one could draw a sharp distinction between the restraint of "destructive competition" and the establishment of "monopoly." [10]

Roosevelt's own thinking on the matter seemed to be about as confused as that of the average man. In his earlier career he had tended to argue both sides of the question, and as President, he still resisted consistency. On the one hand, he admired the principles of Louis Brandeis, was genuinely sympathetic with the problems of small business, and liked to talk about his Administration as a continuation of Wilson's New Freedom. Yet, at the same time, he liked to talk about Theodore Roosevelt's ideas of a "partnership" between government and the better class of businessmen, and he could not get away from the notion that businessmen might gather around a conference table and schedule production so as to eliminate market gluts and stabilize employment. In his message to Congress on February 20, 1935, he recommended a two-year extension of the NRA in modified form, an extension that would retain the labor provisions, but limit future price and production controls to those that were needed to protect small business, check monopolistic practices, prevent destructive competition, or conserve natural re-

[10] Senate Finance Committee, *Investigation of NRA*, 13–31; Marshall's Notes on NIRB Meetings; Blackwell Smith to Richberg, Jan. 10, 1935; "A New NIRA," Dec. 18, 1934, all in NRA Records (Bardsley File, Marshall File); Richberg to FDR, Dec. 22, 1934; Richberg to Marvin McIntyre, Feb. 15, 1935; Marshall to FDR, Feb. 6, 1935, all in PPF 1820, Roosevelt Papers.

sources. "The fundamental purposes and principles of the Act are sound," he declared. "To abandon them is unthinkable. It would spell the return of industrial and labor chaos." [11]

The President's words, however, were largely lost on Congress, especially on the Senate, where a curious coalition of old-line progressives, economic conservatives, Republican politicos, and renegade Democrats seemed bent upon blocking the extension of the NRA even though they could not agree on any program to take its place. It was not surprising either that the Senate should decide that the NRA needed a thorough investigation. The power to conduct one was finally vested in the Senate Finance Committee, and the resulting inquiry, in Richberg's words, soon turned into a "happy hunting ground for the news hound." Disgruntled groups in a variety of fields described in lurid detail the "vicious system" of discretionary powers that was menacing their industries. The unwholesome details of the retail coal conflict and the rubber conspiracy were given a thorough hearing. Consumer and farm spokesmen presented their cases against the NRA. Clarence Darrow testified that "the whole thing was obviously made for the rich man—for big business." And Payson Irwin, deputy administrator for the graphic arts code, admitted to Senator Clark that if anyone used the code's cost-accounting system for income tax purposes, it would "land him in jail." [12]

[11] Raymond Moley, *After Seven Years* (N.Y.: Harper, 1939), 189–90; FDR, *Public Papers and Addresses*, iv (N.Y.: Random House, 1938), 82–83; Rexford G. Tugwell, *The Democratic Roosevelt* (Garden City: Doubleday, 1957), 34, 92, 214, 218–21, 281; Arthur M. Schlesinger, Jr., *The Politics of Upheaval* (Boston: Houghton Mifflin, 1960), 650–51; *New York Times*, Feb. 21, 1935; President Roosevelt's Press Conferences, Feb. 16, March 23, 1934; Jan. 25, 1935, Roosevelt Papers; FDR to Norman Hapgood, Feb. 24, 1936, PPF 2278, Roosevelt Papers.

[12] *Congressional Record*, 74 Cong., 1 Sess., LXXIX, 142–43, 1905–6, 1999, 2003–4, 2736, 3197–201, 4177–83, 4672, 6113–16, 7471; Senate Finance Committee, *Investigation of NRA*, 300–10, 362–63, 524–36, 591–98, 661–68, 744–48, 809–15, 975–84, 999–1004,

The Senate investigation, coupled with renewed criticism and protests from the Federal Trade Commission, also brought a revival of the charges that the NRA was monopolistic, both in terms of its effects on the consumer and in terms of its effects on the "little fellow" or on the innovator. Consequently, for a time, arguments reminiscent of the Darrow Board controversy once again occupied public attention. Friends of the NRA insisted that it had actually helped the "little fellow" by outlawing predatory price-cutting, one of the most effective tools of the monopolist. Most small businessmen, they insisted, sought relief because they could not afford to pay minimum wages, not because they were oppressed by monopoly. The enemies of the NRA, on the other hand, insisted that the agency was dominated by big business and was rapidly eliminating the competitive differentials that made the existence of small business possible. Both sides, moreover, could point to individual cases or specific industries that would prove their respective cases. And because of the conflicting evidence and the different effects of the code system in different industries, it was very difficult to draw up an over-all balance sheet.[13]

1183–96, 1220–24, 1247–70, 1272–75, 1711–24, 1798–1801; Donald R. Richberg, *The Rainbow* (Garden City: Doubleday, Doran, 1936), 199; *New York Times*, Feb. 16, 21, March 1, 7–11, 15, 16, 21, 27, 1935.

[13] Senate Finance Committee, *Investigation of NRA*, 13–14, 203, 243, 300–2, 817–19, 1383–87, 2416–18, 2437–50; House Ways and Means Committee, *Extension of NIRA*, 36–40, 181–86, 677–80, 724–33; *Congressional Digest*, Jan. 1935, pp. 22–24; *Congressional Record*, 74 Cong., 1 Sess., LXXIX, 3197–99; Leverett S. Lyon et al., *The National Recovery Administration* (Washington: Brookings, 1935), 621–22; Schlesinger, *Coming of New Deal*, 167–72; Karl Pribham, in *QJE*, May 1935, pp. 383–93; *Business Week*, March 9, 1935, p. 7; April 27, 1935, pp. 17–18; R&P Div., Report on the Small Firms Problem, Nov. 27, 1935; T. R. Taylor, "NRA and Small Business Enterprises," March 7, 1935; G. C. Gamble, "Status of Small Enterprises under NRA," May 22, 23, 1935; FTC to Richberg, Feb. 4, 1935; Richberg to Ewin Davis, April 5, 1935; Davis to Richberg, April 5, 9, 1935, all in NRA Records (SR&P, Small Business File—CAF, Richberg File).

Whatever the actual effects on the "little fellow," there were members of the Senate Finance Committee who were certain he had not been treated right. And following the hearings, they felt strong enough to defy the President's wishes and substitute a resolution proposed by Senator Bennett Champ Clark, a measure that would extend the NRA only to April 1, 1936, exempt persons whose businesses were wholly intrastate, bar all price fixing except in mineral resource industries, and allow only thirty days for a revision of existing codes to conform with these standards. On May 14, 1935, the Senate approved the Clark resolution by a voice vote, a vote that was said to reflect considerable trading with labor supporters for the passage of the Wagner bill, which would preserve and strengthen the collective bargaining clauses of the National Industrial Recovery Act.

The spotlight now shifted to the House, where the President's recommendations had considerably greater support. On May 16 Administration leader Robert L. Doughton introduced a new measure calling for a two-year extension of the NRA, applying the program to all industries that were engaged in or would "substantially affect" interstate commerce, and allowing price-fixing where it was necessary to stop discriminatory price-cutting, protect small enterprises, deter the growth of monopolies, or prevent the waste of natural resources. On May 20 the House Ways and Means Committee began hearings on the measure; and in conjunction with them, the Industry and Business Committee for NRA Extension arranged for "a great spontaneous demonstration" on the part of some fifteen hundred businessmen who arrived in Washington from some forty states. It seems doubtful, though, that the performance had the desired effect. Senator Nye dubbed it the "Save Our Racket Crusade," and other senators expressed their determination not to be swayed by such pressure.

By late May there was a growing likelihood that a deadlock between the two chambers might block any action at all. Senator Harrison had declared that the Senate would never agree to a two-year extension and had warned the House not to pass one. Yet a vote was scheduled on the Doughton bill for May 28, and every indication pointed to its easy passage. Various compromises were being suggested; but, as it happened, the contemplated deadlock never developed. On May 27, 1935, in a unanimous decision, the Supreme Court ruled that the whole system of codes and all their appendages were unconstitutional.[14]

V

The case that eventually spelled the end of the NRA had its beginnings in June 1934 when Walter Rice of the Justice Department arrived in New York to investigate alleged violations of the live poultry code. A month's quiet investigation of the A. L. A. Schecter Poultry Corporation and its affiliated Schecter Live Poultry Market, the two largest Brooklyn concerns supplying Jewish customers with kosher poultry, amassed enough evidence to obtain indictments against the two concerns and the four Schecter brothers, Joseph, Martin, Alex, and Aaron. In October the defendants were found guilty in district court on nineteen counts, including the disregarding of wage and hour regulations, filing false reports, and selling unfit and uninspected poultry. Upon appeal, in April 1935, the circuit court sustained conviction on seventeen of the counts. The Administration then decided to make the Schecter litigation a test case, particularly in view of the fact that its recent decision to drop an important lumber case had produced a chorus of charges that the

[14] *Congressional Record*, 74 Cong., 1 Sess., LXXIX, 6688, 6749–50, 7470–71, 7483, 7681, 7819–23; *Business Week*, May 25, 1935, p. 16; *Newsweek*, May 11, 1935, p. 7; *Literary Digest*, May 25, 1935, p. 8; *New York Times*, May 2–3, 11, 15–19, 21–26, 28, 1935; House Ways and Means Committee, *Extension of NIRA*, 8–12.

NRA did not dare to face a judicial test. Before the Supreme Court, the Schecters urged three points, all of which had been upheld in a number of lower court decisions. In the first place, they argued, the code system amounted to an unconstitutional delegation of legislative power. In the second place, their business was outside the scope of the commerce power. And in the third place, they were being deprived of liberty and property without due process of law.

A capacity throng gathered in the Supreme Court chamber on the afternoon of May 27 to hear the fateful decision. Chief Justice Charles Evans Hughes, occasionally stroking his beard or shifting in his chair, read the opinion with unusual vehemence. One after the other, he disposed of the government's contentions. "Extraordinary conditions," he said, "do not create or enlarge constitutional power." "Section 3 of the Recovery Act is without precedent. It supplies no standards for any trade, industry or activity. . . . We think that the code-making authority thus conferred is an unconstitutional delegation of legislative power." Nor was it valid to argue that the poultry handled by the defendants was in a "current" or "flow" of interstate commerce and therefore subject to federal regulation. Such an argument proved too much. If conceded, it would bring virtually all activities under federal jurisdiction, something that the makers of the Constitution obviously did not intend to do.[15]

[15] *Schecter Poultry Corp. v. U.S.*, 76 F. (2d) 617; 295 U.S. 495; Thomas R. Powell, in *Harvard Law Review*, Dec. 1935, pp. 202–6, 214–19, 223; Schlesinger, *Politics of Upheaval*, 278–83; *United States Law Review*, June 1935, pp. 283–91; *Yale Law Journal*, Nov. 1934, pp. 91–95, 108; *Newsweek*, April 13, 1935, p. 18; June 1, 1935, p. 5; *New York Times*, March 3, 27, April 2, 5, May 28, 1935; *Literary Digest*, April 6, 1935, p. 8; May 11, 1935, p. 8; Justice Dept. PR, March 25, 1935; NRA Legal Research Section, "Analysis of NIRA Decisions," March 2, 1935, both in NRA Records (Marshall File, NIRA Court Decisions—CAF); Richberg to FDR, April 3, 1935; Stanley Reed to FDR, April 11, 1935, both in OF 466, Roosevelt Papers.

The decision produced a curious mixture of dismay and relief. Businessmen thanked God for the Supreme Court, but at the same time they deluged the White House with appeals to save them from industrial chaos. In the House of Representatives members of the Ways and Means Committee were to meet and report out the Doughton bill. They met, listened to the decision, and adjourned. At the White House, the President conferred with his advisers for over two hours. Finally, Richberg emerged to announce that all codes were now unenforceable as a matter of law. And in New York, General Johnson rose before a convention of the American Booksellers' Association to pronounce an epitaph over the grave of the Blue Eagle. "NRA as written is rolled up tonight," he said. "The principles of NRA, I think, remain. . . . The future depends on whether you and people like you want them hard enough to fight for them." [16]

[16] *New York Times,* May 28–31, 1935; *Newsweek,* June 1, 1935, pp. 5–6; Richberg, *Rainbow,* 8; Hugh Johnson, in *Publishers' Weekly,* June 1, 1935, p. 2110.

CHAPTER 7. THE NRA
IN RETROSPECT

By the time the Supreme Court handed down its decision in the Schecter case in late May 1935, the NRA had already lost most of its popularity and support. Not many congressmen were enthusiastic about the program, and the chances for renewal, even if the court had spared it, had become increasingly slim. Businessmen, too, while they were reluctant to lose the antitrust immunity provided by the National Industrial Recovery Act, generally hailed the Schecter decision as a much needed check against the Roosevelt Administration, as a safeguard against the implied threat of socialization and governmental dictation. And many New Dealers, while they were reluctant to sacrifice the possibility for some form of social planning, seemed glad to be rid of the business-dominated controls and the perplexing administrative problems that the NRA had created. The whole thing, Roosevelt confided to Frances Perkins, had been an "awful headache." Some of the things it had been doing were "pretty wrong." And he did not want to establish a system that would set aside the antitrust laws on a permanent basis.

Consequently, even though a number of Presidential advisers were suggesting ways to get around the Schecter decision, Roosevelt decided against any major effort to restore the NRA. The court's stand on interstate commerce, he told his press conference on May 31, had relegated the nation back to the "horse-and-buggy" era. It had rendered positive regulation impossible; and except for the creation of a temporary, skeletonized agency that would study past operations and encourage voluntary business agreements, he intended to take no further action. An over-all approach would be abandoned in favor of piecemeal legislation, measures like the Wagner and Guffey bills, which might salvage some of the more beneficial portions of the program.[1]

Under the circumstances the President would have found it difficult to do much of anything else. For almost all groups involved, the NRA had been a disillusioning and frustrating experience, one they were not anxious to repeat. The clash of goals, the conflicts of rival pressure groups, the policy stalemate, and a series of fallacious assumptions and administrative mistakes had made the program one of the New Deal's greatest failures, both in terms of the pragmatic goal of stimulating economic recovery and in terms of reorganizing the economy to conform with current visions of what a desirable system should be.

In terms of recovery, to be sure, the economy was in considerably better shape in 1935 than it had been in 1933. The Gross National Product, according to later estimates, had climbed from about fifty-six billion dollars to approximately seventy-two billion, industrial output was up some twenty-eight percent, unemployment had dropped by about two million, the weekly earnings of an average factory worker had increased about twenty percent, and corporate profits, particularly for the larger industrial concerns, were higher than they had been since 1930. Yet such gains were hardly reasons for jubilation. Over ten and a half million workers were still unemployed, approximately twenty million people were still dependent upon relief, basic industries were still operating at little more than half their capacity, and the real income of the

[1] Raymond Moley, *After Seven Years* (N.Y.: Harper, 1939), 306–7; Frances Perkins, *The Roosevelt I Knew* (N.Y.: Viking, 1946), 252; *Business Week*, June 8, 1935, pp. 7–8; June 15, 1935, pp. 9–10; *Nation's Business*, July 1935, pp. 21–22; *Newsweek*, June 8, 1935, p. 7; June 15, 1935, p. 3; *New York Times*, May 29–31, June 1, 5, 1935; President Roosevelt's Press Conferences, May 29, 31, June 4, 1935, Roosevelt Papers.

average family was still thirteen percent below that of 1929.[2] The gains were certainly limited ones, and it was doubtful that even these could be credited to the NRA. More than likely, they were due much less to the NRA codes than to the spending and relief programs, the financial and monetary measures, and the working of natural recuperative forces.

What the NRA might be credited with was a sort of holding action, a program that for a season did provide a psychological stimulant and help check the deflationary spiral, prevent the further erosion of labor standards, eliminate child labor, and implement the share-the-work idea. There was little about it that could generate further expansion, particularly since the Public Works Administration was slow in getting started and since the assumption that businessmen were eager to build up their workers' purchasing power proved to be a fallacious one. On the contrary, in so far as the codes had any effect at all, they moved in the opposite direction, toward restricted output, higher prices, reduced purchasing power, and scarcity profits.[3]

In terms of economic reorganization, too, the NRA was a failure; this was true regardless of the economic philosophy of the reorganizers. The business planners and spokesmen for the "association idea," to be sure, had enjoyed some success. The program did facilitate the organization of new trade associations; it strengthened and reaffirmed existing controls; and it instructed businessmen in the ways of collusion and cartelization. Yet the outcome was far from the rationalized business utopia of profit insurance and financial security that stood as the

[2] Bureau of the Census, *Historical Statistics of the United States* (1960), 92, 139, 141, 166, 409; *Federal Reserve Bulletin*, June 1935, pp. 329–31.

[3] See Arthur M. Schlesinger, Jr., *The Coming of the New Deal* (Boston: Houghton Mifflin, 1959), 172–76; Leverett S. Lyon et al., *The National Recovery Administration* (Washington: Brookings, 1935), 621, 744, 804–9, 844, 863, 876.

objective of "industrial self-government." The proponents
of the business commonwealth, on the whole, were disillusioned with and highly critical of the later phases of
the NRA. And they blamed its failure to achieve recovery
on the abandonment of the "association idea," on its later
tendency to cater to political expediency, issue disturbing
and unsound policy pronouncements, withdraw governmental support, tinker with existing codes, yield to labor
unions, and subject businessmen to the unfriendly supervision of ill-informed, impractical, and unsympathetic bureaucrats. If the original concept had been fully implemented, they insisted, if the Administration had really
established a system of industrial self-government and
then backed the leaders of the system, the depression
would have been a memory.[4]

From the standpoint of the national economic planners, the NRA was also a failure, although again they had
enjoyed some slight degree of success. There had been
some recognition of the desirability of planning, some
acceptance of underconsumptionist theory and the need
for greater economic balance, and some slight concessions
toward a program that would encourage strong labor and
consumer organizations and give them an effective voice
in policy decisions. Yet, as most of the planners saw it,
there had been no real planning at all, only governmental
acceptance of private monopolistic schemes, an approach
that had produced even greater imbalance and made the
situation worse instead of better. They blamed the failure
to achieve recovery on this perversion of the planning idea,
on the NRA's acceptance of restrictionist business views,

[4] See David Lynch, *The Concentration of Economic Power* (N.Y.:
Columbia U. Press, 1946), 156–57; Benjamin A. Javits, *The Com-
monwealth of Industry* (N.Y.: Harper, 1936), 54–56; Nelson B.
Gaskill, *Profit and Social Security* (N.Y.: Harper, 1935), 221; C. A.
Pearce et al., *Trade Association Survey* (TNEC Monograph 18,
1941), 12–13; Clair Wilcox, *Competition and Monopoly in Ameri-
can Industry* (TNEC Monograph 21, 1940), 260, 266; *Business
Week*, March 30, 1935, p. 36.

its lack of effective sanctions and incentives, its reluctance to engage in a central definition of economic goals, and its refusal to create agencies of control that would be broadly representative of all the interests involved. The agency's difficulties, they insisted, stemmed not from the idea of controlling prices and output, but from allowing business to dominate the process.[5]

Finally, from the standpoint of the antitrusters, the NRA was an even greater failure. The theory that it would be used to raise the plane of competition and strengthen the competitive system was largely camouflage to begin with, and although it was finally embodied in official policy, it was never implemented. On the contrary, as the antitrusters viewed the program in operation, they could only conclude that it was spawning new "trusts" everywhere. Those who criticized it from a consumer frame of reference felt that the codes had aggravated the very conditions responsible for the depression, that they had destroyed free markets, rigidified prices, and promoted scarcity at a time when recovery depended upon flexible prices, volume production, and the free adjustment of competitive relationships. Those who criticized the program from a small business frame of reference felt that it worked to the detriment of the "little fellow," removed the differentials that made his existence possible, and added to the concentration of wealth and power that was responsible for the nation's ills. Only in isolated instances or exceptional industries had the codes been designed to aid small business; and in most of these cases,

[5] See Lewis L. Lorwin, in *Plan Age*, Feb. 1935, pp. 6–9; and in *Annals Am. Acad.*, July 1935, pp. 115–18; Rexford G. Tugwell, in *Western Political Quarterly*, Sept. 1950, pp. 403–9; Caroline F. Ware and Gardiner Means, *The Modern Economy in Action* (N.Y.: Harcourt, Brace, 1936), 150–61; Mordecai Ezekiel to Henry Wallace, Jan. 2, 1935, Industrial Section File—CCF, NRPB Records; Schlesinger, *Coming of New Deal*, 173–76; and *The Politics of Upheaval* (Boston: Houghton Mifflin, 1960), 214–17.

they had broken down and the government had refused to enforce them.[6]

II

The NRA, then, was a disappointment, both in terms of producing recovery and in terms of economic reorganization. Its failure was undoubtedly due to many things: administrative mistakes, the attempt to do too much all at once, the failure to get the public works program going when it was most needed, mistaken assumptions about the altruism of businessmen, the basically false analogy that was drawn between its tasks and those of the earlier War Industries Board, and to other errors of commission and omission. The whole program would have worked better if the NRA had limited its operations to a few basic industries, if the PWA had spent its money rapidly, if the administrators could have come up with new sanctions or incentives to win business cooperation, and if there had been more recognition that the problems of depression are basically different from the problems of war. Even if these things had been done, however, there would have still remained the problem of defining goals and developing a consistent line of action. Given the political, economic, and ideological context of the experiment, this was a very difficult problem to solve.

Initially the NRA had appealed to a variety of conflicting economic and ideological groups, each bent upon implementing its own theory of recovery and its own vision of the good society. The business planners and trade association secretaries saw the program as a way of ration-

[6] See NRRB, *First Report to the President* (1934); Jack Levin, "A New Deal for the NRA," Blaisdell File, NRPB Records; Simon Whitney to Charles Roos, March 27, 1934, Dexter Keezer, "Statement for the CAB," Jan. 9, 1935; Leon Henderson, "Price Provisions in Codes," Jan. 9, 1935, all in NRA Records (SR&P, CAB File—MR&D, Henderson File).

alizing economic behavior, reducing competition, and insuring profits. The national planners saw it as a way of
reorganizing economic institutions so as to create the
mass market necessary for recovery. The antitrusters and
champions of small business saw it as a way of strengthening the competitive system and helping small enterprise
through the formulation of rules to keep competition
from evolving into monopoly. And the labor leaders and
social workers saw it primarily as a means of strengthening unions, abolishing child labor, and eliminating sweatshop conditions. Success in achieving all these goals was
impossible; but in the beginning, the conflicts could be
and were glossed over by a high-pressure propaganda campaign. The difficulty came when the propaganda wore off,
the sense of impending national disaster passed, and the
great cooperative effort disintegrated into the original
welter of conflicting and quarreling groups.

The NRA, however, still refused to define its goals or
lay down a consistent policy. On the contrary, the content of the codes was to be determined by economic and
political bargaining, an approach that naturally favored the
highly organized group with a specific and well-articulated
set of demands. Generally speaking, business groups enjoyed a distinct advantage, a favorable position that
stemmed partly from their greater cohesion and power
and partly from the friendly attitude of NRA administrators and the desire to win business cooperation and stay
out of the courts. By and large, though not completely,
the codes reflected the desires of businessmen to erect
economic cartels that could check the forces of deflation.

Once the result had become apparent, though, it was
bound to produce stiff opposition. The outcome was in
conflict with the aims of farmers, laborers, consumers, and
national planners. It intensified the conflicts within the
business community, thus alienating dissenting business
groups. It ran counter to traditional antimonopoly sentiment and the growing feeling that "big business" was

somehow responsible for the depression. Once the public began to realize that the government was openly fostering monopolistic arrangements instead of denouncing them as it had traditionally done and was supposed to do, the result was a wave of shocked moral outrage. As Senator Lewis put it, "We yield to the demand of business. . . . They promptly create a monopoly, violate the law, rob the consumer and dishonor the republic." [7]

Public opinion, rallying from this blow, demanded that its illusions be made good, that government officials at least pay lip service to the antitrust ideal. These demands strengthened the hand of those who advocated a basic reorientation in policy. And slowly, in the face of public criticism, congressional attacks, pressure from rival agencies, and mounting internal controversy, the NRA moved in the direction of freer markets and greater control over the code authorities. It could not move far, however, without alienating business support and destroying the whole basis of business-government cooperation. Typically, an announced change in policy would be followed by a retraction or by failure to implement the change in practice. The announcement in regard to open-price plans, that relating to labor and consumer advisers on the code authorities, and the highly controversial Office Memorandum 228 were all obvious cases in point. The result was a marked divergence between declared policy and actual practice, a situation in which the NRA was saying one thing and doing another. On one level, that of policy principles, it accepted the goal of a free market, declared that trade practice provisions should help to strengthen competition, and stressed the need for close supervision of the code authorities. Yet on a second level, that of the code provisions and code authority activities, it was still accepting arrangements that were designed to fix minimum prices, restrict and allocate production, divide up

[7] Quoted in *New York Times*, July 9, 1934.

markets, create cartels, and establish "industrial self-government."

The resulting stalemate made it difficult to do anything at all; yet it was also very difficult to overcome. Open and active support of the arrangements written into the codes was likely to bring on a political storm that would endanger the whole program. It was something NRA officials could do only in exceptional areas where they could find something other than market control to justify their action. Yet any major attempt to revise the codes and implement declared policy would alienate business support, complicate the compliance problem, impel industries to "turn in" their codes, and perhaps set off the whole deflationary process again. The business-oriented administrators of the NRA felt that any such action would lead to disaster, and even some of the market restorers realized that it was not politically feasible. Consequently, no general code revision took place. Only in isolated instances or in highly competitive or atomistic industries where the attempted controls had broken down, could industries be persuaded to give up their code provisions. The dilemma persisted, heightening the sense of frustration and disappointment on the part of all the groups involved. It was passed on to Congress and again threatened to end in deadlock when the Supreme Court put an end to the whole process.

III

Much of the NRA's ineffectiveness was due to internal conflict and its inability, given the political, economic, and ideological setting, to define and implement a consistent line of policy. And it seems doubtful, even if the court had spared the program, that it could ever have generated much expansion or brought much in the way of economic recovery. What it might have done in other settings is a matter of speculation, but considering the intensity of the debate at the time, one cannot resist venturing some opinions.

Suppose, for example, that the business planners had been able to implement their dream of the business commonwealth and set up a government-backed system of economic cartels. In theory, perhaps, this might have produced a workable economy, at least if the directors of the system really possessed the social vision and know-how they claimed to possess and if they could have found some way to settle intra-business conflicts, create new markets, and stimulate new investment. If the NRA experience or that with the associational activities of the nineteen twenties were any indications of probable business behavior, however, the more likely result would have been economic stagnation, permanent unemployment, and the perpetuation of a depression standard of living, at least for the great majority of the people. Probably, if such a system had been established, the American people in desperation would have moved along the same road as the Germans, toward more and more state controls, totalitarian institutions, desperate efforts to build export markets, and perhaps even rearmament and foreign adventures.

Suppose, on the other hand, that it had been politically and legally possible for the national economic planners to implement their vision of over-all planning. Again, in theory, this might have produced a workable system. They at least recognized the need for expansion and the desirability of raising consumption rather than lowering production. It seems doubtful, though, that a centrally planned economy could have been established without an initial period of confusion, an initial loss in output, and a substantial and probably permanent sacrifice of individual freedom, private enterprise, and democratic institutions. Even if the problems of motivation, lack of essential information, and inexperienced personnel could have been solved, there would have remained the necessity of reshaping the whole economic power structure.

Business leaders, if they could not dominate the planning process, would probably have sabotaged it and refused to cooperate. And the planners, if they were to get anything done at all, would have been forced to resort to more and more coercion, a larger and larger network of government controls, and the nationalization of a number of basic industries.

As a third possibility, let us suppose that the antitrusters had been able to implement their vision of a super trade commission capable of strengthening the competitive system, preventing collusion, reversing the process of economic concentration, and eliminating practices that were conducive to monopoly. Again, if the underlying assumptions of the antitrusters were valid, this approach might have brought recovery. If the competitive model represented the best possible system, if departures from it were really responsible for the depression, and if these departures were really due to the use of unfair practices and the enjoyment of special privileges, then presumably the elimination of these practices and privileges would restore not only a workable system, but the best possible system. Such an approach, however, would certainly have encountered its share of problems and difficulties, and it probably would have revealed that some of the basic assumptions underlying it were not really valid.

There would have been the problem of reconciling the interests of small business with those of the consumer or the public in general. Although many antitrusters denied it, the conflict here was a real one. There were large and important areas of the economy where the size-efficiency dilemma was applicable, where the tendency of the antitrust rationale to identify the maintenance of competition with the preservation of small competitors was simply unjustified, and where aid to small business would involve the perpetuation of inefficiency, sweatshop conditions, technological backwardness, and a high-priced product. A policy of encouraging smallness, discouraging economic concentration, and diverting a larger share of the national income to small businessmen, although it might indeed be desirable on social or sentimental grounds, was not likely to bring much economic expansion or result in a higher over-all standard of living. Yet, if one chose the other horn of the dilemma and stressed efficiency, vigorous competition, and low prices, he might end with a situation in which the very competition that induced the most efficient use of resources would induce the survival of organizations so large and so few that competition itself would disappear.

In addition, it was doubtful that a policy of enforcing competition could ever be very effective. Antitrust action in the past had usually been a lengthy, complicated, and generally futile process, one in which the courts had repeatedly frustrated the trustbusters, businessmen had discovered new devices to replace the outlawed ones, and the effects on price rigidity had been minimal or nonexistent. Apparently, if the feat was possible at all, it would take a major economic reorganization and a large and permanent policing operation to force the more highly concentrated industries into competitive patterns, especially if competition was defined as competition in price rather than salesmanship. Nor had the idea of writing rules to keep competition fair ever worked well in practice. Too often the resulting rules facilitated collusion rather than strengthening competition. Too often they were unenforceable. And too often the whole underlying assumption, the notion that the growth of monopoly and price rigidity was due to unfair competitive practices, was not really valid.

Finally, to the extent that an antitrust policy was effective, it was likely to be deflationary, at least for a long initial period. It would probably frighten businessmen, discourage investment, and bring a further contraction in the economy. To be really effective, it would involve putting the economy through the wringer, subjecting it to a round of debt repudiation, wholesale bankruptcies, corporate reorganization, and major price and wage readjustments. Such a process, to be sure, might eventually bring recovery, provided it did not produce a revolution first. From a practical standpoint, it was never a realistic alternative.

It was probably just as well that the efforts of the various theoretical reformers tended to cancel each other out. In retrospect, a major reorganization of the business structure with all its attendant costs and problems was not really necessary. Recovery might have been achieved and a fairly workable economy restored through a sharp increase in public spending, particularly on social services, coupled perhaps with measures to bring about a more even distribution of income and encourage labor and consumer organization. The National Industrial Recovery Act might have been relatively successful had the emphasis been placed on the public works program and had the codes been limited to minimum labor standards, collective bargaining, consumer protection, and a few rules against dishonest and sharp business practices. It is doubtful that many codes of this type could have been written, but those written would have had a beneficial effect rather than a detrimental one. Some New Deal officials felt that the whole program would have worked much better if a man like Johnson had been in charge of the PWA and a man like Harold Ickes in charge of the NRA.[8] While this analysis was undoubtedly oversimplified, there was a good deal of truth in it.

IV

The realm of the "might have been," however, must remain a matter of speculation. One is on sounder grounds

[8] Schlesinger, *Coming of New Deal*, 109.

when he considers the general effects of the NRA experience on the subsequent course of reform and on the attitudes of the various groups involved. While the antitrusters, the national economic planners, and the proponents of the business commonwealth all retained hopes of putting their respective programs and ideas into effect, there were numerous individuals in each group who felt they had learned "lessons" from the NRA experience and were reluctant to become entangled again in anything similar.

In business circles, there was still considerable support for publicly sanctioned cartelization. Yet now that the sense of crisis had passed, the majority of business leaders, particularly in the more highly concentrated and more strongly organized industries, made it clear that they needed no help from labor, consumers, or the government in setting up and running their cartels. Any new program of economic planning or business-government cooperation, they felt, should contain safeguards to prevent it from turning into another NRA with all its disappointments and frustrations and all its implied threats of bureaucratic control, labor domination, and socialization. It should, in other words, guarantee freedom of action to industrial groups, protect the rights and prerogatives of management, and provide effective barriers against the attempts of non-business groups to take over the business system. As a matter of fact, most business leaders realized that under the existing Administration and from the standpoint of political realism such a program was highly unlikely, that any type of antitrust immunity actually obtainable would probably fail to compensate for the concessions that business would have to make to other groups. Consequently, in the post-NRA period, most industries concentrated on building a system of private controls, defending that system by appealing to the tradition and ideology of laissez-faire, and disclaiming all further interest in the idea that business and government should again join in cooperative planning.[9]

The national economic planners, too, felt they had learned something from the NRA experience. They had become more aware of the complexity of the economy, the ideological and political obstacles to central planning, the lack of essential information, and the dangers of allowing businessmen to dominate the administrative agencies and operate them in the interest of scarcity profits. Any new attempt at planning, they thought, must avoid making the same mistakes again. It should strive for abundance rather than scarcity, bring workers and consumers into the decision-making process, and provide for some type of incentive, something like production payments or guarantees against loss, to induce businessmen to expand their operations and profit from high volume rather than high prices. But after the NRA experience, most of the planners realized that a program of direct administrative controls was not politically feasible; and a few of them had concluded that under present conditions it was not even technically feasible. For the most part, they were willing to work for a less drastic and more politically acceptable program. Some hoped to begin with some type of economic council or advisory planning agency. Some accepted Keynesian ideas and laid more emphasis on what the government might do through its fiscal or monetary policies. Still others were content to work for partial planning and piecemeal legislation, for measures that would strengthen labor unions, add to the bargaining power of

[9] Lynch, *Economic Power*, 156–57; Whaley-Eaton Service, *American Letter*, July 6, 1935; April 4, 1936; May 8, 1937; Paul T. Homan, in AEA, *Readings in the Social Control of Industry* (Philadelphia: Blakiston, 1942), 252–54; Beverly Ober to Leighton Peebles, Oct. 2, 1935; W. R. McComb to Ober, Oct. 1, 1935; George Meyercord to Roos, Sept. 27, 1935, all in Attitude of Industry Toward NIRA File—CAF, NRA Records; George Sloan to Daniel Roper, March 5, 1937, OF 3Q, Roosevelt Papers.

consumers, aid particularly depressed groups, and achieve a more even distribution of income.[10]

Finally, the NRA experience also affected the attitudes of the antitrusters. It reinforced their conviction that "planning" or "regulation" would not work, that almost inevitably the regulated interests would control the regulators and use the resulting rules to enhance their private power and swindle the public. Once again, the antitrusters felt, it had been amply demonstrated that the real solution, if Americans wanted to remain free men and retain the system of free enterprise, was to destroy private monopolies, not sanction them or turn them into public monopolies. Consequently, in the post-NRA period, they tended to shy away from the idea of a broad administrative or regulatory agency and to stress other measures that presumably would help to restore a competitive, self-adjusting system, such measures as a tax on bigness, reform of corporate financing, the dismantling of holding company pyramids, stricter antitrust laws, competitive yardsticks, limitations on size, and increased use of traditional antitrust prosecution.[11]

In general, then, each school of thought tended to regard the NRA experience as confirmation of its own point of view, and the result was a heightening of mutual suspicions and a reluctance to be duped again. Business lead-

[10] Ware and Means, *Modern Economy*, 137–57, 197–204, 222–25; Schlesinger, *Politics of Upheaval*, 215–19; Mordecai Ezekiel, *$2500 a Year* (N.Y.: Harcourt, Brace, 1936), 73–104; *Plan Age*, July 1935, pp. 18–22; Jan. 1936, pp. 25–26; Dec. 1936, pp. 11–19; Nov. 1938, pp. 237–38; Arthur Dahlberg et al., *Recovery Plans* (TNEC Monograph 25, 1940), 4, 40–41, 107–9, 114–15, 125–26.
[11] Schlesinger, *Politics of Upheaval*, 219–21, 391–92; William Borah, in *Congressional Record*, 75 Cong., 1 Sess., LXXXI, 5362; Leon Henderson and Theodore Kreps, "On the Necessity for a Broad Inquiry into the Present Status of Competition," Dec. 30, 1935; Corwin Edwards to Thomas Blaisdell, June 17, 1938, both in Blaisdell File, NRPB Records; Benjamin V. Cohen, "Outline of a Program to Solve the Problem of Concentration of Economic Power," Cohen File, NPPC Records.

ers, antitrusters, and planners were all wary of another broad industrial program, unless, of course, it could be established on their own terms; and this meant in effect that there would be no such program. The antitrusters and national planners regarded any suggestion of industrial self-government with the deepest suspicion. Organized business fought strenuously against every effort to dismantle private controls or engage in social planning. And the planners and antitrusters continued to accuse each other of doing more harm than good. Under the circumstances, only limited actions of either type were possible. Planning in the post-NRA period could be only of the exceptional, partial, piecemeal variety, the type that was backed by a strongly organized lobby, justified on grounds other than market control, and masked in such a way that it could be slipped inside the charges of monopoly. Similarly, antitrust action could be taken only in special areas, in cases where gross abuses or prolonged investigations had produced enough political support to overcome the power of entrenched interest groups and push aside the arguments of the planners or business apologists. Recovery, as it turned out, would come largely through government spending rather than a reorganization of the economic structure.

PART II

ECONOMIC PLANNING IN THE POST-SCHECTER ERA

Private enterprise is ceasing to be free enterprise and is becoming a cluster of private collectivisms; masking itself as a system of free enterprise after the American model, it is in fact becoming a concealed cartel system after the European model.

Franklin D. Roosevelt.

CHAPTER 8. THE FADED DREAM
OF THE BUSINESS COMMON-
WEALTH

As a matter of practical politics, the death of the NRA marked the end of serious attempts to repeal the antitrust laws and establish a general program of publicly supported cartelization. Yet the dream of the business commonwealth was not completely dead; nor were the business planners completely silenced. In the immediate post-Schecter era, a number of former NRA officials, men like Donald Richberg, Prentiss Coonley, Howell Cheney, and James O'Neill, were still proposing ways to get around the court decision and re-establish a policy of "cooperative self-regulation," a program that would "defend industry from the chiseler" and "protect the source from which good wages have been paid." Some labor spokesmen, like George Berry, were still hopeful that a new cooperative effort could be worked out. From trade association circles came proposals like the one set forth by F. J. Stippe of the National Woven Wire Products Association. The federal government, Stippe felt, should grant every national organized trade association the right to call an industrial convention, elect its own "Industrial Governor," write its own code, and legally enforce its own set of ethics.

The ideology behind such proposals also received further development, particularly in the proposals and writings of such men as Fred Kent, Nelson Gaskill, Oswin Willcox, and Benjamin Javits. Kent revived his earlier scheme for coupling government-sponsored cartels with the insurance of key industries against loss. Gaskill argued that the whole theory of value and prices should be reconsidered and recognition given to the need for a selling price that would cover the full cost of production. Will-

cox, in a study published in 1936, concluded that cartelization was an inevitable and natural development, that
when industry reached the "supersaturation phase," the
"urge to self-preservation" arose, and men instinctively
drew together in defense against the "economic man."
And Javits, in books, pamphlets, and letter after letter to
President Roosevelt, set forth an elaborate scheme for
business planning. Each industry, he proposed, should be
organized under a trade association, the trade associations
under "super trade associations," and the latter under a
National Economic Council, which would act as the central planning and governing body. Agreements might then
be drawn up covering such things as minimum prices,
production quotas, accounting procedures, product standards, and labor practices. Once these were formulated and
enforced, they would bring recovery by putting an end to
the "capital-and-job-destroying competition" that prevented "a fair return to the investor." [1]

The fact remained, though, that proposals like the
Javits plan were significant only as indications of what the
business planners dreamed of doing. The friendly, pro-
business Administration and public atmosphere that
would have been necessary to implement such a scheme
had long since disappeared. The same business leaders

---

[1] Raymond Moley, *After Seven Years* (N.Y.: Harper, 1939), 306;
Oswin W. Willcox, *Can Industry Govern Itself?* (N.Y.: Norton,
1936), 266–67, 274–77; Nelson B. Gaskill, *Profit and Social Security* (N.Y.: Harper, 1935), 236–57; and *The Regulation of Competition* (N.Y.: Harper, 1936), 150–58; Benjamin A. Javits, *The
Commonwealth of Industry* (N.Y.: Harper, 1936), 54–56, 61–62,
68–69, 90, 99; and *Industrial Commonwealth Platform* (1938),
5–7; W. M. Kiplinger, in *Today*, Feb. 6, 1937, pp. 6–7; *Business
Week*, June 15, 1935, pp. 9–10; George Berry to FDR, June 20,
1935; James O'Neill to FDR, June 28, July 15, 1935; Howell
Cheney to FDR, July 10, 1935; Prentiss Coonley to FDR, Dec. 5,
1935; Benjamin Javits to FDR, May 26, 1936; June 22, 1937; Jan.
13, 1938; Fred I. Kent to FDR, June 4, 10, 1935, all in Roosevelt
Papers (OF 466, PPF 3174, 3577, 744); National Woven Wire
Products Association, *Bulletin No. 10*, May 1936, CIC File, NRA
Records.

who in 1933 had hailed Franklin D. Roosevelt as "a leader of courage, resourcefulness and trustworthiness" were now grumbling about "that man" in the White House and the coterie of economic crackpots, fuzzy-minded socialists, labor demagogues, and political racketeers that he had gathered about him. And if current trends continued, it seemed likely that this political breach would grow considerably wider before it was healed.[2]

II

The possibilities for cooperative planning, then, had been greatly diminished by the growing quarrel between organized business and the Roosevelt Administration. Yet the break had not been a sudden one, nor even a steadily deepening one. Instead, relations tended to run in cycles. Mutual recriminations were followed by waves of harmony, new laws by "breathing spells," and verbal attacks by efforts at conciliation. After each cycle, however, the gap seemed to grow a little wider.

The first major wave of business criticism had come in the fall of 1933 and the first part of 1934. It was touched off by Roosevelt's "currency tinkering," particularly the gold purchase plan, and the resulting fear that such a policy could destroy faith in the monetary system and produce an uncontrolled spiral of inflation. It was then kept alive by business reaction to such things as the transfer of the air mail service to army fliers, Dr. William Wirt's charges of communism in the government, the shifting policies of the NRA, the development of the power program, the new securities legislation, the relief activities, the Pecora investigation of banking, and the growing militancy of labor. Businessmen, so they said,

---

[2] Frederick L. Allen, *Since Yesterday* (N.Y.: Harper, 1940), 230–34; Arthur M. Schlesinger, Jr., *The Coming of the New Deal* (Boston: Houghton Mifflin, 1959), 471–80; and *The Politics of Upheaval* (Boston: Houghton Mifflin, 1960), 270–74; Arthur Krock, in *New York Times*, May 5, 1935; *Washington Star*, May 7, 1933.

were increasingly perturbed about the unbalanced budget, the growing tax burden, the danger of inflation, the alleged attack on the "profit system" and "private enterprise," and the fact that the President's advisers included so few conservative, practical, experienced businessmen. Clearly, the initial sense of crisis had passed. The "patient," in the words of one observer, was "feeling better" and wanted to know now when he might "give up his medicines" and what the "doctor's bill" would be.

In conjunction with the business criticism, moreover, conservative politicians were again speaking up and depicting the New Deal as a power-mad, bureaucratic tyranny that was not only hindering recovery, but also undermining the qualities of initiative and self-reliance that had made America great. There was a need, they felt, for a bipartisan organization to fight this menace. And accordingly, in August 1934, a group of conservative Democrats and wealthy businessmen established the American Liberty League, designed, so its sponsors said, to "combat radicalism," "preserve property rights," and "preserve the Constitution." Soon the League had become another engine of business propaganda against the New Deal.[3]

[3] Frederick L. Allen, *The Lords of Creation* (N.Y.: Harper, 1935), 450–51; Schlesinger, *Coming of New Deal*, 244–45, 277–79, 434–39, 444, 451–54, 457–65, 471–72, 480–88; George Wolfskill, *The Revolt of the Conservatives* (Boston: Houghton Mifflin, 1962), 12, 14–15, 20–25, 65–67; Ohio Chamber of Commerce, *An Appraisal of the New Deal by Ohio Business* (1934); *Literary Digest*, Nov. 11, 1933, p. 7; Dec. 2, 1933, p. 6; *Business Week*, Nov. 25, 1933, pp. 5–6; Dec. 23, 1933, p. 22; *Review of Reviews*, Dec. 1933, pp. 31–32; *Nation*, Dec. 6, 1933, pp. 653–54; *Nation's Business*, April 1934, pp. 17–19, 56, 58–59; May 1934, pp. 19–20; June 1934, pp. 15–19, 71; Rinehart J. Swenson, in *Annals Am. Acad.*, May 1935, pp. 136–37; Frederick Rudolph, in *AHR*, Oct. 1950, pp. 19–22; *New York Times*, Aug. 23, 1934; May 5, 1935; Directors' Statements, U.S. Chamber of Commerce, March 3, Sept. 21, 1934; Report of the New England Council, Sept. 22, 1934; Marc Rose, Address, Sept. 21, 1934; George Sloan to Hugh Johnson, March 15, 1934; Certificate of Formation of American Liberty League, Aug. 22, 1934, all in Roosevelt Papers (OF 105, 172, 466, PPF 3146).

In the face of this mounting criticism, Roosevelt grew increasingly disillusioned with businessmen, increasingly resentful over their continual carping, their lack of social responsibility, and their apparent willingness to block any measure of social reconstruction and pursue a policy of "rule or ruin." The country, he told some of his associates, was "going through a repetition of Jackson's fight with the Bank of the United States," and there was strong evidence that the bankers and big industrialists were deliberately conspiring against him. The President's conservative advisers, however, men like Raymond Moley, Donald Richberg, and Daniel Roper, kept trying to reestablish some basis for mutual understanding. They encouraged and worked with such "liberal" business groups as Allie Freed's Committee for Economic Recovery; they urged the President to call business leaders into consultation more frequently; and they finally persuaded him to make some overtures of conciliation and harmony. In his speech before the American Bankers' Association on October 24, 1934, the President called for an "all-America" recovery team, an "alliance of all forces intent upon the business of recovery." And business leaders, following the elections of 1934, did seem willing to make peace. The Chamber of Commerce renewed its pledge "to cooperate to the fullest"; others joined in the chorus; and the great majority seemed to agree with the President that 1935 could become a "genuine period of good feeling." [4]

[4] Harold L. Ickes, *Secret Diary*, I (N.Y.: Simon & Schuster, 1953), 108–9, 217; Ernest K. Lindley, *Halfway with Roosevelt* (N.Y.: Viking, 1937), 419, 426; Schlesinger, *Coming of New Deal*, 498–502; Moley, *After Seven Years*, 291–300; FDR, *Public Papers and Addresses*, III (N.Y.: Random House, 1938), 439; IV, 25; *Newsweek*, Nov. 24, 1934, p. 7; *New York Times*, Nov. 6, 1934; FDR to Johnson, Jan. 24, 1934; Daniel Roper to Louis Howe, Aug. 30, 1934; Roper to FDR, Sept. 28, 1934; Thomas J. Watson to Roper, Aug. 28, 1934; Allie S. Freed to Marvin McIntyre, June 4, 1935; Memo. re Committee for Economic Recovery, Nov. 9, 1934; H. I. Harriman to FDR, Nov. 16, 1934; Samuel B. Pettengill to FDR,

The era of "harmony," though, proved to be short-lived. As the New Deal program unfolded in 1935, there was a sharp increase in both the volume and intensity of business criticism. The work relief program, businessmen claimed, would delay recovery, undermine constitutional government, destroy moral fiber, and produce inflation, chaos, and bankruptcy. The proposed banking act would create a "currency dictatorship"; the social security program would increase unemployment; the proposed labor legislation would intensify industrial conflicts; and the attempt to break up utility holding companies would impair efficiency, delay expansion, and wipe out the savings of millions of innocent investors. At the annual convention of the Chamber of Commerce in April 1935 Roosevelt and all his works were roundly denounced in speech after speech; and in the summer of 1935, as Congress debated such measures as the Wagner Act, the Public Utilities Holding Company Act, and the "soak-the-rich" tax scheme, the torrent of criticism and abuse became stronger than ever. There was little doubt, said *Business Week*, that Business and Roosevelt had now "reached the divorce courts."

Through most of these attacks ran a theme of impending catastrophe and shocked moral outrage, a feeling that was probably rooted much more in a sense of psychological loss than in reasoned self-interest. Ideologically, the New Deal was tampering with some of the most revered dogmas of the business creed; and psychologically, it was striking at the foundations of business prestige and class security. Denunciations of the New Deal, moreover, were often blended with bitter personal attacks on the President himself. In the eyes of the wealthy, Roosevelt had

Sept. 15, 1934; FDR to Edward M. House, Nov. 21, 1933; FDR to Felix Frankfurter, Nov. 2, 1934, all in Roosevelt Papers (OF 466, 3, 1150, 1354, 105, PPF 1474, 222, 866); NEC Proceedings, March 20, 1934, pp. 12–13.

become a traitor to his class, a man who "suddenly, out of a clear sky, after a lifetime of cultured, pampered existence," had blossomed as a "Messiah that is a cross between Rex Tugwell and Jesus Christ." And this alleged apostasy added to the bitterness of those who felt they had been betrayed. Through the channels of the rich flowed a torrent of scurrilous stories, depicting the President as a liar, a thief, a madman, a syphilitic, and a communist.[5]

On the other side, for both personal and political reasons, Roosevelt was drifting further to the left and relying more and more upon his so-called "liberal" advisers, upon such individuals as Harry Hopkins, Henry Wallace, Harold Ickes, and Felix Frankfurter. Personally, he could scarcely help but resent the attitude of business leaders and the tactics they were using. And politically, he could not ignore the increasing radicalism of public opinion, the mass following of such popular demagogues as Huey Long, Francis Townsend, and Charles Coughlin, and the fact that Congress was demanding action and repeatedly threatening to seize the initiative on such matters as labor legislation, spending, and debt relief. To a large extent, perhaps, the widening gulf between business and the Administration was merely a reflection of a changed political

[5] Schlesinger, Coming of New Deal, 404–6, 472, 567–69; and Politics of Upheaval, 270–72, 297, 314, 319–20, 333; James M. Burns, Roosevelt (N.Y.: Harcourt, Brace, 1956), 205, 239–40; Wolfskill, Revolt of Conservatives, 107–10; New York Times, Jan. 10, 26, 28, Feb. 5, 8, 17, March 11, 18, April 4, 10, 25, 29, 30, May 1–3, 5, July 7, 1935; Ernest T. Weir and John C. Gall, in Vital Speeches, April 22, 1935, pp. 476–80; June 17, 1935, pp. 610–13; Nation's Business, May 1935, pp. 17–18; June 1935, pp. 15–17; July 1935, pp. 36–42; Aug. 1935, pp. 25–26, 47; Marquis Childs, in Harper's, May 1936, pp. 634–35, 639–40; Rudolph, in AHR, Oct. 1950, pp. 20–21, 32; Newsweek, May 11, 1935, pp. 5–6; Business Week, July 13, 1935, pp. 8–9; July 20, 1935, p. 32; Aug. 31, 1935, pp. 7–8; Whaley-Eaton Service, American Letter, April 6, 1935; Mrs. C. C. Moses to Harold Ickes, Jan. 10, 1936, Political File, Ickes Papers.

climate, of a growing gap between business and the public at large.[6]

Again, though, following the adjournment of Congress in 1935, Roosevelt tried to placate his business critics. In a carefully staged publication of a letter to Roy W. Howard of the Scripps-Howard Newspapers, he intimated that his "basic program" had now reached "substantial completion" and the time for a "breathing spell" had arrived. Once more there was talk of conciliation and harmony, but again the truce proved to be a short one. The atmosphere at the bankers' and manufacturers' conventions in late 1935 was one of open and avowed hostility. Roosevelt's annual message to Congress in early 1936 was a "fighting speech," in which he excoriated "entrenched greed" and "resplendent economic autocracy." And the legislative program in 1936, particularly the new tax on undistributed corporate surpluses, drew sharp fire from business critics. Sentiment in the business world, noted Raymond Clapper, had now become "so overwhelming" that only an "exceptionally sturdy individual" could "stand up against his associates and be for Roosevelt." One businessman told William Hard: "If I find any

[6] James M. Burns, in his biography of Roosevelt, notes the pressure from the left, but lays great stress on the cumulative effect of attacks from the right in explaining Roosevelt's shift in policy. As Burns sees it, the critical moment was sometime in early 1935 when Roosevelt was still precariously balanced between the two wings of his Administration. If businessmen had acted in the great conservative tradition of "reforming to preserve," Roosevelt might have continued his efforts to maintain a government of national crisis. Instead, they acted more and more like reactionaries. The Chamber of Commerce lambasted his whole program, while the Supreme Court, amid cheers from the business community, vetoed parts of it. In the legislative measures of the summer of 1935, business got its answer. See Burns, Roosevelt, 185, 213–14, 218–21, 224–26, 238–39. See also Moley, After Seven Years, 296, 302, 305; Ickes, Diary, 1, 363; Schlesinger, Politics of Upheaval, 274, 290; James A. Farley, Behind the Ballots (N.Y.: Harcourt, Brace, 1938), 249–50; Willard Kiplinger, in Nation's Business, March 1935, p. 22; Aug. 1935, pp. 15–16; Raymond Clapper, in Review of Reviews, Aug. 1935, pp. 18–19; New York Times, March 15, May 22, 1935.

of my executives voting again for Roosevelt, I'm going to fire them. . . . Anybody who is for Roosevelt is just too stupid to be of any good to me."

As the campaign of 1936 got underway, the case of business versus the New Deal was embodied in a steady stream of business speeches and publications. The New Deal, with its burdensome taxes, bureaucratic controls, and alien philosophy, so businessmen charged, was impairing credit, weakening confidence, and retarding recovery. Its extravagant spending could end only in a capital levy, repudiation, or worse. And its reliance on the dole was paving the way for dictatorship by destroying initiative, undermining moral fiber, and creating a self-perpetuating political machine. To the public at large, however, most of this talk about liberty and the Constitution sounded essentially hollow, especially when it emanated from organizations like the American Liberty League, the Chamber of Commerce, and the National Association of Manufacturers. Nor did it take any political wizard to see the incongruity behind the effort of Republican politicians to play up the monopoly issue. They might resurrect the Democratic plank of 1912, denounce a system of "Government protected monopolies," and condemn the NRA; yet their business supporters were in effect trying to maintain a private NRA. As one observer noted, "Landon's supporters want to control by themselves the machinery of stabilization, and they are trying to beguile the voters into agreeing with them by asserting that 'private initiative' in economic control is the 'American way of life.' " [7]

[7] Moley, *After Seven Years*, 317–18, 330–32; Dwight L. Dumond, *America in Our Time* (N.Y.: Holt, 1947), 559–60, 567–68; Schlesinger, *Politics of Upheaval*, 337–38, 499–500; FDR, *Public Papers*, v, 13–18; Farley, *Behind the Ballots*, 289, 293–95, 304; American Liberty League, *Twenty-Eight Facts about the New Deal* (1936); *Newsweek*, Sept. 14, 1935, pp. 10–11; Dec. 14, 1935, p. 10; May 9, 1936, p. 36; *Business Week*, Sept. 14, 1935, p. 7; Nov. 30, 1935, pp. 10–11; Dec. 14, 1935, pp. 9–10; March 14, 1936, p. 48; May 2, 1936, pp. 15–16; June 20, 1936, p. 48; *Time*, Nov. 25, 1935, p. 63; *New York Times*, Sept. 7, Nov. 11–12, 26, Dec. 6, 15,

Following Roosevelt's overwhelming victory in 1936, duly awed business spokesmen again talked of "cooperation," and for a time the bitter exchange of mutual recriminations did subside. In early 1937, however, came the Supreme Court reorganization plan and the wave of sit-down strikes. In these, businessmen found new objects for criticism, and this time there was a considerable echo of popular support. At last, it seemed, conservatives had discovered symbols that they could manipulate with some success.

For a variety of reasons, then, organized business and the Roosevelt Administration were at loggerheads; because of this, a revival of the NRA or anything similar had become politically impossible. Roosevelt's strongest supporters and most influential advisers were now deeply suspicious of any proposal for relaxing the antitrust laws. And given the current policies and attitudes of government officials, business leaders suspected that any new cooperative effort would result in some form of rigid control or in the transfer of power to other economic groups, a price they did not intend to pay.[8]

1935; April 5, 10, May 29, June 9, 12, 14, July 24, Oct. 27, 1936; *Literary Digest*, Dec. 14, 1935, p. 5; Raymond Clapper, in *Washington Post*, Dec. 6, 1935; William Hard, in *Survey Graphic*, Jan. 1936, p. 16; *Nation's Business*, May 1936, pp. 52–53; June 1936, pp. 35–38, 78–80; Ernest T. Weir, in *Fortune*, Oct. 1936, pp. 118–22, 198; Merle Thorpe, in *Saturday Evening Post*, May 23, 1936, pp. 102, 104; Charles A. Beard, in *Current History*, Feb. 1936, pp. 513–15; Rudolph, in *AHR*, Oct. 1950, pp. 23–30; Stephen Early to Roy Howard, Aug. 6, 1935; Early to Moley, Aug. 26, 1935; Howard to FDR, Aug. 26, 1935; FDR to Howard, Sept. 2, 1935; Orval Adams, Address, Nov. 11, 1935; NAM, Open Letter Reviewing Legislative Measures Affecting Industry, Sept. 1936; Peter Van Horn to Marvin McIntyre, Feb. 14, May 12, 1936, all in Roosevelt Papers (PPF 68, 1820, OF 8246, 1974); George Hurley to George Berry, Aug. 5, 1936, Cohen File, NPPC Records.
[8] Burns, *Roosevelt*, 295, 298–99, 307–15; Schlesinger, *Politics of Upheaval*, 385–92; Joseph P. Kennedy, in *Saturday Evening Post*, Jan. 16, 1937, pp. 10–11; L. W. Moffett, in *Iron Age*, Jan. 6, 1938, pp. 56–58; Frank R. Kent, in *Wall Street Journal*, Dec. 18,

III

The political limitations upon what the business planners could do in 1935 and 1936 were readily apparent in the general failure of their efforts to revive the NRA codes on a voluntary basis. Following the Schecter decision, it will be recalled, the President recommended the extension of the NRA as a temporary, skeletonized agency that could conduct research and approve voluntary business agreements. Congress, after amending the proposal to require that all voluntary agreements comply fully with the antitrust laws, agreed to a nine-month extension. Roosevelt then abolished the National Industrial Recovery Board and appointed James O'Neill to head the extended agency.

Aside from its research activities and historical studies, however, the remnant of the NRA accomplished little. Its Labor Advisory Board insisted upon labor participation in the negotiation, administration, and enforcement of any business agreements, something that industry was not willing to grant. And the Federal Trade Commission, anxious to avoid any program that could be used as a cloak for violating the antitrust laws, insisted that it be given full jurisdiction over trade practice provisions, that these provisions "merely prohibit what was already forbidden by Criminal Statute and by the Federal Trade Commission Act," and that the administration of them rest with governmental agencies, not with industrial groups. Such an attitude, declared F. Sims McGrath of the Asphalt Shingle and Roofing Institute, removed "all incentive to further effort." In practice, it meant that "parties to a

1936; *New York Times*, Nov. 14, 17, 20, 22, 29, 1936; *Literary Digest*, Feb. 13, 1937, pp. 5–8; June 26, 1937, pp. 3–4; *Business Week*, April 10, 1937, p. 72; July 31, 1937, p. 48; Whaley-Eaton Service, *American Letter*, Nov. 7, 1936.

voluntary agreement will . . . obtain no exemption whatever from the antitrust laws."

As a result, the few industries that did submit voluntary agreements soon lost all interest. The ladies' handbag, braided non-elastic, and solid braided cord industries withdrew even before hearings were held. The wholesale tobacco trade failed to show that the negotiators of the agreement were properly representative. The fertilizer industry, after protracted negotiations, lost interest and refused to attend further conferences. In five other cases, the Administration refused to grant approval because industrial representatives proposed to lower the labor standards established by their former codes. Thus, when the extended NRA expired on April 1, 1936, total accomplishments under this phase of its program amounted to zero.[9]

Even after the last vestiges of the NRA had disappeared, however, some business groups still hoped to salvage their code provisions through the Federal Trade Commission's trade practice conference procedure. Yet again they found the FTC generally unsympathetic and unwilling to revise its "outmoded" economic ideology. It was "indisposed," they complained, to allow rules that would "cover selling

[9] *Congressional Record*, 74 Cong., 1 Sess., LXXIX, 8875, 8900, 9188–91, 9318–19; FTC, *Annual Report* (1935), 7–8; (1936), 98; *Newsweek*, June 15, 1935, p. 3; June 22, 1935, pp. 7–8; May 2, 1936, p. 14; *Monthly Labor Review*, Aug. 1935, pp. 354–55; Feb. 1936, p. 334; May 1936, pp. 1234–37; *New York Times*, June 5, 7, 11, 15, 17, July 26, Oct. 1, 6, Dec. 24, 1935; March 17, 27, April 1, 17, 1936; Exec. Order 7075, June 15, 1935; Report of Committee on Changes in Labor and Trade Practice Standards, Jan. 4, 1936; Memo. re NRA Functions, Oct. 15, 1935; Burr T. Ansell, Memo. re Conference between FTC and NRA, Oct. 16, 1935; F. S. McGrath to Beverly Ober, Nov. 23, 1935; NRA PR's, June 24, Sept. 30, 1935; LAB to Leighton Peebles, Oct. 25, 1935; Peebles to Charles March, Feb. 18, 24, 1936, all in NRA Records (MR&D, CIC File, Voluntary Agreements File—CAF, Procedure for Voluntary Agreements File—CAF); Ewin L. Davis to FDR, Aug. 19, 1935; Stanley Reed and John Dickinson to Homer Cummings, Aug. 13, 1935; Howell Cheney to FDR, Dec. 11, 1935; L. J. Martin to FDR, Dec. 30, 1935, all in OF 466, Roosevelt Papers.

prices or margins of markup." It insisted that rules against loss leaders, price discrimination, and sales below cost conform to "the cumbersome language and the burdensome provisions of Section 2 of the Clayton Act." And instead of trying to retain "the benefits of the Recovery Act," it was actually piling up a record number of complaints against arrangements and practices that the NRA had once sanctioned and encouraged. Consequently, most business leaders failed to show much enthusiasm for the FTC version of business-government cooperation. The Commission did approve some thirty trade practice conference agreements during the period from September 1935 to the end of 1938; but, with a few notable exceptions, the bulk of the industries involved could be characterized as minor, insignificant, or exotic rather than vital to the industrial life of the nation.[10]

The same attitudes also hampered the activities of Major George L. Berry, the former labor leader and NRA administrator whom Roosevelt had appointed Coordinator for Industrial Cooperation in September 1935. Berry had hopes of working out a new legislative program through a conference between representatives of industry, labor, and consumers, but neither the New Dealers nor the businessmen were overly enthusiastic about his prospects. Even if industry did make constructive proposals, said W. Jett Lauck, "they would not go beyond 'industrial self-government,' which, of course, would be unacceptable

---

[10] FTC, *Annual Report* (1935), 94–96; and *Trade Practice Rules* (1946); John P. Miller, *Unfair Competition* (Cambridge: Harvard U. Press, 1941), 227–28, 272–82; Benjamin S. Kirsh and Harold R. Shapiro, *Trade Associations in Law and Business* (N.Y.: Central, 1938), 125; Felix Bruner, in *Nation's Business*, Nov. 1936, pp. 17–19; *Business Week*, July 13, 1935, p. 16; Sept. 7, 1935, pp. 20–21; Nov. 23, 1935, p. 12; Nov. 7, 1936, pp. 29–30; *N.A.R.D. Journal*, Sept. 3, 1936, p. 1194; Whaley-Eaton Service, *American Letter*, Nov. 9, 1935; *New York Times*, July 7, 21, 28, Sept. 30, Nov. 19, 1935; CIP Proceedings, March 12, 1936, pp. 22-23; Edwin George to AC, Oct. 16, 1935, both in NRA Records (CIC File, Voluntary Agreements File—CAF).

to Labor and the Public." In business circles, the proposed conference was denounced as a move to "regiment business enterprise" and create another "legislative mess." The trade associations in such major industries as steel, petroleum, automobiles, electrical manufacturing, and chemicals rejected Berry's invitations, and the majority of the business delegates that did gather in Washington on December 9, 1935, were openly hostile toward his suggestions. After an initial meeting, at which Berry got involved in a heated exchange of insults with Alfred P. Haake of the National Association of Furniture Manufacturers, hundreds of businessmen returned to their hotels, packed their grips, and left. Only about three hundred attended the subsequent round-table meetings, and most of these were representatives of small businessmen in the less highly organized areas of the economy.

Sparse attendance, though, did not prevent Berry from organizing a Council for Industrial Progress, an organization supposedly representative of all economic interests and therefore qualified to solve the nation's economic problems. But, from the beginning, the Council was little more than a joke. Out of it came a paper organization, some committee meetings, a second conference in December 1936, and a series of reports and recommendations, none of which seemed to impress anyone. The newsmen, noted Peter Van Horn, were referring to Berry as the "man who went wild with publicity and Johnsonian whoopee," the fellow who allowed "a little clique of advisers from N.R.A." to fill him with the "Big Man hop," thus "making jobs for themselves." And business leaders regarded Berry's activities only as an object of ridicule and contempt. "The Council for Industrial Progress," commented Henry Ralph, "appears to be taken seriously by almost nobody but the Major himself. The fact that for various reasons the leaders in most businesses have not seen fit to attend the Berry meetings does not deter the Major. If a couple of filling station operators show up, he considers that the oil industry is represented." In practice, the Council seemed to exert almost no influence whatsoever; and when Berry was appointed senator from Tennessee in 1937, it was allowed to die a natural death.[11]

The collapse of Berry's Council left Secretary of Commerce Daniel Roper's Business Advisory Council, a carry-over from NRA days, as the only formal link between the Administration and organized business. In spite of periodic storms and threats of resignation, Roper had managed to keep this agency intact, and repeatedly had urged the President to make greater use of it. Yet, so far as the newspapers could see, its business consisted principally in having a new letterhead printed every sixth month. One enterprising reporter asked the Secretary just what his Council did do, and Roper, in his best Uncle Dan style, explained only that "still waters run deep." [12]

[11] Schlesinger, *Politics of Upheaval*, 386; CIC, *Council for Industrial Progress* (1936); and *Council for Industrial Progress* (1937); Herbert Corey, in *Nation's Business*, Oct. 1936, pp. 103–7; *Business Week*, Oct. 5, 1935, p. 36; Nov. 16, 1935, p. 8; Dec. 14, 1935, p. 7; Jan. 18, 1936, pp. 11, 14; Nov. 21, 1936, p. 11; Dec. 19, 1936, p. 12; Whaley-Eaton Service, *American Letter*, Oct. 12, Nov. 9, 1935; *Time*, Dec. 16, 1935, p. 19; *N.A.R.D. Journal*, Dec. 19, 1935, p. 1525; Henry D. Ralph, in *Chicago Journal of Commerce*, Dec. 8, 1936, p. 3; *New York Times*, Oct. 28, Dec. 8–11, 20, 1935; Jan. 7, May 7, 1936; W. J. Lauck, Memo. re Conference with Berry, Nov. 5, 1935; Lauck to Blaisdell, Nov. 13, 1935, both in Blaisdell File, NRPB Records; Exec. Order 7193, Sept. 26, 1935; Charts tabulating favorable and unfavorable replies to conference invitations, Nov. 1935; Proceedings of Industrial Conference Called by the CIC, Dec. 9, 1935; Samuel Green to Colonel Value, Dec. 10, 1935; CIC PR's, Dec. 9, 1935, Jan. 8, 1936; Peter Van Horn to Berry, Dec. 28, 1935; Draft of Bill to Prevent Unfair Competition; Robert Cook to F. G. Grimes, Jan. 28, 1937; Otis Swift to Lyle Brookover, Dec. 4, 1936; CIP Proceedings, Dec. 10–11, 1936; George Brady, "Notes on a Permanent Council to Preserve Industrial-Labor Gains," March 1936, all in NRA Records (MR&D, CIC File); Stephen Early to FDR, Nov. 16, 1936; Summary of CIP Report; Berry to FDR, Jan. 3, 1936; March 25, 1937, all in Roosevelt Papers (OF 2452-a, 466, Industrial Recovery File—PSF).

[12] Corey, in *Nation's Business*, Oct. 1936, p. 104; Daniel Roper to FDR, Oct. 29, 1935; March 3, 1937; Ernest Draper to Roper, Oct. 28, 1935; Henry Kendall to Marvin McIntyre, Oct. 21, 1935; Stanley High to FDR, Nov. 12, 1936, all in OF 3Q, Roosevelt Papers.

Such criticism, however, was perhaps exaggerated. The Council did provide a vehicle for the ideas of Donald Richberg, who by the end of 1936 was emerging as the chief spokesman for those who still wanted a government-sponsored program of business cooperation. The antitrust laws, he told the American Bar Association in August 1936, should be rewritten and "monopoly" redefined so as to recognize that competition could be destructive and that price and production controls could sometimes be properly employed to protect public interests. A new commission should then be established to apply and enforce the law, and businessmen should be encouraged to enter into cooperative agreements, subject, of course, to approval by an administrative agency and subject to review by the enforcement commission if they proved to be harmful. A program of this sort, Richberg informed the President, could win the support of all the various groups that were suffering from "ruthless industrial competition" and thus put an end to the pressure for piecemeal legislation. Already, he noted, it had the backing of the American Trade Association Executives, "many labor organizations," and a "great many representative industrialists, economists, lawyers, publicists and officials of long experience in this field." Already it was obtaining "the same type of support from conflicting economic groups that brought universal support to the original N.I.R.A."

In March 1937 the Business Advisory Council asked Richberg to submit a proposal combining his plan of business cooperation with the pending wage and hour bill, a task that he attempted to carry out by defining "unfair methods of competition" so as to include not only objectionable trade practices but also such labor abuses as substandard wages, excessive hours, and the use of child labor. On April 8 the Council approved Richberg's "approach and objectives" and instructed its committee on antitrust policy, headed by William Y. Elliott, to assist in the drafting of specific legislation. Eventually, the committee enlisted the aid of several other former NRA officials, including Blackwell Smith, Edwin George, Donald Nelson, and Ralph Flanders, and before long it was making a number of proposals reminiscent of the days of the NRA. Elliott wanted to revive the NRA emergency price procedure; Assistant Secretary of Commerce Ernest Draper suggested that the Department of Commerce be empowered to approve business agreements; and Blackwell Smith was in favor of devising a set of standards, whereby an appropriate agency could determine whether or not a business agreement was in the public interest.

Politically speaking, however, such suggestions were simply not feasible, since both the liberal politicians and the business leaders viewed them with deep suspicion, and neither was willing to grant what the other really wanted. The Roosevelt Administration could not, as a matter of public policy, relax the antitrust laws so as to permit the creation of business cartels; and organized business would fight tooth and nail every effort to redistribute income and place more purchasing power in the hands of the masses. Once, in the crisis of 1933, these mutual desires had resulted in a trade, but the trade had not worked well, and neither side felt it was advantageous to trade again. "A burnt child fears the fire," remarked one businessman, and both sides felt they had been burned.[13]

[13] Donald R. Richberg, in *U. of Penn. Law Review*, Nov. 1936, pp. 7, 11–13; in *Vital Speeches*, Feb. 1, 1937, p. 239; and *The Rainbow* (Garden City: Doubleday, Doran, 1936), 248–49, 263–67; Kiplinger, in *Today*, Feb. 6, 1937, p. 7; *Business Week*, Jan. 9, 1937, p. 5; Whaley-Eaton Service, *American Letter*, July 6, 1935; April 4, 1936; May 8, 1937; Richberg, "Civilizing Competition," Nov. 16, 1936; Richberg to FDR, Feb. 19, Oct. 28, 1937; Richberg, "Fair Competition and Wages and Hours," Feb. 1937; BAC Resolution, April 8, 1937; Roper to FDR, March 3, 1937; George Sloan to Roper, March 5, 1937, all in Roosevelt Papers (PPF 2418, OF 1961, 3Q); Blackwell Smith, "Federal Regulation of Industry," Nov. 11, 1937; Draper to Walter White, Nov. 20, 1937; William Elliott, Proposed Report of Committee on Antitrust Policies, Nov. 1937; Jacob Baker, "Consumer Representation and Present Points of Concern or Pressure," March 1937, all in Blaisdell File, NRPB

IV

In the post-Schecter era, most industries preferred to rely upon private controls to keep competition within reasonable bounds. If the picture drawn by governmental investigations, court decisions, and the reports and complaints of the FTC had any validity at all, the use of such controls was the rule rather than the exception. A high degree of concentration, coupled typically with price leadership, oligopolistic understandings, cartel agreements, interlocking relationships, or the control of key patents, had largely eliminated price competition in such important and widely varying industries as automobiles, chemicals, motion pictures, farm implements, aluminum, cigarettes, newsprint, anthracite coal, glass containers, optics, lead, sulphur, and tin plate. The basing-point system also facilitated price stabilization in such basic industries as steel and cement. The FTC uncovered a wide variety of price-fixing, market-sharing, exclusive dealing, and production-restricting arrangements in such industries as plate glass, building supplies, caps, paper containers, print cloth, and petroleum refining. And such NRA innovations as the garment label, the automobile dealers' "Guide Book," and the copper cartel persisted long after the Blue Eagle was dead.

Trade associations, also, continued to carry on a wide variety of activities, including the formulation of elaborate codes of ethics, the constant preaching of mutual restraint, continued emphasis upon cost education, and the administration of extensive statistical programs, sometimes accompanied by interpretative guides that were intended to bring about unified action in response to a given relationship in statistical reports. Nor did the associations always

Records; Ober to Peebles, Oct. 2, 1935; W. R. McComb to Ober, Oct. 1, 1935; George Meyercord to George Roos, Sept. 27, 1935, all in Attitude of Industry toward NIRA File—CAF, NRA Records.

act independently. Another notable trend in the post-Schecter era was the growth of management engineering companies that administered the affairs of large groups of trade associations. For example, the firm of Stevenson, Jordan, and Harrison administered some thirty national associations, shaped their policies, provided them with executives, and became one of the frankest advocates of the principles of mutual restraint and market sharing. For this private NRA and for others of the same type, public support of business planning seemed superfluous.[14]

In any event, business leaders made it clear that they had no intention of sharing the prerogatives of management with the government. Experience with governmental agencies under the NRA and in the post-NRA period had convinced them that the type of antitrust immunity that might be acquired would fail to compensate for the concessions they would have to make. It was far better, they concluded, to let the whole issue remain quiet, rely upon unauthorized private controls, and hope that these would be little disturbed by antitrust action. Consequently, most of them were once again expounding the principles of Social Darwinism, reciting the credo of Adam Smith, professing their deep love for "constitutional government," insisting that depression and recovery was a "natural" process, and denying heatedly that they wanted government aid or that they had ever wanted it.

[14] Clair Wilcox, *Competition and Monopoly in American Industry* (TNEC Monograph 21, 1940), 69, 98, 113–20, 193–202, 237–40, 249–56, 266; David Lynch, *The Concentration of Economic Power* (N.Y.: Columbia U. Press, 1946), 153–54, 175–82, 227–34; TNEC, *Investigation of Concentration of Economic Power*, Pt. 5-A (1939), 2323–33; C. A. Pearce et al., *Trade Association Survey* (TNEC Monograph 18, 1941), 13, 51–58, 185–86, 195, 238–39; Dept. of Justice, *Grounds for Action in Investigation of Management Engineering Companies* (1939); FTC, *Annual Report* (1936), 51–57; (1937), 43–52; (1938), 42–56; *Business Week*, July 13, 1935, pp. 16–17; June 27, 1936, p. 22; FTC, "Report on Monopolistic Practices and Other Unwholesome Methods of Competition" (1938), 8–15, 25–29, 31–35, 40–42, 57–58, OF 100, Roosevelt Papers.

This attitude, moreover, coupled with the growing influence of the antitrusters and the reluctance of business planners to come before the public with proposals that were immediately vulnerable to charges of "monopoly," meant that the proponents of the business commonwealth had little chance of seeing their dreams realized. Cartelization and business planning might take place, but they would have to be done privately, not openly and as a matter of public policy. Only in a few areas, where the policy could be masked behind such ideals as conservation, social justice, or the preservation of the "little fellow," could the government openly encourage the organization and operation of economic cartels.[15]

[15] Paul T. Homan, in AEA, *Readings in the Social Control of Industry* (Philadelphia: Blakiston, 1942), 252–54; Whaley-Eaton Service, *American Letter*, July 6, 1935; April 4, 1936; Hurley to Berry, Aug. 5, 1936, Cohen File, NPPC Records; Sloan to Roper, March 5, 1937, OF 3Q, Roosevelt Papers.

CHAPTER 9. THE MIRAGE
OF NATIONAL PLANNING

FOR leftist-oriented national economic planners, the NRA experience had been even more disillusioning than it had for the proponents of the business commonwealth. In the post-Schecter period, they watched in dismay while the remnants of an over-all, organic, operational approach gave way before the onslaught of the antitrusters, disgruntled businessmen, and particularistic economic pressure groups bent upon saving themselves, promoting scarcity, and securing special concessions. The result, said George Galloway, was "a nation more planned against than planning." Ernest Griffith agreed that most of the planning being done was of the "bastard type," the type of partial, piecemeal, pressure-group planning that merely lent government support to the ambitions of economic cartels and served in the end to "discredit government intervention and planning of any sort."

Under the circumstances, a number of those who had once advocated an over-all planning approach were now changing their views. Some had concluded that the sheer complexity of the task and the technical difficulties involved were simply too great, that lack of knowledge, the diversity of the industrial structure, and the difficulty of securing a competent and disinterested personnel made it virtually impossible to compensate for the forces of change and chance or to predict the effects of a given course of action. And even if the technical difficulties could be overcome, there were almost insurmountable political, legal, and ideological obstacles. American politicians, by and large, remained convinced that centralized planning was incompatible with Americanism, the Constitution, democracy, individual liberty, and the institution of private property. Perhaps, some of the planners reasoned, a better, or at least a more feasible, solution might be found in the use of the taxing and spending powers, in changes in the monetary system, or in measures that would build up the economic power of organized laborers and consumers. Perhaps, if such limited governmental intervention could stimulate growth and achieve a more even distribution of income, then overhead planning would be unnecessary.

Not all the planners, however, were completely disillusioned and ready to turn to other approaches. For some, the piecemeal legislation of the post-Schecter era was merely "patching" and "tinkering," and the increased reliance on government spending was merely a way of postponing the fundamental surgery that was really needed. Admittedly, said Lewis Lorwin, the NRA had applied the planning idea "badly," but "the bad application of a good idea should not be used to decry the idea itself." [1]

II

Economic planning, then, was not completely discredited. In spite of the NRA experience, it continued to enjoy the support of a number of men who had been closely associated with the early New Deal, such men as George Galloway and Arthur Dahlberg, who had worked in the NRA's Research and Planning Division, Lewis Lorwin, a Brookings Institution economist in the employ of the National Resources Committee, and Harold Loeb and Walter

[1] Ernest S. Griffith, *The Impasse of Democracy* (N.Y.: Harrison-Hilton, 1939), 231; Griffith and M. H. Hedges, in *Plan Age*, Jan. 1936, pp. 25–26; April 1939, pp. 98–99; George B. Galloway et al., *Planning for America* (N.Y.: Holt, 1941), 46–49, 66–86; Galloway, in *Common Sense*, June 1938, pp. 20–23; Galloway, "Can We Have Both Democracy and Economic Planning?" Plans File, TNEC Records; Arthur Dahlberg et al., *Recovery Plans* (TNEC Monograph 25, 1940), 4, 63; Gerhard Colm, in Max Ascoli and Fritz Lehman, eds., *Political and Economic Democracy* (N.Y.: Norton, 1937), 32–39; Arthur M. Schlesinger, Jr., *The Politics of Upheaval* (Boston: Houghton Mifflin, 1960), 215–19, 236, 390–91; L. M. Graves, in *Harper's*, Feb. 1938, pp. 274–78; Lewis L. Lorwin, in *Annals of Am. Acad.*, July 1935, p. 118.

Polakov, who had conducted the National Survey of Potential Product Capacity for the Civil Works Administration. Outside the government, too, the concept had the support of an able group of publicists, such men as the historian Charles A. Beard, the philosopher John Dewey, the sociologist Robert S. Lynd, the Catholic leader Father John Ryan, and the popular economist Stuart Chase. In intellectual circles, the periodical *Common Sense*, edited by Alfred Bingham and Selden Rodman, set forth the views of John Dewey's League for Independent Political Action and served as a sort of unofficial mouthpiece for the over-all planning view. In Washington, interested officials could attend the monthly meetings of the National Economic Planning Discussion Group. Planners throughout the nation could join the Economic and Social Planning Association (ESPA), which, through the pages of its official organ, *Plan Age*, provided an outlet for those, both in and out of government, who cared to occupy their time in devising a blueprint for the future.[2]

[2] Lewis L. Lorwin, *Time for Planning* (N.Y.: Harper, 1945), xiv–xv; John Dewey, *Liberalism and Social Action* (N.Y.: Putnam's, 1935), 87–93; Stuart Chase, *Government in Business* (N.Y.: Macmillan, 1935), 275–90; John A. Ryan, *A Better Economic Order* (N.Y.: Harper, 1935), 87–88, 178–90; Robert S. Lynd, *Knowledge for What?* (Princeton: Princeton U. Press, 1939), 209–50; Schlesinger, *Politics of Upheaval*, 146–61; Harold Loeb et al., *The Chart of Plenty* (N.Y.: Viking, 1935), 5–6, 161–65; Lorwin, in *Annals Am. Acad.*, July 1935, pp. 114–18; Charles A. Beard, in *Today*, Sept. 14, 1935, pp. 3–4; *Plan Age*, Dec. 1934, pp. 12–14; Jan. 1935, pp. 9–10; Memo. re National Economic Planning Discussion Group, March 1934; Notes on Meeting of National Economic Planning Discussion Group, Nov. 21, 1935; Thomas Blaisdell to W. J. Lauck, July 5, 1935, all in NRPB Records (Lorwin File, Blaisdell File); Arthur Dahlberg to Wesley Mitchell, Nov. 7, 1934, SR&P, NRA Records; Galloway, "Can We Have Both Democracy and Economic Planning?" Plans File, TNEC Records. It should be noted, however, that some of those mentioned here later changed their views. By 1938, for example, Dahlberg had rejected the idea of direct administrative controls in favor of a type of strategic planning stressing a tax on idle money. See Dahlberg, *When Capital Goes on Strike* (N.Y.: Harper, 1938), 68–100, 109–42, 193–96; Dahlberg et al., *Recovery Plans*, 4, 67–77.

The real stronghold for the planners of the post-NRA period, however, was in the Department of Agriculture. Here, under the tutelage of Henry Wallace, were the planners par excellence, men like Rexford Tugwell, Jerome Frank, Mordecai Ezekiel, and Louis Bean, men who argued for centralized, nationwide planning and the coordination of industry with agriculture into one integrated program. Here, it will be recalled, had been one of the centers of opposition to the NRA's price and production policies. And in the post-Schecter era, the Department remained the chief vantage point from which the economic planners argued the necessity for direct governmental intervention that would lower industrial prices and create the basis for volume production.[3]

Still another sanctuary for the economic planners was the industrial section of the National Resources Committee,[4] particularly after Gardiner Means took over as director of research in 1935. As originally conceived, the section was to assist in relief work by studying industrial plant capacity and employment opportunities. However, Means argued that any agency concerned with physical planning might justifiably explore the broader aspects of social and economic planning as well. Accordingly, he had soon embarked on a number of extensive research projects that were designed to "consider the problem of over-all balance,"

[3] Jerome Frank, Save America First (N.Y.: Harper, 1938), 256–63, 354–65; Henry A. Wallace, Technology, Corporations, and the General Welfare (Chapel Hill: U. of N.C. Press, 1937), 78–79; Mordecai Ezekiel, $2500 a Year (N.Y.: Harcourt, Brace, 1936), 73–104; Louis H. Bean, in Plan Age, July 1935, pp. 18–22; Graves, in Harper's, Feb. 1938, pp. 270–71; Schlesinger, Politics of Upheaval, 215–17.

[4] This agency, chiefly concerned with physical and public works planning, was known as the National Planning Board from July 1933 to July 1934, the National Resources Board from July 1934 to June 1935, and the National Resources Committee from June 1935 to July 1939. It later became the National Resources Planning Board. NPB Minutes, July 30, 1933; NRB Minutes, July 2, 1934; June 13, 1935, all in CCF, NRPB Records; Federal Register, July 1, 1939, p. 2727.

provide "a sort of preview of the future Modern Democracy," and discover "what would constitute a balance of production and consumption at a high level." One project examined industrial capacity, the available resources, and the patterns in which resources were being used. Another concentrated on the consumption side of the equation, examining and sampling consumer incomes and expenditures. And a third dealt with the general structure of industry, the extent of concentration, and the techniques of control. Together, it was hoped, such studies might provide the guidelines and some of the basic data necessary for effective planning.[5]

Not all of these planners, of course, were in complete agreement. They still disagreed among themselves as to the amount of planning that would be necessary, the degree to which detailed controls should be established, and the extent to which businessmen had developed a "social conscience" and might be enlisted in a cooperative effort. Yet, in spite of their differences, they did share a number of common assumptions and goals. Almost all of them felt that the competitive system had broken down so badly that it was beyond repair, that the real choice was not between a free economy and a controlled one, but between a privately planned economy and one that was subject to public control, between a system of gigantic trusts directed by the big capitalists and a system of genuine social planning in which all economic groups would participate. The first

[5] Arthur M. Schlesinger, Jr., *The Coming of the New Deal* (Boston: Houghton Mifflin, 1959), 352; and *Politics of Upheaval*, 218–19; NRB Minutes, July 11, 1934; Gardiner Means to Charles Merriam, Jan. 23, 1937, in Advisory Committee Minutes; Industrial Committee Minutes, March 30, 1935; Means to E. J. Coil, Dec. 16, 1937; Frederic Delano to Harold Ickes, Dec. 2, 1935; Thomas Blaisdell to W. W. Alexander, Oct. 10, 1935, all in NRPB Records (CCF, Industrial Section File—CCF, Blaisdell File). The studies conducted by the NRC included Gardiner Means, *Patterns of Resource Use* (1935); NRC, *Consumer Incomes in the United States* (1938); NRC, *Consumer Expenditures in the United States* (1939); Means, *The Structure of the American Economy* (1939).

alternative, they agreed, would necessarily lead to restricted production, scarcity profits, and economic stagnation. Only the second gave hope of producing the overall balance, increased purchasing power, and expansion of production that were necessary for economic recovery.

The ideology of the planners tended to flow from three basic postulates concerning the nature and functioning of the American economy. The first of these, as documented in the writings of Adolf Berle, Gardiner Means, and Arthur R. Burns, held that free competition was rapidly disappearing from the American economic system. In industry after industry, the market-centered economy was giving way to an administered system, privately planned and directed by a few industrial leaders. This development, said the planners, was not necessarily the fault of greedy monopolists. It was the inevitable product of the economic organization and technological advance that made possible mass production techniques and a higher level of output.

The second postulate, most fully developed by economists Gardiner Means and Mordecai Ezekiel, held that the private administration of prices, the ability of business groups to fix prices and hold them rigid over long periods of time, lay at the core of the country's economic difficulties. Concentrated economic power had made it possible to hold up prices in the face of technological advances and increased productivity; and this, in turn, had led to maldistribution, the accumulation of excess savings, the failure of mass purchasing power, and a decline in private investment opportunities. It meant, first, that a disproportionate share of the national income was being withheld as savings. It meant, secondly, that real purchasing power was being diverted from consumers, farmers, and laborers, the classes that created the mass market, upon which the profitable investment of these accumulated savings depended. And thirdly, it meant that the natural forces of adjustment could no longer bring about economic recovery. In the face of falling demand, the normal choice of the businessman was to cut production in preference to lowering prices, a choice that threw laborers out of work, reduced their income, and thus cut purchasing power that much more.

The third basic postulate held that the antitrust approach of breaking down and destroying concentrated economic power was outmoded, impractical, and undesirable. Any policy that would make competition truly effective would impair efficiency and lower the standard of living. Consequently, the only real answer lay in transferring the power over economic decisions to new agencies of control, agencies that would represent all interested parties and would successfully counteract the restrictive influences inherent in the making of business policy. Moreover, the planners felt that such a policy was actually far less radical than any attempt to atomize industrial organizations. Since, as Berle and Means had demonstrated, the ownership and control of business had been substantially divorced from each other, the locus of control might be shifted without greatly altering the patterns of private ownership.[6]

On the whole, the planners regarded most of the New Deal measures as grossly inadequate; yet the majority of them were not socialists in the generally accepted sense of the term. Their economic and political ideology sprang from such men as Thorstein Veblen, Simon Patten, and

[6] Adolf A. Berle, Jr., and Gardiner Means, *The Modern Corporation and Private Property* (N.Y.: Macmillan, 1933), 18, 119–25, 352–57; Means, *Industrial Prices and Their Relative Inflexibility* (Senate Doc. 13, 74 Cong., 1 Sess., 1935), 1–17; Caroline F. Ware and Gardiner Means, *The Modern Economy in Action* (N.Y.: Harcourt, Brace, 1936), 11–43, 115–28, 137–61; Mordecai Ezekiel, *Jobs for All through Industrial Expansion* (N.Y.: Knopf, 1939), 68–70, 248–54; Arthur R. Burns, *The Decline of Competition* (N.Y.: McGraw-Hill, 1936), 40–42, 564–65, 589–90; Dahlberg et al., *Recovery Plans*, 10–11; Ben W. Lewis, in *Journal of Political Economy*, Aug. 1935, pp. 548–54; Donald H. Wallace, in *QJE*, Feb. 1937, pp. 374–87; George Galloway and William H. Hale, in *Common Sense*, June 1938, p. 20; July 1938, pp. 17–19; Means, "NRA and AAA and the Reorganization of Industrial Policy Making," Oct. 15, 1934, Bardsley File, NRA Records.

Herbert Croly, not from Karl Marx. Their heroes were the engineer, the technician, and the ultimate consumer, not the factory worker. Their central concepts stressed economic balance and unified cooperation, not class struggle and the rule of the proletariat. Nor did they favor government ownership and operation, except perhaps for the transportation and natural resource industries. They would be satisfied if the businessman's power over basic economic decisions could be shifted to representative agencies that were more likely to use it in the interests of the community as a whole.

Repeatedly, the planners expressed their concern about the preservation of democracy. They did hope, on the one hand, to create a planned system of abundance, one that would make the most efficient use of technological advances, distribute the proceeds equitably among all claimants, and provide adequate security for everyone. Yet they also hoped, on the other, to maintain a democratic system of procedure, a system based on compromise, conciliation, persuasion, and popular consent. The two objectives, perhaps, were not necessarily incompatible, but the achievement of both required great faith in the efficacy of the conference table, the sweet reasonableness of mankind, and the ability of disinterested experts to resolve interest conflicts through scientific research and the amassing of factual material.

Accordingly, the advocates of planning usually called, first, for some sort of central board or council to think about national economic problems, formulate broad objectives, and lay down central lines of policy. Second, they called for group or functional representation on the policy-making agencies. Third, they envisioned some type of neutral, fact-finding secretariat to provide the basic data necessary for informed decisions. The central idea in most of the plans was to organize and provide representation for all major economic groups, both business and non-business, to secure for them effective participation in the policy-making process, and thus to shift the locus of control in such a way that the final decisions would be more likely to result in expanded output, increased employment, a more equitable distribution of income, and a better balance of prices.[7]

III

Price imbalance seemed to be the problem with which the planners of the Department of Agriculture and the National Resources Committee were chiefly concerned. The failure of the NRA, they felt, stemmed in part from its inability to hold down industrial prices. In early 1937, as price increases seemed to be paving the way for a new recession, they began to search for new ways to cope with the problem.

One suggestion was that the President call a national "productivity conference," at which he would try to persuade business, labor, and farm leaders to forego their restrictive controls and cooperate jointly in a program designed to increase national production. The basic difficulty, according to such economists as Louis Bean and Mordecai Ezekiel, was that partial, piecemeal planning was leading to an economy of scarcity. Each economic group was trying to secure, at the expense of the others, a larger piece from a pie that was steadily dwindling in size. Something had to be done to break the vicious cycle of high prices, restricted production, and falling demand. A dramatic national conference, said Jacob Baker of the National Resources Committee, might succeed in focusing attention on the problem. It might, like Theodore Roosevelt's Rural Life Conference of some thirty years ago, establish

[7] Lorwin and Galloway, in *Plan Age*, Feb. 1935, pp. 6–9; Nov. 1938, pp. 237–41; Lorwin, in *Annals Am. Acad.*, July 1935, pp. 115–18; Rexford G. Tugwell, in *Western Political Quarterly*, Sept. 1950, pp. 403–9; Schlesinger, *Politics of Upheaval*, 151, 162, 215–16; Wallace, *General Welfare*, 78–79; Ware and Means, *Modern Economy*, 14–25, 152–61, 200–8; Frank, *Save America First*, 343–65; Ezekiel, *Jobs for All*, 261, 276–77, 282–87.

a "bench-mark of social progress" from which the nation could move forward to an income that was sufficient "to supply all the needs of all its people, all the time."

Consequently, the conference idea was urged upon the President, both by the Department of Agriculture and the National Resources Committee. Roosevelt, though, doubted that any such device could recapture the earlier enthusiasm for cooperation. For the present, he suggested, efforts should be limited to a "series of trial conferences" and "further explorations of the larger aspects of the problem." The conference, therefore, was never held. The only practical result of the agitation was the creation of a Presidential "study group," which was to keep abreast of the economic situation, report on emerging problems, and explore the possibilities of cooperative planning.[8]

If it had been politically possible, however, the planners would have gone a good deal further than the holding of "productivity conferences." Those in the Department of Agriculture were apparently convinced that the same devices that were being used to bring about agricultural restriction could also be used to bring about industrial expansion. Accordingly, in their blueprint for the future, the ever-normal granary, the Bureau of Agricultural Economics, the Agricultural Adjustment Administration, the agricultural processing tax, and the local farmer committees would all have their counterparts in an ever-normal warehouse, a bureau of industrial economics, a central planning

[8] Harold L. Ickes, *Secret Diary*, II (N.Y.: Simon & Schuster, 1954), 114–15; Advisory Committee Minutes, March 6, April 6, May 8, 1937; Charles Eliot, Memo. re Conference with Secretary of Agriculture, Feb. 15, 1937; Wallace to Delano, Feb. 17, 1937; Ezekiel to Wallace, Feb. 15, 1937; Bean to Wallace, Feb. 16, 1937; Memo. re Dinner Conference on Economic Outlook, Feb. 18, 1937; Eliot to Henry Dennison, April 10, 1937; Eliot to Delano, Feb. 17, 1938; Merriam to Ickes, March 12, 1937, with accompanying memo. by Jacob Baker; Ickes to FDR, March 29, 1937; Baker to Industrial Committee, May 18, 1937, with attached memo., all in NRPB Records (CCF, Industrial Section File—CCF, Industrial Committee—Production File—CCF, Blaisdell File).

board, production taxes, and code authorities made up of representatives from all interest groups. Louis Bean, Jerome Frank, Henry Wallace, and Gardiner Means all suggested plans of this sort. But the proposal that attracted the most support, the one that crystallized the rather nebulous suggestions of the other planners and presented them in their most concrete, lucid, and specific form, was the plan for "industrial expansion" set forth by Mordecai Ezekiel. "Outside of the Socialists," noted one observer, "one would be at a loss to name a person who has given the thought and has displayed the ingenuity and the command of economic facts in planning the complete industrial activity of the nation that Mordecai Ezekiel has done."

For years Ezekiel had been in the employ of the federal government, first with the Census Bureau and the Bureau of Agricultural Economics, later as assistant chief economist for the Federal Farm Board, and finally as economic adviser to the Secretary of Agriculture. These years had convinced him that planning was both essential and possible, not only in the agricultural sector of the economy, but in the industrial sector as well. As early as 1934 he had worked out his blueprint for the future, and in two major works, published in 1936 and 1939, he set forth a vision of a rational, cooperative system, one that would escape the cycle of high prices, low wages, and restricted production, and through planned expansion, would achieve an economy of abundance.

Blended into the scheme were a variety of concepts that were current at the time. Like Harold Loeb and the Technocrats, Ezekiel had caught a vision of what the American economy might achieve, if only it were freed from the shackles of "effective demand." Like the plans of Malcolm Rorty, Fred Kent, and other business leaders, his scheme provided for industrial benefit payments or government insurance against loss, devices that might be used to enlist industrial cooperation. Like most of the proposals of the academic planners, the scheme called for a system in which functional code authorities, under the supervision of a central planning board, would cooperate to achieve economic balance and lift the country from the slough of depression.

Specifically, Ezekiel's plan called for the establishment of "industrial authorities," consisting of representatives from labor, management, consumers, and the government. Such authorities were then to work out a program of planned expansion for each industry, a program that would make it possible through greater volume to reduce selling prices, increase wages, and raise profits, all at the same time. Once these programs had been drawn up, they would be coordinated and approved by "inter-industry agencies" and a central planning board, assisted by a bureau of industrial economics. Once they were approved and in operation, the government would contract to purchase, at a discount, any portion of the programmed production that remained unsold. An additional incentive would also be provided by levying an industrial tax and then returning most of the proceeds to cooperating concerns. Finally, there would be two special programs, one to modernize and expand the housing industry, and the other to retrain workers stranded by technological change.

Ezekiel argued, moreover, that his proposal would not result, as some of his critics claimed, in a rigid, stagnant, and wasteful economy. Flexibility could be retained by establishing both minimum and maximum prices and production quotas, so that within these limits individual initiative and competitive forces would continue to operate. Since a portion of the total planned production would also be reserved for new concerns and new industries, there would be no danger of creating a closed system. In Ezekiel's view, too, the government guarantee against loss should create no special problem. If faulty planning led to temporary surpluses, the government could store them in an "ever-normal warehouse" and take them into account when the programs were computed for the following year.

The real need, he insisted, was to get the American economy off dead center, to provide it with an expanding market and start it producing again. Once this was done, minor defects could be ironed out.[9]

IV

By 1937 Ezekiel's plan had begun to pick up some support, not only from his colleagues in the Department of Agricul-

[9] Ezekiel, $2500 a Year, 83–104, 137–38, 145–48, 160–85, 204–5, 210–14, 267, 299–306; and Jobs for All, 17, 20–28, 42–43, 58–63, 88–90, 109–11, 118–20, 141, 183–88; Loeb et al., Chart of Plenty, 162–65; Schlesinger, Politics of Upheaval, 215–19; Who's Who in America? (1952–3), 763; Dahlberg et al., Recovery Plans, 105–10; N. J. Stone, in Plan Age, June 1939, pp. 190–91, 194; M. C. Rorty, in Harvard Business Review Supplement, April 1932, pp. 389–91; New York Times, Feb. 12, 1933; Ezekiel, in Common Sense, June 1937, pp. 10–12. The major difference between the plan set forth in $2500 a Year and that in Jobs for All was that the former envisioned the organization of virtually all industries and emphasized the idea of benefit payments, while the latter would be confined to key industries and would utilize insurance against loss. The similarities between the plans proposed by Bean, Frank, Wallace, and Means and that proposed by Ezekiel are also obvious. Bean, like Ezekiel, stressed the need for a coordinated expansion program that would make use of functional representation, inter-code authorities, planning agencies, insurance against loss, and an "ever-normal reserve." The same general elements are to be found in the Frank plan, in the form of supercode authorities, inter-industrial councils, guarantees against loss, an ever-normal warehouse, and the use of sliding-scale dividends to induce industry to lower prices and increase production. Henry Wallace, too, felt that the way to bring "economic democray" to industry was through an ever-normal warehouse, functional representation, and production planning. Means advocated a similar approach, although he did tend to be less specific and more aware of the existing lack of knowledge and the technical difficulties involved. Similar plans were also being advocated at the time by Donald R. Taft of the University of Illinois and J. M. Clifford of Oregon State Agricultural College. See Bean, in Plan Age, July 1935, pp. 18–22; Frank, Save America First, 314, 354–65; Wallace, General Welfare, 47–49, 78–79; Ware and Means, Modern Economy, 129–61, 201–8; Wallace to FDR, Aug. 8, 1938, PPF 1820, Roosevelt Papers; Donald R. Taft to Means, June 8, 1935, with accompanying memo., Industrial Studies File—CCF, NRPB Records; J. M. Clifford to Joseph O'Mahoney, Nov. 23, 1938, with memo., Plans File, TNEC Records.

ture but also from a number of radical congressmen and the group of semi-socialist planners associated with the periodical *Common Sense*. Particularly strong support came from Thomas R. Amlie and his American Commonwealth Federation, which had been set up in July 1935 to coordinate radical third party movements and advocate a program of "production for use." The organization was the direct descendant of the Farmer-Labor Political Federation, which had been established in 1933 by John Dewey's League for Political Action. By 1937 it had more or less formal contacts with a number of radical state groups, with such organizations as the Progressive Party of Wisconsin, the Farmer-Labor Party of Minnesota, the Washington Commonwealth Federation, and the Commonwealth Federation of New York. In all of these areas Amlie and the writers associated with *Common Sense* were trying, with some success, to rally radical support behind the Ezekiel proposal. By the end of 1937 a bill had been drafted and introduced, a Committee for the Advancement of the Industrial Expansion Act had been formed, propagandists and speakers had been dispatched to spread the word, and *Common Sense* was heralding the Ezekiel plan as a program around which all progressives might unite.

In Congress, the plan appealed especially to the so-called "mavericks" or "Young Turks," the group of young liberal representatives led by Maury Maverick of Texas. In addition to Maverick himself, the group included such men as Amlie, Robert G. Allen of Pennsylvania, Jerry J. O'Connell of Montana, H. Jeremiah Voorhis of California, and Henry G. Teigan of Minnesota. In April 1937 a number of them attended the Commonwealth Congress for Progressive Social Legislation, meeting in New York under the sponsorship of the Commonwealth Federation. There, in collaboration with Ezekiel, Harold Loeb, Stuart Chase, and others of the planning persuasion, they succeeded in translating Ezekiel's proposals into specific legislative form.

On June 1, 1937, Maverick, Amlie, Allen, and Voorhis introduced identical bills based upon the Ezekiel plan.

Specifically, the Industrial Expansion Bill called for the creation of an Industrial Expansion Administration, a nine-man Industrial Expansion Board, consisting of five experts and four cabinet members, and an Office of Consumers' Counsel, to protect the interests of consumers. Together, these agencies were to prepare an annual industrial expansion plan, setting forth both immediate and long-range goals. They were also to choose the industries that were to be included under the plan and help these industries to organize industrial authorities, upon which management, labor, and the consumer would have equal representation. Such authorities would then estimate the effect of the proposed increase in output upon their industry's employment, wages, hours, prices, and profits; and from these estimates, individual programs would be worked out, minor adjustments made, national totals prepared, and the programs published.

Any approved program, however, would have to increase worker income, expand production, keep prices down, and limit profits to not more than ten percent of the proposed increase in payrolls. Only if these conditions were met, would the upper and lower limits for prices and production go into effect, and only after they became effective, would the government agree to purchase any unsold goods at the minimum price. The government, moreover, in order to insure compliance, would levy a steep production tax, ninety-five percent of which would be returned to the firms that cooperated. Essentially, as its sponsors pointed out, the idea was to use machinery similar to that of the NRA and AAA to secure full production instead of restricted output. The alternatives, they thought, were either increasing confusion or the regulation of all monopolistic concerns in the manner of public utilities.

Probably the great majority of New Dealers, though,

were not convinced that all the alternatives had been exhausted. A number of critics, remembering the experiences of the NRA, doubted that the scheme could ever bring the reduced prices and increased purchasing power that it promised. On the contrary, they argued, businessmen were likely to use the cost clauses to soak the government and insure themselves against failure. Surpluses were apt to be piled up and new enterprises attracted to protected industries. Consumer safeguards, too, would probably be ignored, labor and management would combine to vote for higher prices and higher wages, and the problems of the "ever-normal granary" would be duplicated a thousandfold when industrial warehouses began to fill up with goods of all kinds, grades, sizes, styles, and qualities good, bad, and indifferent, probably mostly bad. Such a program, its opponents insisted, would be immensely wasteful and expensive, and it was likely to establish a fruitful field for downright stealing, graft, and fraud.[10]

v

Consequently, the concept of over-all national planning, like the broad plans for a business commonwealth, never got much beyond the stage of discussion. Except for a few fringe groups, like the American Commonwealth Federation and its affiliated organizations, the planners never at-

[10] Dahlberg et al., *Recovery Plans*, 103, 107–10; Schlesinger, *Politics of Upheaval*, 142–46, 150–51, 217–18; Donald R. McCoy, *Angry Voices* (Lawrence: U. of Kans. Press, 1958), 39–40, 80–85, 94–100; *Congressional Record*, 75 Cong., 1 Sess., LXXXI, 5235–36; Herbert Harris, in *Survey Graphic*, April 1938, pp. 227–37, 246–48; *Common Sense*, Aug. 1935, pp. 8–9; May 1937, p. 24; June 1937, pp. 3–4; Oct. 1937, p. 23; Stanley High, in *Saturday Evening Post*, May 22, 1937, pp. 10–11, 105–9; *Nation*, Jan. 1, 1938, p. 7; Graves, in *Harper's*, Feb. 1938, pp. 271–77; Stone, in *Plan Age*, June 1939, pp. 196–200; Clair Wilcox, *ibid.*, Jan. 1939, pp. 8–17; H.R. 10924, June 14, 1938, 75 Cong., 3 Sess., in Industrial Committee Minutes—CCF, NRPB Records; William Hanneman to James Roosevelt, July 19, 1937; Jerry Voorhis to FDR, May 6, 1938, both in OF 172, Roosevelt Papers.

tracted much of an audience or aroused much real enthusiasm. The New Deal, after all, was essentially a mixture of pressure-group politics with traditional American ideals, and the concept of over-all planning ran counter to both. It was overly radical and in conflict with the traditions of individualism, antimonopoly, and limited government. It offered no immediate, specific gains for which lobbyists usually worked. It threatened important vested interests. And it smacked too much of the NRA, with all its problems, conflicts, and disappointments.

Even the less radical proposals of the economic planners usually received short shrift. The idea of a bureau of industrial economics, for example, was endorsed by business leaders, antitrusters, and planners alike, but during the nineteen thirties it was never established. Much the same was true of the idea of an advisory economic council. Such a council had been proposed by Senator Robert M. LaFollette, Jr., in 1931, but in spite of voluminous hearings, his measure was never reported to the Senate. In 1935 Senator Robert J. Bulkley revived the idea, and once again extensive hearings were held before the Committee on Manufactures. This time, too, numerous and varied economic groups endorsed the idea; yet there was rarely any agreement upon the composition and powers of the proposed council. And consequently, Bulkley's investigation produced nothing.[11]

Under the circumstances, the New Deal could engage only in partial, piecemeal planning that could be justified on other grounds and described in other terms. Yet the

[11] Schlesinger, *Politics of Upheaval*, 217–18; Galloway et al., *Planning for America*, 38–46; Donald C. Blaisdell, *Economic Power and Political Pressures* (TNEC Monograph 26, 1941), 187–89; Senate Committee on Manufactures, *Establishment of a National Economic Council* (72 Cong., 1 Sess., 1931); *National Council Conference* (75 Cong., 3 Sess., 1938); and *Discussion of a National Economic Council* (75 Cong., 3 Sess., 1938); Tugwell, in *Western Political Quarterly*, Sept. 1951, p. 480; Galloway and Theodore J. Kreps, in *Plan Age*, Dec. 1936, pp. 11–19; Nov. 1938, pp. 237–38.

planners continued to hope, particularly after the recession of 1937 brought a new period of economic adversity and a new sense of crisis and despair. They reintroduced the Industrial Expansion Bill and argued anew that it offered the only adequate solution to the nation's economic problems.[12] The great majority of their countrymen, however, did not agree. Their vision was to remain essentially a mirage, a phantasy that produced tantalizing glimpses of the promised land but remained outside the realm of economic, political, and practical reality.

[12] Galloway et al., *Planning for America*, 46–49; Griffith, *Impasse of Democracy*, 231; Dahlberg et al, *Recovery Plans*, 129–46; *Congressional Record*, 75 Cong., 3 Sess., LXXXIII, 9347–48; 76 Cong., 1 Sess., LXXXIV, 11117; Galloway, in *Plan Age*, Nov. 1938, pp. 237–44; *Common Sense*, Feb. 1938, pp. 13–14; April 1938, p. 5; July 1938, p. 5; H.R. 7504, Aug. 4, 1939, in Industrial Legislation File —CCF, NRPB Records.

CHAPTER 10. THE CONCEPT
OF COUNTERORGANIZATION

As New Deal economists and reformers viewed the problem of concentrated economic power in 1935, they still tended to think in terms of two general solutions, one involving industrial atomization to restore a self-adjusting economy, the other involving centralized planning and detailed regulation. Yet from a political standpoint, both approaches were, and seemed likely to remain, unrealistic. A more feasible alternative was needed. Gradually, haltingly, incoherently, almost haphazardly, another possibility was emerging, one that sprang not from any preconceived plan, but rather from the process of political compromise, the conflict of ideals, and the interplay of power between rival pressure groups. As yet, the policy had no well-articulated rationale behind it, nothing at least beyond a vague sympathy for the underdog, a pragmatic willingness to experiment, and a shrewd assessment of political realities. The ideology would come later, as a rationalization after the event. But if one insisted on a dominant theme, he could probably find it in the concept of counterorganization, in the idea of using the government to promote the organization of economically weak groups, thus restoring economic balance, pitting one power concentrate against another, and developing an economy of "countervailing powers" capable of achieving the full utilization of resources that a free market was supposed to achieve.

The advantages of stronger economic organization had long been stressed by labor, farm, and small business groups. The relatively new element was the attempt of these groups to enlist governmental aid in developing market power. Labor leaders had now abandoned their former devotion to "voluntarism" and were urging that the government foster unionization, absorb the unemployed, and regulate wages and hours. Farm leaders, beginning in the nineteen twenties, had abandoned their earlier emphasis on an antitrust approach and started advocating their own government-supported price and production controls. Then, with the onset of the depression, small merchants and declining or highly competitive industries had also turned toward a program of government-fostered and government-enforced cartelization. Each of these groups, moreover, had developed elaborate arguments explaining why it should receive a larger share of the national product and why its own recovery was a basic prerequisite for general recovery.

To some extent this concept of counterorganization found its way into the early New Deal. There were elements of it in the farm program, in Section 7(a) of the National Industrial Recovery Act, in the gestures toward labor and consumer representation, in the efforts to organize consumer councils, and in the attempts of some industrial groups to use their codes as a means of redistributing the burden of the depression, either by developing market power of their own or by placing restrictions on the market power of their rivals. By no stretch of the imagination, though, could one regard counterorganization as the dominant policy of the early New Deal. The early New Dealers tended to take a paternalistic outlook, to think in terms of having the government or business do something for the underprivileged, not in terms of organizing economic power blocs that could look out for themselves. Consequently, the whole emphasis was upon cooperation, preferably voluntary cooperation, not upon the compulsion that would flow from the development of countervailing powers. The idea, essentially, was to persuade or induce businessmen to use their economic power in the public interest, raise the income of farmers and laborers, and thus build the mass market that was necessary for sustained growth. And the practical effect was to accentuate economic imbalance and strengthen the groups that were already dominant.

The programs of the early New Deal, however, had generated a new organization consciousness among previously weak and relatively unorganized groups. For the farmer and the laborer, the independent grocer or druggist, the coal mine operator, used car dealer, and crude oil producer, the trucker, barber, and beauty shop operator, and for others that lacked market power in an economic world where price and production control had become increasingly characteristic, the NRA and AAA had been eye openers. Public power, they learned, could be used to reinforce private power and control markets; and the group that could develop sufficient political strength and a plausible ideological rationale could secure governmental intervention of this type, particularly from an increasingly progressive Congress and from an Administration that was now quarreling with big business, shifting to the left, and actively seeking the support of farmers, laborers, and small businessmen.

Even the antitrusters seemed willing to go along, especially if the departure from competitive standards could be justified on grounds other than market control and especially if there was an appeal to public sympathy for the underdog, for the "little fellow" struggling against sinister, organized interests. So long as the alleged enemy was "big business," the desired legislation could often be presented as an extension of the long-standing antitrust tradition. Only upon closer examination did it become obvious that there were striking differences, that in reality the new economic control measures were based upon assumptions that ran directly counter to traditional antitrust concepts. Under the older view, public control was justified only in cases of natural monopoly, in areas where competition could not be made effective. Under the new, the justification was not too little competition, but too much; not protection for the consumer or the public, but protection for the producer. The initiative came not from the government or an aroused public, but from the industrial group itself. Some producers, it seemed, were trying to gain a public utility status quite as zealously as their forerunners had opposed it.

The general tendency, therefore, was to foster cartelization and economic organization in previously competitive or unorganized areas. Yet again, it must be emphasized that this objective was never clearly set forth. Nor did it necessarily follow that those who had been the weakest and most underprivileged in the past would now receive the greatest benefits. The legislation, on the whole, was piecemeal, pressure-group legislation, designed to satisfy immediate economic and political needs. Generally, the prizes still went to the groups with the greatest cohesion, the strongest political organization, and the most plausible arguments for linking their own special interests with the current conception of the public interest. The position of the Administration, moreover, was never wholly clear. In some cases it fostered the new cartels; in others it merely acquiesced in the legislative *fait accompli* of a particularly vociferous lobby; in still others it opposed the projected legislation, but failed to hold the legislators in line. A new policy was emerging, but largely by default rather than by design.[1]

[1] John P. Miller, *Unfair Competition* (Cambridge: Harvard U. Press, 1941), 283–84, 330–35, 400; John K. Galbraith, *American Capitalism* (Boston: Houghton Mifflin, 1962 ed.), 55–56, 110–65; Gardiner Means, *Industrial Prices and Their Relative Inflexibility* (Senate Doc. 13, 74 Cong., 1 Sess., 1935), 12–15; David Lynch, *The Concentration of Economic Power* (N.Y.: Columbia U. Press, 1946), 143, 164–66, 168–69; Arthur M. Schlesinger, Jr., *The Coming of the New Deal* (Boston: Houghton Mifflin, 1959), 38–39, 89–92, 129–30, 136–37, 179–84, 401–4, 407–8; John H. Cover et al., *Problems of Small Business* (TNEC Monograph 17, 1941), 164; Ewald T. Grether, *Price Control under Fair Trade Legislation* (N.Y.: Oxford U. Press, 1939), 6, 10; Calvert Judkins, in Benjamin Werne, ed., *Business and the Robinson-Patman Law* (N.Y.: Oxford U. Press, 1938), 167–68; Basil Rauch, A *History of the New Deal* (N.Y.: Creative Age, 1944), 203–6; Mordecai Ezekiel to Henry Wallace, Jan. 2, 1935; Leon Henderson and

II

The two largest economic groups that might be organized to counterbalance big business were farmers and laborers. Consequently, even though developments in the fields of agriculture and labor lie largely outside the scope of this book, one cannot ignore the new power structures there, the special governmental favors they were able to obtain, and the implications of these developments for business policy. In agriculture, for example, the decade of the nineteen twenties had witnessed the rise of strong farm organizations, the improvement of agricultural lobbying techniques, and the emergence of a powerful farm bloc in Congress. With the advent of the New Deal, the farm organizations, led and coordinated by the American Farm Bureau Federation, had been able to implement their earlier proposals. And the result was the elaborate system of planning and controls embodied in the Agricultural Adjustment Act and the later amendments to it, a system designed, so the Act said, to "re-establish prices to farmers at a level that will give purchasing power . . . equivalent to the purchasing power of agricultural commodities in the base period," such base period being for most crops the five-year span from 1909 to 1914.

The chief method of raising and maintaining farm prices was through restriction of production. Typically, this took the form of agreements with farmers to reduce acreage or output in return for benefit payments from the proceeds of a tax levied on the primary processors of the product. Supplementing this central program, too, were such devices as marketing agreements and such arrangements as those designed to subsidize exports, divert sur-

Theodore Kreps, "On the Necessity for a Broad Inquiry into the Present Status of Competition," Dec. 30, 1935, both in NRPB Records (Industrial Section File—CCF, Blaisdell File).

pluses to relief, discover new uses for farm products, and provide commodity loans that would enable producers to hold goods off the market. Finally, in such lines as tobacco, cotton, and potatoes, marketing quotas and special penalty taxes had been established to force agrarian "chiselers" into line.

The justification for such a program stressed the theory that recovery could not be achieved until the balance of market power between agriculture and industry had been restored, particularly since agriculture was presumed to be the "fundamental" economic activity upon which all others rested. The protracted agricultural depression of the nineteen twenties, the farmers insisted, had been a primary cause of the general depression; and general recovery would therefore require the channeling of more purchasing power into the hands of the farmers. Coupled, too, with the argument for parity were the powerful political symbols of the family farm and the yeoman farmer, the sturdy, honest, independent, morally upright individual that was supposed to constitute the very foundation of America's individualistic and democratic ideals. Farming, so it was said, was a "way of life," an occupation that was somehow purer, cleaner, and morally better than other occupations. It mattered little that this agrarian dream corresponded only slightly with the realities of commercial farming and tenant relationships. It still had a powerful appeal. To many people, farmers and non-farmers alike, it justified the salvation of farming as a way of life. And it explained in part why agriculture was able to dodge most of the anti-monopoly agitation and find ways of using governmental powers to fix prices, plan production, and regularize markets.

When the first Agricultural Adjustment Act was declared unconstitutional in January 1936, it became necessary to achieve the same objective indirectly. Accordingly, another powerful and sacred symbol was brought into play, that of conservation. The result was the Soil Conservation and Domestic Allotment Act, under which farmers could be paid for diverting acreage to soil-conserving crops or adopting soil-building practices. Restriction of production was now made to look like conservation of resources; the term "soil-depleting crops" was usually defined to include those in which surpluses existed, and a market control program was thus erected in the guise of a conservation measure.

Finally, in 1938, after the Supreme Court had changed its mind about the scope of federal power and after the bumper crops of 1937 had piled up new and unmanageable surpluses, a second Agricultural Adjustment Act was passed, one that restored all the control provisions of the earlier measure and added a few more, including Henry Wallace's pet project of the "ever-normal granary." As if by some strange paradox, a planned economy had come first to what had traditionally been the most individualistic area of the American economy. And it had all come with a minimum of conflict, thanks to the political power of the farmers and the use of effective symbols that justified a departure from traditional competitive standards.[2]

In some areas, too, where federal controls were unavailable or insufficient, the farmers were able to secure state controls. In California, where the producers' associations were particularly strong, the farm forces pushed through an agricultural prorate act, an agricultural adjustment act, a milk control act, and a processed foodstuffs act. In Or-

[2] Broadus Mitchell, *Depression Decade* (N.Y.: Rinehart, 1947), 187–99, 205–7; Edwin G. Nourse et al., *Three Years of the Agricultural Adjustment Administration* (Washington: Brookings, 1937), 35–50, 450–57; Joseph S. Davis, *On Agricultural Policy, 1926–38* (Stanford U. Press, 1939), 24–26, 232–39; Christiana M. Campbell, *The Farm Bureau and the New Deal* (Urbana: U. of Ill. Press, 1962), 33–67; Murray R. Benedict, *Farm Policies of the United States, 1790–1950* (N.Y.: 20th Century Fund, 1953), 283–84, 349–52, 375–79; Lowry Nelson, in *American Quarterly*, Fall 1949, pp. 232–34; Louis B. Schmidt, in *Agricultural History*, April 1956, pp. 53–57; *Congressional Record*, 73 Cong., 1 Sess., LXXVII, 1392–9; 74 Cong., 1 Sess., LXXIX, 9460, 9484–85.

egon, Washington, and Idaho "little AAA" laws were also passed. In Georgia the state commissioner of agriculture could fix prices for fruits, vegetables, and truck crops. In Florida a citrus commission could fix minimum prices. And in Texas the commissioner of agriculture could accept and enforce citrus marketing agreements. Perhaps the most extensive effort at state control, however, was that undertaken in the milk and dairy industry. During the period from 1933 to 1940 some twenty-one states adopted milk control laws, all of them empowering some state agency or board to fix producer prices, and most of them providing for wholesale and retail price fixing, pooling arrangements, production quotas, and entry controls. Sometimes, certainly, such laws were fitted out with a rationale that justified them on the ground of protecting the public health, but in most cases they amounted to little more than a public underwriting of private arrangements between producers and distributors.[3]

III

For the farmers, particularly the larger commercial farmers,[4] counterorganization was well underway; and businessmen, they felt, should not complain because the "whole

[3] FTC, *Report on Agricultural Income Inquiry*, Pt. II (1938), 623–25; WPA, *State Milk and Dairy Legislation* (1941), 1, 7, 26, 36–41, 48–51, 58; and *State Price Control Legislation* (1940), 381, 453–67; Nourse et al., *Three Years of AAA*, 240; Wilcox, *Competition and Monopoly in American Industry* (TNEC Monograph 21, 1940), 272–73; Grether, *Price Control*, 78–81.

[4] It has occurred to me that a profitable exploration might be made of the whole area of policy conflict between generally dominant views of the commercial farm organizations interested chiefly in market power and business values, the old agrarian ideal of the small, self-sufficient, yeoman farmer, and the new ideal of a collectivized and planned agricultural system. In several respects, it would appear, this conflict was similar to the struggles relating to business policy. The present study, however, makes no attempt to deal with agricultural policy beyond pointing out some of the obvious implications for business policy.

philosophy" behind the program was simply "to apply business principles to agriculture." Somewhat the same might also be said of the labor program, for here, too, the effort to enlist governmental aid in the development of market power was making steady progress. Less than two months after the Schecter decision, Senator Robert F. Wagner, with the backing of the President, piloted the National Labor Relations Act through Congress, thus salvaging and fortifying the collective bargaining provisions of Section 7(a). The new law declared a variety of employer practices, including such things as discriminatory hiring and firing or support of company unions, to be unfair and illegal. It gave official sanction to the majority rule, the principle that an organization representing a majority of workers should be the sole bargaining agent for all the workers in a given plant. It established a powerful governmental agency, the National Labor Relations Board, to enforce the rules, hold elections, determine appropriate bargaining units, and require that employers bargain in good faith.

The government made no effort to interfere in the substantive matter of labor disputes or to direct in detail the course of labor organization; yet there is little doubt that the Wagner Act did open the way to counterorganization by removing legal obstacles and curbing the power of labor's opponents. If it did not stimulate, it certainly facilitated the rise of the Congress of Industrial Organizations and the success of its organizational campaign during the period from 1935 to 1939. Big labor, like big agriculture, was being called into existence to counterbalance big business. And, as in the case of agriculture, the violation of competitive standards and the individualistic tradition was generally justified on grounds other than market control, on such grounds as social justice, humanitarianism, the need to combat big business, or the need for economic balance.

The urban laborer, like the farmer, was depicted as an

underdog, as an exploited individual worthy of public sympathy and entitled to public intervention on his behalf. At the very least, he was entitled to a decent living and protection from overt oppression; and if prosperity was to be restored, he was entitled to much more. The failure to divert a large enough share of the national income to the laboring classes, so the argument ran, had been one of the primary causes of the depression; and general recovery could not be achieved until labor was sufficiently organized to correct this imbalance. Consequently, even the New Dealers that believed in restoring competition in business generally made a place in their program for labor organization and social legislation.[5]

In other ways, too, the New Deal worked to protect laborers from the full brunt of deflationary forces. For one thing, the government absorbed surplus labor, first through such makeshift agencies as the Federal Emergency Relief Administration and the Civil Works Administration, and later through the more comprehensive program of the Works Progress Administration. The doctrine that labor was not a commodity, that a man was entitled to the essentials of life regardless of whether there was an economic demand for his services, was an increasingly accepted doctrine that no government could ignore. Eventually, the government moved to establish a minimum floor beyond which wages could not fall, partly for humanitarian reasons, partly with the idea that increased wages and shorter hours would lead to fuller employment, increased purchasing power, and the eventual restoration of economic prosperity. The first attempt along this line, following the invalidation of the NRA codes, was the Walsh-Healey Act of 1936, a measure requiring that government contractors

[5] Mitchell, Depression Decade, 277–79; Irving Bernstein, The New Deal Collective Bargaining Policy (Los Angeles: U. of Calif. Press, 1950), 100–4, 115–28, 148–49; Lloyd K. Garrison, in Survey Graphic, Dec. 1935, pp. 596–98, 634; Monthly Labor Review, Aug. 1935, pp. 369–70; Congressional Record, 74 Cong., 1 Sess., LXXIX, 7565–73, 9461, 9692, 9711.

observe a maximum forty-hour week, refrain from using child labor, and pay the prevailing wages in their locality, as determined by the Secretary of Labor. Then, in 1938, after protracted agitation and preparation, came the Fair Labor Standards Act, abolishing child labor and providing initially for a floor of twenty-five cents an hour and a ceiling of forty-four hours per week, with higher standards contemplated for subsequent years and with payment of time and a half for all hours worked over the maximum figure. In spite of numerous exemptions in the law, labor's long struggle to divert competition into more "honorable" fields than chiseling off the earnings of workers had finally culminated in a partial victory.

For agriculture and labor, then, the development of "countervailing power" was well underway. What had been an essentially monolithic economy in 1929, one dominated for the most part by the business-financial element, was being converted into something basically different, an economy of great countervailing forces in which organized collective groups fought each other for their respective shares of the national income and appealed to political power to aid them in this struggle. For agriculture the government had moved into the marketplace and by the use of public power had given the farmers the advantages of corporate organization without forcing a collectivization of actual operations. For labor governmental intervention in the bargaining process had not been so complete, but labor organization and the growth of labor power were certainly encouraged to the extent that the Administration maintained a friendly attitude, established minimum standards, absorbed surplus labor, required recognition of unions, and restrained a number of employer practices that had been used to break unions in the past.[6]

[6] Elizabeth Brandeis and Selig Perlman, in Milton Derber and Edwin Young, eds., *Labor and the New Deal* (Madison: U. of Wis. Press, 1957), 208–10, 218–31, 366–67; Arthur S. Link, *American Epoch* (N.Y.: Knopf, 1955), 602; Mitchell, *Depression Decade*, 315–26; Adolf A. Berle, Jr., in *Virginia Quarterly Review*, Summer

IV

Some critics, however, doubted that the new power structures in agriculture and labor were really conducive to greater production, more employment, and fuller utilization of resources. In reality, they pointed out, farmers and laborers were using their power not as a means of counteracting the restrictive tendencies of big business, but rather to establish their own restrictions and sometimes to join forces with businessmen in the quest for scarcity profits. Union leaders, in other words, were often much more interested in high wages and job security than in fuller employment, and frequently, both during the NRA period and after, were willing to help businessmen fix prices and restrict production in return for wage increases or greater security. Most farm leaders were interested primarily in higher farm prices, not in a high volume of low-priced industrial goods. Those agricultural administrators who did want to use the farm program to achieve the second objective, men like Jerome Frank, Frederic Howe, and Gardner Jackson, quickly lost out in the so-called "purge" of 1935.[7]

If consumer purchasing power was to be increased, the critics felt, the real need was for consumer organization and protection, although, as yet, there was little agreement upon just how to go about providing them. Some consumer spokesmen, like Frederick Schlink of Consumers' Research, stressed the need for more information, expert

---

1938, p. 331; Paul H. Douglas and Joseph Hackman, in *Political Science Quarterly*, Dec. 1938, pp. 491–515; March 1939, pp. 29–47; Beulah Amidon, in *Survey Graphic*, Nov. 1938, pp. 538–39; *Monthly Labor Review*, Aug. 1936, pp. 368–72.

[7] Caroline F. Ware and Gardiner Means, *The Modern Economy in Action* (N.Y.: Harcourt, Brace, 1936), 150–57; Schlesinger, *Coming of New Deal*, 75–80; Horace M. Kallen, in *Christian Century*, June 27, 1934, pp. 858–60; Henry A. Wallace, *Technology, Corporations, and the General Welfare* (Chapel Hill: U. of N.C. Press, 1937), 47–49.

research, and testing agencies that could provide scientific data and turn the consumer into an informed buyer. Others, like Rexford Tugwell, Gardiner Means, and Paul Douglas, would concentrate upon political representation and the development of effective political pressure groups that could influence legislation and give the consumer an effective voice in policy making. Still others would try to emulate the trade unions and develop organizations capable of engaging in collective bargaining or of using such economic weapons as the strike, the boycott, and the blacklist. Finally, there were those who believed that the real answer lay in consumer cooperatives similar to those in the Scandinavian nations. Such cooperatives, they felt, could eventually provide the consumer with buying power, bring about a more even distribution of income, and thus restore the economic balance necessary for a workable and expanding economy.

In spite of repeated proposals and considerable agitation, however, the movement for consumer organization made little progress. One could note, of course, some increase in the amount of business done by cooperative associations, some interest in consumer education and rating organizations, some abortive attempts to set up a national organization, and occasional efforts to organize buyers' strikes, "cost of living" conferences, protective committees, and consumers' councils. Yet such activities, even when considered as a whole, constituted only the most meager of beginnings. The consumer cooperatives still did less than one percent of the total retail business. Consumer agitation was usually weak and sporadic. And the vision of a closely knit, nationwide organization run by professional experts and able to act swiftly and ruthlessly in the consumer's interest remained only a dream.

The great majority of American consumers remained unorganized, inarticulate, and indifferent. Most of them, in fact, continued to think of themselves as producers rather than consumers; and as producers, their primary objective was to earn more money, not to maximize the purchasing power of such income as they had. The latter course smacked too much of penny-pinching, of miserliness and grubbiness that was somehow un-American. Consequently, the advocacy of the consumer's cause was left largely to eccentrics, nonconformists, misfits, dilettanti, and amateur enthusiasts; to such groups as college professors, club-women, social workers, recent immigrants, and a few professional agitators, none of whom could wield much political power or speak for any well-organized constituency.

The lack of political power, moreover, meant that New Deal policy-makers frequently failed to show much concern for the interests of the consumer. The consumer agencies in the NRA, the AAA, and the National Bituminous Coal Commission turned out to be mostly window dressing. The activities of the Consumers' Project in the Department of Labor and the Bureau of Home Economics in the Department of Agriculture never went beyond the realm of research and education. And the repeated proposals of such men as Leon Henderson, Jacob Baker, and Thomas Blaisdell for a federal Department of the Consumer failed to make much of an impression on practical politicians. The only hope extended to the consumer advocates was that the proposed Department of Public Welfare in 1937 might include a consumers' bureau, and even this possibility disappeared after the President's reorganization plan was defeated. Perhaps, Robert Lynd remarked, the value of such an agency was problematical anyway. It was unrealistic to suppose that "the direction of the road-bed" would be deflected "by coupling on another box car to the train." [8]

[8] Helen Sorenson, *The Consumer Movement* (N.Y.: Harper, 1941), 15–20, 21–22, 33, 70–72, 82, 93, 102, 111–22, 139–40, 212; Rexford G. Tugwell, *The Battle for Democracy* (N.Y.: Columbia U. Press, 1935), 268–69; Horace M. Kallen, *The Decline and Rise of the Consumer* (N.Y.: Appleton-Century, 1936), XII, 139–49; Bertram B. Fowler, *Consumer Cooperation in America* (N.Y.: Vanguard, 1936), 223; Persia Campbell, *The Consumer Interest*

Roosevelt's generally friendly attitude toward consumer cooperatives was also largely cancelled out by his sensitivity to protests from independent retailers. In 1936, soon after reading Marquis Childs' Sweden: The Midlle Way, he appointed a special commission to study cooperative enterprise in Europe and report on its applicability to America. Included on the commission were a number of cooperative leaders and sympathizers, men like Jacob Baker, Leland Olds, and Robin Hood. Consequently, there was some speculation about the possibility of a special governmental program. In its report, however, the commission confined itself almost exclusively to activities in Europe, with the implication that these had little pertinence for the United States. Extensive governmental promotion or subsidization of cooperatives, it felt, would never work; for the present, any program should be limited to equitable treatment of the cooperatives and the establishment of a government agency to provide them with information and advice. Yet even these limited proposals could not be implemented. Small retailers protested vigorously about the very existence of the commission, and the President reacted by playing down the whole idea and giving reassurances that he was

(N.Y.: Harper, 1949), 464, 616–69, 633, 643–44; J. B. Matthews, Guinea Pigs No More (Washington, N.J.: Consumers' Research, 1936), 248–49, 259, 311; Robert S. Lynd, in Political Science Quarterly, LI (Dec. 1936), 495–96, 513–15; E. J. Lever, J. J. Schalet, and Dayton McKean, in New Republic, Nov. 15, 1933, pp. 20–21; May 6, 1936, pp. 359–60; Frederick J. Schlink, Paul H. Douglas, Gardiner Means, and Leon Henderson, in Annals Am. Acad., March 1934, pp. 103–6, 121–22; May 1934, pp. 13–16; Jan. 1936, pp. 270–71; Donald E. Montgomery, in Survey Graphic, April 1938, pp. 213–17; Business Week, Dec. 5, 1936, pp. 24, 26; April 22, 1939, pp. 40–43, 45–46, 50, 52; Fortune, March 1937, pp. 140–44; Kallen, in Christian Century, June 27, 1934, pp. 858–59; Ruby Black, in Independent Woman, Nov. 1935, pp. 377–78; Jacob Baker, "The Area of Consumer Representation and Present Points of Concern or Pressure," March 1937; Baker to Isador Lubin and others, March 10, 1937, both in Blaisdell File, NRPB Records; Thomas Blaisdell, "The Consumer Agencies," May 13, 1935, Richberg File, NRA Records.

still deeply concerned about the problems of "small individual business concerns."

In other ways, too, the Administration's concern with the political realities of the issue stymied efforts to improve the position of the cooperatives. In 1936, when Byron N. Scott of California was pushing for the creation of a new system of banks to loan money to cooperatives, the Administration gave the measure virtually no encouragement, and it attracted little support. And similar political considerations led the President to postpone a projected census and survey of existing cooperatives until after the election of 1936. Such a survey, it was feared, might be cited as evidence that the Administration planned to foster the growth of consumer cooperatives, and if such a construction "registered with millions of small business men," warned James Fitzgerald of the Department of Labor, "the effect would be serious at the polls." The only area in which the Administration showed much interest in fostering consumer cooperation was that of rural electrification, where the REA helped to organize and finance some 670 rural cooperative associations during the period from 1935 to 1940. In this area, there were special circumstances involved. The problem was one of providing new facilities, not displacing old ones; and since the private power companies, already badly discredited, refused to cooperate in providing these facilities, cooperation became the logical alternative.[9]

[9] Henry Slattery, *Rural America Lights Up* (Washington: National Home Library Foundation, 1940), 76, 109–10; Twentieth Century Fund, *Electric Power and Government Policy* (N.Y., 1948), 440–46; American Retail Federation, *Consumers Cooperatives* (1936), 1–3; House Banking and Currency Committee, *To Establish Consumers' Administration and Cooperative Bank* (74 Cong., 2 Sess., 1936), 1–7, 18–19; *Fortune*, March 1937, pp. 137–38; Florence E. Parker, in *Annals Am. Acad.*, May 1937, p. 97; *Monthly Labor Review*, May 1937, p. 1182; Commission of Inquiry to Study Cooperative Enterprises in Europe, *Report* (1937), 273, 338–39, 365, 377, 380–84; Robert L. Van Boskirk, in *Nation's Business*, Oct. 1936, p. 17; Whaley-Eaton Service, *American Letter*,

The only other field in which the New Deal registered much of a gain for the consumer was that of protective legislation. The Wheeler-Lea Act of 1938 broadened the power of the Federal Trade Commission over deceptive practices and false and misleading advertising, and the Federal Food, Drug, and Cosmetic Act of the same year extended the jurisdiction of the Food and Drug Administration to cover cosmetics and therapeutic devices, broadened the definitions of adulteration and misbranding, established new labeling requirements, required special permission for the introduction of new drugs, and strengthened enforcement procedures. Yet, even in this area, consumer groups found that they were no real match for the food and drug lobby. Passage of these acts came only after five years of debate, repeated delays, numerous revisions, and the addition of a number of crippling amendments that made the final measures a far cry from the original Tugwell bill of 1933.[10]

v

In many respects, then, the consumer remained the "forgotten man" of the New Deal, the most prominent gap in the new organizational economy. Inarticulate, indif-

Oct. 31, 1936; Marvin McIntyre to Walter Turner, July 30, 1936; Stephen Early to Rudolph Forster, Aug. 4, 1936; James V. Fitzgerald to Early, July 31, 1936; Donald Montgomery to Early, Aug. 11, 1936; Ben Glasgow to FDR, Aug. 22, 1936; McIntyre to Glasgow, Aug. 25, 1936; Paul Appleby to L. E. Linnan, Aug. 26, 1936; Thomas Hennings to FDR, July 25, 1935; FDR to Hennings, Aug. 8, 1936, all in OF 2246, Roosevelt Papers; Jacob Baker to McIntyre, Jan. 4, 1937, Relief Plans File, Hopkins Papers; President Roosevelt's Press Conferences, June 23, 1936, Roosevelt Papers.

[10] Ruth D. Lamb, *American Chamber of Horrors* (N.Y.: Farrar & Rinehart, 1936), 278–332; Charles W. Dunn, comp., *Federal Food, Drug, and Cosmetic Act* (N.Y.: Stechert, 1938), 23 *et seq.*; T. S. Harding, in *Commonweal*, July 8, 1938, pp. 290–92; and in *Christian Century*, June 29, 1938, pp. 814–16; *American Journal of Public Health*, Sept. 1938, pp. 1114–16; Schlesinger, *Coming of New Deal*, 355–59.

ferent, and unorganized, he could wield little economic or political power; and so long as he remained weak, a policy of counterorganization, in and of itself, could never solve the problem of economic imbalance. Furthermore, any attempt to provide consumers with the necessary power was bound to encounter serious obstacles, politically, economically, and ideologically. To be successful, it would require a drastic change in the whole temperament and outlook of the American people, a change that the Roosevelt Administration had neither the means nor the desire to bring about. It was far easier, the Administration found, to work within the existing producer psychology, to organize conflicting producer groups, balance them off against each other, and compensate for their restrictive tendencies and the resulting imbalance by a program of government spending.

Farmers and laborers were not the only producer groups that the government was helping to organize. Within the business community itself, a number of formerly competitive, atomistic, or "sick" industries were soon trying to revive their NRA codes and secure public sanction and support for monopolistic arrangements that would give them increased control over price and output. These business groups, too, thought in terms of counterorganization and partial planning. And where they could develop the necessary political strength and take advantage of effective political symbols, they were able to win government support.

CHAPTER 11. PARTIAL PLANNING IN SICK AND NATURAL RESOURCE INDUSTRIES

Ａs the economist Paul Homan surveyed New Deal policy in 1936, he concluded that the dominant theme was a type of partial planning or government-supported cartelization. Many industries were no longer interested in such programs; others were unwilling to pay the price of public supervision; still others could not win the necessary political support. But for those that wanted government aid and that possessed the right combination of public sympathy, acute problems, political strength, internal cohesion, and effective symbols for justifying a departure from competitive standards, the aid was available. Two such industries were bituminous coal and crude oil production. Both were competitive industries in which private arrangements had failed to achieve market stability. Both possessed an effective lobby, one through the influence of a politically powerful labor union, the other through tightly-knit trade associations and the support of oil-state politicians. Both were natural resource industries, in which the potent symbol of conservation could be used to overcome the objections of antitrusters and mask a program of market controls.[1]

II

Bituminous coal had long been a sick industry, one characterized by market gluts, chronic losses, frequent bankrupt-

[1] Paul T. Homan, in *Political Science Quarterly*, June 1936, pp. 169–72, 178–84; and in AEA, *Readings in the Social Control of Industry* (Philadelphia: Blakiston, 1942), 252–54; Merle Fainsod and Lincoln Gordon, *Government and the American Economy* (N.Y.: Norton, 1948), 621–54; Waldo E. Fisher and Charles M. James, *Minimum Price Fixing in the Bituminous Coal Industry* (Princeton: Princeton U. Press, 1955), 309–313.

cies, and starvation wages. Essentially, its problem was one of overcapacity. High prices during World War I, cheap transportation costs, and postwar labor disturbances, which stimulated the opening of new mines in unorganized areas, had all contributed to the expansion of the industry. Then had come a shrinkage in demand, a development that was due partly to the substitution of natural gas, petroleum, and electrical power, partly to inventions that permitted new economies in the use of coal, partly to slower growth rates in consuming industries. The result was a price that did not cover the costs of production; and the existence of some six thousand mines, scattered over thirty states and operated by approximately four thousand different companies, made it almost certain that private controls would be ineffective. Under the circumstances, coal operators tried desperately to cut costs, usually by depressing wage rates. Consequently, the United Mine Workers had early joined with management in efforts to mitigate competition and obtain publicly supported price and production controls.[2]

The industry's NRA code had provided for minimum labor standards, minimum prices, and marketing agreements, and in spite of compliance difficulties, it had been a qualified success. Wages had gone up, strikes had ended, coal companies had started showing profits, and both the operators and miners had become convinced that the solution lay in stricter controls, not in a return to com-

[2] Ralph H. Baker, *The National Bituminous Coal Commission* (Baltimore: Johns Hopkins Press, 1941), 14–37; National Bureau of Economic Research, *Report of the Committee on Prices in the Bituminous Coal Industry* (N.Y., 1938), 12–19; NRC, *Energy Resources and National Policy* (House Doc. 160, 76 Cong., 1 Sess., 1939), 69–72; Walton Hamilton and Helen Wright, *The Case of Bituminous Coal* (N.Y.: Macmillan, 1936), 166–99; F. E. Berquist et al., *NRA Work Materials 69 (Economic Survey of the Bituminous Coal Industry)*, 16–26, 76–77; Fisher and James, *Price Fixing in Coal*, 8–19; Theodore A. Veenstra and Wilbert G. Fritz, in *QJE*, Nov. 1936, pp. 106–12, 125–26; H. O. Rogers, in *Survey Graphic*, June 1937, pp. 326–27.

petition. As early as May 1934 they had begun discussing a stronger law. And in the fall of 1934, Harry Warrum of the UMW had drafted a bill for a special coal commission, under which guarantees of collective bargaining and minimum labor standards would be coupled with minimum prices, marketing agreements, production quotas, a rehabilitation program for displaced miners, and a special program allowing the Secretary of the Interior to buy up excess coal properties and place them in a national coal reserve.

In January 1935 Senator Joseph Guffey and Representative J. Buell Snyder, both of Pennsylvania, agreed to introduce the Warrum bill. But at first it made little headway against the strong opposition of the railroads, power utilities, and other large consumers of coal. There was some opposition, too, within the industry itself, particularly from West Virginia operators, who felt that production control based on previous tonnage would discriminate against them and in favor of the older mining regions. In effect, they argued, it would grant an "old-age pension to a coal mine." Following the Schecter decision, though, most operators were anxious to find a substitute for their NRA code. Their spokesmen quickly agreed to a revised measure under which the establishment of production quotas would be postponed. President Roosevelt, by stressing the probability of legislative action, managed to avert a threatened coal strike and arrange for the extension of the existing wage agreement.

In Congress there were strong doubts about the constitutionality of the measure, but Roosevelt managed to overcome some of them with a letter to Congressman Samuel B. Hill, in which he declared the situation to be "so urgent" and the benefits of the legislation "so evident" that all "doubts as to constitutionality, however reasonable," should be resolved in its favor. On August 19, after the provisions for production quotas and a national coal reserve had been dropped, the House passed the measure, and three days later, after Senator Borah had added his customary amendment striking out any specific exemptions from the antitrust laws, the Senate gave its approval.[3]

As finally passed, the Guffey-Snyder Act was to be administered by a five-man National Bituminous Coal Commission, a three-man Bituminous Coal Labor Board, and a Consumers' Counsel to look after the interests of consumers. The Commission, working with some twenty-three district boards, each consisting of one labor member and from two to sixteen operators, was to determine the weighted average cost of production and use this as a basis for schedules of minimum prices in some nine minimum price areas. If necessary, it could also fix maximum prices on the basis of cost of production plus a reasonable profit, and it could approve and enforce trade practice and marketing agreements. For labor, too, there were a number of benefits, including a guarantee of collective bargaining, the right of miners to select their own check-weighmen, and the maintenance of those wage and hour standards agreed upon by producers of two-thirds of the annual national tonnage and the representatives of a majority of the mine workers. Finally, to secure compliance, there was a penalty tax, a levy of fifteen percent on the selling price of coal, ninety percent of which would be returned to all operators who complied with the law.

[3] Baker, *NBCC*, 43–52; Ellery B. Gordon anl William Y. Webb, in Donald H. Wallace, ed., *Economic Standards of Government Price Control* (TNEC Monograph 32, 1941), 255–57; Fisher and James, *Price Fixing in Coal*, 26–28; House Committee on Ways and Means, *Stabilization of Bituminous Coal Mining Industry* (74 Cong., 1 Sess., 1935), 1–17, 20, 24–28, 157, 160, 219–20, 236–39, 312–14, 322–23, 648; Senate Commerce Committee, *Stabilization of Bituminous Coal Industry* (74 Cong., 1 Sess., 1935), 1–10, 134, 181, 196, 237, 299, 467; *Congressional Record*, 74 Cong., 1 Sess., LXXIX, 868, 957, 5411, 9254, 12908, 13195, 13433–37, 13449–56, 13666–67, 13968, 14084, 14362–64; W. Jett Lauck, in *Annals Am. Acad.*, March 1936, pp. 134–36; *Business Week*, June 8, 1935, pp. 16–17; *New York Times*, June 2, 5, 9, 12, 15, 30, July 7, 14, 27, 31, Aug. 13, 1935; Walter A. Jones to FDR, Feb. 28, 1934; FDR to Samuel B. Hill, July 6, 1935, both in OF 175, Roosevelt Papers.

In September 1935 the President appointed the first coal commission. The chairmanship went to Charles S. Hosford, a former coal operator, and the remaining positions to Percy Tetlow, an Ohio labor leader, Clarence Smith, a West Virginia editor, George Acret, a California lawyer, and Walter Maloney, another lawyer from Missouri. Soon, it was hoped, the industry could recover its cost of production. Yet in practice the Commission made little headway, partly because it had great difficulty in getting the producers to agree among themselves, partly because its authority was seriously crippled by court orders. By the end of 1935, over eighty cases were in the courts, and most of them had resulted in restraining orders against the collection of the penalty tax. Under the circumstances, the Supreme Court agreed to accept an appeal directly from the lower courts; and on May 18, 1936, in the Carter coal case, it ruled that the labor provisions of the act were invalid and that the price provisions were so intimately connected with them that the two could not be separated.[4]

Neither the miners nor the operators, however, were ready to call it quits. Both felt that they would benefit from a simple price-fixing law and that the court might uphold such a measure. Again Senator Guffey sponsored the proposal; and after an initial setback in 1936, when Senator Rush Holt of West Virginia blocked action by a threatened filibuster, he was successful in piloting it through Congress. The Guffey-Vinson Act of early 1937 revived in a slightly modified form the price-fixing, taxing, marketing, and fair practice provisions of the earlier law. The major innovations were the elimination of the labor provisions, the enlargement of the Coal Commission to

[4] 49 *U.S. Statutes* 991, Public, No. 402, 74 Cong.; Baker, *NBCC*, 52–61, 325, 328; *Carter v. Carter Coal Co.*, 298 U.S. 238; Gordon and Webb, in Wallace, ed., *Government Price Control*, 260–62; *Monthly Labor Review*, July 1936, pp. 68–74; *Business Week*, Nov. 2, 1935, p. 14; *New York Times*, Sept. 1, 21, 1935; May 19, 1936; NBCC Minutes, Sept. 28, Oct. 9, 23, 1935, NBCC Records.

seven members, a requirement that hearings be held to determine whether intrastate transactions had a direct effect on interstate commerce, and a provision strengthening the Consumers' Counsel and allowing him to report directly to Congress.[5]

Once more, the President appointed a coal commission. Hosford, Smith, Maloney, and Tetlow would continue as members, and the remaining positions would go to John C. Lewis, a former union official, Thomas Haymond, a former coal operator, and Pleas Greenlee, an Indiana editor. All of these appointments, so it was charged in Congress, were made to repay political debts, and in operation, the Commission did become a haven for deadweight political appointees and the scene of bitter patronage quarrels. Added to these were divisions over policy. The majority, consisting of Hosford, Haymond, Smith, and Maloney, tended to side with the coal operators. They insisted that the cost data remain confidential, that cost hearings be closed to the public, and that large coal consumers, like the railroads and utilities, were not entitled to special price concessions. Their job, they felt, was to help the coal industry counteract the buying power of large consumers; and the position taken by the minority and Consumers' Counsel John Carson was in effect a boon to "reactionary forces," a view that failed to show any understanding of the "economic and social disaster" it might produce.

There were also difficulties in getting the producers to agree among themselves, particularly when it came to establishing coal classifications and common price floors that might give one producer or one district an advantage over others. Not until November 1937 were minimum prices and marketing rules promulgated; and once promulgated, they brought a storm of protests, especially from railroads,

[5] Baker, *NBCC*, 63–78; *Congressional Record*, 74 Cong., 2 Sess., LXXX, 7565, 9608–37, 10538–43; 75 Cong., 1 Sess., LXXXI, 64, 2126, 3145; 50 *U.S. Statutes* 72, Public, No. 48, 75 Cong.

municipal purchasing agents, and other large buyers of coal. The Commission, so it was charged, had simply ignored its critics, denied all access to the cost data, and failed to hold the public hearings required by law. Almost immediately, its action was attacked in the courts. And in early 1938, after the court of appeals for the District of Columbia ruled that failure to hold public hearings justified an injunction against the price schedules, the Commission gave up, suspended all minimum prices, and started over again.

Shortly thereafter, in March 1938, Hosford resigned, Tetlow took over as chairman, and the Commission reversed some of its earlier policies. In the future, it announced, public hearings would be held at each stage of the price-fixing procedure; and at these hearings, the cost data of individual producers would be admissible as evidence. It was now the turn of the coal operators to protest. They refused to abide by the new ruling, and not until January 1939, when the Supreme Court ruled in favor of the Commission, were they forced to do so. In January 1940 the hearings were finally completed. The proposed prices were then reviewed by the Department of the Interior's Bituminous Coal Division, which had replaced the NBCC under the President's reorganization plan of May 1939, and eventually, on October 1, 1940, they went into effect. After a lapse of five and one-half years, the expenditure of millions of dollars, and the taking of some forty thousand pages of testimony, a planned economy had finally come to the coal industry.[6]

[6] Baker, NBCC, 80, 89, 109–21, 135, 143–48, 152–53, 156, 159–78, 185, 233–39, 325–26; Persia Campbell, *Consumer Representation in the New Deal* (N.Y.: Columbia U. Press, 1940), 93–95; Committee on Public Administration Cases, *The Consumers' Counsel and the National Bituminous Coal Commission* (Washington, 1950), 33–94, 112–16; Harold L. Ickes, *Secret Diary*, II (N.Y.: Simon & Schuster, 1954), 630; House Appropriations Committee, *Hearings on the Interior Department Appropriations Bill for 1939* (75 Cong., 3 Sess., 1938), 127, 167–75; NBCC, *Annual Report* (1937), 1–3; (1938), 5–12; NBCC Consumers' Counsel, *Annual*

During the nineteen thirties, then, the Guffey Act failed to provide much relief; yet it was a major example of the type of partial planning in which the government had become involved. The assumption underlying the law was not that competition had disappeared, but that it was excessive and destructive and that the government should help producers to escape its consequences. To men like Senator William Borah such an approach was liberalism in reverse. "Next will come the textile industry," he predicted, "and they will set up their commission. . . . Next will come the steel industry. Next will come another industry; and eventually the country will be operating under commissions, with the Sherman law entirely repealed." [7]

III

A second industry with problems similar to those of bituminous coal was that of crude oil production. Here, too, the basic problem was overcapacity, particularly after the opening of the East Texas field in 1930. And since demand was relatively stable, the number of producers relatively large, and the urgency to produce, because of capital investments, royalty arrangements, and the law of capture,

Report (1938), 4; Congressional Record, 75 Cong., 3 Sess., LXXXIII, 2472–76, 4817, 4827–30; Newsweek, May 15, 1937, p. 14; Nov. 15, 1937, p. 15; March 28, 1938, p. 10; Business Week, Aug. 28, 1937, pp. 18, 20; John T. Flynn, in Collier's, July 9, 1938, pp. 49–50; Utah Fuel Co. v. NBCC, 306 U.S. 56; New York Times, Oct. 12, Nov. 11, 1937; Washington Star, Oct. 11, 1937; Washington News, Aug. 2, 1937; John C. Lewis to NBCC, Nov. 9, 1937; Lewis to FDR, Nov. 10, 1937; James Roosevelt to FDR, Feb. 21, 1938; Charles Hosford to FDR, March 10, 1938, all in OF 172, Roosevelt Papers; Compendium of Protests Filed with the Commission, Feb. 5, 1938; Hosford to James Roosevelt, Feb. 15, 1938, both in Tetlow File, NBCC Records.

[7] Baker, NBCC, 221; Senate Commerce Committee, To Regulate Interstate Commerce in Bituminous Coal (74 Cong., 2 Sess., 1936), 185; House Committee on Ways and Means, House Report 1800 (1935), 59; Congressional Record, 75 Cong., 1 Sess., LXXXI, 2996–3012.

relatively great, the result was low prices that did not begin to cover the costs of production, except perhaps for the newer fields.

The oil producers had turned first to the state governments, and along with arguments for stabilization, had stressed the need for conservation and the idea that unrestricted output led to a reckless waste of resources. As early as 1927 Oklahoma passed the first compulsory proration law. Other oil states followed suit. In 1931 the governors of Texas and Oklahoma went so far as to declare martial law and close wells by military order. In spite of the state controls, however, "hot oil," produced in violation of them, continued to flow out of Texas and Oklahoma. Consequently, the demand for some type of federal control grew more and more insistent.[8]

In early 1933 a number of oil control plans were discussed in Washington, but eventually all of them were set aside in favor of the National Industrial Recovery Act and its provision for federal control of "hot oil." The resulting code provided for production quotas, import limitations, and minimum prices, but in practice the price provisions were never invoked. Instead, the industry relied primarily upon production control to restore a so-called "parity" price for crude oil, a price that was theoretically determined by a high-sounding, pseudo-scientific formula,[9] but one

[8] Ronald B. Shuman, *The Petroleum Industry* (Norman: U. of Okla. Press, 1940), 62–64, 267; Myron W. Watkins, *Oil: Stabilization or Conservation?* (N.Y.: Harper, 1937), 26–31, 43–52, 194; Eugene V. Rostow, *A National Policy for the Oil Industry* (New Haven: Yale U. Press, 1948), 16–21; William J. Kemnitzer, *Rebirth of Monopoly* (N.Y.: Harper, 1938), 29–31, 129–32; NRC, *Energy Resources*, 390–91; Northcutt Ely, in AEA, *Social Control*, 324–25; Report of the Committee of Fifteen representing Governor's Conference and Major and Independent Oil Producers, March 29, 1933, OF 56, Roosevelt Papers.

[9] NRA, *Code of Fair Competition for the Petroleum Industry* (1933). Article III, Section 6 stated that the parity price per barrel should "be determined by multiplying the average Group 3 tank car price per gallon of U.S. motor gasoline of 60-64 octane rating during the preceding calendar month by the constant 18.5. The

that soon settled down at the convenient rule-of-thumb figure of a dollar per barrel. Under the system, the Bureau of Mines furnished forecasts of consumer demand. The Oil Administrator then set quotas for each of the oil-producing states, and these in turn were allocated, either by state agencies or industrial groups, to individual fields and wells. These arrangements, moreover, although they were not equally satisfactory to all factions of the industry, did achieve their major purpose. The flow of "hot oil" dwindled to a trickle, and by October 1933, when the second allocation order was issued, the price of crude oil had risen to a dollar per barrel.[10]

The first attempt to replace the code with a special oil control law came in the spring of 1934, when Oil Administrator Harold Ickes became alarmed over adverse court decisions and crippling injunctions. A group of officials from the Petroleum Administrative Board, under the supervision of Nathan Margold, solicitor for the Department of the Interior, drafted an oil control bill. After it had been adjusted to meet objections from industrial representatives, the measure was introduced by Senator Elmer Thomas and Representative Wesley Disney, both of

---

constant 18.5 represents the relationship, during the period 1928–1932, between the average price per barrel of Mid-Continent crude petroleum of 36°–36.9° A.P.I. gravity and the average Group 3 price per gallon of U.S. Motor gasoline of 57–65 octane rating or 58–60 U.S. Motor gasoline. . . . Fair and equitable differentials between the price of 36°–36.9° Mid-Continent crude petroleum . . . and the prices quoted for other crude petroleums shall be observed."

[10] Watkins, *Oil*, 59–70, 73–75, 93–100, 106–15, 175–80; Kemnitzer, *Rebirth of Monopoly*, 137–39; Rostow, *Policy for Oil*, 21–22; David Levine, *The Petroleum Industry* (WPA Study 1040, 1938), 78–79; Irene Till, *The Price of Gasoline* (NRA Consumer Report 4, 1934), 6, 37, 46, 49–50; *Business Week*, Oct. 7, 1933, pp. 10–11, Sept. 1, 1934, pp. 21, 23; TNEC, *Investigation of Concentration of Economic Power*, Pt. 14 (1939), 7447–48; House Commerce Committee, *Petroleum Investigation* (73 Cong., 1934), 1300-1; Petroleum Administrator, Report to NEC (1935), NEC File, Ickes Papers.

Oklahoma. Under it, the Secretary of the Interior might prescribe production quotas, and if necessary, allocate them to individual pools, fields, and wells. In May the Senate Mining Committee reported the bill favorably, but in the House, Commerce Committee chairman Sam Rayburn decided that recent court decisions had made the measure unnecessary and that his committee was too busy to consider it. As a result, all that Ickes could get was a House resolution calling for an extensive investigation of the oil industry.

Gradually, too, as the immediate crisis passed, the attitude of the industry itself began to change. The major companies had originally endorsed the Thomas-Disney bill, but by the fall of 1934 a majority of the Petroleum Institute's directors had decided that such a measure was unnecessary and would involve too much governmental "interference," a trend that was getting out of hand anyway. The Petroleum Administrative Board, they complained, was becoming dictatorial and domineering. The decisions of the industry's planning and coordination committee were being overruled. And Secretary Ickes was alarming everyone with his talk about turning the oil industry into a public utility.[11]

Under the circumstances, then, industrial spokesmen seemed determined to prevent any further expansion of the federal program; and this attitude led to a revival of the interstate compact idea, a proposal with a long history

[11] Kemnitzer, *Rebirth of Monopoly*, 141–44, 207–9; Samuel B. Pettengill, *Hot Oil* (N.Y.: Economic Forum, 1936), 251–64, 270–82; Ickes, *Diary*, I, 158–59, 164, 169; House Commerce Committee, *Petroleum Investigation*, 1754–56, 1985–86, 2416–20, 2619–20; Senate Committee on Mines and Mining, *Federal Petroleum Act* (73 Cong., 2 Sess., 1934), 1–30; *National Petroleum News*, Nov. 21, 1934, pp. 11–14, 17; *Congressional Record*, 73 Cong., 2 Sess., LXXVIII, 7633–5, 9068, 9790; Harold Ickes, Address, Nov. 14, 1934, Speeches File, Ickes Papers; Ickes to FDR, June 2, 1934; Henry Kannee to Marvin McIntyre, June 4, 1934, both in Roosevelt Papers (OF 6, 56); Howard Cowden to James Warbasse, June 6, 1935, Blaisdell File, NRPB Records.

dating back to the recommendations of the Federal Oil Conservation Board in the nineteen twenties. In late 1934 Governor E. W. Marland of Oklahoma resurrected the idea; and eventually, at a meeting in Dallas, Texas, in February 1935, the representatives of Oklahoma, Texas, California, and New Mexico reached a common agreement. Each state was to pass conservation and proration laws, bar from commerce any oil produced in violation of them, and appoint a representative to a supervisory Interstate Oil Compact Commission.[12]

In the meantime, the Supreme Court was striking sharp blows at the existing controls. In January 1935, in the Panama oil case, it ruled that the Presidential control of "hot oil" was an unconstitutional delegation of legislative power. Only three months after this breach had been repaired by the passage of the Connally Act, spelling out in detail what the President might do, came the Schecter decision invalidating all the NRA codes. It now became necessary to work out some new program. Since the American Petroleum Institute and other industrial spokesmen wanted only limited federal controls, Congress was reluctant to accept the revised version of the Thomas-Disney bill that Secretary Ickes was still backing. Instead it seemed to favor a much milder measure introduced by Representative William P. Cole, one that provided only for import limitations, voluntary agreements, "hot oil" controls, and an interstate compact. To Ickes, who thought it a "thoroughly vicious bill," its worst feature was that the proposed administrative agency would be an independent one outside the Department of the Interior. "After careful

[12] The Interstate Oil Compact was eventually ratified by all the major oil-producing states except California and Louisiana. See NRC, *Energy Resources*, 397–98; Levine, *Petroleum Industry*, 81–82; B. M. Murphy, ed., *Conservation of Oil and Gas* (Chicago: American Bar Assoc., 1949), 559–70; Pettengill, *Hot Oil*, 198–201, 284–87; Ely, in AEA, *Social Control*, 323, 326–27; J. Stanley Clark, *The Oil Century* (Norman: U. of Okla. Press, 1958), 191–92, 197–98; Northcutt Ely, *Oil Conservation through Interstate Agreement* (Washington: GPO, 1933), 18–24.

consideration," he wrote the President, "I have come to the conclusion that no oil legislation would be preferable to the Cole bill."

The President, though, was reluctant to support a strong law, especially since most of the oil state representatives were fighting it. The initiative and the outcome, he told Ickes, should "be left strictly up to the Congress." There, on August 14, the Senate passed the Connally bill, which would merely ratify the interstate compact, limit imports, and make the "hot oil" law permanent. This, Ickes declared, was preferable to Cole's solution, and Cole then reacted by scrapping his proposal and substituting a simple ratification of the interstate oil compact. To this both the House and Senate agreed. Congress adjourned without further oil legislation. The later attempt of the industry to secure FTC approval for its trade practice conference agreement of 1931 also came to naught.[13]

The failure to pass a comprehensive law in 1935 left the system of control resting on a number of individual programs. On the state level were the proration laws, now coordinated and made more uniform by the deliberations, studies, and recommendations of the Interstate Oil Compact Commission. In general, these measures allowed state agencies to limit and allocate production, usually on the basis of so much per well, per acre, per day, or per month. Theoretically, they were justified as conservation measures,

[13] Kemnitzer, *Rebirth of Monpoly*, 144–45; Pettengill, *Hot Oil*, 264–68; Ickes, *Diary*, I, 413–14, 416–18: Levine, *Petroleum Industry*, 80; *Panama Refining Co. v. Ryan*, 293 U.S. 388; 49 *U.S. Statutes* 30, Public, No. 14, 74 Cong.; 49 *U.S. Statutes* 939, Public Res., No. 64, 74 Cong.; Senate Committee on Mines and Mining, *Federal Petroleum Act* (74 Cong., 1 Sess., 1935), 16; *Congressional Record*, 74 Cong., 1 Sess., LXXIX, 2141–44, 9258–61, 13054, 13058–60, 14486, 14583–93; *Business Week*, Aug. 10, 1935, p. 24; *New York Times*, May 28, June 6, 8, Aug. 5–7, 10, 14, 15, 25, 1935; Sept. 5, 1937; Ickes to FDR, May 21, Aug. 7, 1935; FDR to Ickes, Aug. 8, 1935; FDR to Samuel Rayburn, May 23, 1935; Charles Fahy to Ickes, May 15, 1935; James Farley to FDR, April 16, 1935; A. H. Meadows to Farley, April 15, 1935; FTC PR, Sept. 5, 1937, all in Roosevelt Papers (OF 6, 56, 100).

but in reality the rate of withdrawal bore little relation to what a geologist might regard as the rate necessary to minimize waste. The state allowables, in fact, rarely deviated from the monthly estimates of the Federal Bureau of Mines, estimates that in effect merely stated how much crude oil would be needed to meet the demand for gasoline at the existing price level.[14] Under the Connally Act, the federal government also continued to control "hot oil" shipments, and through the tariff law and a voluntary agreement between the Secretary of the Interior and the principal importing companies, it limited and controlled imports.

Supplementing these government controls, too, were a number of private arrangements. The American Petroleum Institute maintained an extensive statistical service, coupled with quarterly suggestions on the steps necessary to balance supply and demand. In California, where a proration law was rejected by a popular referendum, the oil producers established their own private system and hired an oil umpire to allocate production quotas. In the transportation, refining, and marketing phases of the industry, the major integrated companies reached oligopolistic understandings, operated buying pools to take the surplus gasoline of small independents off the market, and managed to achieve a fairly high degree of market stability.

Taken as a whole, the system seems to have worked well. There were some critical periods like that in late 1936, when the Texas Railroad Commission upped the Texas allowable some 56,470 barrels above the daily aver-

[14] The formula for estimating market demand was a complicated one, but essentially it rested on estimates of the number of motor vehicles in use and the average consumption of gasoline per vehicle, estimates that had been derived from automobile registration records and gasoline tax receipts. The total estimate was then broken down among refining districts by a study of inter-regional gasoline shipments and the normal source of petroleum for each district. After adjustments for imports, exports, natural gasoline, losses, and the amount consumed in field operations, the estimated need for each state could be determined.

age advised by the Bureau of Mines and the oil authorities in Kansas and Oklahoma threatened to pull out of the interstate compact and take retaliatory action. Peace, however, was soon restored and a more business-like policy resumed. In its later review of the oil controls, the Small Business Committee concluded that taken together the controls formed a "perfect pattern of monopolistic control over oil production, the distribution thereof among refiners and distributors, and ultimately the price paid by the public." [15]

Thus, in many respects, the program for oil was similar to that for bituminous coal. Both industries could take advantage of the conservation argument. Both possessed powerful lobbies and the other necessary prerequisites for a program of public assistance. And each, after making some minor concessions to opposing groups, the competitive ideal, and existing court interpretation, had been able to secure a program of public-sponsored cartelization.

There were important differences, however, in the structures of the two industries, their political strength, and public attitudes toward them. One difference was the generally greater concern with the conservation of oil, since proven oil reserves ran only a few years into the future.

[15] David Lynch, *The Concentration of Economic Power* (N.Y.: Columbia U. Press, 1946), 131–34, 164–66, 176–77; Roy C. Cook, *Control of the Petroleum Industry by Major Oil Companies* (TNEC Monograph 39, 1941), 6–7, 16, 28, 36; Rostow, *Policy for Oil*, 27–30, 34–38; Watkins, *Oil*, 87–88, 95–96, 253; NRC, *Energy Resources*, 202–7, 212–14, 394, 398–401; Ely, in AEA, *Social Control*, 323, 325–29, 338–42; Murphy, ed., *Conservation*, 580–81, 696–702; Shuman, *Petroleum Industry*, 269; Melvin G. de Chazeau and Alfred E. Kahn, *Integration and Competition in the Petroleum Industry* (New Haven: Yale U. Press, 1959), 163–66; TNEC, *Investigation of Concentration of Economic Power*, Pt. 14, 7447; House Commerce Committee, *Petroleum Investigation*, 1298–99; Attorney-General, *Annual Report* (1938), 307–10; Dept. of the Interior, *Annual Report* (1935), 365; (1938), 194–95, 360–61; Senate Small Business Committee, *Senate Report* 25 (81 Cong., 1 Sess., 1949), 13; *U.S. v. Socony-Vacuum Oil Co.*, 310 U.S. 150; *Business Week*, Nov. 23, 1935, p. 22; Dec. 12, 1936, pp. 26–27; *New York Times*, Nov. 7, 1937.

A second was the lack of acute labor problems in the oil industry and the absence there of any powerful industrial union comparable to the United Mine Workers. A third was the higher degree of private organization in the petroleum industry, which meant that once the crisis of 1933 had passed, the major companies became fearful of governmental dictation and "socialization." A fourth was the previous history of state oil controls and the reluctance of state agencies to surrender their powers to the federal government. Finally, there was the old suspicion of the "oil trust," a creature that had no counterpart in coal. The oil industry, after all, had once been dominated by a single firm; it still had monopolistic characteristics. Consequently, any attempt to lend open public support to market controls brought vehement denunciations from the antitrusters or from dissident groups within the industry itself.

All of these differences affected the political and ideological climate in which the proponents of market controls had to work. In doing so, the differences naturally affected the final outcome, the fact that the oil industry tended to rely more upon state controls, to emphasize production quotas rather than minimum prices, to be less concerned with labor practices, and to be more wary of federal regulation, at least in the form that it was politically obtainable.[16]

IV

A third sick industry, which tried but failed to secure special legislation, was that of cotton textiles. Here again the basic problem was one of overcapacity, declining demand, and intense competition for a shrinking market. The in-

---

[16] Kemnitzer, *Rebirth of Monopoly*, 150–51, 207–9; Fainsod and Gordon, *Government and Economy*, 624–25, 634–35; Shuman, *Petroleum Industry*, 113–16; Senate Mining Committee, *Federal Petroleum Act* (1935), 53–56, 119–20, 137–41, 169–74; Watkins, *Oil*, 194; Lynch, *Economic Power*, 131–34, 317–18.

dustry had been hit hard by changes in fashion, competition from cheap Japanese textiles, and the increasing use of such substitutes as rayon, burlap, and paper. It suffered, too, from the buying power of distributors and large industrial consumers, who, under depression conditions, had been able to dictate prices and rearrange distributive patterns to their own advantage. Finally, the tendency of the industry to migrate to the South, where labor was unorganized and wages were lower, left the New England textile mills in a particularly depressed state.[17]

The situation, as the millowners saw it, called for counterorganization, production quotas, and a reduction of capacity. Since the private controls sponsored by the Cotton Textile Institute had been ineffective, they welcomed the National Industrial Recovery Act and were the first to take advantage of it. Under their NRA code, they were able to limit machine hours to two forty-hour shifts per week, restrict the installation of new machinery, and strengthen their position in relation to buyers and distributors. New England textile men were also well-satisfied with the labor provisions, since they had managed to cut the North-South wage differential to only 2½ cents per hour. Overproduction, however, still persisted, and in 1934 the code authority secured a new curtailment order cutting the allowable shift from forty to thirty hours. Labor, thus confronted with a twenty-five percent cut in wages, struck back with a bitterly fought strike, and although President

[17] House Labor Committee, *To Rehabilitate and Stabilize Labor Conditions in the Textile Industry* (74 Cong., 2 Sess., 1936), 622–25; Stephen J. Kennedy, *Profits and Losses in Textiles* (N.Y.: Harper, 1936), 155, 197–98, 200–5; Jules Backman and M. R. Gainsbrugh, *Economics of the Cotton Textile Industry* (N.Y.: National Industrial Conference Board, 1946), 17–19, 54–55, 147–48; H. E. Michl, *The Textile Industries* (Washington: Textile Foundation, 1938), 82–105, 133–56, 164–67, 175–84; President's Cabinet Committee on the Cotton Textile Industry, *Report on the Conditions and Problems of the Cotton Textile Industry* (Senate Doc. 126, 74 Cong., 1 Sess., 1935), 4, 30–31, 46–47, 81–95, 112; George R. Dickson, "NRA Code History 1" (Cotton Textiles), 104–7, CHF, NRA Records.

Roosevelt managed to settle this through a special Textile Labor Relations Board, it was obvious that no one was really satisfied. Accordingly, in April 1935, following a conference with the governors of the New England states, Roosevelt turned the problem over to a newly appointed Cabinet Committee on the Cotton Textile Industry under the chairmanship of Secretary of Commerce Daniel Roper.

By the time the Cabinet Committee reported in August 1935, the Schecter decision had swept away the NRA and made the need for action even more urgent. Consequently, the committee did favor a variety of legislative and administrative remedies, including machine hour limitations, a purchase or leasing system for retiring surplus or obsolete equipment, the establishment of minimum labor standards, larger purchases by government relief agencies, further restrictions on Japanese imports, and the promotion of research to find new uses for cotton textiles. Similar proposals were also being discussed by the textile men themselves. Some, for example, advocated a plan associated with the Federation of Master Spinners' Associations in England, a plan under which the industry might enter into pooling agreements, establish individual quotas, and set up a surplus spindleage board to buy up and scrap spindles with funds provided by a levy on the spindles still in operation. Others favored a scheme that would allow the textile mills to lease their machinery to a central corporation at a nominal rental and then rehire it at a rental so calculated that it would not pay to rehire unless they could earn a normal return of five percent. Still others favored an export subsidy plan, under which the government would pay a drawback or tolerance on cotton that was manufactured into textiles and exported.[18]

[18] Kennedy, *Textiles*, 200–7; Cabinet Committee, *Report*, iii–v, 4–8, 14, 124–26; House Labor Committee, *To Rehabilitate Textile Industry*, 624; Michl, *Textile Industries*, 261–65, 271–75; *Congressional Record*, 75 Cong., 1 Sess., LXXXI, Appendix, 150; *Newsweek*,

The most important proposal for national textile legislation, however, was the one drafted in 1935 by the United Textile Workers and introduced in Congress by Henry Ellenbogen of Pennsylvania. The bill would establish initial labor standards, outlaw a number of unfair trade practices, and then allow a National Textile Commission to promulgate and enforce minimum wage scales, guarantee collective bargaining, regulate job classification and work assignments, and prescribe the number of work shifts or other controls necessary to prevent overproduction. At the hearings on the measure in early 1936, it enjoyed strong support from labor spokesmen, the Textile Converters' Association, the silk mills, and a number of New England politicians and millowners. Yet the majority of the millowners, particularly those from the South, strongly disapproved of the labor provisions and felt that the bill in its present form would do more harm than good.

In retrospect, it seems doubtful that the Ellenbogen bill ever had any real chance of being passed. The textile union, when compared with its counterpart in coal, was weak and ineffective. The millowners, too, were divided and reluctant to accept public control over their labor practices, particularly after the improved conditions in the industry in 1936 gave some hope that private agreements to limit machine hours might be successful. The necessary ideological rationale was also lacking. The industry could not appeal to past precedents; it enjoyed no special place in the national mythology; and it could claim no close and vital connection with such things as defense, conservation, public safety, or the national health. Finally, there were the legal and constitutional objections, particularly after the Carter decision invalidated the Guffey Coal Act. "Pass

Sept. 8, 1934, pp. 7–8; *Literary Digest*, Oct. 6, 1934, p. 9; *Monthly Labor Review*, Oct. 1935, pp. 944–46; *New York Times*, Aug. 22, 1935; Daniel Roper to FDR, April 19, 1935; FDR to Secretaries of State, Agriculture, Commerce, and Labor, April 26, 1935, OF 355, Roosevelt Papers.

the word to Ellenbogen," Roosevelt told his secretary, "that the Supreme Court issue seems to be coming to a head and in the long run it has got to be settled the right way first." Ellenbogen reintroduced his bill in 1937, but it no longer received serious consideration. The combination of circumstances was such that the pattern followed by the coal and oil industries was not repeated.[19]

v

There were similar proposals for "Guffeyizing" such sick industries as lumber, the apparel trades, and anthracite coal. Yet none of these possessed the basic prerequisites necessary to secure a program of publicly supported market controls, at least in any form that its leaders would be willing to accept. Generally speaking, the proposed programs could not be adequately disguised. They lacked the support of a powerful, cohesive lobby with the right political connections. And their supporters were unable to come up with strong alternative ideals that could be used to justify a departure from competitive standards.[20]

There were other areas of the economy, however, where these basic prerequisites did exist. In the transportation industries, and to some extent in the distributive and serv-

[19] Michl, *Textile Industries*, 276–77; *Congressional Record*, 74 Cong., 1 Sess., LXXIX, 12766, 14024–25; 75 Cong., 1 Sess., LXXXI, 29; House Labor Committee, *To Rehabilitate Textile Industry*, 1–15, 31–34, 49, 89, 137–39, 147–51, 160–61, 302, 403–4, 411, 423–25, 437, 453–54, 500–8, 739; and *To Regulate the Textile Industry* (75 Cong., 1 Sess., 1937), 1–32; *New York Times*, June 6, Aug. 8, 1935; Jan. 26, 28, April 20, 24, May 21, Nov. 15, 1936; *Textile World*, Feb. 14, 1936, pp. 57, 97; Feb. 14, 1937, p. 53; Feb. 28, 1937, pp. 102–13; Notes re phone conversation between Peter Van Horn and James P. Davis, Oct. 7, 1935, Attitude of Industry toward NIRA File—CAF, NRA Records; FDR to McIntyre, June 4, 1936, OF 355, Roosevelt Papers.

[20] Dwight E. Robinson, *Collective Bargaining and Market Control in the New York Coat and Suit Industry* (N.Y.: Columbia U. Press, 1949), 165–68; Constant Southworth, in *Plan Age*, Sept. 1937, pp. 180–87; *Newsweek*, Jan. 31, 1938, pp. 32, 34.

ice trades, it was possible to develop programs and rationales similar to those for bituminous coal and crude oil production. Consequently, it seems advisable to consider these areas next and note the trends toward partial planning and counterorganization that were underway there.

CHAPTER 12. PARTIAL PLANNING
IN THE TRANSPORTATION
INDUSTRIES

I N the United States the term "public utility" generally
conjures up a vision of an inherently monopolistic industry providing essential public services, one in which
the nature of the service, the large amounts of capital required, and the presence of high fixed costs all combine
to produce large economies of scale and make any competitive duplication of facilities wasteful and inefficient. It
is usually conceded, too, that in dealing with such "natural monopolies," society may resort to public regulation.
Since the purpose of this presumably is to protect consumers, the industries concerned are expected to resist its
establishment as long as possible. But under depression
conditions like those of the nineteen thirties, these commonly held assumptions were of doubtful validity. On the
contrary, for a number of declining, overly competitive, or
particularly depressed industries, the status of a public
utility became a means of economic salvation, a way to
enter the haven of publicly regulated monopoly and use
the power of the state to stabilize prices, reduce competition, and insure profitable returns on overcapitalized structures.

One field in which this perversion of the public utility
concept was especially noticeable was that of transportation. Under depression conditions and in view of the
threat posed by newer forms of transport, the leaders of
the older transportation industries had begun advocating
a broad extension of the public utility approach, an extension they justified by appealing to past precedents, arguing
that transportation was a "natural monopoly," or stressing
things like public safety or national defense. And the result was a mixture of controls, protection, subsidies, and

publicly sponsored cartels, a system in which the government became not only a regulator, but a protector, supporter, and provider as well.[1]

II

For a long period in America, inland transportation had meant railroad transportation. During the nineteen thirties, the railroad industry remained a highly important one. It still hauled approximately two-thirds of the nation's freight, employed about a million men, and used about one-fifth of the nation's coal, fuel oil, steel, and lumber. In terms of total investment, it was outranked only by agriculture; and since a large proportion of railroad securities were held by financial and fiduciary institutions, distress for the railroads could spell financial disaster for the whole community, a fact that made politicians extremely reluctant to tamper with railroad financing.

For a number of years, however, railroading had been a declining industry. The advent of automobiles had produced a steady drop in passenger traffic, a decline of about sixty-six percent from 1920 to 1933. A good deal of freight, too, was being diverted to motor trucks, barges, and pipelines. And such developments as the shift from coal to natural gas or the tendency to locate plants closer to raw materials and markets had also reduced the demand for railroad services. Finally, on top of these problems, came the depression. Demand fell sharply; the newer forms of

[1] John H. Gray and Jack Levin, *The Valuation and Regulation of Public Utilities* (N.Y.: Harper, 1933), 1–5; Martin G. Glaeser, *Public Utilities in American Capitalism* (N.Y.: Macmillan, 1957), 8, 218–19, 414–16; Ford P. Hall, *The Concept of a Business Affected with a Public Interest* (Bloomington: Principia, 1940), 146–54; David Lynch, *The Concentration of Economic Power* (N.Y.: Columbia U. Press, 1946), 168–69; Horace M. Gray, in AEA, *Readings in the Social Control of Industry* (Philadelphia: Blakiston, 1942), 282–98; Ralph L. Dewey, in AER, March 1941, pp. 16–19; NRPB, *Transportation and National Policy* (1942), 10–11, 202–16, 355–56.

transportation captured an even larger share of the market; and the result was a drastic decline in railroad revenue, a drop of about fifty percent from 1929 to 1933. Under the circumstances, a sanely financed and conservatively managed industry would have been in trouble. The railroads, with their fixed costs, heavy bonded indebtedness, overexpanded and obsolescent plant, and legacy of financial manipulation, never had a real chance. By 1933 one-sixth of the nation's railroad mileage was in the hands of receivers, and many of the remaining companies were nearly bankrupt.[2]

In the face of declining demand, railroad managers tended to blame their difficulties upon excessive competition or unfair subsidization of their rivals. The solution, they seemed to think, was a program of cartelization, under which the power of the state could be used to control facilities, raise rates, protect invested capital, and restrict their competitors. By 1933, such a program was already well advanced. Even before World War I the railroads had developed an elaborate system of rate-making conferences, which in practice initiated most rate changes and inhibited rate cutting. Following the war, the Transportation Act of 1920 gave legal sanction to the cartel principle, to the idea of equalizing returns between weaker and stronger systems and adjusting rates so that the carriers as a whole (or in separate rate groups) would earn a fair re-

[2] Thor Hultgren, *American Transportation in Prosperity and Depression* (N.Y.: National Bureau of Economic Research, 1948), 9–13; Harold G. Moulton et al., *The American Transportation Problem* (Washington: Brookings, 1933), 49–66, 87–90, 97–98, 173–77, 283–84, 289–91, 301, 471, 660–66, 714; NRPB, *Transportation*, 33–40; William N. Leonard, *Railroad Consolidation under the Transportation Act of 1920* (N.Y.: Columbia U Press, 1946), 57–64; ICC, *Annual Report* (1930), 147; (1934), 99; and *Coordination of Motor Transportation* (1932), 4–5, 10–18; Ralph Sucher, in *Current History*, Dec. 1935, pp. 254–55; Julius H. Parmalee, in *Annals Am. Acad.*, Jan. 1934, pp. 155–58; *Fortune*, Aug. 1939, pp. 50–51.

turn of 5.5 percent on the value of their property. With the onset of the depression, the demands for financial assistance, further consolidation, and higher rates had brought some aid from the Hoover Administration. The Reconstruction Finance Corporation, for example, had made government loans available; a new bankruptcy law had facilitated financial reorganization; and the ICC had allowed some rate increases.[3]

With the advent of the New Deal, railroad leaders and investors renewed their demands for economic aid, and because of past precedents and the special position of the industry, the new Administration listened sympathetically. After consulting with industrial spokesmen, a special transportation committee, headed by Joseph Eastman of the ICC, worked out a plan for a federal coordinator of transportation. After further adjustments to meet the objections of the railroad unions and other interested parties, the plan resulted in the Emergency Railroad Transportation Act of 1933, a measure that seemed thoroughly compatible with the prevailing philosophy of industrial self-government. Under its provisions, the nation's railroads were divided into three regional groups, each under a coordinating committee chosen by the member carriers. Such committees, together with the Federal Coordinator, were to devise measures for reducing waste, pooling facilities, and eliminating any unnecessary duplication of services. If they refused to act on their own, the Coordinator might issue orders and compel action. Nothing, however, was to be done if it would reduce the level of railroad employ-

---

[3] Moulton et al., *Transportation Problem*, 56, 67–68, 377–78, 882–95; Earl Latham, *The Politics of Railroad Coordination, 1933–36* (Cambridge: Harvard U. Press, 1959), 8–15, 33–34; Arne C. Wiprud, *Justice in Transportation* (N.Y.: Ziff-Davis, 1945), 12–13, 48–56, 76–87; *Harvard Law Review*, Nov. 1933, pp. 18–20; NRPB, *Transportation*, 29–31; *Business Week*, Feb. 22, 1933, pp. 6–7; *New York Times*, Jan. 16, March 30, Nov, 16, 19, Dec. 2, 18, 1932, Jan. 10, 1933.

ment below that of May 1933 (minus an annual five percent allowance for normal attrition).[4]

In philosophy, then, the railroad program was similar to the business planners' version of the National Industrial Recovery Act, and in practice the experiences of Federal Coordinator Joseph Eastman were somewhat similar to those of the more liberally oriented NRA administrators. He noted that the railroad managers operated like feudal chieftains, jealous of their independence and determined to preserve their salaries, perquisites, and status positions. They also took the position that any real economies would require the elimination of jobs, and when Eastman refused to go along, they reacted by rejecting almost all of his recommendations. His plans for a freight car pool, a transportation clearinghouse, improved passenger services, and a central bureau of scientific research were all rejected as impractical and useless. So, since he was reluctant to use compulsion, he could accomplish little beyond the filing of learned reports and the introduction of some minor economies.

Gradually, too, after the crisis of 1933 had passed and after the Association of American Railroads had been set up in 1934 as a private coordinating agency, the leaders of the railroad industry came to the conclusion that they no

[4] The Act of 1933 also contained provisions affecting the powers of the Interstate Commerce Commission. It repealed the recapture clause of the Transportation Act of 1920, brought railroad holding companies under ICC jurisdiction, modified the rate-making formula so as to eliminate the objective of a fair return on the value of railroad property, and provided that the ICC might veto an RFC loan if it felt that the carrier needed financial reorganization. Latham, *Railroad Coordination*, 35–78; R. W. Harbeson, in *Journal of Political Economy*, Feb. 1934, pp. 106–26; *Congressional Record*, 73 Cong., 1 Sess., LXVII, 2860, 2908, 4267–69, 4283, 4441, 4853, 4999, 5393–98, 5430–35; 48 *U.S. Statutes* 211, Public, No. 68, 73 Cong.; House Commerce Committee, *Emergency Railroad Transportation Act of 1933* (73 Cong., 1 Sess., 1933), 69, 191, 209, 291; *New York Times*, April 2–4, 6, 28, May 5, 11, 20, 28, June 6, 9, 10, 17, 1933.

longer needed a federal coordinator, particularly one who was "dictatorial," "impractical," "doctrinaire," and prone to "socialistic" statements. The labor leaders were also willing to get rid of Eastman, especially after the railroads guaranteed dismissal compensation in the Washington agreement of May 1936. Accordingly, since both the unions and management opposed any further extension of the Emergency Railroad Transportation Act, Congress allowed it to expire in June 1936. The railroad companies were still far from being financially healthy, but they were in better shape than they had been in 1933. And the railroad leaders, like their counterparts in other industries, had decided that the type of aid available under the Act of 1933 was not worth the price paid for it; that if continued too long it could result in a drastic shift of power to federal officials or perhaps the nationalization of the industry itself.[5]

III

The Emergency Railroad Transportation Act was not the only attempt to legislate prosperity for the railroads. After all, most of the "destructive competition" seemed to come from the newer forms of transportation; consequently, it was not surprising that the railroads should attempt to do

[5] Latham, *Railroad Coordination*, 40, 48–51, 94–100, 119–33, 165–68, 201–12, 244–60; Claude M. Fuess, *Joseph B. Eastman* (N.Y.: Columbia U. Press, 1952), 211–21, 232–44; Samuel T. Bledsoe, in Academy of Political Science, *Transportation Development in the United States* (N.Y.: Columbia U. Press, 1937), 119–24; NRPB, *Transportation*, 146–48; ICC, *Annual Report* (1936), 1–5; Harbeson, in *Journal of Political Economy*, Feb. 1934, pp. 125–26; W. J. Cunningham, in *Harvard Business Review*, Spring 1937, pp. 269–73; Carl B. Swisher, in *Public Administration Review*, Winter 1945, pp. 44–46; *Monthly Labor Review*, June 1936, pp. 1503–5; *Railway Age*, June 8, 1935, p. 885; Aug. 31, 1935, p. 267; June 20, 1936, p. 985; *Business Week*, Sept. 22, 1934, pp. 15–16; June 27, 1936, p. 34.

something about this threat from their newer rivals. The trucking industry, in particular, had become a major worry, had inspired a long series of railroad-sponsored motor carrier bills, and had produced a growing conviction on the part of railroad leaders, their dependents, and their allies on the state and federal railroad commissions that the public would benefit greatly if trucking could be converted into a public utility.

During the nineteen twenties the truckers themselves were far from enthusiastic about the alleged benefits of public regulation. But with the coming of the depression, the drastic drop in demand, and the resulting struggle for available markets, the attitude of some of the larger trucking firms began to change. Their position, they felt, was seriously threatened by the appearance of cut-rate, "fly-by-night" operators, who, with the aid of truck dealers and manufacturers, managed to get a truck on credit, to eke out a living on cut rates until they lost it, and in the process to force down wages and disrupt the whole rate structure. Under the circumstances, there was growing support in trucking, bus, and teamster circles for some type of regulation, some system that would establish minimum rates and wages and eliminate irresponsible operators.

In 1933, then, many truckers welcomed the establishment of an NRA code. Most of them, particularly the smaller truckers and contract carriers, continued to prefer the code to any type of special legislation. The suggestions for a separate motor carrier act continued to come primarily from the railroads, the railroad commissions, or the Federal Coordinator of Transportation; and, as trucking spokesmen pointed out, they almost invariably proposed that the new controls be entrusted to the "railroad-minded" Interstate Commerce Commission. This was true of the Wheeler bill that was passed by the Senate in April 1935. For a time, this measure encountered strong opposition, not only from shippers and automobile manufacturers, but also from the American Trucking Associations and most other trucking leaders.[6]

The turning point came with the Schecter decision, which in effect converted the American Trucking Associations from an opponent into an active sponsor of special legislation. As a result, the Wheeler bill now moved through Congress with relative ease and by August 1935 had become the Motor Carrier Act, a measure that gave the ICC broad regulatory powers over most interstate motor carriers. Common carriers now had to secure certificates of public convenience and necessity, contract carriers to secure permits, and brokers to secure licenses, all of which would be issued as a matter of right to those operating in June 1935, but whose issuance in the future would depend upon the discretion of the ICC. The Commission could also fix maximum and minimum rates for common carriers and minimum rates for contract carriers; it could supervise the issuance of trucking securities; and it could establish maximum hours and safety rules, not only for common and contract carriers, but for private carriers as well. Thus, through control over entry, required adherence to filed rates, and the establishment of higher standards of financial responsibility, safety, and labor prac-

[6] Donald V. Harper, *Economic Regulation of the Motor Trucking Industry by the States* (Urbana: U. of Ill. Press, 1959), 21–22, 27–31, 33–40; William J. Hudson and James A. Constantin, *Motor Transportation* (N.Y.: Ronald, 1958), 462–76; Moulton et al., *Transportation Problem*, 521–22; Latham, *Railroad Coordination*, 218–21, 226–31; ICC, *Coordination of Motor Transportation*, 2, 97–98, 102–3, 115–19; Senate Commerce Committee, *To Amend the Interstate Commerce Act* (74 Cong., 1 Sess., 1935), 1–37, 44–45, 97, 147–65, 241–43, 255–58, 263, 265, 271, 305–7, 403, 417–18, 433–35, 471, 484–506; *Congressional Record*, 74 Cong., 1 Sess., LXXIX, 1420, 5650–55, 5737; Federal Coordinator of Transportation, *Report* (House Doc. 89, 74 Cong., 1 Sess., 1935), 14–18, 59–62; James C. Nelson, in *Journal of Political Economy*, Aug. 1936, pp. 464–70; Meyer H. Fishbein, in *Social Forces*, Dec. 1955, pp. 171–78; *Business Week*, March 17, 1934, p. 24; Aug. 10, 1935, pp. 11–12; C. H. Becker and D. H. O'Connell, "NRA Code History 287" (Trucking), 17, 100–110, CHF, NRA Records.

tices, the ICC could reduce competitive disturbances, both within the industry and between the truckers and the rail-roads.

In practice, there was a good deal of complaint about the time-consuming, cumbersome, and cautious manner in which the act was implemented. Enforcement, too, was difficult, and the friction between the railroads and truck-ers persisted, resulting in frequent charges of favoritism on both sides. Yet there was little disposition to do away with the act. It did bring greater stability, a minimum-rate floor, fewer and larger trucking firms, more rate bureaus, and a reduction in the cost advantage of low-cost carriers. In both trucking and railroad circles, there was a general feel-ing that the new system provided some protection against the cut-rater and the chiseler and that consequently, even though the trucking industry possessed few of the traits of a "natural monopoly," the policy of treating it as a public utility should be continued.[7]

IV

Another transportation industry in which regulation and partial planning were mixed with government subsidies was that of shipping. Here, too, the underlying rationale relied partly on the argument that the industry was a "natural monopoly," one in which capital requirements were large, fixed costs were high, and rivalry was wasteful,

[7] *Congressional Record*, 74 Cong., 1 Sess., LXXIX, 11813, 12196–12200, 12204–34, 1279, 12863; 49 *U.S. Statutes* 543, Public, No. 255, 74 Cong.; House Commerce Committee, *Amending Motor Carrier Act* (75 Cong., 3 Sess., 1938), 27–29; ICC, *Annual Report* (1936), 72–74, 82, 88; (1938), 83; Wiprud, *Justice in Transporta-tion*, 32–37, 60; Hudson and Constantin, *Motor Transportation*, 466, 476–78; Ernest W. Williams, Jr., *The Regulation of Rail-Motor Rate Competition* (N.Y.: Harper, 1958), 205–6, 209–12, 220–23; NRPB, *Transportation*, 110–14, 217–30; Nelson, in *Journal of Political Economy*, Aug. 1936, pp. 470–94.

inefficient, and conducive to rate wars. Probably an even more potent argument was the one advanced by nationalists and mercantilists, the contention that a nation's security and prosperity depended upon its possession of an adequate merchant marine, even though economically there might be no justification for it. The United States, like other nations, had acted on this premise. The result had been the establishment of various types of public aid. Since 1817, American vessels had enjoyed a legal monopoly of the coastwise and intercoastal trade. Governmental development of inland waterways and navigation facilities was also a long established policy. For shipping firms engaged in foreign trade, subsidization had gone even further. Under the merchant marine acts of 1920 and 1928 such firms could buy government ships at a small fraction of their original value; they could obtain low-interest construction loans; and they could sign generous mail contracts under which the government paid many times the actual cost of carrying the mail.

Still, shipping remained a "sick" industry. World War I, economic nationalism, and worldwide shipping subsidies had stimulated the building of far more ships than were warranted by available cargoes. The depression, with its accompanying trade restrictions, produced a further decline in foreign trade. The result was an industry plagued by excess capacity and cutthroat competition. The United States Shipping Board, which had been given some power over maximum rates and unfair practices, could do little to reduce competitive pressures. Even the international shipping conferences, with their elaborate market-sharing and rate-making machinery, could not prevent the outbreak of disastrous rate wars. American shipowners, moreover, were in a particularly adverse position. To be eligible for subsidies, they had to use American-built ships; yet the cost of building such ships was higher than in any other major nation in the world, partly because of relatively high wage scales, partly because of expensive materials and backward methods.[8]

Subsidies, it seemed, were necessary to keep American ships afloat. Yet in practice the subsidy approach had not worked well. It had failed to stimulate new construction or modernization. It had produced excessive lobbying activities. And there were strong indications that much of the subsidy money had not been used for the purposes intended. In 1933 complaints from independent shipping firms led to extensive governmental investigations; and in the months that followed, the Post Office, an Interdepartmental Committee on Shipping Policy, and a special committee headed by Senator Hugo Black uncovered a wide variety of abuses. Many of the mail contracts, they learned, were the result of collusion rather than competitive bidding, and much of the money had been siphoned off into fat bonuses and salaries, huge lobbying fees, and excessive service charges by subsidiaries and affiliates. Large sums, it appeared, were being spent, but the country was receiving little in return.

In spite of the scandals, though, Roosevelt insisted that a merchant marine was necessary for national defense and national security. Subsidization, he told Congress in March 1935, would have to continue, although the abuses of the system might be prevented by doing away with the subterfuge of mail contracts and substituting direct subsidies and tight controls. The shipping companies, too, seemed willing to go along with this approach. Ira Campbell, the counsel for the American Steamship Owners' Association,

[8] Moulton et al., Transportation Problem, 511–13, 874; Daniel Marx, Jr., International Shipping Cartels (Princeton: Princeton U. Press, 1953), 19–23, 31–40, 105–7, 299–302; Paul M. Zeis, American Shipping Policy (Princeton: Princeton U. Press, 1938), 166–69; Congressional Digest, Feb. 1936, pp. 38–40; R. J. Baker, in Annals Am. Acad., Jan. 1934, pp. 195–96; Clarence N. Weems, Jr., in Foreign Policy Reports, Jan. 1, 1938, p. 239; John G. B. Hutchins, in QJE, Feb. 1939, pp. 238–40, 243–48; William Adams, in Nation, Sept. 5, 1934, p. 263; Fortune, Sept. 1937, pp. 61, 65–66, 112, 166, 169.

helped to draft an appropriate bill. Senator Royal Copeland of New York and Representative Schuyler Bland of Virginia agreed to sponsor it; and in June 1935, after its minimum-rate features had been deleted, the measure was passed by the House. In the Senate, though, it ran into stronger opposition, particularly from Senator Black, who favored a government-operated merchant marine. Consequently, substantial modifications had to be made. Copeland himself began to add more safeguards. Senator Guffey introduced a whole new measure, providing for still tighter restrictions and for the possibility of government ownership. Eventually, by a process of negotiation, compromise, and amendment, a hybrid version emerged, one to which Black, Guffey, and their allies succeeded in adding a number of safeguards. And it was this hybrid version that became the Merchant Marine Act of June 1936.[9]

In its final form the new law created a five-man Maritime Commission with power to equalize American and foreign costs by subsidizing American builders and operators. If an operator wished to acquire a new vessel, the government would have it built in the United States, and then, providing the maximum discount was no greater than thirty-three and one-third percent (fifty percent if four commissioners agreed), would sell it to the operator on generous credit terms at a figure representing the construction costs of his foreign competitors. Operators could

[9] FDR, *Public Papers and Addresses*, IV (N.Y.: Random House, 1938), 90–92; Kenneth S. Crawford, *The Pressure Boys* (N.Y.: Messner, 1939), 148–58; Zeis, *Shipping Policy*, 159–65, 167–75, 186–92; House Merchant Marine Committee, *Hearings to Develop an American Merchant Marine* (74 Cong., 1 Sess., 1935), 1098–1111, 1122–37; Special Senate Committee, *Investigation of Air Mail and Ocean Mail Contracts* (72 Cong., 1933), I, 802–5, 838, 1364–65; *Congressional Record*, 74 Cong., 1 Sess., LXXIX, 5617–24, 5721, 9740, 10074–79, 10092–125, 10193, 10209, 10289, 14255–64; 74 Cong., 2 Sess., LXXX, 2900, 4367, 9885, 9899–902, 9915–17, 10069–78, 10569–76; Ralph L. Dewey, in *AER*, June 1937, pp. 241–43; *Fortune*, Sept. 1937, pp. 54–55, 76–78, 184; *Congressional Digest*, Feb. 1936, pp. 36–37, 40–41, 46–49.

also get subsidies to compensate for the lower operating costs of foreign ships. In addition, if the Commission agreed unanimously, special payments might be made to offset the subsidies of foreign nations. Along with these subsidies, too, went an elaborate system of controls, some of them desired by the industry, some imposed by Senator Black and his camp. The Commission, for example, could establish minimum wage and manning scales, fix maximum rates, prescribe routes, regulate trade practices, require uniform accounts, control intercompany relationships, limit salaries, and recapture excessive profits. Finally, there was the possibility of government ownership and operation. If the Commission felt that subsidies were not providing an adequate merchant fleet, it could build ships on its own and charter them to private operators; or if no reasonable contract could be made, it could operate the ships itself.

In various ways, then, the Act of 1936 went beyond the earlier program, although the underlying approach remained the same, the rationale behind it was similar, and the problem of restoring a prosperous, expanding, privately owned merchant marine remained largely unsolved. There were still few commitments to build, even after a further liberalization of the law in 1938. The public, it seemed, was still reluctant to invest in a depressed industry dependent upon government support; and it was not until the approach of World War II that large-scale government investment led to a rapid expansion of the merchant fleet.[10]

The Act of 1936, of course, applied primarily to shipping firms engaged in foreign trade, but this did not mean

[10] Hutchins, in *QJE*, Feb. 1939, pp. 251–58; Dewey, in *AER*, June 1937, pp. 243–48; *Fortune*, Sept. 1937, pp. 188, 190, 193–94; Weems, in *Foreign Policy Reports*, XIII (Jan. 1, 1938), pp. 241–47; Zeis, *Shipping Policy*, 193–205; 49 *U.S. Statutes* 1985, Public, No. 835, 74 Cong.; 52 *U.S. Statutes* 953, Public, No. 705, 75 Cong.

that the other branches of the industry enjoyed no governmental protection or support. The coastal shipping companies continued to enjoy a monopoly of the coastwise and intercoastal trade. After 1936 they could also borrow from the government on the same terms as the subsidized operators. And through legislation in 1933, 1936, and 1938 they were able to establish a rate-filing system and a government-supported minimum-rate floor. Inland waterways, too, would eventually be subjected to public utility regulation, although here the demand for such action came more from the railroads and their allies than it did from the water carriers themselves. Inland water carriage, so the rail spokesmen argued, was in reality an expensive and uneconomic form of transportation, one that could compete successfully with the railroads only because it enjoyed such artificial advantages as toll-free waterways, unregulated rates, and freedom from burdensome restrictions like the long-and-short-haul clause. The government, they insisted, should equalize the competitive situation. Ultimately, these demands would produce the Transportation Act of 1940, bringing the water carriers under ICC jurisdiction and subjecting them to the same type of entry, rate, and financial controls as had been applied to other areas of transportation.[11]

[11] Latham, *Railroad Coordination*, 235–40, 318–19; D. Philip Locklin, *Economics of Transportation* (Homewood: Irwin, 1954), 761–78, 778–86; Wiprud, *Justice in Transportation*, 18–19, 41–42, 61–63; Moulton et al., *Transportation Problem*, 129–30, 465–66, 511–13; NRPB, *Transportation*, 379–82; Carl E. McDowell and Helen M. Gibbs, *Ocean Transportation* (N.Y.: McGraw-Hill, 1954), 400–1; 47 *U.S. Statutes* 1425, Public, No. 415, 72 Cong.; 49 *U.S. Statutes* 1985, Public, No. 835, 74 Cong.; 52 *U.S. Statutes* 953, Public, No. 705, 75 Cong.; 54 *U.S. Statutes* 899, Public, No. 785, 76 Cong.; Dewey, in *AER*, March 1941, pp. 15–26; Harold D. Koontz, in *Journal of Political Economy*, April 1938, pp. 153–54, 167–68; G. L. Wilson and H. S. Perry, in *Annals Am. Acad.*, Jan. 1934, p. 215; Truman C. Bigham, in *Southern Economic Journal*, July 1941, pp. 2–9, 14–16.

V

Still another industry receiving special treatment was that of aviation. It, too, was represented as a special case, one in which special circumstances justified governmental assistance and intervention. Rapid development of the industry, so the argument ran, was vital to the national defense; yet because it was still in the pioneer stage, risky, speculative, and unable to offer assured returns, the industry on its own could never attract the large capital outlays that were necessary for rapid expansion. The answer was government support, and under the aviation acts of 1925, 1926, and 1930 the government had stepped in to provide safety controls, generous mail subsidies, and a wide variety of promotional and navigational aids.

The subsidy program, however, like that for shipping, had soon become the subject of numerous abuses. As Senator Hugo Black's investigating committee discovered in 1934, competitive bidding on contracts had been largely replaced by negotiation and the so-called "spoils conferences." Independents had been frozen out, most of the mail contracts had gone to three large aviation holding companies, and much of the subsidy money had gone into the pockets of a few insiders, promoters, and financial manipulators. Taking advantage of these revelations, the smaller independents began agitating for the cancellation of existing contracts. In February 1934, on the recommendations of Senator Black, the Post Office, and the Department of Justice, President Roosevelt announced that the contracts were the result of collusion and would therefore be cancelled. The Army, he said, would carry the mail during the emergency.

Subsequent events, though, proved that the Army Air Corps was ill-prepared for such a mission. A combination of inadequate equipment, lack of experience, and extremely bad weather produced a series of disasters, a total of sixty-six accidents in which twelve pilots lost their lives. In the face of mounting public and congressional protest, the President quickly retreated. On March 10 he announced that the air mail service would be returned to private hands as soon as possible, and by May 8 the private lines were again carrying the mail under temporary three-month contracts.[12]

In the meantime, Congress was considering further legislation, and after a heated debate, produced the Air Mail Act of 1934, a measure that was both promotional and punitive in its effects. Under it, the Postmaster General might still award and extend mail contracts, control routes and schedules, and prescribe standards of performance. The contracts, however, were to be the result of competitive bidding. Rates were not to exceed thirty-three and one-third cents per mile for less than three hundred pounds (or forty cents a mile, in any case). Mergers between competing contractors on parallel routes were prohibited. Contracting companies were to divest themselves of all outside interests and interlocking relationships, pay no individual salaries in excess of $17,500 a year, and receive no more than three contracts, only one of which could cover a primary route. Once the contracts were let,

[12] Francis A. Spencer, *Air Mail Payment and the Government* (Washington: Brookings, 1941), 30–32, 41–44, 53–66; John P. Frank, *Mr. Justice Black* (N.Y.: Knopf, 1949), 65–73; Moulton et al., *Transportation Problem*, 749–56; Arthur M. Schlesinger, Jr., *The Coming of the New Deal* (Boston: Houghton Mifflin, 1959), 448–54; John H. Frederick, *Commercial Air Transportation* (Chicago: Irwin, 1946), 8–9, 243–47, 491–504; Henry L. Smith, *Airways* (N.Y.: Knopf, 1942), 88–102, 125–28, 159–71, 190–96, 202–82; Paul T. David, *The Economics of Air Mail Transportation* (Washington: Brookings, 1934), 153–57, 188–97, 205–6; M. R. Werner, *Privileged Characters* (N.Y.: McBride, 1935), 388–433; FDR, *Public Papers*, III, 93–94, 138–42; Special Senate Committee, *Air and Ocean Mail Contracts*, I, 1443–57, 1483–1504, 1549–57, 1678–79, 1720–22, 1801, 1829–31, 1868, 2733–40, 2849, 2979–97; Elmer Davis, in *Harper's*, May 1934, pp. 633–36; *Fortune*, May 1934, pp. 85–89, 140, 142, 144, 153–54, 156, 158; *Aviation*, April 1934, pp. 117–18; June 1934, pp. 187–89.

moreover, the rate of compensation would be subject to the jurisdiction of the Interstate Commerce Commission, which might examine the contractors' books, determine the costs of service, and lower rates that resulted in excessive profits. In a sense, the act represented a qualified victory for the champions of small business and enforced competition. Unlike most of the transportation laws of the nineteen thirties, it did make some effort to restore competition rather than eliminate it.

In practice, though, the act worked badly. Under it, the airlines were losing money, the new independents were providing substandard service, and a number of the new rules were administratively unworkable. In early 1935 the Federal Aviation Commission, an investigatory agency set up by the act, recommended a number of changes, and in August 1935 Congress amended the law in several particulars. Contracts were now to run for three years instead of one, routes were consolidated, and the ICC was empowered to raise rates as well as lower them and to deal with various types of unfair competitive practices. However, authority remained divided between the ICC and the Post Office, resulting in a good deal of friction between the two agencies over such matters as the policing of accounts, the methods of cost and rate determination, and the desirability of compensating the airlines for non-mail losses. Generally speaking, the Post Office had less sympathy for the airlines, and since it could rearrange schedules and payloads, it could virtually nullify the increased rates allowed by the ICC.[13]

In view of these conflicts, there was growing support

[13] Spencer, *Air Mail*, 76–100, 105–6, 112, 121–44, 186–91, 225–26; Frederick, *Air Transportation*, 247–48; Smith, *Airways*, 284–90; ICC, *Annual Report* (1936), 30–32; *Congressional Record*, 73 Cong., 2 Sess., LXXVIII, 4041–42, 5384, 5694–96, 5756–58, 6727–33, 7609–29, 8543–56, 8587–88, 9869–80, 11161; 74 Cong., 1 Sess., LXXIX, 4378–99; 48 *U.S. Statutes* 933, Public, No. 308, 73 Cong.; 49 *U.S. Statutes* 614, Public, No. 270, 74 Cong.; W. B. Courtney, in *Collier's*, Feb. 9, 1935, pp. 10–11, 40–41; *Newsweek*, Aug. 17, 1935, p. 26.

for centralizing all aspects of the aviation program under one agency. The difficulty came in deciding which one, since some favored the ICC, some the Post Office, some the Department of Commerce, and some an independent regulatory commission. Roosevelt, however, had indicated his preference for ICC regulation. Accordingly, Senator Pat McCarran and Representative Clarence Lea drafted measures to accomplish this, enlisted the support of the aviation industry, and nearly succeeded in getting their program through Congress in 1937. The chief stumbling block was opposition from rival agencies, particularly from the Post Office and the Department of Commerce. But, in the end, a threatened filibuster by Senator Kenneth McKellar, the chairman of the Senate Post Office Committee, prevented any action in the 1937 session.

In late 1937 the President appointed an interdepartmental committee on aviation, which eventually recommended the creation of an independent commission. Roosevelt then indicated his willingness to go along; McCarran and Lea revised their bills, which, in 1938, moved through Congress with relative ease. Most of the debate was over the relationship that should exist between the regulatory agency and the President. The issue here was finally compromised by making the proposed authority independent, but giving the President control over the Administrator, an official charged with carrying out administrative and promotional tasks. In May both houses of Congress gave their approval, and in June the measure became the Civil Aeronautics Act of 1938.

When contrasted with the Act of 1934, the new law reflected a general abandonment of the idea of enforcing competition. Under it, competitive bidding for air mail contracts was to give way to a system of negotiated, noncompetitive certificates. Entry into the industry was to be controlled through the issuance of certificates of convenience and necessity. The new five-man Civil Aeronautics Authority had full power to control routes, prevent unfair practices, maintain labor and safety standards, and prescribe rates for mail, passenger, and express service. The act also removed most of the restrictions of the 1934 measure. The CAA now had discretionary power to allow mergers, pools, interlocking directorates, and subleasing of contracts. Finally, attached to the Authority were two semi-independent agencies: the Administrator, who would handle executive and promotional functions; and an Air Safety Board, which would investigate air crashes and recommend ways to prevent them.

Like most of the other transportation laws, then, the Civil Aeronautics Act provided for a blend of subsidies, cartelization, and public controls, one that was justified by stressing such things as the "infant industry" argument, the requirements of national defense, the need for public safety, and the similarities of the industry to other "natural monopolies." There was, undoubtedly, some hesitation before this program was adopted. In the heated atmosphere of 1934 there was even some disposition to force the industry into a competitive pattern. But such sentiments proved to be short-lived. In the end, the opposite policy prevailed; the airlines, like the railroads, motor carriers, and shipping companies, entered the haven of publicly regulated monopoly.[14]

VI

By 1938, the main trends in transportation policy seemed firmly established. When declining demand led to excess

[14] Spencer, Air Mail, 78, 89–90, 227–30, 233–38; Smith, Airways, 301–6; Stuart Daggett, Principles of Inland Transportation (N.Y.: Harper, 1941), 852–63; FDR, Public Papers, IV, 68–70; Congressional Record, 75 Cong., 1 Sess., LXXXI, 64, 1769, 5095, 8882–92, 8968–78, 8983–86, 9202–4, 9226; 75 Cong., 3 Sess., LXXXIII, 2897, 5379, 6406–10, 6627–29, 6635–37, 6724–32, 6854–68, 6879, 7104, 8843–69, 8963, 9616; 52 U.S. Statutes 973, Public, No. 706, 75 Cong.; Aviation, Aug. 1937, pp. 61–62; Sept. 1937, p. 64; Nov. 1937, p. 55; Dec. 1937, p. 57; Jan. 1938, p. 55; Feb. 1938, pp. 67, 69; March 1938, p. 55; June 1938, pp. 52–53; July 1938, pp. 53–55.

capacity and intense competition, the transportation leaders reacted by advocating some type of cartelization. In case after case, the use of the appropriate symbols had produced the desired results. Public sympathy had been won, the defenders of competitive values had been silenced, and the government had moved in to establish rate floors, control entry, promote coordination and consolidation, provide special favors, and keep out the chiselers. Most transportation leaders and regulatory officials, moreover, remained convinced that a return to competition would be "unnatural" and "economically dangerous." When confronted with a new crisis in the late nineteen thirties, they reacted by advocating a further departure from competitive standards.

In retrospect, though, it seemed obvious that such measures had failed to overcome the real difficulties confronting the transportation industries. The central problem, after all, was lack of volume, and there was little in the existing program that could stimulate demand. At least it seemed this way to critics of an antitrust orientation, who doubted that transportation was really a special case and who suspected that the concepts of "destructive competition" and "natural monopoly" were largely the creation of industrial propagandists. The country, they argued, never had too much transportation; it simply had too much high-priced transportation. And it was now time to stop worrying about railroad investors and vested interests, accept obsolescence and technological changes, and reverse the whole attitude toward competition.

It seemed doubtful, however, that such a change would ever take place, since politically speaking, the transportation policy was a going concern. It did satisfy to some extent the desire of industrial pressure groups for planning, rationalization, and security. Yet by avoiding unpopular extremes, perverting the public utility concept, making skillful use of competitive symbols, and stressing such things as national defense and public safety, it managed to accomplish the task with a minimum of political disturbance. Consequently, the transportation industries, like the farmers, coal operators, and oil men, could avoid most of the agitation against monopoly, claim that they constituted a special case, involve the government in partial planning, and win support for a program of publicly sponsored cartels.[15]

[15] NRPB, *Transportation*, 233–37, 281–82; Leonard, *Railroad Consolidation*, 244–50; Wiprud, *Justice in Transportation*, 4–10, 69–71, 138–42, 167; Gray, in AEA, *Social Control*, 287–88, 293–94; Lucile S. Keyes, *Federal Control of Entry into Air Transportation* (Cambridge: Harvard U. Press, 1951), 72–105; Leslie Craven, in *Atlantic Monthly*, Dec. 1938, pp. 767–76; Bigham, in *Southern Economic Journal*, July 1941, pp. 2, 20–21; *Congressional Record*, 75 Cong., 3 Sess., LXXXIII, 6635; *Fortune*, Aug. 1939, pp. 82–84, 86–88, 90; *Current History*, March 1938, pp. 27–30; Feb. 1939, p. 52; Thurman Arnold, "The Right to Transport," Folder 4, Arnold Papers.

CHAPTER 13. PARTIAL PLANNING IN THE DISTRIBUTIVE AND SERVICE TRADES

WHEN the small merchant denounced "monopoly" in the nineteen thirties, he meant big business crushing little business, not the use of artificial controls to exploit consumers or discourage innovation. To him the monopolist was the chain store, mail order house, supermarket, or some other large-scale rival. Paradoxically, though, he used the vocabulary of the antitruster to advocate a program of market controls, a system under which governmental power would be used to foster cartels, freeze distributive channels, and preserve profit margins. "Competition," he assumed, was synonymous with small business; he, like the farmer, argued that his "way of life" was of social value, that it was worth preserving even at the cost of inefficiency, and that if it was not preserved, the consumer would eventually be at the mercy of a few giant organizations.

At one time, as economists pointed out, the small merchant had been something of a monopolist himself, or at least a "partial monopolist" with a tilted rather than horizontal demand curve. The relative immobility of consumers, coupled with product and enterprise differentiation, had limited effective competition to localized areas where any given retailer was typically in close, immediate competition with only a small number of others. Partly because of this, the drive for efficiency, lower costs, and economies of scale came relatively late to the retail field. Once it came, however, in the nineteen twenties and thirties, it seemed to threaten the very existence of the small merchant. The advent of the mass distributors, along with greater consumer mobility and the growth of nationally advertised brands, tended to break down local controls, destroy small specialists, disrupt traditional channels of trade, and bring the crossroads store into direct competition with the metropolis. The process, moreover, seemed likely to continue, since the larger units benefited not only from greater volume and internal economies, but also from their buying power, their ability to bargain with manufacturers and win special price concessions, allowances, and discounts.[1]

Then, with the advent of the depression, the lot of the small merchant became even more precarious. Driven from their regular jobs, thousands of the unemployed tried to eke out a living by opening subsistence stores, small units that sophisticated NRA administrators referred to as the "Mama, Papa, and Rosy stores." Yet while the number of retailers was growing, demand was shrinking; and the result was intense rivalry for available markets. Before long, it seemed, almost every line had its cut-raters, institutions like the "supermarket" in the grocery field, the "pineboard" in the drug trade, the discount house and bargain basement in other lines. Using cheap equipment, fast-moving items, price appeal, and loss-leader advertising, these new establishments could undercut traditional merchants and drive them out of business.

Consequently, small distributors and their suppliers were particularly receptive to the type of reasoning that underlay the NRA codes. The cut-raters, they felt, were predatory, immoral, or misguided chiselers, and depressed markets were due primarily to price cutting, "unfair" practices, and retail "monopolies," things that should be legis-

[1] Ewald T. Grether, *Price Control under Fair Trade Legislation* (N.Y.: Oxford U. Press, 1939), 210, 225–35; Gerrit A. Dommisse, *The Regulation of Retail Trade Competition* (N.Y.: Colonial, 1939), 15–6, 21–27; Joseph C. Palamountain, Jr., *The Politics of Distribution* (Cambridge: Harvard U. Press, 1955), 6–10, 17–20, 26–30, 40, 189; John H. Cover et al., *Problems of Small Business* (TNEC Monograph 17, 1941), 157; Clair Wilcox, *Competition and Monopoly in American Industry* (TNEC Monograph 21, 1941), 112; FTC, *Report on Resale Price Maintenance* (1945), 252–53; and *Final Report on the Chain Store Investigation* (1935), 85–86.

lated out of existence. In a number of respects, too, the distributive codes did reflect their point of view, particularly in the provisions for confining distribution to recognized channels, eliminating the buying advantages of large units, and prohibiting loss leaders. Most of them also contained some type of loss limitation provision prohibiting sales below cost plus a given mark-up. For instance, in the general retail code, the price floor was finally fixed at ten percent above cost, in the grocery trade at six percent, and in the drug, tobacco, and book trades resale prices were set by the manufacturers and publishers. These codes, to be sure, often worked badly. They were irritating, inconvenient, and hard to enforce. Yet when all was said and done, small merchants had acquired a new organization consciousness and a conviction that they were on the right track. Their vocal spokesmen at least wanted to strengthen the code controls, not junk them.[2]

II

Following the Schecter decision, then, independent retail groups were keenly interested in salvaging their former code provisions, particularly those designed to reduce the

[2] Albert Haring, *Retail Price Cutting and Its Control by Manufacturers* (N.Y.: Ronald, 1935), 34–39; Dommisse, *Retail Trade*, 45–47; Mark Merrell et al., *NRA Work Materials 57* (*Restriction of Retail Price Cutting*), 10–11, 47, 59–61, 65, 70–75, 161–72; Palamountain, *Politics of Distribution*, 15, 93, 104–5, 192–95, 245–46; Grether, *Price Control*, 386–87; Cover et al., *Small Business*, 163–64; Herbert F. Taggart, *Minimum Prices under the NRA* (Ann Arbor: U. of Mich. Press, 1936), 140–50; CIA, *The National Recovery Administration* (House Doc. 158, 75 Cong., 1 Sess., 1937), 152–56; Senate Finance Committee, *Investigation of the National Recovery Administration* (74 Cong., 1 Sess., 1935), 1353, 1801–6, 1825–33, 1881–91; Kenneth Dameron, in *Journal of Business*, Jan. 1935, p. 8; M. M. Zimmerman and F. R. Grant, in *Nation's Business*, March 1937, pp. 20–22, 96–98; Frederic B. Northrup, "NRA Code History 182" (Retail Food and Grocery), 99–103, 109–16; R. C. Rogers et al., "NRA Code History 60" (Retail Trade), 186–87; R. C. Rogers, "NRA Code History 60A" (Booksellers' Trade), 137, all in CHF, NRA Records.

buying advantages of large-scale units. Small merchants, they felt, "should be able to buy . . . at prices as low as the largest buyer." Politically speaking, moreover, it seemed that now was the time to strike. The Federal Trade Commission, after completing a six-year study of the chain store system, had recommended action to deal with "unfair" and "unjust" discrimination. Congressmen like Carl Mapes, George Huddleston, and John Bankhead had introduced bills based upon these recommendations. And a special committee was investigating the American Retail Federation, a lobbying organization dominated by the chain stores and mail order houses. The Federation, so the independents claimed, was "a diabolically clever scheme . . . to promote the growth of great retail monopolies." Further, Wright Patman of Texas, as chairman of the investigating committee and chief spokesman for the small merchants, had been using the hearings to dramatize the whole chain store issue.[3]

[3] Palamountain, *Politics of Distribution*, 172–73, 188–89, 195–200, 208–9; Godfrey M. Lebhar, *Chain Stores in America, 1859–1959* (N.Y.: Chain Store Publishing Corp., 1959), 182–229; John P. Nichols, *The Chain Store Tells Its Story* (N.Y.: Institute of Distribution, 1940), 157–59; Corwin D. Edwards, *The Price Discrimination Law* (Washington: Brookings, 1959), 21; *Congressional Record*, 74 Cong., 1 Sess., LXXIX, 1202, 1292, 3354–55, 3419, 6338, 8646–47; FTC, *Final Report on Chain Store Investigation*, 1, 96–97; House Judiciary Committee, *To Amend the Clayton Act* (74 Cong., 1 Sess., 1935), 2–3, 91–92; Special House Committee, *Investigation of the Lobbying Activities of the American Retail Federation* (74 Cong., 1 Sess., 1935), 46–58, 123–28, 430–38, 465–71; Charles D. Evans, in *Virginia Law Review*, Dec. 1936, pp. 140–42; Frank P. Stockbridge, in *Today*, Nov. 7, 1936, pp. 6–7; *N.A.R.D. Journal*, March 21, 1935, pp. 328, 330; April 4, 1935, p. 382; May 2, 1935, pp. 497, 500–1, 505–6; *Business Week*, Dec. 14, 1935, p. 16. It should be noted here that the Clayton Act already contained provisions banning certain types of price discrimination; yet there were numerous qualifications that allowed price differences when they did not substantially lessen competition, when they were made "on account of differences in grade, quality, or quantity," when they made only "due allowances" for differences in selling or transportation costs, or when they were made "in good faith to meet competition." The goal of the independents, generally speaking, was the elimination of most of these qualifications.

Consequently, the independent merchant associations looked to Patman as the logical sponsor of anti-chain legislation. H. B. Teegarden, counsel for the United States Wholesale Grocers' Association, drafted a suitable bill, one that would empower the FTC to control quantity discounts, brokerage payments, and advertising allowances. Patman agreed to sponsor it. By late June 1935 rumors were circulating that politically it was a "sure bet," that it reflected both the widespread resentment against chain stores and the general disappointment among retail groups over the death of the NRA. On June 26 Senator Joseph Robinson, the majority leader himself, introduced the bill in the Senate. Patman, though, was never able to win the support of the Administration; accordingly, passage of the Robinson-Patman Act did not come without a stiff fight and intense lobbying, which in turn produced such phenomena as congressional contact committees, anti-chain movies, and giant "National Independents' Day" rallies.

By early 1936 a bitter, three-cornered struggle had developed. In one corner were the small independents, striving to eliminate the buying advantages of large units and preserve traditional channels of trade. The chain stores, they insisted, were undesirable, monopolistic, alien institutions, organizations that deceived their customers, sapped community life, and crushed the little merchant, who, after all, was the mainstay of economic democracy. In the second corner were the mass distributors, trying to maintain the status quo and therefore stressing such things as economic efficiency, consumer service, and laissez-faire. If passed, they argued, the Patman bill would constitute a "drastic and dangerous interference with business," one that would do an "incalculable" amount of damage, since the danger of monopoly from large-scale retail enterprise was negligible when compared to the "huge, continuous, and futile cost of retail operation on a wastefully and incompetently small scale." In the third corner were the manufacturers and raw materials producers, advocating restrictions on chain buying power, but opposed to anything that might limit their own freedom of action. Finally, added to this conflict, was the reluctance of the legislators to break too sharply with the antitrust tradition, a reluctance that was strong enough to force the bill's sponsors to make a number of concessions to the competitive ideal.[4]

In the Senate, where the conflicting claims had produced a good deal of confusion about the bill's objectives, there was a general willingness to add any and all proposed amendments and leave the final content to the conference committee. As a result, a number of amendments were adopted, some tightening up enforcement procedures and facilitating proof of illegal price discrimination, some exempting such items as mineral products, imports, and semi-manufactured goods, and one simply adding a more moderate price discrimination bill backed by Senators William Borah and Frederick Van Nuys. In the House the power of the independents was stronger, but not strong enough to ward off two major concessions, one striking out an anti-basing point provision, the other eliminating a

[4] Palamountain, *Politics of Distribution*, 42, 89, 159, 169–71, 189, 196–97, 200–4, 208–22, 233; Paul Cherington and Wheeler Sammons, in Benjamin Werne, ed., *Business and the Robinson-Patman Law* (N.Y.: Oxford U. Press, 1938), 34–37, 102–6, 109–10; Wright Patman, *The Robinson-Patman Act* (N.Y.: Ronald, 1938), 367–70, 386–90; Nichols, *Chain Store*, 159–60; Edwards, *Price Discrimination Law*, 21–26; House Judiciary Committee, *To Amend the Clayton Act* (1935), 1–2, 9, 42; (1936), 391–98, 431–32; and *House Report* 2287 (74 Cong., 2 Sess., 1936), Pt. 2, pp. 1–10; Senate Judiciary Committee, *Price Discrimination* (74 Cong., 2 Sess., 1936), 2–14, 21; *Congressional Record*, 74 Cong., 1 Sess., LXXIX, 9081, 10129; Evans, in *Virginia Law Review*, Dec. 1936, p. 145; Stockbridge, in *Today*, Nov. 7, 1936, pp. 24–25, 27; *New York Times*, Feb. 23, 27, March 5, 22, 1936; *Business Week*, Jan. 25, 1936, p. 11; March 7, 1936, p. 9; March 21, 1936, pp. 9–10; April 18, 1936, p. 20; May 16, 1936, p. 52; *N.A.R.D. Journal*, Oct. 17, 1935, pp. 1278–79; March 5, 1936, pp. 270–71; March 19, 1936, pp. 350–51; J. A. O. Preus to FDR, March 4, 1936; Wright Patman, "Critics of Robinson-Patman Bill Answered," March 7, 1936; Patman to FDR, Nov. 11, 1935; Patman to Marvin McIntyre, Nov. 30, 1935; McIntyre to FDR, Dec. 13, 1935, all in Roosevelt Papers (OF 2175, 288).

customer classification clause. The conference committee, moreover, made little effort to work out a consistent and logical compromise. It merely combined the House and Senate bills and passed the task of reconciling and interpreting them on to the Federal Trade Commission. Yet it did provide one guideline of major significance. It rejected the view that the anti-price-discrimination clause would require manufacturers to spread their total distributive costs evenly over each unit of output, thus forcing mass distributors to pay for services they did not use. As a result of this interpretation, the FTC eventually adopted a view that made the act largely ineffective for the purposes intended by its original sponsors.[5]

As finally passed, in June 1936, the prohibition of price discrimination contained in the Robinson-Patman Act was hedged about with numerous qualifications. Sellers might still select their own customers, prices could be changed "in response to changing conditions," and price differentials were permissible for goods of different grade or quality, when they made "only due allowance" for differences in costs, or when quoted in good faith to meet an equally low price of a competitor. The act also contained various other provisions. It prohibited the use of brokerage commissions as discounts from selling or buying prices, forbade advertising allowances unless they were available on "proportionately equal terms" to all customers, contained the Borah-Van Nuys amendment prescribing criminal penalties for unfair discounts, geographical price discrimination, and predatory price cutting, and allowed the FTC to limit quantity discounts in cases where available quantity purchasers were "so few as to render differentials on account thereof unjustly discriminatory or promotive

[5] Palamountain, *Politics of Distribution*, 201, 204–7, 223–29; Edwards, *Price Discrimination Law*, 27–28, 34–36; *Congressional Record*, 74 Cong., 2 Sess., LXXX, 6276–87, 6346–51, 6425–36, 8139–40, 8223–42, 9413–22, 9902–4; House Judiciary Committee, *House Rept.* 2287, Pt. 2, 8–10; *Business Week*, March 7, 1936, p. 9; May 9, 1936, p. 32.

of monopoly." The sponsors of the measure hoped that it would save "thousands of small retailers," but in order to get it through, they had been forced to make numerous concessions. The result was a vague law, the actual effects of which would depend upon its administration and interpretation.[6]

III

For some independent merchants the Robinson-Patman Act might be the "greatest news of the century," but for others it was only one step toward "relief from uneconomic, predatory price competition." The druggists, in particular, believed that the act had got "somewhat off the track," that the real need was for resale price maintenance or "fair trade," an arrangement, in other words, requiring retailers to charge resale prices set by manufacturers. This, they thought, was more suitable for the drug trade, where the real enemy was the cut-rater and the department store, not the drug chains. Because of their relatively high degree of group cohesion and the extremely weak position of drug consumers, the druggists felt they could make the arrangement work. With legal backing they could apply pressure to manufacturers, force them to fix resale prices, and thus eliminate price competition, do away with loss leaders, and protect normally high retail margins.

For years, in fact, retail druggists had dreamed about fair trade laws. During the progressive period they had supported the American Fair Trade League. During the nineteen twenties they had been chiefly responsible for

[6] Edwards, *Price Discrimination Law*, 54–65; Palamountain, *Politics of Distribution*, 231–34; 49 *U.S. Statutes* 1526, Public, No. 692, 74 Cong.; Reynolds Robertson, in *Fortune*, Nov. 1936, pp. 96–97, 174; Melvin T. Copeland and Charles F. Phillips, in *Harvard Business Review*, Winter 1935, pp. 156–73; Autumn 1936, pp. 70–75; FTC, *Data on Robinson-Patman Act* (1936), 2–24; N.A.R.D. *Journal*, June 18, 1936, p. 774; *New York Times*, June 23, 1936.

nearly thirty fair trade bills. Under the NRA they had written resale price maintenance into their code. After the NRA, they concentrated on special state and federal legislation and on economic pressure designed to force manufacturers into line and get them to issue fair trade contracts. They found, too, that they could enlist considerable support from such retail groups as booksellers, tobacconists, stationers, and liquor dealers, all of whom were keenly interested in a device that would reduce price competition and prevent the use of their particular merchandise as loss leaders.

Before long the National Association of Retail Druggists had created a powerful lobby, one based on the so-called "captain plan" and complete with a "captain" in each trading area, a "colonel" in each county, a national Fair Trade Committee, and "contact committees" in every congressional district. This political pressure, moreover, was soon getting results. By the end of 1936 some fourteen states had passed "fair trade" laws, most of them modeled on the law of California and therefore containing the critical "non-signer clause," which provided that a contract with one distributor, coupled with appropriate notices to others, would establish a resale price that was legally binding on all non-contracting third parties.[7]

[7] Palamountain, *Politics of Distribution*, 84, 92–106, 235–39, 242–43; Merell et al., *Work Materials 57*, 1–2, 10–11, 383–84; Grether, *Price Control*, 18–21, 97–99, 102–5, 139–59, 239; E. R. A. Seligman and R. A. Love, *Price Cutting and Price Maintenance* (N.Y.: Harper, 1932), 29, 37–41, 479–84; Harry S. Kantor, NRA *Work Materials 16 (Resale Price Maintenance Legislation)*, 33–56; FTC, *Resale Price Maintenance*, 39–55, 64–65, 144, 266, 362, 453; Saul Nelson, in *Harper's*, Aug. 1937, p. 323; *N.A.R.D. Journal*, Aug. 1, 1935, p. 884; Feb. 6, 1936, p. 140; June 18, 1936, p. 774; *Druggists' Circular*, Jan. 1936, p. 17; July 1936, p. 15; *American Druggist*, Sept. 1936, p. 144; Sept. 1937, pp. 58, 132–33, 136–37, 140–1; *Publishers' Weekly*, June 15, 1935, p. 2283; *Business Week*, Oct. 5, 1935, pp. 10–11; Aug. 28, 1937, p. 40. The states that had passed fair trade laws by the end of 1936 were California, Illinois, Iowa, Louisiana, Maryland, New Jersey, New York, Ohio, Oregon, Pennsylvania, Rhode Island, Washington, Wisconsin, and Virginia.

For a time it appeared as though the courts might invalidate the state laws. But in December 1936 the Supreme Court upheld those of California and Illinois. In the months that followed, the fair trade forces launched a new campaign that threatened to carry all before it. Fair trade, they insisted, was really beneficial to everyone. It would help manufacturers to protect their reputations and maintain "normal" trade channels. It would protect honest retailers from predatory chiselers, would-be monopolists, and ignorant cut-raters. And it would assure consumers of quality goods, decent service, and ready access to a full line of merchandise. Most state legislators, moreover, seemed to agree. By August 1937 twenty-eight new laws were on the books, bringing the grand total of "fair trade" states to forty-two. Vetoes saved Delaware and Vermont from a similar fate, and the legislatures were not in session in Mississippi and Alabama. Only in Texas and Missouri had the opposition developed enough strength to defeat the proposed bills.[8]

By this time, the proponents of fair trade were pushing for national legislation that would exempt resale price maintenance from the Sherman Antitrust Act, relieve "fair-minded" manufacturers from the risk of federal prosecution, and make it unnecessary for resale price fixers to employ such dodges as domesticating in each state, selling on consignment, or relying on omnibus contracts between wholesalers and retailers. In 1935 Herbert Levy, counsel for the National Association of Retail Druggists, had

[8] Grether, *Price Control*, 22–24; FTC, *Resale Price Maintenance*, XXVII–XXVIII, 52, 65; Palamountain, *Politics of Distribution*, 244–45; House Judiciary Committee, *Resale Price Maintenance* (75 Cong., 1 Sess., 1937), 10–20, 66–69; WPA, *State Price Control Legislation* (1940); *Old Dearborn Distributing Co. v. Seagram Distillers Corp.*, 299 U.S. 183; *Business Week*, Dec. 12, 1936, pp. 13–14; Aug. 28, 1937, pp. 41–43; *N.A.R.D. Journal*, Jan. 7, 1937, p. 36; May 6, 1937, p. 720; June 17, 1937, p. 920; *American Druggist*, Sept. 1937, pp. 136–37, 140–41. Mississippi passed a fair trade law in 1938, Alabama in 1939, and Delaware in 1941. Texas, Missouri, Vermont, and the District of Columbia never had fair trade statutes.

drafted an appropriate bill. Levy's old law partner, Senator Millard Tydings of Maryland, had been persuaded to sponsor it, and even though the House had failed to act in 1936, the druggists expected the measure to pass with relative ease in 1937. Opposition was growing, particularly from mail-order houses, department stores, and farm and consumer groups, but the fair trade forces were stressing the idea that the Tydings bill was merely an enabling act, one that would allow the states to determine their own policy, and most congressmen seemed to agree.[9]

Then, in what the druggists regarded as a "bolt from the blue," the Administration stepped into the picture. In the Treasury Department, both Secretary Morgenthau and Herman Oliphant, the general counsel, were afraid that the bill would raise prices and put an end to the case that the FTC was bringing against the leading whiskey makers. In April 1937 Morgenthau called these matters to the President's attention. After Roosevelt had received a similar opinion from the FTC and similar protests from the Departments of Agriculture, Labor, and Justice, he decided to intervene. The "present hazard of undue advances in prices," he said, made it "most untimely" to legalize any marketing practice that might produce a further increase in the cost of living.

The druggists, however, felt that the White House had been "badly advised." Consequently, they redoubled their lobbying efforts and began looking for a new opening. Their chance came on July 2, when a Senate committee began considering a routine tax bill for the District of Co-

[9] FTC, *Resale Price Maintenance*, 59–62; Palamountain, *Politics of Distribution*, 237–41, 248; House Judiciary Committee, *House Report 382* (75 Cong., 1 Sess., 1937), 3; Senate Judiciary Committee, *Resale Price Maintenance* (75 Cong., 1 Sess., 1937), 14–30, 44; *Congressional Record*, 74 Cong., 2 Sess., LXXX, 1007, 8433, 8622; 75 Cong., 1 Sess., LXXXI, 34, 66; *N.A.R.D. Journal*, Sept. 5, 1935, pp. 1032, 1035; Nov. 7, 1935, pp. 1342–43; April 1, 1937, pp. 504–5; *American Druggist*, Nov. 1935, pp. 20–21; Jan. 1936, p. 29; March 1937, p. 45; *Druggists' Circular*, June 1935, p. 17; Nov. 1935, p. 11; Feb. 1936, p. 24; Feb. 1937, pp. 32–33.

lumbia and Senator Tydings succeeded in adding his "fair trade" measure as a committee amendment. Wright Patman then suggested that an amendment might be worked out to meet the Administration's objections; Roosevelt told him to see Attorney-General Homer Cummings. On July 10, Tydings emerged from a series of conferences with an amendment prohibiting horizontal price-fixing agreements and with a statement that the Administration was no longer opposed. The Senate then passed the bill, rider and all, the conference committee accepted it, and on August 6 the measure went to the White House.

There, for nine long days, the bill lay on the President's desk, while Administration leaders like Homer Cummings, M. L. Wilson, and Herman Oliphant continued to criticize it. Finally, however, after he had strongly condemned the "vicious practice" of attaching unrelated riders to tax bills, the President added his signature, and the measure became the Miller-Tydings Act of 1937. In its final form, it exempted resale price maintenance contracts from the antitrust laws, subject to three major qualifications. First, the contracts could apply only to identifiable products that were in "free and open competition" with goods of the same general class. Second, they must be legal under the law of the state in which resale took place. And third, they must not facilitate horizontal price-fixing arrangements among manufacturers, wholesalers, or retailers. The act, in spite of its concessions to the competitive ideal, represented a considerable victory for the druggists, their independent allies, and the political lobby that had made "fair trade" its number one objective.[10]

[10] FTC, *Legalization of Contracts for Minimum Resale Prices* (Senate Doc. 58, 75 Cong., 1 Sess., 1937), 1–4; and *Resale Price Maintenance*, LXII–LXIII, 3–4, 63–65; *Congressional Record*, 75 Cong., 1 Sess., LXXXI, 6871, 7487–97, 8134–43, 8166–68, 8478, 9628; FDR, *Public Papers and Addresses*, VI (N.Y.: Macmillan, 1941), 171–76, 333–34; 50 *U. S. Statutes* 673, Public, No. 314, 75 Cong., Title VIII at 693–94; *Druggists' Circular*, May 1937, pp. 28–29; Aug. 1937, p. 18; *N.A.R.D. Journal*, May 6, 1937, p. 684; June 17, 1937, pp. 921, 996; July 15, 1937, pp. 1124–25; Aug. 5,

IV

Alongside the drives for "fair trade" and restrictions on chain buying power, there were other legislative campaigns, movements that were chiefly confined to the state level, but which threatened at any moment to erupt on the national scene. One such movement, for example, was the agitation, particularly on the part of independent grocers, for reestablishing the loss limitation provisions of the NRA codes. "Fair trade," the grocers argued, was really unsuited to their problems. If one really wanted to restrain chiselers, eliminate "unfair competition," and do away with loss leader advertising, it would be much better simply to prohibit any sales below a certain defined cost.

The resulting drive for loss limitation laws, or as the grocers usually called them, "unfair practices" or "unfair sales" acts, remained largely on the state level. In 1935, California was the first state to pass such a law. Other states followed suit, and by the end of 1939 the grocer associations, with some aid from tobacconists, bakers, druggists, and filling station operators, had secured some type of loss limitation measure in a total of twenty-eight states. The goal of all these was to establish a minimum-price floor by prohibiting sales below cost, but they differed considerably in their definitions of cost and in methods of enforcement. Some states, for example, tried to define all elements of cost; others used invoice, replacement, or merchandise cost plus mark-ups of six to twelve percent. Some also relied upon civil suits for enforcement, while others

1937, p. 1177; Aug. 26, 1937, p. 1242; *Business Week*, Aug. 7, 1937, p. 17; Aug. 21, 1937, p. 16; Aug. 28, 1937, p. 17; *American Druggist*, June 1937, p. 49; Sept. 1937, pp. 40–41, 44–45, 108, 140; *New York Times*, July 10, 30, Aug. 5, 19, 1937; John H. Crider, in *Nation's Business*, Nov. 1937, p. 22; Henry Morgenthau to FDR, April 6, 1937; Ayres to FDR, April 14, 1937; FDR to Garner and Bankhead, April 24, 1937; Herman Oliphant to FDR, July 27, 1937; Patman to McIntyre, Aug. 9, 1937; M. L. Wilson to FDR, July 26, 1937, all in OF 277, Roosevelt Papers.

established special commissions or allowed the use of cost surveys to determine the cost of doing business. In nearly all of the acts, too, in order to bring them into line with state constitutions and disguise them as antimonopoly measures, the legislators found it necessary to insert clauses stating that sales below cost were illegal only when they were made with the intent and effect of destroying competition. In practice, these clauses severely limited the program's effectiveness for the purposes intended.

There were also occasional suggestions for a national loss limitation law, but generally speaking, the grocers and their allies lacked the necessary cohesion, political strength, and ideological appeals to secure such a measure. They had no high-pressure lobby comparable to that of the National Association of Retail Druggists. They were never able to overcome the tendency of antitrusters to look upon their program as price-fixing and associate it closely with the discredited NRA codes. In addition, they faced a growing conviction that a national law would be administratively and legally unworkable, particularly after it became apparent that most of the state laws were extremely difficult to administer, almost impossible to enforce, and highly disappointing in their effects. Therefore, the proposals for a national act never received serious consideration, and the movement never got beyond the state level.[11]

[11] Grether, *Price Control*, 27–42, 127–30, 159–60, 239, 355–57, 364–73; FTC, *Resale Price Maintenance*, LII–LIII, 87–91, 272–74, 852–58; Herbert F. Taggart, *The Cost Principle in Minimum Price Regulation* (Ann Arbor: U. of Mich. Press, 1938), 1–2, 4–5, 123–28, 152, 155; Merrell et al., *Work Materials 57*, 208–13; Robert Taunenbaum, *Cost under the Unfair Practices Acts* (Chicago: U. of Chicago Press, 1939), 19–24, 29–36, 42; Wenzil K. Kalva and Donald C. Beckley, *The Retailer* (N.Y.: Prentice-Hall, 1950), 325–26; Palamountain, *Politics of Distribution*, 84–85; Burton A. Zorn and George J. Feldman, *Business under the New Price Laws* (N.Y.: Prentice-Hall, 1937), 317–18, 321–26, 423–33; House Judiciary Committee, *To Amend the Clayton Act* (74 Cong., 2 Sess., 1936), 83–89, 145, 225–27; WPA, *State Price Control Legislation*, L–LVI (also contains texts of all state unfair practices acts);

A second and simultaneous movement that was also confined largely to the state level was the one agitating for anti-chain taxes, for special levies that would either drive the chain stores out of existence or reduce their competitive advantages. Here again, the appeal was primarily to antimonopoly sentiment, with the chains cast in the role of "big business" and with their managers depicted as agents of "Wall Street," as cogs in an evil, monopolistic conspiracy that was responsible for impoverishing local communities, depressing farm prices, cheating consumers, destroying small business, and turning a society of independent proprietors into a "nation of clerks." For although the movement had no well-organized lobby behind it, it did enjoy the support of numerous political agitators, of small business champions like Wright Patman, popular demagogues like Huey Long, and colorful rogues like W. K. (Old Man) Henderson who used his radio station to appeal for twelve-dollar memberships in the "Merchant Minute Men" and to offer the public a chance to aid the cause by buying coffee at a dollar a pound, when it was retailing for half that price.

The first flurry of state anti-chain taxes had come during the period from 1927 to 1933, particularly after the onset of the depression. Then, with the passage of the National Industrial Recovery Act, the movement had temporarily subsided, only to emerge again in the post-Schecter era. During the years 1935 to 1939, twenty-four new acts were passed, and although the courts invalidated some of these, the majority remained in force. By the end of 1939 some nineteen states were still taxing the chains, most of them through graduated license laws, under which the tax increased in direct proportion to the number of stores in a

N.A.R.D. *Journal*, April 15, 1937, p. 597; *American Druggist*, June 1936, pp. 44–45; *Newsweek*, May 22, 1939, p. 44; Lorenzo A. McHenry, in *Journal of Marketing*, Oct. 1937, pp. 126–28; *Business Week*, May 7, 1938, pp. 25–26; April 29, 1939, p. 39.

chain. Indiana, for example, levied a tax beginning at three dollars a year on the first store and increasing by graduated steps to 150 dollars on all stores over twenty. A few states also levied graduated gross sales taxes, under which the percentage of taxation increased in proportion to the magnitude of gross sales. Still others experimented with more drastic provisions. Louisiana, for example, levied a tax based upon the total number of stores in the chain, regardless of whether the stores were located within the state. Tennessee levied one based upon the amount of floor space occupied by all stores in a chain. In general, though, the state taxes were far from excessive, and the chains found that such moderate burdens were relatively easy to evade, pass on, or absorb.[12]

The first serious proposal for a national tax came in early 1938, when Wright Patman and some seventy-two cosponsors introduced a measure calling for a special levy that would range from fifty dollars per store for chains of ten to fifteen units up to one thousand dollars per store for those containing over five hundred units and that would then be multiplied by the number of states in which the chain operated. Chains with outlets in all states and the District of Columbia, for example, would pay $49,000 per store for all units over five hundred. At no time, however, did the Patman bill ever stand much chance of passage. By the time it was introduced, the chains had

[12] Theodore N. Beckman and H. C. Nolen, *The Chain Store Problem* (N.Y.: McGraw-Hill, 1938), 228–39, 244, 247–57, 333–35; Palamountain, *Politics of Distribution*, 161–68, 184–87; FTC, *Chain Stores* (1934), 78–80, 108–10; Maurice W. Lee, *Anti-Chain-Store Tax Legislation* (Chicago: U. of Chicago Press, 1939), 5–21; Nichols, *Chain Store Story*, 130–50, 178–79; Lebhar, *Chain Stores*, 121–64; Charles F. Phillips, in *Harvard Business Review*, Spring 1936, pp. 350–59; Frederick K. Hardy, "The Special Taxation of Chain Stores," Ph.D. Dissertation, U. of Wis. (1934), 95, 101–4, 109–12, 120–21, 176. The states having anti-chain tax laws in December 1939 included Alabama, Colorado, Florida, Georgia, Idaho, Indiana, Iowa, Louisiana, Maryland, Michigan, Minnesota, Mississippi, Montana, North Carolina, South Dakota, South Carolina, Tennessee, Texas, and West Virginia.

launched an organized counteroffensive. Through the use of special food promotion campaigns, collective bargaining agreements, more attention to public relations, and more emphasis on consumer and community welfare, they were convincing large numbers of farmers, laborers, businessmen, and public officials that anti-chain taxes were not in the public interest. Such prominent New Dealers as Henry Wallace and Harry Hopkins attacked the Patman bill publicly, and since its supporters were unable to develop an effective lobby, the majority of congressmen remained aloof. Here the size-efficiency dilemma was revealed in bold relief. Confronted with it, most Americans would eventually choose economic efficiency over littleness per se.[13]

V

There were other legislative campaigns as well, other attempts by small businessmen to enlist the power of the state and use it to solve the problems of some particular trade or alleviate conditions in a particularly depressed area. In the service trades, there was considerable agitation for government action to stabilize prices, eliminate cutthroat competition, and reduce the pressure from thousands of new establishments set up by the unemployed. The NRA service codes, however, with their ambitious schemes of price control, had proved to be dismal failures.

[13] Palamountain, *Politics of Distribution,* 163, 173–81; Lee, *Anti-Chain-Store Tax Legislation,* 24–25, 65; Nichols, *Chain Store Story,* 163–65, 169, 173–83; Carl Byoir et al., *Current Trends in Chain Store Taxation* (1939), 3–6; Lebhar, *Chain Stores,* 232–83, 303–4; *Business Week,* Dec. 26, 1936, pp. 21–22; Feb. 5, 1938, pp. 17–18; Helen Woodward, in *Nation,* Dec. 11, 1937, pp. 638–40; *American Druggist,* March 1938, p. 56; *Newsweek,* Sept. 5, 1938, p. 40; *Congressional Record,* 75 Cong., 3 Sess., LXXXIII, 1921; Appendix, 598–99; House Ways and Means Committee, *A Bill Providing for an Excise Tax on Retail Stores* (76 Cong., 3 Sess. 1940), 681, 775, 793, 874, 966, 1060, 1078, 1105, 1114, 1121, 1127, 1345, 1362, 2255–57; Patman to FDR, Nov. 25, 1938, OF 288, Roosevelt Papers.

Consequently, in the post-NRA period, legislation for the service trades was limited largely to the state and city levels, where a wide variety of laws appeared. The states of Alabama, California, Iowa, and Minnesota authorized cities to approve local codes when a specified percentage of the trade was willing. A number of other states enacted minimum price laws for the barbering, beauty parlor, laundering, and dry cleaning trades. In Wisconsin a "little NRA" law allowed the governor to approve codes of fair competition, containing both labor and trade practice provisions and providing for schedules of minimum prices in the cleaning and dyeing, barber, beauty parlor, shoe repair, and bowling trades. Frequently, these measures worked badly, but their sponsors continued to hope that some type of guild regulation or publicly sponsored cartelization would solve their problems.[14]

Still another group with similar problems was the automobile dealers, who were suffering particularly from the exercise of vertical power on the part of the manufacturers, power that forced the dealer to stock and use only factory parts, to finance his sales through the manufacturers' finance companies, and to promote the sale of a maximum number of cars even if this meant highly excessive allowances on trade-ins. The result was furious retail price competition through concessions on trade-ins. The solution, so many dealers felt, was to invoke the power of the state to establish and enforce maximum used-car allowances. Under the NRA, they had been able to do this. Their code had forbidden sales below a list price and had established a code "Blue Book" of maximum used-car values, some-

[14] Wilcox, *Competition and Monopoly*, 59–60, 273–77; Taggart, *Minimum Prices*, 128–33; WPA, *State Price Control Legislation*, 381–82, 473–94; Grether, *Price Control*, 77, 398–400; Wisconsin Trade Practices Commission, *Report* (1937), 4–6; *Wisconsin Code Law for Certain Service Trades*, I (1939), 5, 9, 12; and *Reasonable Cost Schedules* (1936); *Monthly Labor Review*, March 1936, pp. 628–31; William F. Brown and Ralph Cassady, Jr., in *QJE*, Feb. 1947, pp. 312–25, 335–38.

thing they were naturally reluctant to give up. For a time, following the Schecter decision, they hoped to salvage the code through a trade practice conference agreement, but in the end the FTC turned down most of the proposed rules. And since private adherence to the "Used Car Guide" was difficult to enforce and vulnerable to antitrust action, the dealers were soon agitating for new legal sanctions.

At first most of the agitation was on the state level. And state after state did respond with "financial responsibility" laws, measures that required automobile dealers to obtain licenses, demonstrate that they possessed adequate financial resources, and refrain from using "unfair trade practices," a term that was often construed to cover "excessive" trade-in allowances. Such measures often appeared in the guise of consumers' legislation, but consumers had virtually nothing to do with their promotion, and a number of them were obviously designed to eliminate competition. As Louis Milan, secretary of the Wisconsin dealers' association, boasted in 1938, the plan adopted there had already greatly reduced "overallowances" and eliminated "760 competitors."

State regulation, however, was still insufficient, and once again the dealers turned to the federal government. In 1937 Gardiner Witherow of Wisconsin and Sherman Minton of Iowa sponsored a resolution calling for an FTC investigation of automobile manufacturers, and the sentiments expressed at the resulting hearings left little doubt that the dealers expected this investigation to lead to federal legislation on their behalf. These expectations, though, were never realized. The FTC's report proved to be much more critical of the dealers than of the manufacturers. This, when combined with the refusal of unorganized dealers to go along, the opposition of automobile manufacturers, and the fact that consumers tended to be highly price conscious when buying a car, meant that Wright Patman's proposed "Motor Vehicle Act" never stood much of a chance. The manufacturers, to be sure, did make some limited concessions, but the general problem of manufacturer-dealer relations remained an unsolved one that became the center of other monopoly inquiries in the post-World War II years.[15]

VI

On the national level, the Robinson-Patman and Miller-Tydings acts were all that small merchants were able to secure. Because their passage required numerous concessions, both to other economic groups and to the competitive ideal, the two laws were not very effective for the purposes intended. It was difficult, after all, to disguise a measure as an antimonopoly statute and then use it to eliminate competition and arrest technological change.

In the case of the Robinson-Patman Act, for example, the original proposal was diluted by the inclusion of the "good faith" competition clause, the broader interpretation of "due allowance" for cost savings, and the Borah-

[15] Palamountain, *Politics of Distribution*, 108–28, 130–42, 158; FTC, *Report on the Motor Vehicle Industry* (House Doc. 468, 76 Cong., 1 Sess., 1940), 151–72, 176–80, 213–49, 260–87, 367–406, 415, 1074–76; Albert Abrahamson, *The Price of Automobiles* (NRA Consumers' Report 5, 1934), 60–66; Grether, *Price Control*, 171; Wilcox, *Competition and Monopoly*, 277; WPA, *State Price Control Legislation*, 202–3; Wisconsin State Banking Commission, *Law Relating to the Licensing of Motor Vehicle Dealers* (1937); *Congressional Record*, 75 Cong., 1 Sess., LXXXI, 5114, 5744–46; 75 Cong., 2 Sess., LXXXII, 721; House Commerce Committee, *Hearings on H. J. Res. 389* (75 Cong., 2 Sess., 1938), 3–10, 82–83; Senate Commerce Committee, *Automobile Marketing Practices* (84 Cong., 2 Sess., 1956), 2–6, 170–75; Neil M. Clark, in *Saturday Evening Post*, July 30, 1938, pp. 23, 33–35, 39; Ruth Brindze, in *Nation*, April 27, 1940, pp. 539–40; *Business Week*, Nov. 9, 1935, p. 10; May 23, 1936, p. 31; Feb. 6, 1937, p. 42; July 24, 1937, p. 44; Jan. 1, 1938, pp. 22, 27–28; Oct. 1938, pp. 34–35; Jan. 20, 1940, pp. 15–16; March 16, 1940, p. 30; *Time*, May 9, 1938, pp. 55–56, 58; *Fortune*, June 1938, pp. 39–41, 114, 116; C. H. Barber, "NRA Code History 46" (Motor Vehicle Retailing), 20, Enclosure B; Harley Barton to FDR, Jan. 5, 1937, both in NRA Records (CHF, CIC File).

Van Nuys amendment, all concessions that enabled the FTC and the courts to adopt a "rule of reason," allow price discrimination if the practice was used by the seller's competitors, and stress an interpretation under which the act might really be used to strengthen competition rather than protect small competitors. In practice, too, the act had something of a boomerang effect. It forced manufacturers and wholesalers to re-examine their discount structures, something that led many of them to realize that prices charged for small orders were insufficient to cover the costs of handling them. The restrictions on brokerage payments and advertising allowances seemed to do more harm to voluntaries, cooperative groups, and food brokers than they did to corporate chains. The latter were usually able to offset the effects of such provisions by promoting their own brands, producing their own goods, purchasing the entire output of small producers, or securing other types of concessions.[16]

"Fair trade" also proved disappointing to many retailers, particularly to independent grocers and other trades where group solidarity was lacking and entry was relatively easy. Actually, it was only in the drug, liquor, and book trades that resale price maintenance did much to raise prices and enhance profit margins. And even in these areas it was far from an unqualified success. Manufacturers were reluctant either to raise prices or reduce their own profit margins. Department stores evaded the law by establishing "book clubs" and promoting private brands. Some wholesalers, to the dismay of the independents, persuaded manufacturers to sign contracts forbidding them to grant retailers

[16] Palamountain, *Politics of Distribution*, 228–34; Edwin George, Wheeler Sammons, and Blackwell Smith, in Werne, ed., *Robinson-Patman Law*, 90–98, 100–1, 106–8, 236–48; FTC, *Robinson-Patman Act* (1942), 40–48; Zorn and Feldman, *New Price Laws*, ix–xii, 19–26; Edwards, *Price Discrimination Law*, 111–13, 130, 151–52, 321–23, 619–33; Blackwell Smith and Joseph H. McConnell, in *Dun's Review*, Jan. 1938, pp. 7–13, 45–48; Edwin George, *ibid.*, March 1937, pp. 11–15; John H. Crider, in *Nation's Business*, Aug. 1937, pp. 38, 114–17; *New York Times*, June 13, 1937.

the customer discounts. The promise of known price levels and guaranteed margins attracted new proprietors and worsened the problem of overcapacity. Under the circumstances, contracts guaranteeing "full" or "normal" retail margins were rare. Later, when the druggists tried to set up a national organization to force manufacturers into line, their plans collapsed in the face of internal conflicts, the threat of federal prosecution, and growing public disillusionment with the "fair trade" laws.

On balance, then, the Robinson-Patman and Miller-Tydings acts were largely ineffective for the purposes intended by their sponsors. Yet insofar as they had any effect at all, it was certainly not in the direction of stimulating economic expansion and adding to consumer purchasing power. On the contrary, like most of the other attempts at counterorganization and partial planning, they tended to restrict production, prevent change, hold up prices, and bilk the consumer. If, as John Galbraith argued later, the chain stores were really the American counterparts of European cooperatives, then a real policy of counterorganization should have encouraged chain buying power. Instead of attacking the mass distributors, penalizing efficiency, and encouraging an anti-consumer alliance between manufacturers and small merchants, it should have been promoting chain growth, encouraging small merchants to join voluntaries or cooperative buying groups, and making every effort to develop organizations that could offset the power of manufacturers, reduce the costs of distribution, and pass the economies along to consumers.

From a political standpoint, however, such a policy was impossible. The chains, unlike the small merchants, lacked the necessary political strength and political symbols. Consequently, counterorganization in the distributive trades as elsewhere followed a political pattern that was essentially restrictive in nature. Something else would have to be found to stimulate expansion and bring recovery.[17]

[17] FTC, *Resale Price Maintenance*, XXIX, 145–49, 210–11, 226–28, 233–34, 333–34, 703–4; Grether, *Price Control*, 101–5, 118–23, 149–51, 162–65, 254–55, 300–7, 321, 334, 347–52; Cover et al., *Small Business*, 192–96, 199–203; Conference Board Economic Forum, *The Fair Trade Question* (1955), 11–13; Edgar H. Gault, *Fair Trade* (Ann Arbor: U. of Mich. Press, 1939), 41–46; Palamountain, *Politics of Distribution*, 249–52; John K. Galbraith, *American Capitalism* (Boston: Houghton Mifflin, 1962 ed.), 117–22, 126–28, 141–44; Ralph Cassady, Jr., in *QJE*, May 1939, pp. 455–64; Corwin Edwards, in *AER Supplement*, March 1940, pp. 113–14; Reinhold Wolff and Duncan Holthausen, in *Dun's Review*, July 1938, p. 47; Marvin Frankel, in *Journal of Business*, July 1955, pp. 193–94; *Business Week*, Sept. 4, 1937, pp. 14–15; *Publishers' Weekly*, Jan. 21, 1939, pp. 188–90; Dept. of Justice, "Operation of Resale Price Maintenance Laws," 1–2, 15–17, Special Studies File, TNEC Records.

CHAPTER 14. NEW DEAL
ECONOMIC PLANNING
IN RETROSPECT

As one considers the economic legislation of the post-NRA period, he is forced to conclude that most New Deal planning was in the nature of government-sponsored cartelization. It came at the behest of organized economic groups intent upon strengthening their market positions through legal sanctions or government supports. It came, moreover, in a disjointed, almost haphazard manner, in response to specific pressures, problems, and needs, and without benefit of any preconceived plan or integrating theory. And its purpose, although this was often disguised as something else, was to help individual industries or particularistic pressure groups to promote scarcity and thus balance their output with demand, regardless of the dislocations that such action might bring in other areas of the economy. This was true, noted Ernest Griffith, of most of the NRA codes and of "almost the whole of our agricultural output limitation . . . and marketing agreements, our various tariff acts, the Robinson-Patman Act, the Miller-Tydings Act, the Walsh-Healey Act, the Guffey Coal Act," and "most of our wage and hour . . . legislation." Such measures might be justified on "other and more general grounds," but the "genesis of all of them was in group utilitarianism," and their combined effect ran directly counter to the over-all expansion that planning should produce.[1]

From a political, ideological, or practical standpoint, however, over-all or centralized planning was not a realistic alternative, especially after the NRA experience and the resurgence of antitrust sentiment. An approach like that proposed by Mordecai Ezekiel and backed by the

[1] Ernest S. Griffith, *The Impasse of Democracy* (N.Y.: Harrison-Hilton, 1939), 230–31; and in *Plan Age*, April 1939, pp. 98–99.

American Commonwealth Federation seemed too complicated, too gimmicky, too visionary, too alien to American traditions. As a practical matter, it seemed unworkable, a virtual impossibility in view of the lack of pertinent data, trained personnel, and suitable administrative procedures. Ideologically, it failed to make the necessary concessions to inherited ideals, to the antitrust tradition, the aversion to big government, the fear of socialism, and the objections on constitutional and legal grounds. Politically, it lacked support from the organized economic groups that shaped legislative action, groups that were now suspicious of each other, wary of cooperative schemes, determined to maintain their power and prerogatives, and bent upon winning immediate, short-run gains for themselves. Influenced by the depression psychology, such groups almost necessarily worked for restrictive cartelization rather than planned expansion, particularly since the latter would involve major shifts in the economic power structure.

An open, avowed, and generalized policy of cartelization, though, was just as unrealistic as a policy of planned expansion. In the political climate of 1935, with its rising agitation against "big business," the widening rift between business and government, and the growing radicalism of public and congressional opinion, any proposal for repealing the antitrust laws on a permanent basis or for the economy as a whole was unlikely to attract much support. A program like the one advocated by Benjamin Javits, or even the one proposed by Donald Richberg, was immediately vulnerable to charges of "monopoly." In the eyes of farmers, laborers, antitrusters, and liberal politicians, such an approach would amount to turning the economy over to big business. Even in business circles, it no longer had much support. The majority of business leaders had concluded that government-supported market controls were no longer necessary, particularly since private controls were again in working order and since the support would have to come from an unfriendly government, one that was likely to insist upon burdensome restrictions, limitations on the prerogatives of management, and unwarranted concessions to non-business groups.

II

Under the circumstances, planning was possible only in special areas, on a partial, group-by-group basis, and only when the right combination of factors was present. First of all, there had to be a strong desire for government support on the part of the group concerned, a desire strong enough to override internal divisions and make the group willing to pay the necessary political price. For business groups this usually meant benefits for labor and the acceptance of at least a modicum of public regulation or supervision; consequently, the industries willing to pay the price were generally those that were suffering acutely from technological changes or those that were atomistic in structure, lacking in market power, and unable to develop private controls. Secondly, there had to be an organization capable of exerting political pressure, one that could articulate the group's program, line up political support, and administer political rewards and penalties. Finally, there had to be a covering rationale, an ideological appeal that would make the group a special case, identify its interest with the national or public interest, and justify a departure from competitive standards. Planning, if it was to be done at all, had to be disguised and undertaken not as a means to enhance the group's market power, but rather as a way to promote conservation, save the "little fellow," protect the public from "natural monopolies," provide for the national defense, attain social justice, or preserve a socially valuable "way of life."

Two areas that possessed the necessary characteristics and in which partial and limited planning was possible were those of agriculture and labor. In agriculture the inability of farmers to develop their own private controls had produced a strong demand for government support. This demand had stimulated the development of powerful political organizations. And these organizations could take advantage of potent ideological symbols, of a rationale that stressed the physiocratic legend, the myth of the yeoman farmer, the ideal of soil conservation, and the vision of social justice embodied in the concept of parity. Consequently, once the Supreme Court had withdrawn its constitutional objections, the farmers were able to secure an extensive program of government aid, one that included production controls, price supports, marketing quotas, surplus removal, conservation payments, and a variety of other special subsidies. In the labor field, too, there was a similar development. Again there was a strong desire for government support. This was coupled with the development of an increasingly powerful political organization that could appeal to potent political symbols, to the image of the downtrodden worker, the ideal of social justice, and the vision of economic balance. The result was a broad program of government support, one that fostered unionization and collective bargaining, established minimum labor standards, absorbed surplus labor, and attempted to protect workers from some of the hazards of an industrial way of life.

There were also industrial groups, particularly in the natural resource and transportation fields, who wanted government support, were willing to pay for it, and were able to secure it by putting together the right combination of political pressure and ideological appeals. In the bituminous coal industry, the operators and miners were able to achieve a semblance of unity, to apply the necessary political pressure, and to make a strong case for market controls on the grounds of conservation, labor stability, and the rehabilitation of a "sick" industry. As a result, they did win government support for price-fixing and marketing agreements. If the operators could only have agreed among themselves, they might have secured production controls as well. In the oil industry, too, a powerful lobby appealing primarily to the conservation angle was able to secure the type of controls it wanted, to enlist federal support in limiting imports, estimating market demand, controlling the flow of "hot oil," and enforcing state proration laws. Finally, in the transportation industries, similar programs appeared, programs that blended public utility regulation with government-supported market controls and generous subsidies, especially for the railroads, shipping companies, and airlines, and programs that again were the products of political pressure and ideological appeals, of a combination of powerful and well-developed lobbies, public concern over railroad finances, appeals to past precedents, skillful emphasis on such things as national defense and public safety, and a general willingness to treat transportation as a "natural monopoly."

In the distributive trades, the pattern was somewhat different. Here, too, there was the desire for government support, coupled with political pressure and appeals to alternative ideals. There were, for example, the claims of the druggists that they were professional "men in white," the claims of the booksellers that they were the transmitters of the cultural heritage, and the claims of all independent merchants that they were the "backbone" of the nation, that they stood for community progress and community pride and were therefore worthy of preservation.[2] Yet none of these symbols was really strong enough to justify a program of outright cartelization. Consequently, the measures passed had to be put through in the guise of restoring competition. Littleness became synonymous with free enterprise; chain stores were equated with "monopoly"; and the preservation of competition was confused with the preservation of small competitors. The result, paradoxically, was an anticompetitive program that was made pos-

---

[2] See, for example, the appeals in *Druggists' Circular*, Aug. 1935, p. 15; Wisconsin Trade Practices Commission, *Report* (1937), 38; and R. C. Rogers, "NRA Code History 60A" (Booksellers' Trade), 79–80, CHF, NRA Records.

sible by the use of competitive symbols, a program of market controls that was presented to the public under such favorable symbols as "fair trade." Rather than justify a departure from competitive values, distributive groups claimed they had never abandoned them.

Such an approach, however, had its weak points as well as its strong ones. It often necessitated some real concessions to competitive values; and since the resulting laws were usually couched in the language of the competitive model, they were often administered in ways that their sponsors had never intended. The good-faith competition clause and other concessions, for example, lessened the intended impact of the Robinson-Patman Act. The fair trade laws and anti-chain taxes were weakened by the necessity of disguising them an antimonopoly statutes. The anticompetitive objectives of automobile dealers were frustrated by the reliance of the Federal Trade Commission on competitive values. Generally, the supports granted to small merchants were weak to begin with, and in practice they proved to be relatively ineffective for the purposes intended.

There were also other groups who tried but failed to secure special legislation, groups who lacked the desire, the unity, the political strength, or the covering ideology that made such legislation possible. The efforts to use the government to foster consumer organization and enhance the market power of consumers were probably foredoomed to failure, since consumers in general had neither the desire nor the political organization nor the well-developed consumer ideology that would have been necessary to establish anything more than a token program. The attempts to enact federal loss limitation laws and anti-chain taxes, to set up special programs for the service trades and automobile dealers, and to pass special laws for the textile, lumber, anthracite coal, and garment industries all suffered from one or more of the same basic deficiencies. The necessary lobbies or symbols were lacking, or conditions were such that substantial factions within the industrial groups involved were opposed to government-supported controls or were unwilling to accept the labor provisions and public safeguards that would have been required to get such measures through.

III

It was extremely difficult to discern any over-all pattern or integrating theme in the politically-inspired partial planning of the post-NRA period. Yet insofar as there was any common thread at all, it could probably be found in the concept of counterorganization, in the idea of using the government to promote the organization of economically weak groups so that they might hold their own against stronger rivals. Theoretically, such an approach might have been used to promote economic expansion, which after all was the crying need of the time. If the government could have selected and built up the right groups, those whose natural interests lay in a larger output, fuller employment, and low-cost, high-volume operations, if it could have distinguished between original and countervailing power and concentrated on developing the latter, and if it could have persuaded or forced the organized groups involved to follow their long-range interests, then it might have been possible to increase consumer purchasing power, build a mass market, and thus achieve the economic balance necessary for sustained growth.

In reality, though, the post-Schecter version of counterorganization and partial planning rarely stimulated much expansion, nor was its ability to do so a prime consideration in selecting the areas in which it should be applied. On the contrary, as noted before, government intervention depended upon the desire, political strength, and ideological appeals of the pressure groups involved; and since these groups were producer-oriented and imbued with a depression psychology, the end product was almost always restrictive in nature. In the farm program, for example, the emphasis was upon higher farm prices and restricted output, not upon lower costs, greater consumption, and stiffer bargaining by farm consumers. In labor union circles, the major goals were higher wages and job security, not fuller employment, cheaper goods, and maximum efficiency. In the "sick" industries and the transportation field the typical program was designed to arrest technological innovation and protect inefficiency, not to encourage economic progress or ease the transition to newer, cheaper, and more productive methods of providing the necessary goods and services. And in the distributive trades the whole legislative effort was directed against the mass distributors and aimed at protecting inefficient merchants, penalizing consumers, and preventing the development or use of countervailing power, not at reducing the costs of distribution, offsetting the market power of manufacturers, and passing the economies along to consumers.

The type of planning that was possible, then, might help to check deflationary forces and provide temporary relief to individual groups, but in the process it seemed to make over-all expansion more difficult than ever. As some of the national planners pointed out, it was creating a situation where organized economic groups were fighting furiously against each other for larger shares of an ever-shrinking pie. Unless they changed their attitudes and goals, they would condemn the nation to permanent depression.[3] The great need was for a larger product, for some arrangement or program that would stimulate growth and counteract the restrictive tendencies inherent in pressure-group planning. Since over-all planning for this purpose was politically impossible, a number of planners were now turning to the underconsumptionist and spending ideology associ-

[3] Charles Eliot, Memo. re Conference with Secretary of Agriculture, Feb. 15, 1937, Industrial Section File—CCF, NRPB Records; Henry A. Wallace, *Technology, Corporations, and the General Welfare* (Chapel Hill: U. of N.C. Press, 1937), 44–49.

ated with the British economist, John Maynard Keynes.[4] Under the circumstances, this offered an attractive alternative, one that would avoid the complications and difficulties of structural reform and yet provide a politically feasible way to stimulate expansion.

All along, in fact, the Keynesians had shown much less concern than the planners or antitrusters with the alleged evils of maldistribution and monopolistic rigidity. Oversavings, they argued, would still be possible in a capitalistic economy with a perfectly equal distribution of income. Even a perfectly competitive, frictionless system would not always have full employment. What did matter was the propensity to consume, the expectation of profits, and the attitude toward liquidity, for these factors in turn determined the level of output and hence the level of employment. The trick was not merely to balance savings with investment, as other underconsumptionists advocated, but to balance them at a full employment level, to increase both consumption and investment, which, the Keynesians held, was possible so long as equilibrium had been reached at a point of underemployment.

Accordingly, the Keynesians laid less stress upon price policy and structural reform, more upon compensatory government spending. The government, they held, should spend or withdraw enough funds so that investment was equal to savings at a full-employment level. Some of them felt that this spending program would have to be continued on a more or less permanent basis. The economy, they maintained, had now reached maturity. It had developed built-in tendencies toward economic stagnation, and for the present at least, there were no revolutionary technological changes in prospect and no new areas or markets

[4] See, for example, Caroline F. Ware and Gardiner Means, *The Modern Economy in Action* (N.Y.: Harcourt, Brace, 1936), 69–70, 113–32, 198–99; Mordecai Ezekiel to Thomas Blaisdell, April 15, 1938; Ezekiel, "Elements of a Suggested Program for Action," March 16, 1938; NRC, "Where Are We?" March 18, 1938, all in Blaisdell File, NRPB Records.

to be exploited. The rate of population growth was also slowing down. The old spirit of business enterprise was giving way to an obsession for security. In the future, it seemed that private investment opportunities would never again provide sufficient outlets for a high-savings economy. The gap would simply have to be filled with public investments.[5]

Here, then, was a simple, politically feasible, and apparently workable solution, something that the government could do quickly, with a minimum of difficulty, and with immediate practical results. Eventually, in the crisis of 1937 and 1938, a spending approach would enjoy considerable support in both the planning and antitrust camps. Among the planners there was a growing disillusionment with the effects and results of pressure-group planning, a growing realization that centrally planned expansion was simply outside the realm of political possibilities, and a growing acceptance of Keynesian analysis and Keynesian solutions, at least as the basis for temporary programs or as a supplement to planning activities. Among the antitrusters, too, there was a growing tendency to couple spending with antitrust action, which was a slow process and likely to be deflationary in its initial phases.

[5] See John M. Keynes, *The General Theory of Employment, Interest, and Money* (N.Y.: Harcourt, Brace, 1936), 27–34, 91–98, 107–31, 141–58, 166–74, 248–54, 324–32, 358–84; and in *New Republic*, Feb. 20, 1935, pp. 35–37; Seymour E. Harris, *John Maynard Keynes* (N.Y.: Scribner's, 1955), 191–96; Lawrence R. Klein, *The Keynesian Revolution* (N.Y.: Macmillan, 1947), 42, 53–83, 138, 166–77; D. Hamberg, *Business Cycles* (N.Y.: Macmillan, 1951), 135–59; Henry H. Villard, *Deficit Spending and the National Income* (N.Y.: Farrar & Rinehart, 1941), 92–113; Arthur E. Burns and Donald S. Watson, *Government Spending and Economic Expansion* (Washington: American Council on Public Affairs, 1940), 71–83; Richard V. Gilbert et al., *An Economic Program for American Democracy* (N.Y.: Vanguard, 1938), 15–23, 41–74; Alvin H. Hansen, *Full Recovery or Stagnation* (N.Y.: Norton, 1938), 286–89, 302–29; Oscar L. Altman, *Saving, Investment, and National Income* (TNEC Monograph 37, 1941), 92–106; Henry Wallace, Abstract of Conference with Keynes, May 8, 1936, PPF 1820, Roosevelt Papers.

Before considering this convergence on the spending solution, however, one should note the prior impact of the antitrust tradition, the attempts, in other words, to revitalize competitive markets and the programs and activities that this had produced prior to 1937. The heirs of Louis Brandeis and the New Freedom, after all, had never accepted the basic assumption that planning was necessary. They had their own version of the good society, their own program for attaining it, their own set of pressure groups and political symbols, and their own views as to what caused the depression and what could be done about it. The demand for planning and government-supported cartelization, in fact, had been accompanied by a simultaneous and conflicting demand for antitrust action. This demand, too, the New Deal tried to satisfy, and its attempts to do so form the subject of the next major portion of this book.

PART III

THE ANTITRUST
TRADITION

It is time to make an effort to reverse that process of the concentration of power which has made most American citizens, once traditionally independent owners of their own businesses, helplessly dependent for their daily bread upon the favor of a very few, who, by devices such as holding companies, have taken for themselves unwarranted economic power. I am against private socialism of concentrated economic power as thoroughly as I am against government socialism. The one is equally as dangerous as the other; and destruction of private socialism is utterly essential to avoid government socialism.—*Franklin D. Roosevelt*

CHAPTER 15. THE ANTITRUSTERS
AND THEIR PROGRAM

EVEN during the planning of the New Deal," wrote Hugh Johnson in 1935, "there began to appear—faintly and little considered at first—pressures, and vetoes in advice, from a group then sometimes called 'The Harvard Crowd,' but later, on account of its leader, Prof. Felix Frankfurter, irreverently yclept the 'Happy Hot Dogs.'" This group, Johnson felt, had diverted the New Deal from its original purposes, and it was still bent upon the harassment of business. Frankfurter had gradually "insinuated" his "boys" into "obscure but key positions," where they had become influential "wardens of the marches, inconspicuous but powerful."

Johnson's allusions to "sinister influences," "clever infiltration," and "collectivism" were hardly justified, but he was describing a phenomenon noted by many other observers. Over the years Felix Frankfurter had become a sort of unofficial employment agency for the government service, and since he and Roosevelt had long been friends, the President naturally turned to him for advice, particularly in the search for bright young lawyers to draft and administer reform measures. The result, almost inevitably, was a large group of officials who regarded Frankfurter as their guide and mentor. Included were many of his former students, men like David Lilienthal, Nathan Margold, Charles Wyzanski, Herbert Feis, and Benjamin Cohen, but especially prominent were his star graduates whom he had long rewarded with a year's apprenticeship as secretaries to Justices Holmes and Brandeis. Dean Acheson, James M. Landis, William Sutherland, Paul Freund, and Calvert Magruder had all served as former secretaries to Justice Brandeis, while Thomas Corcoran, Lloyd Landau, Donald Hiss, Alger Hiss, and James Rowe had served their apprenticeship with Holmes.

All of these men, of course, did not act as a unit. Yet a number of them did share a common set of attitudes and intellectual concepts. Their liberalism tended to be of the older Wilsonian-Brandeis vintage; it lacked and distrusted the overtones of planning that characterized the ideas of the original brain trust, the group of advisers drawn chiefly from Columbia University, and it looked with deep suspicion upon the idea of business rationalization so dear to the "Baruch men," the group drawn from the old War Industries Board. The gods in Frankfurter's pantheon were Holmes and Brandeis, and like Brandeis, Frankfurter believed in a world of small business, economic independence, and government action to restore and preserve free competition. He agreed, in fact, with most of Brandeis' assumptions, goals, and prescribed remedies. It was through Frankfurter and his disciples that the Brandeisian philosophy was to have its greatest impact upon the making of New Deal policy.[1]

Of particular importance was the trio of Thomas Corcoran, Benjamin Cohen, and James M. Landis. Corcoran, who, in Moley's words, became "a sort of Washington general manager for Frankfurter," operated out of an office in the Reconstruction Finance Corporation, where he had taken a job in 1932. For a time, following the change of Administrations, he had moved to the Treasury Depart-

---

[1] Harlan B. Phillips, *Felix Frankfurter Reminisces* (N.Y.: Reynal, 1960), 235–40, 247–50; Alpheus T. Mason, *Brandeis* (N.Y.: Viking, 1946), 614–21; Arthur M. Schlesinger, Jr., *The Politics of Upheaval* (Boston: Houghton Mifflin, 1960), 220, 230, 280; J. F. Carter, *The New Dealers* (N.Y.: Simon & Schuster, 1934), 315, 318–23; Raymond Moley, *Twenty-Seven Masters of Politics* (N.Y.: Funk & Wagnalls, 1949), 151–60; Eric F. Goldman, *Rendezvous with Destiny* (N.Y.: Knopf, 1952), 333–37, 363–66; Hugh S. Johnson, in *Saturday Evening Post*, Oct. 26, 1935, pp. 7, 85; Matthew Josephson, in *New Yorker*, Nov. 30, 1940, pp. 27–28; Dec. 7, 1940, pp. 35–38; Dec. 14, 1940, p. 25; Beverly Smith, in *American Magazine*, Feb. 1939, pp. 128–29; Fred Rodell, in *Harper's*, Oct. 1941, pp. 451–55; *Today*, Nov. 2, 1935, pp. 5, 20–22; *Current Biography*, June 1941, pp. 30–31; *Fortune*, Jan. 1936, pp. 88, 90; June 1937, pp. 111–12.

ment as assistant to Undersecretary Dean Acheson, but after Acheson's resignation over the gold purchase policy, he returned to the RFC. In the meantime, Frankfurter had brought Cohen and Landis to Washington to help draft the new securities law, and both men soon became key additions to the Brandeisian reform group. Cohen had an established reputation as a specialist on corporate reorganization, a "lawyer's lawyer," to whom other lawyers took the knotty legal problems they could not solve themselves, while Landis, like Frankfurter, was a brilliantly successful teacher. After graduating at the head of his class in 1924, he served his year's apprenticeship with Justice Brandeis, returned to Harvard Law School as assistant professor of law, and by 1928 had been promoted to full professor and installed in the new chair of legislation.

The stage was set, then, for the early legislative drafting team of Corcoran, Cohen, and Landis. Together they wrote the securities laws, and Landis stayed on to administer them, first as a member of the Federal Trade Commission and later as a member and eventually chairman of the new Securities and Exchange Commission. Cohen, in the meantime, had joined the legal staff of the Public Works Administration, and in 1934 became general counsel to the National Power Policy Committee. In the ensuing years he and Corcoran became almost inseparable. They were the "Brain Twins," the "Gold Dust Twins," the "little hot dogs"; and according to popular repute, they exerted a far-reaching influence through the numerous young lawyers they had placed in key positions.[2]

[2] Raymond Moley, *After Seven Years* (N.Y.: Harper, 1939), 179–80; and *Masters of Politics*, 156; Carter, *New Dealers*, 155–58; Schlesinger, *Politics of Upheaval*, 223–30; Marion L. Ramsay, *Pyramids of Power* (N.Y.: Bobbs-Merrill, 1937), 269–72; Smith, in *American Magazine*, Aug. 1937, pp. 22–23, 125–28; William H. Hale, in *Common Sense*, June 1938, pp. 13–14; Blair Bolles, in *American Mercury*, Jan. 1938, pp. 42–45; Joseph Alsop and Robert Kintner, in *Saturday Evening Post*, Oct. 29, 1938, pp. 77–79; Nov. 12, 1938, pp. 9, 105; Alva Johnston, *ibid.*, July 31, 1937, pp. 5–7, 65; *Newsweek*, May 12, 1934, pp. 15–16.

There were also other influential antimonopolists in the Administration, other men imbued with the same fear of concentrated economic power and the same faith in antitrust action. One key individual was Robert H. Jackson, a highly successful lawyer from upstate New York, who first joined the government as general counsel to the Bureau of Internal Revenue and later took over the Antitrust Division. A second major figure was William O. Douglas of the Yale Law School, who began working for the SEC in 1934, was later appointed to the agency, and eventually became its chairman. A third prominent New Dealer associated with the Brandeisians was Secretary of the Interior Harold Ickes, who early formed the habit of talking over his difficulties "with Tom and Ben." Finally, there was the veteran antitruster Herman Oliphant, a former professor of law at Johns Hopkins University who was now general counsel to the Treasury Department. Oliphant, however, was never really close to the Brandeis-Frankfurter group. Corcoran regarded him as a "dangerous man," as Morgenthau's "evil genius" and a man who was not really a "progressive." The feud between the two men dated from the time that Acheson resigned in protest against the gold purchase plan and Morgenthau and Oliphant moved into the Treasury to put it into operation. Not until 1937, when the antimonopoly campaign really got underway, were they able to compose their differences.[3]

II

If the philosophy of the Brandeis-Frankfurter adherents and their allies could be summed up in one word, that

[3] Schlesinger, *Politics of Upheaval*, 360–61, 393; William O. Douglas, *Democracy and Finance* (New Haven: Yale U. Press, 1940), 6–16; Harold L. Ickes, *Secret Diary*, I (N.Y.: Simon & Schuster, 1953), 342; II (1954), 36, 62, 175, 283–84; Carter, *New Dealers*, 115–16; Marquis Childs, in *Forum*, March 1940, pp. 150–53; Alsop and Kinter, in *Saturday Evening Post*, Oct. 29, 1938, pp. 78, 80; Nov. 12, 1938, pp. 9, 104–5, 108; Max Lerner, in *Nation*, Oct. 23, 1937, pp. 429–32; *Fortune*, Feb. 1938, pp. 119–20; March 1938, pp. 78–80, 132, 136.

word would probably be "decentralization." Centralized wealth, centralized control, and centralized location, they felt, were all complementary, all aspects of a broad general trend that should be reversed. Nor could they see any valid reason why it could not be. Large, monopolistic organizations, they held, were not the result of technological imperatives. They grew instead from the desire to avoid competition, the desire for promoters' profits, and the fact that "finance" simply went out and forcibly merged "a flock of little business concerns for milking purposes." In most industries, they argued, the size of greatest efficiency was reached at a comparatively early stage. Further growth depended upon financial manipulation, monopolistic devices, or the use of unfair practices. It followed that if such devices and practices were eliminated, huge corporations would not be created, or if created, they would not be successful. Competition, in other words, could and should be restored and maintained. The only exception was in dealing with "natural monopolies," with those few areas of economic endeavor where duplication of facilities was obviously wasteful. For such areas, government operation, or at least yardsticks, offered the best solution.

For some of the Brandeisians, too, including the old justice himself, a preference for mere smallness tended to override the desire for competitive efficiency. In the field of retail trade, for example, Brandeis sided with the advocates of "fair trade" and anti-chain legislation. To him, the chain stores were monopolistic, and the restraint of trade by small firms was preferable to further bigness in business. Bigness, in fact, was a social "curse." The huge corporation, with its myriad of employees, its stuffed shirts and high-priced conferences, its absentee ownership and financier control, was a menace to a democratic society. It sapped away the vitality of local communities, corrupted the political process, denied to the great mass of citizens the satisfactions that came from owning and operating their own businesses, and, by taxing human abilities beyond their natural limitations, resulted in an impersonal, machine-like, stultifying process, lacking in imagination, flexibility, and compassion. "Although the simple farm and village community life has a low mechanical efficiency . . . ," said the Brandeisian disciple David Coyle, "it has one healthy and essential quality that we need to cultivate now. It is efficient as a social organism; it does not waste either material or human resources on any such scale as we find in modern business."

Big business, moreover, was not only a curse in itself, but also the primary cause of big government, big labor, and big agriculture. Because of it, society became organized into collective fighting units, each bent upon sabotaging the others, and the result was a "plague of idleness and poverty" for everyone. In order to make such a system work, the government had to take over more and more functions and would eventually end by destroying democracy and individual freedom. Government officials, taxed with problems that were beyond their capacity to solve, would grow fearful, suppress freedom of speech and press, and take refuge in an impersonal, bureaucratic ineptitude, oblivious to the needs and problems of the individual or the local community. The real job of government, as the Brandeisians saw it, was to recreate a system of economic democracy as the basis for political democracy, to establish, in other words, the conditions that would make regulation of prices and production unnecessary, since detailed economic planning in a country as vast as the United States was simply incompatible with a democratic society. As Coyle put it, "The most practical of all industrial plans are plans for making detailed plans unnecessary."

Interwoven, too, with the attack on centralized power was a belief in physical decentralization. The idea of "concentrating and specializing in one area," Brandeis thought, was wrong. Each state, each city, and each village should be partially self-sufficient; industry and agriculture should be balanced; and the whole trend toward urban centralization and absentee control should be checked. The nation, in other words, should try to recapture some of the enduring values of its rural upbringing, recognize that Big Business and High Finance were false gods, and get back to a simpler and more satisfying system.[4]

Decentralization, then, was the key concept in the Brandeisian program. Politically and ideologically the time seemed peculiarly ripe for the revival, spread, and implementation of such an approach. After all, it could draw upon traditions that were deeply rooted in American folklore. It could take advantage of the general disillusionment with business leadership and the yearning for a simpler system. And it could count upon the support of a large and varied group of politicians, publicists, and scholars.

In the political category, President Roosevelt himself had a strong preference for rural values and Jeffersonian ideals. He believed it was now possible to carry to the country and the small towns most of the advantages of the city, and to some extent he tried to implement this idea. There were elements of it, for instance, in the emphasis on cheap power and rural electrification, in the social engineering of the TVA, in the greenbelt settlements, and in the rural rehabilitation program. Roosevelt, moreover, had

[4] Louis D. Brandeis, *The Curse of Bigness* (N.Y.: Viking, 1934), 104–28; Mason, *Brandeis*, 354–56, 615–16; Alfred Lief, ed., *Brandeis Guide to the Modern World* (Boston: Little, Brown, 1941), 4–5, 7–8, 17–24, 70, 180, 185–86, 213–14; and *Brandeis* (N.Y.: Stackpole, 1936), 470, 479; Donald Richberg, in Felix Frankfurter, ed., *Mr. Justice Brandeis* (New Haven: Yale U. Press, 1932), 130–40; David C. Coyle, *Brass Tacks* (Washington: National Home Library Foundation, 1936), 117–21; and *Irrepressible Conflict* (N.Y.: 1933), 16–7; Coyle, in *Virginia Quarterly Review*, July 1935, pp. 322–35, 338; Summer 1938, pp. 373–79; Coyle et al., *The American Way* (N.Y.: Harper, 1938), 24–25; Coyle and Herbert Agar, in Agar and Allan Tate, eds., *Who Owns America?* (Boston: Houghton Mifflin, 1936), 3–17, 94, 103–6; Solomon Bloom, in *Commentary*, Oct. 1948, pp. 317–19; Herbert Agar, *Land of the Free* (Boston: Houghton Mifflin, 1935), 191–207, 274, 288; Schlesinger, *Politics of Upheaval*, 387–89; Clifford B. Reeves, in *Atlantic Monthly*, Aug. 1936, p. 223.

a number of friends who had served their political apprenticeships under Wilson's New Freedom and had not changed their minds much since the campaign of 1912. These included men like Josephus Daniels, who kept urging the President to strengthen and enforce the antitrust laws, or Norman Hapgood, who had edited *Collier's* and *Harper's Weekly* in their crusading, muckraking days, and who now acted as a sort of liaison between Roosevelt and Brandeis. In Congress, there were the Western agrarians, men like William E. Borah of Idaho, Gerald P. Nye of North Dakota, Burton Wheeler of Montana, and Joseph C. O'Mahoney of Wyoming, all of whom drew their intellectual precepts from the old Populist tradition.[5]

The Brandeisian view was also being expounded at the time by an able group of publicists and writers. Walter Lippmann, for example, had finally given up his earlier flirtations with centralized planning and was now writing elaborate defenses of the views associated with the New Freedom. Morris L. Ernst, a liberal New York lawyer specializing in civil liberties cases, had become another Brandeisian champion of the small businessman against the big interests. And David Cushman Coyle, a consulting engineer for the PWA, had become the highly articulate author of numerous books and articles in which he stressed the evils of High Finance and developed the case for a

[5] Daniel R. Fusfeld, *The Economic Thought of Franklin D. Roosevelt and the Origins of the New Deal* (N.Y.: Columbia U. Press, 1956), 54–61, 83–86, 123–24, 152–53; Paul K. Conkin, *Tomorrow a New World* (Ithaca: Cornell U. Press, 1959), 34–35, 82–89, 327–31; Ralph L. Woods, *America Reborn* (N.Y.: Longmans, Green, 1939), 296–302, 306–14; Ernest K. Lindley, *Halfway with Roosevelt* (N.Y.: Viking, 1937), 70–72; FDR, *Public Papers and Addresses* (N.Y.: Random House, 1938), 507–11; Lief, *Brandeis*, 471; Schlesinger, *Politics of Upheaval*, 134–38; *Congressional Record*, 74 Cong., 1 Sess., LXXIX, 2199–2208; Rexford G. Tugwell, in *Western Political Quarterly*, Sept. 1950, pp. 398–402; *New Republic*, Jan. 12, 1938, p. 281; NEC Proceedings, March 20, 1934, pp. 8–9, 12–13; President Roosevelt's Press Conferences, Nov. 23, 1934, Roosevelt Papers; Josephus Daniels to FDR, Jan. 7, 15, 1935; Norman Hapgood to FDR, July 13, Aug. 3, 11, 1935, all in Roosevelt Papers (PPF 86, 2278).

competitive economy of small units. "For gosh sake, Dave, you haven't gone Brandeis, have you?" Jerome Frank is supposed to have remarked upon reading one of Coyle's articles. "Hell, I've always been Brandeis," Coyle replied. "The big battle is coming on, and them that is there will have the fun."

Somewhat similar, too, was the stricter Jeffersonian and agrarian ideology associated with such groups as the distributists, the Catholic Rural Life Conference, the Southern Agrarians, and the back-to-the-land movement. Typically, the leaders of such movements were disillusioned writers, economists, or historians, imbued now with the ideal of returning to an agrarian society of small property owners. One of their most influential spokesmen was Herbert Agar, who, in his syndicated column, "Time and Tide," and in various books and articles, argued effectively for decentralization, wider distribution, and restoration of competition. In 1936 he joined with Allen Tate to edit a symposium written by the leaders of the various agrarian groups. "Our common ground," he wrote, "is a belief that monopoly capitalism is evil and self-destructive, and that it is possible, while preserving private ownership, to build a true democracy in which men would be better off both morally and physically." [6]

[6] Walter Lippmann, The Good Society (Boston: Little Brown, 1937), XIII, 13–18, 31–34, 97–105, 172–76, 362–89; and The Method of Freedom (N.Y.: Macmillan, 1934), 63–71; Lindley, Halfway with Roosevelt, 58–59; Schlesinger, Politics of Upheaval, 70–71, 230–33, 393, 399–400; Conkin, New World, 25–34; Agar and Tate, eds., Who Owns America?, IX, 18–67, 94–109; Coyle, in Virginia Quarterly Review, July 1935, pp. 321–38; Summer 1938, pp. 368–79; Marquis James, in Scribner's, July 1938, pp. 7–11, 58; Morris L. Ernst, in Publishers' Weekly, May 16, 1936, pp. 1932–36; Current Biography, March 1944, pp. 3–6; Who's Who in America? (1954–55), 580; Agar, in Forum, Jan. 1936, pp. 11–13; and in American Review, April 1934, pp. 1–22; Harold Loeb, in Common Sense, Aug. 1936, pp. 7–10; Hapgood to Brandeis, Aug. 3, 1935, PPF 2278, Roosevelt Papers. See also such books as Coyle's Brass Tacks; Ernst's Too Big (Boston: Little, Brown, 1940); Agar's Land of the Free and Pursuit of Happiness (Cambridge: Riverside, 1938); John C. Ransom et al., I'll Take My Stand

In academic circles the idea of decentralization was also espoused by such spokesmen as Henry C. Simons of the University of Chicago, Walter P. Webb of the University of Texas, and Frank A. Fetter of Princeton University. In a widely read little pamphlet, published in 1934, Simons deplored the increasing organization of interest groups and set forth an alternative program for the restoration and maintenance of competition. Webb, too, in his *Divided We Stand*, deplored the decline of the independent entrepreneur and the corresponding growth of a "new feudalism." And Fetter, in a series of speeches and articles, continued to advance the arguments of the classical economists, to blame the nation's ills on a departure from competitive standards, and to call particularly for the abolition of the basing-point system of pricing.[7]

III

The antitrusters also benefited from their ability to absorb new strands of economic thought and weave them into a new and increasingly influential rationale. Blended with the traditional fear of centralization and the indictment of monopoly on social grounds were views that regarded monopoly as the primary cause of depression and the major

(N.Y.: Harper, 1930); Ralph Borsodi, *This Ugly Civilization* (N.Y.: Harper, 1933 ed.); Luigi Ligutti, *Rural Roads to Security* (Milwaukee: Bruce, 1940); and Hilaire Belloc, *The Servile State* (London: Constable, 1927 ed.). For a time the *American Review*, edited by Seward Collins, also acted as the chief organ and mouthpiece for the Southern Agrarians and other "Revolutionary Conservatives." Later it tended to become a spokesman for a reactionary form of fascism. After 1936 *Free America* became the chief organ of the agrarian distributist groups.
   [7] Henry C. Simons, *A Positive Program for Laissez-Faire* (Chicago: U. of Chicago Press, 1934), 3–6, 17–37; and in AER *Supplement*, March 1936, pp. 68–76; Frank A. Fetter, Address, Nov. 12, 1935, Borah Papers; Fetter, in *Annals Am. Acad.*, Jan. 1933, pp. 93–100; in *Journal of Political Economy*, Oct. 1937, pp. 577–605; and in *Proceedings of the Academy of Political Science*, May 1938, pp. 100–7; Walter P. Webb, *Divided We Stand* (N.Y.: Farrar & Rinehart, 1937), 52–59, 110–19, 140–48.

obstacle in the way of recovery. Especially useful here was the so-called "administered price thesis," the view that price rigidity had resulted in maldistribution, oversavings, and economic breakdown. Yet oddly, this theory came primarily from the work of the economic planners, especially from Gardiner Means' *Industrial Prices and Their Relative Inflexibility.*

In the original version of his highly influential pamphlet, Means had set out to explain how the policies of the NRA and AAA might be reoriented to bring about full production. The American economy, he said, had come to consist of two markets. In one, supply and demand were equated by a flexible price; in the other production and demand were equated at an inflexible, administered price. The first, generally speaking, was the world of farm commodities, textiles, coal, and crude oil; the second was the world of steel, cement, automobiles, and farm implements. The price of farm commodities, for example, had dropped sixty-three percent from 1929 to 1933 while production had dropped only six percent. The price of farm implements, on the other hand, had fallen only six percent while production had dropped eighty percent. In this case, as well as in numerous other industries, "modern industrial organization" had "destroyed the free market" and lodged the making of industrial policy in the hands of a few private individuals, who, when confronted with falling demand, would normally cut production rather than prices, a choice that threw laborers out of work, reduced their income, and thus further reduced demand. Where the old economy had set forces in motion to restore a balance, the new set forces in motion that tended to make the situation progressively worse.

For Means and his colleagues in the Department of Agriculture, the only realistic solution was to develop new "techniques of control" that would restore an economic balance. But for the antitrusters the situation seemed to call for a "dislocation of controls." The NRA market restorers argued that greater price flexibility would almost certainly mean larger volume and fuller employment. At the price hearing in early 1935, they used the administered price thesis to support their position. Leon Henderson had Means' charts and tables introduced as evidence, and in his concluding statement, he went to great lengths to refute the notion that there was any correlation between price stability and full employment and to argue for the restoration of flexible prices, particularly in those areas where the greatest reemployment might be expected.[8]

The antitrusters also received an unexpected assist from a highly publicized investigation in Canada. There, in 1935, the Royal Commission on Price Spreads not only "set Canada rocking," but created a considerable tremor elsewhere. Particularly interesting, Henderson thought, was the Commission's "very excellent statement on imperfect competition," a statement that emphasized price disparity and the decline of competition as the factors primarily responsible for the current economic distress. He had Chapter II of the report mimeographed for distribution within the NRA. And Norman Hapgood suggested that

[8] David Lynch, *The Concentration of Economic Power* (N.Y.: Columbia U. Press, 1946), 8–25; Schlesinger, *Politics of Upheaval*, 215–19; Gardiner C. Means, *Industrial Prices and Their Relative Inflexibility* (Senate Doc. 13, 74 Cong., 1 Sess., 1935), 1–17; and in *AER Supplement*, March 1936, p. 28; *Blue Eagle*, Jan. 16, 1935; Means, "NRA and AAA and the Reorganization of Industrial Policy Making," Oct. 15, 1934; E. J. Working to Leon Henderson, Sept. 21, 1934, with accompanying memo.; Henderson to NIRB, Jan. 2, 1935; V. S. von Szeliski to Henderson, April 26, Oct. 19, 1934; von Szeliski, "Effect of Price Levels on Employment," Jan. 24, 1935; R&P Div., Analysis of Statements at the Price Hearing, Jan. 23, 1935; Henderson, "Price Provisions in Codes," Jan. 9, 1935, all in NRA Records (Bardsley File, Henderson File, von Szeliski File, MR&D, Marshall File); Interview with Means, Washington, D.C., Feb. 21, 1957; Rexford Tugwell to FDR, Sept. 8, 1934, PPF 1820, Roosevelt Papers; Mordecai Ezekiel to Henry A. Wallace, Jan. 2, 1935, Industrial Section File—CCF, NRPB Records; Henderson to John Chamberlain, Jan. 29, 1938, Relief Plans File, Hopkins Papers.

if the President did not have the study, he should certainly get it. "I should think," he wrote, "it might be full of ammunition for next year." [9]

In the meantime, a copy of Means' memorandum had gravitated into the hands of Senator William E. Borah, who naturally regarded it as strong corroboration for what he had been saying all along, that the growth of monopoly had brought about the depression and was now making recovery impossible. In January 1935 he offered a resolution calling upon the Secretary of Agriculture to transmit "a certain study, memorandum, or report, prepared by Gardiner C. Means, . . . relative to monopolistic influence upon, or monopolistic control of, industrial prices." The resolution was accepted without discussion, and Means' memorandum was thus elevated to the dignity of a congressional document.

In the report submitted to the Senate and in subsequent articles and books, Means took great pains to point out that since administered prices were more a matter of technological development than of monopolistic collusion, there was little hope of correcting matters by antitrust action. Yet Means' analysis was now passing into the hands of men who did not agree. For the neo-Brandeisians, in particular, the obvious remedy for price rigidity was to make prices flexible again. Although they continued to demonstrate the existence and growth of monopoly by citing the works of economic planners, by appealing, for example, to such studies as Arthur R. Burns' *Decline of Competition*, Harry Laidler's *Concentration of Control in American Industry*, or the widely discussed *Modern Corporation and Private Property* by Adolf Berle and Gardiner

[9] Royal Commission on Price Spreads, *Report* (Ottawa: Patenaude, 1935), 5–12; *Boston Globe*, July 9, 1935; Memo. re Economic Background of Royal Commission on Price Spreads; Henderson to Means, April 30, 1935, both in NRA Records (Hughes File, Henderson File); William Phillips to FDR, July 16, 1935; Norman Hapgood to FDR, July 19, 1935, both in PPF 2278, Roosevelt Papers.

Means, they still disagreed strongly with the explanations and solutions offered by such men. Concentration, they insisted, was due to financial manipulation, unfair practices, judicial confusion, and executive inaction; not to "natural laws" and "overhead costs." The answer was strong antitrust action that would either insure price competition or force businessmen to pursue flexible price policies. "The analogy of unscrambling an omelet," Frank Fetter told Senator Borah, was "quite fallacious." A corporation was not an omelet. It was a "man-made institution shaped and adapted to man-made laws"; men, when they knew what they wanted, were "entirely competent" to change these laws.[10]

Somewhat similar views were characteristic of the consumer-minded economists who had fought the battles against the NRA codes, of men like Leon Henderson, Corwin Edwards, Thomas Blaisdell, and Isador Lubin. Henderson, in particular, continued to speak out against the dangers of price rigidity. In late 1935, he teamed up with Theodore Kreps, former head of the NRA's statistics

[10] Means, *Industrial Prices*, III-IV, 8–13; Caroline F. Ware and Gardiner Means, *The Modern Economy in Action* (N.Y.: Harcourt, Brace, 1936), 5–28, 39–55, 141–61, 196–220; Means, in *Journal of the American Statistical Association*, June 1935, pp. 401–9; and in *AER Supplement*, March 1936, pp. 32–35; Marion C. McKenna, *Borah* (Ann Arbor: U. of Mich. Press, 1961), 314, 317; Lynch, *Economic Power*, 9–16; Schlesinger, *Politics of Upheaval*, 219–35; Coyle, *Brass Tacks*, 114–21; and in Agar and Tate, eds., *Who Owns America?*, 3–17; Simons, *Positive Program*, 3–7, 34–36; *Congressional Record*, 74 Cong., 1 Sess., LXXIX, 141; Fetter, in *Journal of Political Economy*, Feb. 1937, pp. 95–110; Means, "NRA and AAA and the Reorganization of Industrial Policy Making," Oct. 15, 1934; Fetter to Borah, Jan. 15, 1938, with accompanying memoranda; Robert Jackson, Addresses, May 28, Sept. 17, 1937, all in Borah Papers (New Deal File, Monopoly File); Hapgood to FDR, July 13, 1935; W. H. Cameron to Hapgood, July 1935, both in Roosevelt Papers (PPF 2278, 1820). The studies mentioned in the text are Adolf A. Berle, Jr., and Gardiner Means, *The Modern Corporation and Private Property* (N.Y.: Macmillan, 1933); Harry W. Laidler, *Concentration of Control in American Industry* (N.Y.: Crowell, 1931); and Arthur R. Burns, *The Decline of Competition* (N.Y.: McGraw-Hill, 1936).

section, to write a long memorandum setting forth the administered price thesis and advocating "a broad inquiry into the present status of competition," the areas in which it had disappeared, and the methods by which it might be revived. Late in the following year, as consulting economist to the WPA, he warned that unjustified price increases were again hindering recovery and urged that the Administration move against them on a wide front, by antitrust prosecutions, the use of yardsticks, encouragement of co-operatives, lower tariffs, patent law reform, and special taxation. With people like Henderson, however, the subject of bigness tended to be subordinated to recovery considerations. Their approach was more managerial, more pragmatic, more concerned with consumer welfare and the disciplining of price policies, less with the preservation of small business or decentralization as a social good. Price maintenance activities, they felt, were detrimental, regardless of whether they were conducted by big business or little business.[11]

The belief of most antitrusters that monopoly was widely prevalent and growing was also related, at least indirectly, to the revolution that was taking place in abstract economic theory. From the writings of Piero Sraffa, Harold Hotelling, Edward Chamberlin, Joan Robinson, and other theorists there had emerged a new technique of economic analysis, one that regarded monopolistic conditions as

[11] Leon Henderson, in *Annals Am. Acad.*, Jan. 1936, pp. 266–71; Schlesinger, *Politics of Upheaval*, 388–92; Samuel Lubell, in *Saturday Evening Post*, Sept. 13, 1941, pp. 82, 84; Henderson to Benjamin Cohen, Feb. 22, 1937, Cohen File, NPPC Records; Henderson to Harry Hopkins, Nov. 1937, Relief Plans File, Hopkins Papers; Henderson and Theodore Kreps, "On the Necessity for a Broad Inquiry into the Present Status of Competition," Dec. 30, 1935; Jacob Baker to Isador Lubin and others, March 10, 1937, with accompanying memo.; Corwin Edwards to Thomas Blaisdell, June 17, 1938; NRC, "Emerging Industrio-Governmental Problems," Nov. 9, 1937, all in NRPB Records (Blaisdell File, Meetings File—CCF, Presidential Correspondence—CCF); Henderson, "Boom and Bust," March 29, 1937, Industrial Recovery File—PSF, Roosevelt Papers.

ubiquitous and determining, not exceptional and inconsequential, and one that treated the typical seller as a partial monopolist and used the marginal revenue curve as a key analytical tool. For the real world, the new theorists felt, the principles of oligopoly and duopoly were more pertinent than those of free competition, and the task of the economist was to devise a hybrid theory allowing for both monopolistic and competitive elements.[12]

Such writing was usually in highly abstract terms; yet the general orientation did influence practical economists and lead to a general broadening of the definition of "monopoly." The term now came to include all behavior that departed from the concept of pure competition, including a good deal of the oligopolistic rivalry that businessmen regarded as "competition." Politicians, who failed to make the fine distinctions of the economists, tended to equate "oligopoly" and "imperfect competition" with "monopoly," to regard them as being equally productive of social and economic ills, and to assume that "monopoly" was now much more widely prevalent than it had been in the past. Some critics, certainly, suggested that much of the change really represented "the decline of the idea of competition," not the decline of competition itself. Yet most antitrusters believed that the latter was true, and their assumption that monopolistic behavior was a relatively late development reinforced their faith in

[12] General discussions of the new developments in the field are contained in Horace G. White, Jr., "A Review of Monopolistic and Imperfect Competition Theories," AER, xxvi (Dec. 1936), 637–49; R. F. Harrod, "Doctrines of Imperfect Competition," QJE, xlviii (May 1934), 442–70; Lewis H. Haney, History of Economic Thought (N.Y.: Macmillan, 1949 ed.), 699–717; J. R. Hicks, "Annual Survey of Economic Theory," Econometrica, iii (Jan. 1935), 1–20. Representative and significant writings include Piero Sraffa and Harold Hotelling, in Economic Journal, Dec. 1926, pp. 535–50; March 1939, pp. 41–57; Edward H. Chamberlin, The Theory of Monopolistic Competition (Cambridge: Harvard U. Press, 1933); Joan Robinson, The Economics of Imperfect Competition (London: Macmillan, 1933); Fritz Machlup, in AER, Sept. 1937, pp. 445–51.

antitrust action. Monopoly, they insisted, was a malignant growth on the body economic, one that was responsible for the depression and one that must now be eradicated.[13]

Still another group of studies that helped to shape the indictment of monopoly was the one linking the administered price thesis with an underconsumptionist, over-savings theory of the business cycle. Especially significant here was the Brookings Institution's four-volume inquiry into the "Distribution of Wealth and Income in Relation to Economic Progress." In *America's Capacity to Produce* in 1934 a team of economists headed by Harold Moulton measured the nation's productive capacity and concluded that there had been no build-up of un-utilized plant during the period from 1900 to 1930. In *America's Capacity to Consume*, also published in 1934, they explained this phenomenon by arguing that the creation of new plant depended mostly upon consumer demand rather than the level of savings, an explanation borne out by the fact that savings had been growing much more rapidly than consumer expenditures. In *The Formation of Capital* in 1935 they showed that a large portion of these savings had either remained idle, been loaned abroad, or moved into speculative ventures. In the final volume, *Income and Economic Progress*, Moulton explained why savings were excessive in the first place. Price stabilization by business combinations, he concluded, when coupled with technological advances and lower costs of production, had channeled a disproportionate share of the income to those that did most of the savings, and the result had been too much saving by too few.

Moulton's apparent belief that businessmen themselves could be persuaded to lower prices and increase volume

[13] Edward Mason, in AEA, *Readings in the Social Control of Industry* (Philadelphia: Blakiston, 1942), 27–28; Thomas J. Anderson, Jr., and Shorey Peterson, in AER, March 1940, pp. 118–20; March 1957, pp. 60–78; Donald H. Wallace, in QJE, Feb. 1937, pp. 374–87; *Fortune*, March 1938, pp. 75–77, 120, 122, 124, 126, 128.

failed to make much of an impression on New Dealers, but his underlying diagnosis was widely accepted. Here, so the antitrusters felt, was proof that concentration of control and concentration of wealth were but reverse sides of the same coin, that one was simply the product of the other, and that no recovery could be expected until both trends were reversed. "The main thesis," Brandeis wrote to Norman Hapgood, "is our old one: Recovery and well-being must come through reducing prices—not by raising them." [14]

Some antitrusters, too, were accepting elements of the Keynesian analysis and trying to weave the spending and antitrust approaches together. Brandeis, Frankfurter, Corcoran, Cohen, and Coyle, were all advocates of a spending program, and Leon Henderson argued that American capitalism had been sustained from the beginning by federal intervention to create purchasing power. From a variety of angles, spending and antitrust measures could be regarded as supplementary rather than alternative courses of action. Monopolistic industries, after all, could destroy the multiplier effect of government spending by raising prices. Consequently, a spending program would be more effective if it were accompanied by a broad attack

[14] Edwin G. Nourse et al., *America's Capacity to Produce* (Washington: Brookings, 1934), 15–28, 421–30; Maurice Leven et al., *America's Capacity to Consume* (Washington: Brookings, 1934), 1–5, 126–32; Harold G. Moulton, *The Formation of Capital* (Washington: Brookings, 1935), 155–60; Moulton, *Income and Economic Progress* (Washington: Brookings, 1935), 41–46, 117–65; Lynch, *Economic Power*, 13–16; David C. Coyle, *Roads to a New America* (Boston: Little, Brown, 1938), 201–20, 295–98; Arthur F. Burns, in *QJE*, May 1936, pp. 476–523; Moulton, in *Fortune*, Nov. 1935, pp. 77–81, 166, 168, 171–72, 174, 177–78, 180, 182; Reeves, in *Atlantic Monthly*, Aug. 1936, pp. 217–25; Stuart Chase, in *Survey Graphic*, Nov. 1935, pp. 533–36, 566, 570; Henderson and Kreps, "On the Necessity for a Broad Inquiry into the Present Status of Competition," Dec. 30, 1935, Blaisdell File, NRPB Records; Hapgood to FDR, May 25, July 31, 1936, PPF 2278, Roosevelt Papers.

upon monopolies and price-fixing combines. Such a drive might also open up new outlets for private investment in areas that had been roped off by monopolistic combinations. Finally, a spending program might be one way of actually increasing competition. It would place more purchasing power in the hands of consumers, stimulate competition for the consumer's dollar, and bring an expanding market that would reduce the incentives for cartelization.

From various sources, then, the antitrusters were putting together a convincing rationale, and by 1937 they could take advantage of a considerable body of thought linking depression with such phenomena as rigid prices, industrial concentration, maldistribution, and excessive savings. All of these things were believed to be interlinked and each a part of the broad general problem. "To me," said Leon Henderson, "competition and purchasing power are linked—just as concentration, control, rigidity, unemployment, and imbalance are linked. . . . I believe the excessive instability is related to the rigidities in the system, which excess is related to concentration of control." The New Deal, he thought, should be against monopoly, not only because this was an American tradition, but also because "monopoly and concentration of wealth control prices and production to such an extent that depressions are inevitable." [15]

[15] Coyle, New America, 308–35; Schlesinger, Politics of Upheaval, 227, 236–37; Arthur E. Burns and Donald S. Watson, Government Spending and Economic Expansion (Washington: American Council on Public Affairs, 1940), 77, 94–95; Oscar L. Altman, Saving, Investment, and National Income (TNEC Monograph 37, 1941), 91–92, 109; Lynch, Economic Power, 5, 10, 14–16; Harry Hopkins, in Special Senate Committee, Unemployment and Relief (75 Cong., 3 Sess., 1938), 1883–89, 1352–54; Henderson to Chamberlain, Jan. 29, 1938; Henderson to Hopkins, April 1937; Henderson & Beardsley Ruml to Hopkins, April 1938, all in Relief Plans File, Hopkins Papers; Henry C. Simons, "Economic Stability and Antitrust Policy," Box 18, Arnold Papers; Robert Jackson, Addresses, Dec. 26, 29, 1937; Henderson, Address, Jan. 1, 1938, all in NRPB Records (Barrows File, Blaisdell File).

IV

In practice, however, the antitrust ideology seemed to be mostly a negative force. It could be used to thwart or hamper the programs of the planners and business rationalizers, but when it came to positive antitrust action, it was difficult to line up the type of pressure-group support that would make such action possible. Theoretically, of course, one could rely on small business groups, consumers, farmers, laborers, and all those who believed in "the old capitalistic system before it was largely throttled by semifeudalism." But in reality such groups were either unorganized or were interested primarily in creating their own barriers against competition, not in making everyone live by it. For themselves, in particular, they insisted upon antitrust exemptions, or at least executive inaction. Even when the enemy was "big business," their support was often sporadic, divided, and confined to specific problems or specific industries.

Consequently, antitrust action had to be limited, for the most part, to special areas and conducted on a partial, piecemeal, problem-by-problem basis. Like government-supported cartelization, it could be undertaken only when its proponents could develop the necessary political strength or manipulate the right political symbols. This meant that they could act only against isolated or widely hated groups or in situations where there was a strong underlying economic conflict, one in which a disgruntled business group was trying to better its lot by destroying the economic power of a rival group. There were conflicts of this sort in such industries as petroleum, motion pictures, and automobile financing, and it was not surprising that these should become areas of particular concern to the antitrusters. Nor was it surprising that many of their activities, especially during the period from 1933 to 1935, should center about efforts to deal with such popular demons as the Money Power and the Power Trust. Here were groups that were actively hated, particularly after the panic of 1929. For them, it seemed, reform was virtually inevitable. Under the circumstances, the antitrusters were able to shape the resulting measures and enlist general support behind them, often from groups that had no great concern about the monopoly problem as a whole.

These banking, securities, power, and holding company reforms constituted only a small part of what the antitrusters hoped to do. Yet, prior to the recession of 1937, they seemed unable to do much more. They had a general objective, a set of ideals and proposed reforms, and the general guidelines of an economic approach, but they had difficulty in developing the necessary political support. Consequently, their activities, especially during the early New Deal, amounted to little more than skirmishes on the flanks.[16]

[16] Lynch, *Economic Power*, 109–10; Walton Hamilton and Irene Till, *Antitrust in Action* (TNEC Monograph 16, 1941), 3–4, 25, 29, 37–38; Rexford G. Tugwell, *The Democratic Roosevelt* (N.Y.: Doubleday, 1957), 168, 243, 288–89, 366–69, 416, 545–46; Lief, *Brandeis*, 459, 470–72; Richard L. Neuberger, in *Current History*, Sept. 1936, pp. 65–71; Benjamin Ginsberg, in *North American Review*, Spring 1938, pp. 59, 73–75; *Time*, June 6, 1938, p. 48; August 1, 1938, p. 37; *Business Week*, May 28, 1938, pp. 13–14.

CHAPTER 16. THE ANTITRUSTERS
AND THE MONEY POWER

THE great monopoly in this country," Woodrow Wilson had declared in 1911, was "the money monopoly," the control over capital and credit that destroyed the "old variety and freedom and individual energy of development." Shortly thereafter the Pujo Committee had agreed that concentration of credit was "far more dangerous" than the elimination of competition by industrial combines. Since that time the existence of an evil Money Power had remained a central tenet of orthodox progressivism. The great enemy, so Brandeis and other antitrusters had long insisted, was the investment bankers. These masters of finance had become masters of the trusts, and through them the masters of the people, all by the use of "other people's money."

Most of the Brandeisians, then, could expound at length on the rise, dominance, and evils of finance capitalism. They knew how the investment bankers had first fastened their control upon American industry in the eighteen nineties, how this control had been broadened and solidified through a vast network of interlocking directorates, gentlemen's agreements, and communities of interest, and how the bankers had come to dominate both the capital-supplying and capital-using institutions and could therefore dictate the stocks to be issued and the prices to be paid. They were convinced, too, that the system was productive of numerous evils. It encouraged consolidation for speculative ends, for such purposes as profitable stock sales, insider deals, or handsome promotional and underwriting fees. It discriminated against small business and thus encouraged the irresponsibility of absentee ownership and the further concentration of economic power, wealth, and industrial activity. It centralized power in the hands of cautious, pecuniary-minded men, who were much more interested in guaranteed returns upon invested capital than in economic progress, with the result that new inventions were suppressed, economic development was arrested, and new lines of economic endeavor were consistently discouraged. Finally, it enabled the bankers to exact a heavy toll from investors, businessmen, clients, and the community as a whole, a toll that far exceeded the value of their services.[1]

By 1929, there was growing evidence that this Brandeisian indictment was no longer a very accurate one. The relative abundance of capital, coupled with the rise of new investment houses, the growth of direct investments, and the ability of large corporations to finance their own expansion from corporate surpluses, had largely undercut the finance capitalists, shifted power to a new managerial elite, and produced situations where the industrialist rather than the banker could call the tune. Many antitrusters, however, continued to think in terms of 1912. The Money Power, they felt, was still the chief enemy. It had been responsible for the mergers, speculative abuses, corporate pyramids, and other acts of financial chicanery during the nineteen twenties. In order to deal with it, a variety of reforms were now urgently needed. Regulation of securities issues, stock exchanges, and holding companies would reduce the ability of the financiers to build bigness for speculative purposes. Pitiless publicity and full

[1] Louis D. Brandeis, *Other People's Money* (Washington: National Home Library Foundation, 1933), 1–35, 91–92, 102–5, 138–39; George W. Edwards, *The Evolution of Finance Capitalism* (N.Y.: Longmans, Green, 1938), 3–8, 167–79, 193; Merwin H. Waterman, *Investment Banking Functions* (Ann Arbor: U. of Mich. Press, 1958), 27–29, 36–37; David C. Coyle, *Uncommon Sense* (Washington: National Home Library Foundation, 1936), 80–85; William O. Douglas, *Democracy and Finance* (New Haven: Yale U. Press, 1940), 6–13; Rexford G. Tugwell, in *Western Political Quarterly*, Sept. 1950, pp. 398–402; *Congressional Record*, 73 Cong., 1 Sess., LXXVII, 2928–29, 2932–33.

disclosure of facts would help to protect investors and put
an end to excessive charges and insider deals. Strict prohibition of interlocking directorates would reduce banker
influence and eliminate conflicts of interest. And the
divorcement of investment houses from commercial banks,
savings institutions, and industrial enterprises would help
to restore competitive bargaining, lower the price of capital, and relegate investment bankers to their legitimate
role.[2]

II

Some of the reforms advocated by the Brandeisians lacked
political support in 1933, but in one area, that of securities
reform, some sort of legislation had become a virtual certainty. This was particularly true after the Senate Banking
Committee launched a massive investigation in April 1932,
and in subsequent months, began to familiarize the public
with a variety of sensational abuses, with speculative pools,
preferred lists, corporate pyramiding, insider deals, and
numerous devices for unloading worthless securities upon
unsuspecting purchasers. The story was certainly a lurid
one. Together with the distress of stockholders and the
angry bewilderment of those who had lost their savings in
stock speculation, it produced a resolute and implacable
demand for governmental action. Dozens of security bills
were in the hoppers. The Democratic Party had pledged
itself to reform. And President Roosevelt, in his inaugural
address, had denounced the "unscrupulous money chang-

[2] Edwards, *Finance Capitalism*, 5, 228–31; Willard E. Atkins
et al., *The Regulation of the Security Markets* (Washington:
Brookings, 1946), 30, 35–37; Brandeis, *Other People's Money*, xxxi–
xxxvii, 42–43, 62–74, 109–11; 134–36; Thomas C. Cochran, *The
American Business System* (Cambridge: Harvard U. Press, 1957),
92–98; Ferdinand Pecora, *Wall Street under Oath* (N.Y.: Simon &
Schuster, 1939), 37–40; Arthur M. Schlesinger, Jr., *The Politics of
Upheaval* (Boston: Houghton Mifflin, 1960), 220–21; Coyle, *Un-
common Sense*, 62–69, 80–88; Adolf A. Berle, in *Yale Review*,
Sept. 1933, pp. 25–29.

ers" and called for "an end to speculation with other people's money." [3]

Consequently, even before the inauguration, Roosevelt had asked Samuel Untermyer, former counsel for the Pujo Committee, and Huston Thompson, former chairman of the Federal Trade Commission, to prepare suitable bills. On March 29, 1933, he sent the Thompson bill to Congress. A number of congressmen, however, felt that the measure was unworkable, particularly since it would allow the FTC to pass upon the merits of securities. The whole thing, Samuel Rayburn told Raymond Moley, would have to be redrawn. Moley then enlisted the aid of Felix Frankfurter; and, as noted previously, Frankfurter entrusted the job to James M. Landis and Benjamin Cohen, who, with the aid of other interested parties, worked out a revised bill, a measure that, according to its proponents, was "so air-tight that no corporation lawyer in the world could sift through it." In early May the House passed the bill. The Senate then agreed to substitute it for the Thompson version, and on May 27 the President added his signature.

As finally passed, the Securities Act protected investors in a number of ways. It outlawed the sale of securities in interstate commerce by means of false, misleading, or fraudulent statements. It required prospective stock issuers to file detailed registration statements with the Federal

[3] Douglas, *Democracy and Finance*, vi; Emanuel Stein, *Government and the Investor* (N.Y.: Farrar & Rinehart, 1941), 74–75, 114–16; Alpheus T. Mason, *Brandeis* (Princeton: Princeton U. Press, 1933), 45–48; FDR, *Public Papers and Addresses*, ii (N.Y.: Random House, 1938), 12–13; Atkins et al., *Security Markets*, 44–51; Louis Loss, *Securities Regulation* (Boston: Little, Brown, 1951), 15, 65–66, 75–77; Pecora, *Wall Street*, 27–34, 41–69, 100–2, 113–30, 169–88, 226–30; Arthur M. Schlesinger, Jr., *The Coming of the New Deal* (Boston: Houghton Mifflin, 1959), 434–40; Duncan Fletcher, in *Today*, Dec. 30, 1933, pp. 10–11. The investigations of the Senate Banking Committee began in April 1932 and ran well into 1934. The hearings were published under the title *Stock Exchange Practices* (1932–4). See Senate Banking Committee, *Stock Exchange Practices* (Senate Rept. 1455, 73 Cong., 2 Sess., 1934), 1–3.

Trade Commission and to include certain specified items in any prospectus or offering circular. And it made the principal officers of the issuing corporation, along with the accountants, appraisers, and underwriters involved, liable for the accuracy of the statements. A security purchaser might sue to recover the full purchase price if he could show that the registration statement or prospectus contained false or misleading information. As critics pointed out, the act did nothing to insure the soundness of securities, but it did try to insure that the issuers and promoters would tell the truth about them.[4]

In the meantime, other major goals of the Brandeisians were being incorporated into the Banking Act of 1933. This measure had its origins in a bill introduced by Senator Carter Glass in 1932, but not until 1933, when the Senate Banking Committee brought forth new disclosures of financial chicanery, did the drive for passage really gain momentum. Even then, important changes were necessary, including elimination of provisions for branch banking, abandonment of proposed changes in reserve requirements, and the addition of Henry B. Steagall's plan for guarantee of bank deposits, a proposal about which Roosevelt himself was not enthusiastic at the time. The President, however, did hope that the act would bring about a more unified banking system, and on June 16, 1933, he signed it into law. As the Brandeis men had long advocated, it divorced commercial banks from their investment affiliates, allowed the Federal Reserve Board to limit specula-

[4] Raymond Moley, *After Seven Years* (N.Y.: Harper, 1939), 176–83; Stein, *Government and Investor*, 75–86; FDR, *Public Papers*, II, 93–94, 213–15; Schlesinger, *Coming of New Deal*, 440–42; James M. Landis, in T. J. Lowi, ed., *Legislative Politics, USA* (Boston: Little, Brown, 1962), 225–39; *Congressional Record*, 73 Cong., 1 Sess., LXXVII, 937–38, 1006, 2838, 2910–54, 2979–84, 2996–3000, 3891–3903, 4009, 5195; 48 *U.S. Statutes* 74, Public, No. 22, 73 Cong.; Franklyn Waltman, Jr., in *Literary Digest*, July 22, 1933, p. 38; *Newsweek*, April 8, 1933, pp. 20–21; May 12, 1934, p. 16; *New York Times*, March 30, April 1-2, 4, May 3–4, 17, June 4, 1933.

tive loans, and made it much more difficult for bank officials to speculate with "other people's money." [5]

Financial reform, though, was still far from complete. Roosevelt had promised to regulate the stock exchanges, and by early 1934, as Ferdinand Pecora, counsel for the Senate Banking Committee, probed deeper into financial malpractices, the time seemed ripe for action. Again the President put a number of people to work on the problem, and again Benjamin Cohen emerged as the chief legislative draftsman. With the aid of Corcoran, Landis, Pecora, and several members of Pecora's staff, he soon had a bill ready. On February 9, 1934, after Roosevelt had discussed it with legislative leaders, it was introduced by Senator Duncan Fletcher and Representative Sam Rayburn.

Immediately, the Fletcher-Rayburn bill brought a chorus of protests from business and financial leaders, a number of whom seemed to think that Wall Street was perfectly capable of regulating itself. The Securities Act, they claimed, was already producing a dearth of new financing, and passage of this new measure, with its rigid prohibitions and high margin requirements, would dry up the securities market completely. The protests, moreover, did bring some changes. The House Commerce Committee, after consulting with Treasury and FRB officials, revised its measure to lower margin requirements, postpone

[5] Edwards, *Finance Capitalism*, 295–98; Marcus Nadler and Jules I. Bogen, *The Banking Crisis* (N.Y.: Dodd, Mead, 1933), 44–48, 52–54; Schlesinger, *Coming of New Deal*, 442–43; Pecora, *Wall Street*, 284–86; *Congressional Record*, 72 Cong., 1 Sess., LXXV, 2403, 8273, 9885–89, 9974–82, 9999–1007, 10051–59, 10068, 11214–17, 11453; 72 Cong. 2 Sess., LXXVI, 1330–36, 1937–38, 2094–6, 2153–56, 2207–8, 2517; 73 Cong., 1 Sess., LXXVII, 196, 3725–31, 3835–40, 4058, 4182, 5769–5783, 5861–63, 5898, 6198; 48 *U.S. Statutes* 162, Public, No. 66, 73 Cong.; Ray B. Westerfield, in *Journal of Political Economy*, Dec. 1933, pp. 722–26, 735–49; Howard H. Preston, in *AER*, Dec. 1933, pp. 588–607.

the separation of brokers and dealers, relax some of the rules against "insider" operations, and place the control of margins under the Federal Reserve Board. The Senate adopted the Glass amendment vesting regulation in a new and separate commission whose powers would be largely discretionary. The conference committee, while accepting the statutory margin requirements of the House bill, went along with the general idea of a special commission and discretionary control.

As finally approved on June 6, 1934, the new Securities Exchange Act established a five-man Securities and Exchange Commission, empowered it to administer both the new law and the Securities Act of 1933, and attempted to deal with a number of past abuses. It required that all security exchanges register with the Commission and furnish full information about the securities listed with them. It set initial margin requirements at from twenty-five to forty-five percent of the market price, depending upon the value of the stock over the past three years, and empowered the Federal Reserve Board to change these when necessary. It prohibited price manipulation through pools, wash sales, matched orders, and other similar devices. It gave the Commission broad discretionary power to promulgate rules for odd-lot dealers, specialists, "insider" operations, short-selling, options, stop-loss orders, and various trade practices. Finally, it liberalized the civil liability provisions of the Act of 1933. A defendant could now establish an adequate defense by showing that he had acted prudently upon the advice of an expert or that the damages suffered by the purchaser of a security were not due to the false statements of the issuer.[6]

[6] Moley, *After Seven Years*, 284–86; FDR, *Public Papers*, III, 90–92; John T. Flynn, *Security Speculation* (N.Y.: Harcourt, Brace, 1934), 277–94; Schlesinger, *Coming of New Deal*, 456–57; 48 U.S. *Statutes* 881, Public, No. 291, 73 Cong.; *Congressional Record*, 73 Cong., 2 Sess., LXXVIII, 2264–72, 2378, 3058–9, 7693–7716, 8116, 8161–4, 8667–8714, 10185–6, 10248–69, 10847; House

Some of the Brandeisians were disappointed when Roosevelt appointed Joseph P. Kennedy, a former Wall Street operator himself, as chairman of the new commission. But on the whole, they were satisfied with the outcome, and the securities legislation was basically different from the other measures of the early New Deal. The thesis implied in such laws was that the exchanges had failed to provide a free market, and the remedy was not state capitalism or even government control of investment decisions. It was the revival of free and fair competition, the restoration of a system where savers and businessmen could bargain on the basis of all the known facts and arrive at the fair market value of any offered security. The exchanges, in other words, were to be freed of riggers and insiders; decent standards of business morality were to be restored; and exchanges outside New York were to be revitalized, thus making capital more accessible to the small concern. To the economic planners, the securities laws were "nineteenth-century legislation." A foreign observer, contrasting them against the background of the NRA, wondered if they could not properly be regarded as "a convenient vent for national spite." "Nothing," he noted, was "too bad for Wall Street—not even free competition." [7]

Commerce Committee, *Stock Exchange Regulation* (73 Cong., 2 Sess., 1934), 82–83, 151–233, 625–44, 674–700; *Business Week*, Feb. 17, 1934, pp. 8–9; March 24, 1934, p. 28; April 14, 1934, p. 39; *Newsweek*, Feb. 17, 1934, pp. 26–28; Feb. 24, 1934, p. 25; March 3, 1934, p. 25; May 12, 1934, p. 27; June 9, 1934, p. 26; *New York Times*, Jan. 26, 28, Feb. 6, 10, March 20, April 10–12, May 17, 27, 1934.

[7] A. S. J. Baster, *The Twilight of American Capitalism* (London: King, 1937), 91, 209; Moley, *After Seven Years*, 286–90; and in *Today*, Dec. 30, 1933, p. 13; Edwards, *Finance Capitalism*, 315–18; Rexford G. Tugwell, *The Democratic Roosevelt* (Garden City: Doubleday, 1957), 288–89; Schlesinger, *Coming of New Deal*, 444–45, 467–69; George McCabe, in *Commonweal*, Aug. 3, 1934, pp. 341–44; Max Lerner, in *Nation*, Oct. 23, 1937, pp. 431–32; William O. Douglas, in *Yale Review*, March 1934, 521–33; Berle, *ibid.*, Sept. 1933, pp. 42–43.

IV

To some antimonopolists, though, securities reform was only a beginning. They felt that commercial banking, like the investment business, was too highly concentrated; and the Federal Reserve Act, in spite of its original goals, had failed to correct the situation. The New York Federal Reserve Bank, in particular, had continued to dominate the whole system. New York remained the financial center of the nation. Therefore, unless remedial action was taken, monetary and credit policies would continue to favor the Northeastern financial interests.

The traditional solution of agrarians and antitrusters had been decentralization and legal discouragement of branch, chain, or group banking. Yet by 1933 it was obvious that the unit banking system had serious defects. Some banks might be too large, but numerous others were almost certainly too small, too limited in resources to provide the diversification, capital, and management that were necessary for safe and adequate service. Accordingly, more and more progressives were accepting the idea of centralized government controls. If there had to be a financial capital, they felt, then it should be in Washington, not in New York.[8]

The chance to do something about the situation came with the new attempt at banking reform in 1935, a move that had its origins in a memorandum prepared by Marriner Eccles and Lauchlin Currie. Eccles, who had just

[8] Joseph Dorfman, *The Economic Mind in American Civilization*, IV (N.Y.: Viking, 1959), 278–79, 287; Nadler and Bogen, *Banking Crisis*, 25–39; Rudolph L. Weissman, *The New Federal Reserve System* (N.Y.: Harper, 1936), 31–32, 58–62; Edwards, *Finance Capitalism*, 289–93; Tugwell, *Democratic Roosevelt*, 373; John M. Chapman, *Concentration of Banking* (N.Y.: Columbia U. Press, 1934), 6–7, 126–27, 366–73; Ray B. Westerfield, in *Annals Am. Acad.*, Jan. 1934, pp. 17–21; *Congressional Record*, 74 Cong., 1 Sess., LXXIX, 6656–58, 6733, 6800–3, 6916–19, 6971–72, 11842–56, 11914–17.

been offered the governorship of the Federal Reserve Board, had become deeply concerned about the lack of centralized monetary controls, so the measure he now proposed was designed essentially to centralize responsibility, provide the FRB with new powers, and expedite the government's spending program. To the antitrusters, however, the important thing about the bill was the blow it would strike at the Money Power. If passed, they felt, it might put an end to the dominant position of New York and the New York Federal Reserve Bank.

The introduction of the Eccles bill in Congress in February 1935 touched off a prolonged controversy. Supporting the measure were such groups as the farm bloc, the newly monied interests of the West and Southwest, and the majority of the spenders, antitrusters, and monetary reformers. Opposing it were such groups as the radical advocates of nationalized banking, who felt it did not go far enough, the defenders of property rights and laissez-faire, who regarded it as an attack upon localism, individual freedom, and states' rights, and the spokesmen for the Eastern financial interests, who insisted that it would subjugate the Federal Reserve Board to political control, establish a financial dictatorship, and force the banks to accept government securities. Under the circumstances, the strategy of the Administration was to combine the Eccles proposals with provisions that might attract conservative support, particularly with provisions to liberalize the membership requirements of the Federal Deposit Insurance Corporation and to extend the terminal date of the loans that banks had made to their own officials. Conversely, the strategy of the opposition, led by Senator Carter Glass, was to split the measure into separate bills and defeat the objectionable provisions.

Glass never succeeded in breaking up the omnibus bill. But by exploiting the bureaucratic rivalries of the FRB, the Treasury, the FDIC, and the Comptroller, he did win a number of concessions. One new provision deleted a section that would allow the President to remove the chairman and vice-chairman of the Federal Reserve Board. Another eliminated the Secretary of the Treasury and the Comptroller of the Currency as ex officio members. Still others limited the FRB's power to alter reserve requirements and gave the bankers representation on the proposed open-market committee. On July 26 the Senate approved the new version of the bill, and although there were some changes in the conference committee, the final act still bore the marks of Glass' handiwork.

As finally passed, the Banking Act of 1935 placed several new weapons at the disposal of the Federal Reserve Board. It could now approve or reject the appointment of the president and vice-president of Federal Reserve Banks. It could—within limits—change the reserve requirements of member banks. And of greatest importance, it could now control the new Federal Open Market Committee and thus dominate the initiation and conduct of open-market operations. Both Eccles and his opponents praised the new law. In spite of its weaknesses, there was a general consensus that it would go a long way toward transferring control of the money market from New York to Washington.

The act was obviously a compromise measure that tried to reconcile conflicting points of view. It strengthened the powers of the Federal Reserve Board, but the country still had no central bank. As the economic planners pointed out, many of the new powers were essentially negative in nature, designed only to prevent abuses and check unwise policies, not to provide central direction. The unit banking system, with its multitude of small banks and the division of authority between federal and state governments, had also emerged essentially intact. It had been strengthened somewhat by the guarantee of bank deposits and stricter rules, but the more radical proposals, the measures that would establish branch banking, create a unified banking system, nationalize the banks, or socialize the credit function, had all been defeated.

American banking policy, like American economic policy in general, was a curious mixture of planning and decentralization. Elements of it still reflected the attempt to satisfy the competitive ideal, the tradition of localism, and the old aversion to financial concentration. Yet other elements did reflect the needs of a complex industrial civilization, the need for a central money market, over-all economic management, and some way to insure that this concentrated power was used in the public interest. Typically, it seemed, the avowed foes of the Money Power were still undecided as to just which course to pursue. On one hand, there was a growing belief that banking was one of the "natural monopolies," one of those areas of economic endeavor that should be centralized and then subjected to strict controls or transferred to the state. Yet mixed with this view, sometimes in the same individual, was a yearning for past simplicities and a tendency to look upon the small unit bank as a symbol of democracy, as a locally controlled institution, responsive to community needs, with officers that had the welfare of the home folks at heart. The alleged advantages and efficiencies of consolidation, some reformers argued, were illusions or myths, and the only real solution lay in a return to small units and enforced competition.[9]

[9] Marriner S. Eccles, *Beckoning Frontiers* (N.Y.: Knopf, 1951), 166–75, 179–81, 187, 196–229, 269; Tugwell, *Democratic Roosevelt*, 368–69, 373; Edwards, *Finance Capitalism*, 291–95; Weissman, *New Federal Reserve*, 76–87, 91, 120–23, 167–71; John M. Blum, *From the Morgenthau Diaries*, I (Boston: Houghton Mifflin, 1959), 344–53; Schlesinger, *Politics of Upheaval*, 292–301; Pecora, *Wall Street*, 237–38; *Congressional Record*, 74 Cong., 1 Sess., LXXIX, 1501, 1514–24, 6792–93, 6800–4, 6813–20, 6908–9, 6916–19, 6923–25, 6952, 6971–72, 7183–86, 7251–71, 11776–79, 11824–27, 11840–41, 11906, 11935, 13655, 13688–711, 14768; 49 *U.S. Statutes* 684, Public, No. 305, 74 Cong.; Howard H. Preston, in *Journal of Political Economy*, Dec. 1935, pp. 743-62; Frederick A. Bradford, in

V

A similar conflict also existed in the field of monetary and currency policy. For example, the agrarian tradition had once been closely associated with a preference for hard money, with the idea that bankers and "paper capitalists" were somehow artificial and injurious to the interests of the small property owner. During the nineteen thirties, men like Herbert Agar continued to expound this point of view. Easy money and bank credit, they argued, were the root causes of the depression, the devices by which the small owner was betrayed into the hands of the monopolist, and their solution, like that of the Locofocos in the days of Jackson, was to "throw away all the hocus-pocus of wizard finance" and return to sound money that would actually be convertible into gold. More generally, however, the trustbusters tended to be inflationists, a position that was particularly true of the Western progressives and farm leaders, many of whom continued to think in terms of the old Populist ideology. The power to create and destroy money, they insisted, should be exercised exclusively by the federal government, and under the existing circumstances, should be used to expand the money supply, thus raising prices and providing debt relief.

Many of the antitrusters, then, tended to agree with the inflationary ideas that were being pushed by the farm organizations, monetary cranks, and such business groups as the Committee for the Nation. More money, they felt, would help to check financial concentration. Generally speaking, they strongly supported the inflationary experiments of the early New Deal. The Thomas Amendment, for example, which authorized the President to issue green-

AER, Dec. 1935, pp. 663–72; Jacob Viner, in AER *Supplement*, March 1936, pp. 106–19; Marc A. Rose, in *Today*, Sept. 14, 1935, pp. 8–9, 22–23; Sassoon G. Ward, in *Nation*, June 26, 1935, pp. 737–38; Elliott V. Bell, in *Current History*, July 1935, pp. 353–59; A. D. Gayer, in *QJE*, Nov. 1935, pp. 98–99, 103–116.

backs, coin silver, and resort to other inflationary expedients, had the staunch backing of the Western agrarians and other advocates of cheap money. The same general group cheered and supported the abandonment of the gold standard, the torpedoing of the London Economic Conference, the adoption of the gold purchase plan, and the passage of the Silver Purchase Act. Such measures, to be sure, were relatively unsuccessful. Typically, their proponents failed to realize that simply making more money available would not necessarily insure that it would be spent. But still the cheap money idea persisted. As late as 1938 and 1939 Wright Patman, Usher Burdick, Robert L. Owen, Elmer Thomas, and others were still pushing a variety of inflationist schemes, and the arguments for them were still couched in terms of an attack on the Money Power.[10]

Antitrusters and advocates of decentralization were also prominent in the movement for "Constitutional money" or "100% reserves," a reform that was designed to deprive the bankers of their power to expand or contract the

[10] Dorfman, *Economic Mind*, v, 679–81, 685–89; James D. Paris, *Monetary Policies of the United States, 1932–8* (N.Y.: Columbia U. Press, 1938), 17–26, 42–56, 77–80, 103–9; Arthur W. Crawford, *Monetary Management under the New Deal* (Washington: American Council on Public Affairs, 1940), 14, 17–18, 36–46, 53–57, 69–75, 95–114, 198–204, 252–53, 266, 304, 336–52; Schlesinger, *Coming of New Deal*, 195–252; National Monetary Conference, *Honest Money Year Book and Directory, 1940* (Chicago: Honest Money Founders, Inc., 1939), 24–25, 134–42; Irving Fisher, *Stable Money* (N.Y.: Adelphi, 1934), 113–22, 183–92, 360–73; Donald R. McCoy, *Angry Voices* (Lawrence: U. of Kans. Press, 1958), 12–14; Bray Hammond, *Banks and Politics in America* (Princeton: Princeton U. Press, 1957), 35–37, 493–99, 605–26; Herbert Agar, *Land of the Free* (Boston: Houghton Mifflin, 1935), 220–28, 232–33, 265–69; and in *American Review*, Feb. 1935, pp. 432–34; *Congressional Record*, 73 Cong., 1 Sess., LXXVII, 483–88, 2004–5, 2079–83, 2148–50, 2216–32, 2452–57, 2520–22, 2551–52; 73 Cong., 2 Sess., LXXVIII, 963–67, 981–84, 994–96, 999–1002, 1253–54, 1400–4, 1444–61, 6671–73, 9986–92, 11030, 11060; 75 Cong., 3 Sess., LXXXIII, 1010–11, 2015–20, 4812–14, Appendix, 1783–85; 76 Cong., 1 Sess., LXXXIV, 2928–32, 7206–9, 7583–97; P. H. Noyes, in *Nation*, Dec. 6, 1933, p. 654.

money supply and thus create booms and depressions. The underlying idea came from a variety of sources, from the writings of "commodity-dollar" advocates like Irving Fisher, from Lauchlin Currie's *Supply and Control of Money*, from similar reforms that were being advocated abroad, and especially from Henry C. Simons and his colleagues at the University of Chicago. Essentially, it called for the banks to stop their "free and unlimited coinage of debt," to back all their checking deposits with one hundred percent cash reserves, and to lend only from their own capital, savings accounts, or money repaid on maturing loans. And to enable them to do this, a central monetary authority would print the necessary cash, use it to buy banking assets, and adjust the money supply to conform with over-all economic and social goals. The plan, so some of its proponents insisted, would correct the basic defects in the monetary system and render unnecessary any central bank or any socialization of commercial banking operations.

During the period from 1933 to 1939, the "100% reserve" plan was constantly agitated, both in and out of Congress. Henry Simons made it an integral part of his "positive program for laissez faire." Organizations like the National Monetary Conference, the Honest Money Foundation, and the Constitutional Money League endorsed it. Bronson Cutting and Wright Patman introduced it in Congress. Eventually, it found its way into the monetary programs of T. Alan Goldsborough, Gerald P. Nye, Martin L. Sweeney, Charles G. Binderup, and other critics of private banking. Most congressmen, however, seemed reluctant to nationalize the monetary function. Numerous critics felt that the proposal was too drastic, and consequently, nothing came of it. The private bankers managed to retain much of their power over the money supply.[11]

[11] Irving Fisher, *100% Money* (N.Y.: Adelphi, 1935), vii–xiii, 8–17, 20–24; and *Stable Money*, 396–97; Lauchlin Currie, *The Supply and Control of Money in the United States* (Cambridge:

Another undesirable aspect of the financial system, according to antitrusters, was its tendency to discriminate against small businessmen, particularly those who were located in the hinterland. Much of the larger firm's advantage, so the argument ran, stemmed from its access to credit, its ability to borrow at cheaper rates, or its ability to raise capital by issuing new securities. During the nineteen thirties, the demand for liquidity on the part of investors and lenders placed the small firm at an even greater disadvantage. It seemed, in fact, that decentralization and equality of opportunity would no longer be enough, that if small business was to secure the necessary credit and capital, the government would have to provide special facilities.

One possible way to provide such aid was through the Federal Reserve Banks, and there were some efforts along this line. A measure in 1932 allowed the Reserve Banks to provide working capital to businesses that could not obtain loans on a reasonable basis elsewhere. And in 1934 the Industrial Advances Act made it possible for banks to grant five-year loans for working capital, then, after assuming responsibility for twenty percent of any possible loss, to discount the resulting paper at the Reserve Banks. But in practice, these measures were little used. Typically,

---

Harvard U. Press, 1934), 151–56; Charles R. Whittlesey, *Banking and the New Deal* (Chicago: U. of Chicago Press, 1935), 21–24; Crawford, *Monetary Management*, 121–22, 200–2; National Monetary Conference, *Honest Money Year Book*, 100–3, 118, 132–34, 137, 180–82; *Congressional Record*, 73 Cong., 2 Sess., LXXVIII, 10557, 10671; 74 Cong., 1 Sess., LXXIX, 2898–2900, 2961, 11842–45, 14215; 75 Cong., 3 Sess., LXXXIII, 651–52, 7184–85, Appendix, 1693; 76 Cong., 1 Sess., LXXXIV, 2591, 10605–6, Appendix, 1491–1501, 3136–39; Henry C. Simons, *A Positive Program for Laissez-Faire* (Chicago: U. of Chicago Press, 1934), 15–16, 18, 23–26; and in *AER Supplement*, March 1936, pp. 69–70; Albert G. Hart, in *Review of Economic Studies*, II (1934–5), 104–16; James W. Angell, in *QJE*, Nov. 1935, pp. 5–16, 30–35; Harry G. Brown, in *AER*, June 1940, pp. 309–14.

the requirements for collateral and financial soundness were so stringent that small entrepreneurs could not qualify, and even where they could, most bankers continued to feel that long-term small business loans were too risky.

Another agency that might be used to control or supplant the investment bankers and divert a larger share of capital and credit to small enterprises was the Reconstruction Finance Corporation. This idea of helping small business was partially responsible for the agency's new lending powers in 1934. Like the Federal Reserve Banks, it could now supply working capital to established enterprises for periods up to five years, providing the enterprises concerned could not obtain such loans from other sources. As interpreted and administered, though, the measure failed to provide much relief. Jesse Jones, to be sure, had no love for Wall Street. As head of the RFC, he made it clear that the agency would not be used as a backstop for the New York bankers. Yet, at the same time, he also made it clear that he did not intend to supplant private lenders and that he was not running a relief agency for small business. The law, he decided, did not authorize him to extend loans for fixed capital, refunding, construction, or repairs. In providing working capital, he insisted upon sound collateral and a substantial record of financial responsibility. "If the struggling enterprise was strong enough to satisfy the requirements of the Reconstruction Finance Corporation," noted one critic, "it was ordinarily easier to borrow privately." [12]

[12] Rudolph L. Weissman, *Small Business and Venture Capital* (N.Y.: Harper, 1945), 33–45, 74, 78–88; John H. Cover et al., *Problems of Small Business* (TNEC Monograph 17, 1941), 219–28, 231–36; Weissman, *New Federal Reserve*, 145–47; Douglas, *Democracy and Finance*, 20–31; Schlesinger, *Coming of New Deal*, 431–33; *Congressional Record*, 73 Cong., 2 Sess., LXXVIII, 9286–87, 9294–95; 47 *U.S. Statutes* 709, Public, No. 302, 72 Cong.; 48 *U.S. Statutes* 1105, Public, No. 417, 73 Cong.; Berle, in *Yale Review*, Sept. 1933, pp. 28–29, 41; Joseph L. Nicholson, in *Harvard Business Review*, Autumn 1938, pp. 31–33; James C. Dolley, in

Still another possibility was the establishment of special agencies or special banks, and again there were a number of suggestions along this line. In 1934, Adolf Berle worked out a plan for a system of "capital credit" banks, institutions that would seek out new investment opportunities and provide venture capital to men of initiative and ability. The Treasury and the Federal Reserve Board also produced a bill for a chain of intermediate credit banks, and for a time, it seemed that President Roosevelt himself would push the proposal. In March 1934 he recommended the establishment of a dozen credit banks "for the small or medium-size industrialist." After the lending powers of the RFC and the Federal Reserve Banks were extended, however, the proposals for new banking and lending institutions were allowed to languish. A few men, like Herman Kopplemann and T. N. Beckman, kept the idea alive, but not until after the recession of 1937 was it again given serious consideration. Even then, in spite of numerous proposals and a good deal of agitation, the only action taken was another limited extension of the RFC's lending powers. Additional relief and the eventual establishment of a Small Business Administration would have to await the developments of the postwar period.[13]

QJE, Feb. 1936, pp. 236–37, 245–49, 264–74; Marshall D. Ketchum, in *Journal of Business*, April 1944, pp. 84–90; *Fortune*, May 1940, pp. 45–50, 132, 134, 136, 139–40, 142, 144; Grosvenor Jones, "Loans to Small Business," March 27, 1939, Secretary of Commerce File, Hopkins Papers; W. N. Rastall, "NRA and Relations with Other Government Agencies" (Nov. 1935), 13, CTS, NRA Records.

[13] Weissman, *Small Business*, 53–56, 68–72, 74–78, 88–94; Blum, *Morgenthau Diaries*, 415; FDR, *Public Papers*, III, 152–55; Cover et al., *Small Business*, 228–30, 237–39, 278; Schlesinger, *Coming of New Deal*, 432–33; *Congressional Record*, 74 Cong., 1 Sess., LXXIX, 2359, 6915–16, 75 Cong., 3 Sess., LXXXIII, 1382, 1485, 1683, 3008; 76 Cong., 1 Sess., LXXXIV, 1536, 2441–46, 2472–73, 2511–12; 52 *U.S. Statutes* 212, Public, No. 479, 75 Cong.; Ketchum, in *Journal of Business*, July 1944, pp. 164, 169–71; *Business Week*, Feb. 24, 1934, p. 7; March 24, 1934, p. 11; Nov. 17, 1934, pp. 5–6; April 2, 1938, p. 15; Adolf A. Berle, "Banking System for Capital and Capital Credit," May 23, 1939, Statements to Commission

In retrospect, the attempt to destroy the Money Power achieved only limited success, partly perhaps because its opponents were still undecided as to just what it was or how the battle against it could best be conducted. As noted previously, the antitrusters found it difficult to agree among themselves, particularly in regard to monetary policy, special aid for small business, and the merits of a decentralized unit banking system. From the standpoint of the economic planners, most of the Brandeisian ideas were either meaningless or positively harmful. As they saw it, the solicitude shown for little banks and amateur bankers seemed only to weaken the banking system, lower the quality of its services, and prevent its integration into a program of centralized planning. The efforts to subsidize small business and promote decentralization were essentially wasteful and futile. And the attempts to promote fair practices and business honesty bore little relation to the real problems of economic concentration. They did nothing about the power of a self-perpetuating managerial elite, nothing about unsound capital structures, and nothing about the problem of mobilizing capital and regulating its use.

The real need, the planners insisted, was for a government agency that could supervise, evaluate, and regulate the flow of investments. Or alternatively, the government itself might have to take over the investment function. The group that backed Mordecai Ezekiel's Industrial Expansion Plan, for example, thought in terms of placing a prohibitive tax upon private investment bankers and then transferring their functions to a new system of Capi-

File, TNEC Records; Jones, "Loans to Small Business," March 27, 1939; Benjamin Cohen to Stuart Guthrie, May 1, 1939, with accompanying memo. and draft of bill, both in Secretary of Commerce File, Hopkins Papers; *New York Times*, Feb. 16, March 5–6, 19–20, 25, 29, 1934.

tal Issue Banks, institutions that would finance the industrial expansion program, underwrite new stock issues, and market all securities affecting interstate commerce.

It was probable, though, that both the planners and antitrusters were unduly concerned about the power of High Finance. As already noted, the influence of the investment bankers had declined sharply during the nineteen twenties, and during the thirties it declined even further, partly because of the monetary reforms, but perhaps mostly because of the existence of surplus funds and large corporate surpluses, coupled with the fact that corporations needed less money, were less dependent upon capital market flotations, and could therefore ignore or bypass the bankers. Near the end of the decade various studies showed that investment banking was no longer a highly lucrative business, that the extent of banker control over key industries had declined markedly, and that in spite of various charges to the contrary, there was little evidence of any banker conspiracy to fix rates or prices.[14]

In some respects, it seems that the Money Power was only a phantom evil, a menace that existed more in the past than in the present. Consequently, its opponents

[14] Loss, *Securities Regulation*, 78–80, 264–68, 920–21; Weissman, *Small Business*, 62–63; Edwards, *Finance Capitalism*, 312–18, 332–37; Atkins et al., *Security Markets*, 35–41, 57–74, 85–91, 115–16; Waterman, *Investment Banking*, 60–92; T. K. Haven, *Investment Banking under the Securities and Exchange Commission* (Ann Arbor: U. of Mich. Press, 1940), 38–39, 82–97, 140, 149–50; Oscar L. Altman, *Saving, Investment, and National Income* (TNEC Monograph 37, 1941), 62–63, 89–91; Cochran, *Business System*, 179–83; Tugwell, *Democratic Roosevelt*, 230, 240, 264, 368–69; Caroline F. Ware and Gardiner Means, *The Modern Economy in Action* (N.Y.: Harcourt, Brace, 1936), 103–12, 216–17, 223; *U.S. v. Henry S. Morgan* (Civil Action 43–757, U.S. Dist. Ct., S.D.N.Y., 1954), 43–44, 117–33, 168–73, 213–14, 294–96, 415–16; Irving B. Altman and W. J. Lauck, in *Common Sense*, April 1935, pp. 22–25; Aug. 1938, pp. 9–10; *Nation*, Feb. 28, 1934, p. 232; Nov. 28, 1934, pp. 613–14; Feb. 27, 1935, p. 236; June 24, 1939, p. 713; Paul T. Homan, in *Political Science Quarterly*, June 1936, pp. 164, 167; H.R. 7480, Aug. 3, 1939; Claude Watts to Thurman Arnold, April 5, 1940, both in Box 14.2, Arnold Papers.

could never really hope to solve the problem of concentrated economic power by financial reform alone. Their ability to pose as dragon slayers, however, did produce some useful reforms, particularly in the way of new monetary and credit controls, stock exchange regulation, and the promotion of business honesty. Elsewhere, too, the antitrusters were making some progress. Another evil dragon they were determined to slay, for example, was the Power Trust, and it seems advisable to turn next to their efforts along this line.

CHAPTER 17. THE ANTITRUSTERS
AND THE POWER TRUST

As Norman Hapgood looked back over the New Deal reforms in 1936, he could find only two areas in which the struggle against monopoly had made any real gains. One was the area of corporate finance, where the advocates of decentralization, the "true" liberals, were responsible for the securities legislation and other restrictions on Wall Street. The other was in the battle against the Power Trust, where the TVA and the Holding Company Act constituted about the "only steps ahead since Wilson." In these areas, antitrusters had taken on two of the most hated enemies in progressive demonology, and they had won some significant victories.

In both areas, however, antitrusters had difficulty in agreeing upon a course of remedial action. Consequently, the power measures, like the financial reforms, often failed to fit any logically consistent pattern. Some antitrusters would accept the power industry as a "natural monopoly" and then either nationalize it or subject it to comprehensive regulation. Others proposed setting up "government yardsticks" to lower rates and provide a standard for regulation. Still others wanted to combine regulation with trustbusting so as to break up large units, destroy the political strength of the power interests, and make the industry amenable to local control.

The search for new approaches to the power problem stemmed largely from the failure of public utility regulation in the nineteen twenties. Too often, it seemed, the local regulatory commissions had degenerated into "boards of arbitration," agencies that were concerned chiefly with adjusting private disputes rather than protecting the public. Too often, rate bases had been inflated and regulation turned into a safe haven for guaranteed profits. And too often the regulatory agencies had passed under the domination of the very interests they were supposed to regulate. The states, moreover, had been unable to prevent or control the growth of giant interstate holding companies with highly complex financial structures. The result, in the words of William Z. Ripley, was all sorts of "prestidigitation, double shuffling, honeyfugling, hornswoggling, and skullduggery," all sorts of devices for inflating rates, milking investors, plundering the operating companies, and influencing public opinion.[1]

Long before 1933, then, progressive reformers had been trying without much success to bolster state regulation with federal laws and public competition. Twice Senator George W. Norris had piloted a bill through Congress calling for public operation of the federal power facilities at Muscle Shoals, and twice the measure had been vetoed. There were indications, though, that the situation was changing. In 1928 the Senate had defied "the mightiest lobby ever assembled in Washington" by voting for a full-scale probe of holding company activities and had thus set in motion one of the most widely publicized and extensive investigations of all time. Year by year, Robert Healy and a dedicated band of FTC investigators plowed through the jungles of holding company accounting, uncovering some of the weirdest and most disastrous financing the nation

[1] James C. Bonbright and Gardiner Means, *The Holding Company* (N.Y.: McGraw-Hill, 1932), 153–87, 221–22; Twentieth Century Fund, *Electric Power and Government Policy* (N.Y., 1948), 42–43, 243–45; Rexford G. Tugwell, *The Democratic Roosevelt* (Garden City: Doubleday, 1957), 168, 366; John Bauer and Nathaniel Gold, *The Electric Power Industry* (N.Y.: Harper, 1939), 133–34, 141–66; Stephen Raushenbush, *The Power Fight* (N.Y.: New Republic, 1932), 15–45, 79–109; William Z. Ripley, *Main Street and Wall Street* (Boston: Little, Brown, 1927), 303; Richard L. Neuberger, in *Current History*, Sept. 1936, pp. 65–71; Frederick R. Barkley, in *Outlook and Independent*, Dec. 17, 1930, pp. 614–16, 635–36; Burton Wheeler, in *Congressional Record*, 74 Cong., 1 Sess., LXXIX, 4596–97; Leland Olds, in *Yale Review*, June 1935, pp. 704–23; Norman S. Buchanan, in *Journal of Political Economy*, Feb. 1936, pp. 45–53; *Fortune* Feb. 1938, pp. 62, 128; Norman Hapgood to FDR, Feb. 13, 1936; Hapgood to William Borah, May 30, 1936, PPF 2278, Roosevelt Papers.

had ever known. Then, as the depression deepened and the creations of Samuel Insull and other power magnates collapsed about their founders, the House Commerce Committee had begun a second investigation, retaining for that purpose Dr. Walter M. W. Splawn of the University of Texas. In the Federal Power Commission, too, there were signs of new life, as Frank McNinch, the newly appointed member from North Carolina, joined with Claude Draper of Wyoming to challenge conservative control. By 1933, reform was clearly in the air. Whatever else the incoming Administration might do, it would have to do something about the Power Trust.[2]

President Roosevelt, moreover, had long had well-defined views on the power question. As governor of New York, he had waged a campaign for cheap electricity, both by giving wide publicity to studies of comparative power rates and by appointing the New York Power Authority to foster the development of public power. Repeatedly, he

[2] Marion L. Ramsay, *Pyramids of Powers* (N.Y.: Bobbs-Merrill, 1937), 12, 173–79; Carl D. Thompson, *Confessions of the Power Trust* (N.Y.: Dutton, 1932), xix–xx, 19–20; C. H. Pritchett, *The Tennessee Valley Authority* (Chapel Hill: U. of N.C. Press, 1943), 12–18; Preston J. Hubbard, *Origins of the TVA* (Nashville: Vanderbilt U. Press, 1961), 219–36, 286–97, 309–14; Robert D. Baum, *The Federal Power Commission and State Utility Regulation* (Washington: American Council on Public Affairs, 1942), 28; Joseph S. Ransmeier, *The Tennessee Valley Authority* (Nashville: Vanderbilt U. Press, 1942), 56–60; House Commerce Committee, *Public Utility Holding Companies* (74 Cong., 1 Sess., 1935), 55–57, 121; Senate Commerce Committee, *Public Utility Holding Company Act of 1935* (74 Cong., 1 Sess., 1935), 70–75, 98–102; FTC, *Summary Report on Economic, Financial, and Corporate Phases of Holding and Operating Companies of Electric and Gas Utilities* (Senate Doc. 92, Pt. 72-A, 70 Cong., 1 Sess., 1935), 1–17. The FTC investigation lasted approximately seven years and resulted in the eventual publication of some eighty-four volumes plus numerous supplements and exhibits. These were published under the title of *Utility Corporations* (Senate Doc. 92, 1928–35). The investigations of the House Commerce Committee were published in six volumes in 1934 under the title of *Relation of Holding Companies to Operating Companies in Power and Gas Affecting Control* (House Report 827, 73 Cong., 2 Sess., 1934).

had championed such things as holding company control, regulation of power company financing, and the establishment of the "prudent investment" principle of rate-making. And during the Presidential campaign, he had called for the development of four great public projects to act as a "national yardstick," one on the St. Lawrence River, one at Muscle Shoals, one at Boulder Dam, and one on the Columbia River.[3]

Consequently, it was not surprising that Roosevelt should deal promptly with the Muscle Shoals question. In January 1933 he and Senator Norris visited the Tennessee Valley area. And on April 10 he sent a message to Congress asking for the creation of a Tennessee Valley Authority. As approved on May 18, the TVA combined the objective of cheaper and more plentiful power with a program designed to provide navigation and flood control, attract new industries, and inaugurate an experiment in rural rehabilitation. In one sense, it was an experiment in planning, paternalism, and public enterprise; yet the advocates of decentralization also found much to praise in the TVA program. They saw it not only as an instrument to smash the Power Trust, but also as an experiment in decentralized administration, regional development, and the encouragement of small integrated communities in which the workers might still be attached to the land and yet have access to factories as a source of supplementary income. Here in the Tennessee Valley, they hoped, one might achieve the dream of a balanced rural-industrial society, a society of small units based upon cheap and flexible power, good transportation, and the latest technology.

In the meantime, the New Deal was moving against the

[3] Daniel R. Fusfeld, *The Economic Thought of Franklin D. Roosevelt and the Origins of the New Deal* (N.Y.: Columbia U. Press, 1956), 134–53; Ramsay, *Pyramids of Power*, 183, 188–92, 197; Ernest R. Abrams, *Power in Transition* (N.Y.: Scribner's, 1940), 21–22; FDR, *Looking Forward* (N.Y.: Day, 1933), 139–54; in *Forum*, Dec. 1929, pp. 327–32; and *Public Papers and Addresses*, 1 (N.Y.: Random House, 1938), 727–42.

Power Trust along other fronts. One line of attack took the form of PWA subsidies and loans to municipalities to enable them to construct their own power plants or distribution services. A second took the form of an electric rate survey and the publication of comparative rates by the Federal Power Commission. A third was represented by the development of such national projects as the Bonneville and Grand Coulee dams, and a fourth by the creation of the Rural Electrification Administration to provide funds that would enable rural cooperatives to construct their own distribution systems. From a variety of angles the Roosevelt Administration was attacking the power problem. Thus, in time, an abundance of cheap and easily accessible power might be forthcoming, power that would do more than any prohibitory law to promote decentralization, reinvigorate the hinterland, and encourage a society of small competitive units.[4]

II

By late 1934, the Roosevelt Administration was preparing to move against the chief citadel of the Power Trust,

[4] Pritchett, TVA, 27–30; David E. Lilienthal, TVA (N.Y.: Harper, 1944), 22–24, 141–51; Abrams, Power, 27–37, 46–60, 198–200; Twentieth Century Fund, Power and Government Policy, 149, 491–94, 575–76; David C. Coyle, Roads to a New America (Boston: Little, Brown, 1938), 221–25; FDR, Public Papers, I, 886–88; II, 122–29; Arthur M. Schlesinger, Jr., The Coming of the New Deal (Boston: Houghton Mifflin, 1959), 319–20, 323–26; and The Politics of Upheaval (Boston: Houghton Mifflin, 1960), 376–83; 48 U.S. Statutes 58, Public, No. 17, 73 Cong.; FPC, Annual Report (1934), 4–5, 9–13; (1935), 6–7; and Preliminary Report of the Electric Rate Survey (1935), 4–5, 8; Jonathan Mitchell, in New Republic, Oct. 18, 1933, pp. 272–74; Henry T. Hunt, ibid., Feb. 27, 1935, pp. 71–73; Paul Hutchinson, in Scribner's, Oct. 1934, pp. 196–200; Joseph S. Lawrence, in Review of Reviews, Jan. 1934, pp. 21–22; Thomas Blaisdell, Address, Dec. 29, 1934, Blaisdell File, NRPB Records; Hapgood to Walter Lippmann, July 5, 1935; Frank McNinch to FDR, Aug. 13, 1934; Jan. 23, 1935; Harold Ickes to FDR, Sept. 8, 1934, all in Roosevelt Papers (PPF 2278, OF 235, 466B).

against the complicated financial structure created by its pyramids of holding companies. The investigations of the FTC and the House Commerce Committee were now nearing completion, and the indictment they were framing was a long one. The chief purpose of pyramiding, they charged, was to enable a minimum investment to control a maximum of operating facilities, and the result was a wide variety of abuses. The power companies had loaded their capital accounts with arbitrary or imaginary amounts to establish a base for excessive rates. Holding companies had entered into transactions with subsidiaries for the express purpose of recording arbitrary profits or fixing valuations unjustified by market values. Company executives had issued excessive obligations, manipulated security markets, paid dividends from capital, and milked the operating companies through such devices as excessive service charges and "upstream loans." And to add insult to injury, the power interests had exerted improper influence over newspapers, political assemblies, schools, teachers, and religious bodies. The different and questionable acts, concluded the FTC, ran well into the hundreds; and unless the government took action, there was every prospect that the process of pyramiding would continue until a nationwide monopoly had been established.[5]

The first shot in the Administration's campaign came in July 1934 when the President appointed Harold Ickes

[5] Thompson, *Power Trust*, 19, 118–19, 191–97, 269–72, 283–86, 330–92, 417–22, 632–48; FTC, *Summary Report on Holding and Operating Companies of Electric and Gas Utilities* (Senate Doc. 92, Pt. 73-A, 1935), 61–65; *Efforts by Associations and Agencies of Electric and Gas Utilities to Influence Public Opinion* (Senate Doc. 92, Pt. 71-A, 1934), 391–94; and *Publicity and Propaganda Activities by Utilities Groups and Companies* (Senate Doc. 92, Pt. 81-A, 1935), 245–46; Senate Commerce Committee, *Holding Company Act*, 70–71, 108–12; Westmore Hodges, "Notes on Public Utility Holding Companies"; FTC, "Conclusions and Recommendations" (Jan. 1935), 9–12, 14, both in Roosevelt Papers (OF 293, 100).

chairman of a National Power Policy Committee,[6] which was to consider legislation "on the subject of holding companies and for the regulation of electric current in interstate commerce." The task of drafting an appropriate bill naturally devolved upon the Committee's general counsel, Benjamin V. Cohen. Accordingly, the team of Corcoran and Cohen soon had a measure ready for consideration, one that would prohibit a number of specific abuses and give the Securities and Exchange Commission broad powers to regulate the financing of utility holding companies and compel simplification of their corporate structures. Suggestions were also pouring in from other quarters. The FTC favored the use of graduated taxes, levied in proportion to the holdings of one company in others and the amount of income that such a company derived from its subsidiaries. The Treasury was backing the proposals of Herman Oliphant and Robert Jackson for taxation of intercorporate dividends. Dr. Splawn, now with the Interstate Commerce Commission, advocated the complete abolition of holding companies. And the FPC wanted authority to regulate all electrical utilities engaged in the interstate transmission of power.

All the various proposals were eventually referred to an interdepartmental committee headed by Attorney-General Homer Cummings. Out of its meetings came a composite draft, one that was based largely on the work of Corcoran and Cohen, but which also included, at the President's insistence, a mandatory "death sentence" for all utility holding companies. Such companies were to be dissolved within a period of five years unless the Federal Power Commission certified that their continuance was necessary for the operation of an economic unit in contiguous states, and

[6] The committee included Morris L. Cooke, Robert Healy, David Lilienthal, Edward Markham, Frank McNinch, Elwood Mead, and T. W. Norcross. See NPPC, "Report on Public Utility Holding Companies," March 7, 1935, Barrows File, NRPB Records.

in such cases, the remaining holding companies would be limited to a single tier. In this form, the bill was introduced by Senator Burton K. Wheeler and Representative Sam Rayburn on February 6, 1935.[7]

The power companies, of course, immediately filed a strong protest and set about mobilizing support from their stockholders. Regulation, they declared, was one thing; "malicious" and "wanton" destruction, like that envisioned under the Wheeler-Rayburn bill, was another. Such a law would bankrupt numerous operating units and force the liquidation of securities at distress prices, thus retarding recovery, holding back the flow of new capital, ruining thousands of innocent investors, and wiping out the savings of poor "widows and orphans." The whole measure, moreover, was based upon false premises. It ignored the obvious advantages of the holding company, its ability to diversify risk, raise capital, and provide cheaper and better engineering and management services. Also, it accepted the unfounded allegations of the FTC, whose report was nothing but a "vicious piece of dirt-digging," one that catered to the "proponents of public ownership," was prepared by "fearful subordinates," and contained "incredible distortions of fact and false theories."[8]

[7] Senate Commerce Committee, *Holding Company Act*, 9–49, 70–75, 143, 155–56, 239–40; Schlesinger, *Politics of Upheaval*, 303–6; FTC, *Summary Report on Holding and Operating Companies*, 66–74; *Congressional Record*, 74 Cong., 1 Sess., LXXIX, 1525, 1624; Joseph Alsop and Robert Kintner, in *Saturday Evening Post*, Nov. 12, 1938, pp. 9, 102; *New York Times*, Jan. 22–23, Feb. 6–7, 1935; Benjamin Cohen to Felix Frankfurter, Nov. 23, 1934; Cohen to Healy, Nov. 25, 1934; Feb. 1, 1935; Ickes to FDR, Jan. 18, 1935; Cohen to Ickes, Feb. 8, 1935; President's letter creating NPPC, July 9, 1934, all in Cohen File, NPPC Records; Homer Cummings to FDR, Feb. 6, 1935; Herman Oliphant to Henry Morgenthau, Dec. 18, 1934; Ewin L. Davis to FDR, Feb. 9, 1935; FTC, "Conclusions and Recommendations," all in Roosevelt Papers (OF 10, 137, 100).

[8] Schlesinger, *Politics of Upheaval*, 308–9; National Industrial Conference Board, *Public Utilities Holding Company Bill* (N.Y.: 1935), 8–9; Senate Commerce Committee, *Holding Company Act*, 287–360, 533–623; House Commerce Committee, *Utility Holding*

On March 12 the President sent the report of the National Power Policy Committee to Congress, along with a scathing denunciation of the "propaganda" against the Wheeler-Rayburn bill. It was "idle," he said, to talk about the continuation of holding companies on the assumption that regulation could deal with them. Regulation had "small chance of ultimate success" against that kind of "concentrated wealth and economic power," and it was time now to reverse the whole process, to come to grips with a system that had made "most American citizens, once traditionally independent owners of their own businesses, helplessly dependent for their daily bread upon the favor of a very few." Such passages probably reflected the fact that Tom Corcoran had now become the President's leading speechwriter. In any event, they made Roosevelt sound like a confirmed antitruster, and most advocates of decentralization hoped that they were not mere rhetoric. The basic objective, in the eyes of men like Corcoran, Senator Wheeler, and Justice Brandeis, was the simplification of the utility structure so as to allow a return to localized control and decentralized management. Such action was a necessary step in the restoration of "economic and political democracy," and if Roosevelt could put the measure through, the country would have "achieved considerable toward curbing Bigness." [9]

Companies, 587–88, 909–50, 1334–53; Wendell L. Willkie, in *Vital Speeches*, Feb. 11, May 20, 1935; pp. 297–99, 538–41; *Business Week*, April 6, 1935, pp. 27–28; June 8, 1935, p. 29; *New York Times*, Feb. 8, 17, March 18, May 18, 1935; Hodges, "Notes on Public Utility Holding Companies"; Henry L. Doherty to Security Holders of Cities Service Co., Feb. 18, 1935, both in OF 293, Roosevelt Papers.

[9] FDR, *Public Papers*, IV, 98–103, 138–39; Schlesinger, *Politics of Upheaval*, 307; *Congressional Record*, 74 Cong., 1 Sess., LXXIX, 1525, 3425–26, 4594–97; Senate Commerce Committee, *Holding Company Act*, 1–9, 65–68, 177–81; *Business Week*, March 16, 1935, p. 26; *New York Times*, March 13, April 29, 1935; NPPC Report, March 7, 1935, Barrows File, NRPB Records; Cohen to Willkie, March 21, 1935, Cohen File, NPPC Records; Hapgood to FDR, June 16, 1935; Memo. re Death Sentence, both in Roosevelt Papers (PPF 2278, 1820).

For a time, though, it seemed doubtful that the "death sentence" could be carried against the opposition of what President Roosevelt termed the "most daring lobby" ever to function in Washington. Operating through the Committee of Public Utility Executives, the American Federation of Utility Investors, and the public relations firm of Lee and Ross, the power companies raised a huge war chest and urged their investors to swamp Congress with letters and telegrams. Many of these letters were undoubtedly genuine, but others were simply "manufactured" for the occasion. Investors, for example, received "key letters," from which the writer could pick paragraphs that were applicable to his particular situation. Employees were instructed to secure a specified number of letters or lose their jobs. And in one case, a representative of the Associated Gas and Electric Company simply dictated some thirteen hundred telegrams and signed them with names taken from a city telephone directory.

Such pressure seemed to have little effect on the Senate. The Senate Commerce Committee rejected all efforts to cancel the "death sentence," attempts to amend the measure on the Senate floor were unsuccessful, and the measure that the Senate passed on June 11 differed little from the original bill. In the House, though, it was a different story. There the Commerce Committee rejected the original "death sentence" and reported a substitute measure that would allow holding companies to continue indefinitely, providing the SEC found this to be in the public interest. The committee's recommendations, moreover, made it virtually impossible to salvage the "death sentence" on the House floor. On July 1 the House rejected the provisions of the Senate bill, and the next day it passed its own version by a substantial majority and sent the measure to conference.

For the moment it seemed that the Administration had suffered a serious defeat, but paradoxically its enemies came to the rescue. Representative Ralph Brewster of

Maine now charged that Tom Corcoran had threatened to stop work on Maine's Passamaquoddy Dam project unless Brewster voted for the "death sentence," and these charges had soon touched off a highly publicized lobbying investigation that greatly strengthened the President's hand. In hearings before the House Rules Committee, Corcoran was able to explain his conduct so as to imply that Brewster had sold out to the Power Trust. Brewster, he noted, had always been regarded as a "great anti-Power Trust champion." He had participated in legislative planning, had agreed to make a speech in favor of the bill, and in order to get PWA action on the Passamaquoddy project, had given assurances that the Maine legislature would set up a state power authority. Then he had made a trip to Maine, and upon his return, had claimed that his political situation was "so delicate" that he could no longer vote for the "death sentence." Confronted with this about-face, Corcoran had reacted with "brutal frankness." "You know perfectly well I can no longer trust you on the 'Quoddy project in the future," he told Brewster. The investigating committee, after hearing both sides of the argument, concluded that there was "no suggestion of corruption or moral turpitude" in the conduct of either man.

Even more influential in shaping public opinion was the investigation conducted by a special Senate committee under the chairmanship of Senator Hugo Black. Once the committee had been established, Black quickly expanded his activities to take in the whole lobbying field. The resulting disclosure of the methods used by the power lobby gave new strength to the Senate conferees. The outcome was a conference report that contained a modified "death sentence," a plan known as the Barkley compromise although it had actually been drafted by Felix Frankfurter. Under its terms, systems containing more than three tiers of companies were to be abolished completely, and the SEC was to move as soon as practicable after January 1, 1938, to limit the smaller ones to single, integrated public utility systems. For the latter, however, it might grant exceptions if simplification would mean the loss of substantial economies, if necessary to achieve geographical integration, or if the excepted companies were not too large for localized management, efficient operation, and effective regulation.

In addition to the revised "death sentence," the new Public Utility Holding Company Act required all utility holding companies to register with the SEC, to furnish it with detailed financial information, and to secure its approval before undertaking most financial transactions, including the issuance or acquisition of securities, alteration of security rights, payment of dividends, allowances for depreciation, and plans for reorganization, dissolution, liquidation, or receivership. The Commission might also prescribe rules governing such matters as proxy solicitation, intra-system loans, intercompany transactions, service contracts, and methods of accounting. Finally, Title II of the measure authorized the Federal Power Commission to regulate the rates, security issues, and financial transactions of operating companies engaged in the interstate transmission of electricity.[10]

[10] Ramsay, *Pyramids of Power*, 258; Twentieth Century Fund, *Power and Government Policy*, 279–84, 350; John P. Frank, *Mr. Justice Black* (N.Y.: Knopf, 1949), 75–81; Kenneth G. Crawford, *The Pressure Boys* (N.Y.: Messner, 1939), 55–71; Schlesinger, *Politics of Upheaval*, 313-24; Special Senate Committee, *Investigation of Lobbying Activities* (74 Cong., 1 Sess., 1935), 5–7, 61–67, and *passim*; House Rules Committee, *Investigation of Lobbying on Utility Holding Company Bill* (74 Cong., 1 Sess., 1935), 2–13, 23–33; and *House Report 2081* (74 Cong., 2 Sess., 1936), 1–2; House Commerce Committee, *Utility Holding Companies*, 1752, 1762, 1767–69; and *House Report 1318* (74 Cong., 1 Sess., 1935), 3–6, 44; Senate Commerce Committee, *Senate Report 621* (74 Cong., 1 Sess., 1935), 4–17; *Congressional Record*, 74 Cong., 1 Sess., LXXIX, 7445, 9040–53, 9065, 10022, 10301–15, 10353–56, 10508–12, 10555, 10589, 10637–40, 10659–60, 10806–10, 11003–5, 14469–73, 14600–27; 49 *U.S. Statutes* 803, Public, No. 333, 74 Cong.; Raymond Clapper, in *Review of Reviews*, Aug. 1935, p. 18; *Business Week*, July 6, 1935, p. 8; Aug. 31, 1935, p. 8; *New York Times*, May 9, June 12, 18, July 2, 3, Aug. 22–25, 27, 1935.

As finally passed, the Public Utility Holding Company Act represented a substantial victory for the foes of economic concentration. It was a victory, however, that still lacked the sanction of the courts. Accordingly, most utility holding companies, operating on the assumption that the act was unconstitutional, simply refused to register. Not until March 1938, in the Electric Bond and Share case, did the Supreme Court finally uphold the registration requirements of the law. Not until August 1938 did the SEC ask the holding companies to submit programs for simplification. Not until 1940 did hearings on these programs begin. And even after the latter date, the SEC proceeded slowly, usually on the basis of voluntary reorganization plans.[11]

III

While the holding companies were appealing their case to the courts, a similar stalemate was developing in the program designed to provide cheaper and more plentiful power. The TVA found itself stymied in efforts to acquire distribution facilities and expand operations. The agreement upon a division of territory that it had negotiated with the Commonwealth and Southern Corporation was due to expire in 1936, and the company was now insisting that the TVA sell to no one else outside its own area, not even to public agencies. Such a demand, declared TVA director David Lilienthal, was a brazen attempt to secure a power "monopoly." Instead of acceding to it, he had

[11] Emanuel Stein, *Government and the Investor* (N.Y.: Farrar & Rinehart, 1941), 173–78; William O. Douglas, *Democracy and Finance* (New Haven: Yale U. Press, 1940), 127–33; Louis Loss, *Securities Regulation* (Boston: Little, Brown, 1951), 90–92; Twentieth Century Fund, *Power and Government Policy*, 333–34; SEC, *Annual Report* (1937), 42–43; (1938), 6–13, 46–48; (1939), 63–85; (1940), 11–18; *Electric Bond and Share Co. v. SEC*, 303 U.S. 419 (1938).

pushed through a resolution barring any further area limitations.[12]

In the hope of reaching a new agreement satisfactory to both parties, the President turned to the idea of a jointly-owned grid transmission network.[13] To explore this idea, he invited representatives of the power companies to a power pooling conference. But the conference could reach no agreement, since each side was highly suspicious of the other and in no mood to "cooperate." The private companies kept accusing the government of bad faith because it continued to subsidize municipal power systems. The government claimed that the utilities were acting in bad faith because they continued to seek court injunctions against public power operations. And progressives, like Norris and LaFollette, kept charging that the whole operation was a "sell-out" to the Power Trust. Consequently, after a district court in December 1936 issued a sweeping injunction virtually paralyzing the TVA's power activities, the President vetoed the whole idea and turned out the conferees.[14]

The issue was further complicated by the growing rift between TVA directors David Lilienthal and Arthur E.

[12] Pritchett, TVA, 66–70, 190; Schlesinger, Politics of Upheaval, 364, 367–68; Joseph Barnes, Willkie (N.Y.: Simon & Schuster, 1952), 104–5; Christian Century, Oct. 14, 1936, pp. 1350–51.

[13] The President thought the British gridiron would be a good example to follow. "But, then," he noted, "the Britishers do not everlastingly rush to the Supreme Court but instead sit round the table with the Government in good faith—and get results." FDR to Hapgood, Feb. 24, 1936, PPF 2278, Roosevelt Papers.

[14] Pritchett, TVA, 70–71; Schlesinger, Politics of Upheaval, 368–69; Louis B. Wehle, Hidden Threads of History (N.Y.: Macmillan, 1953), 161–75; Barnes, Willkie, 106–9; Business Week, Jan. 23, 1937, pp. 13–14; Basil Manly to FDR, Sept. 12, 29, 1936; Jan. 12, 1937; Robert La Follette, Jr., to FDR, Sept. 26, 1936; Louis B. Wehle to Marvin McIntyre, Oct. 19, 1936; Wehle to FDR, Oct. 26, 1936; Alexander Sachs to FDR, Jan. 16, 1937; FDR to Frederic Delano, Jan. 25, 1937; White House PR, Sept. 20, 1936; Sachs, Memo. re Power Pool Conference, Sept. 30, 1936; Sachs to FDR, Jan. 25, 1937, all in Roosevelt Papers (OF 42, 1893); President Roosevelt's Press Conferences, Jan. 26, 1937, Roosevelt Papers.

Morgan, a conflict that was in part a personality clash but also had overtones of basic policy differences. Morgan, who tended to think in terms of cooperative action and over-all economic planning, was convinced that his fellow directors had first conspired to depose him as general manager and then had put through a number of undesirable policies, such policies, for example, as the claim of "yardstick significance" for TVA power rates, the administration of the fertilizer program through land grant colleges, the disposition to cater to local established interests, and the tendency to make cheap power the primary rather than a secondary function of the agency. Lilienthal, on the other hand, was a former Frankfurter student, deeply imbued at the time with a Brandeisian antipathy toward Big Business and High Finance. Morgan, he thought, had a highly visionary, impractical, and unrealistic streak, as exemplified by his concern with the revival of folk arts, his arguments for a separate coinage system in the Tennessee Valley, and his notion that the government could cooperate and make deals with the power companies. By 1936 the clash had become a bitter one, and it was partially responsible for the breakdown of negotiations with the power companies. Morgan felt that Lilienthal was deliberately sabotaging the power pool idea, while Lilienthal was convinced that Morgan would sell out to private power interests.[15]

Still another impasse was reached in 1937 in efforts to extend the TVA type of program to other areas of the nation. In January of that year President Roosevelt appointed a new National Power Policy Committee, which

[15] Pritchett, TVA, 46–47, 148–58, 162–65, 186–94; Schlesinger, Politics of Upheaval, 363–73, 387; Joint Committee on the TVA, Investigation of the TVA (75 Cong., 3 Sess., 1938), 6, 24–35, 48–52, 58–59, 98–113, 151–91, 865–68; Willson Whitman, in Harper's, Sept. 1938, pp. 352–61; J. C. Poe, in Nation, Oct. 3, 1936, pp. 385–86; Time, Jan. 25, 1937, pp. 12–13; Today, Feb. 6, 1937, pp. 14–15, 28–30; Morris L. Cooke, "Eddies in National Power Policy," Nov. 20, 1937, PPF 1820, Roosevelt Papers.

soon began consideration of a proposal to establish eight regional planning authorities. As embodied in an Administration bill drafted by Benjamin Cohen and introduced by Representative Joseph J. Mansfield, the new agencies would be limited chiefly to planning functions, although there was a possibility that they might eventually develop into regional power authorities. At the same time, Senator Norris and Representative John Rankin introduced a measure that would go one step further and duplicate the TVA set-up in six other areas of the nation. Neither Norris nor Mansfield, however, could get much of a hearing for their proposals. An increasingly rebellious Congress, torn by the court fight and absorbed in trying to deal with the recession of 1937, promptly relegated such bills to the background and never gave them serious consideration.

Consequently, the "seven sisters" proposal never became a reality, and it was not until 1938 that the legal logjam confronting the existing power agencies began to break up. In January of that year the Supreme Court upheld the right of the PWA to make grants for municipal power plants. Confronted with this decision, the private power companies began to dispose of their properties to public agencies. The real breakthrough came the following year when the constitutionality of the TVA operations was upheld and the Commonwealth and Southern Corporation sold its entire Tennessee Electric Power system to the government.

In the meantime, the Morgan-Lilienthal feud had come to a head, resulting in the removal of Arthur Morgan and an extensive congressional investigation. In 1937 Morgan became convinced that Major George Berry's claim for damages to his marble properties because of the flooding of the Norris reservoir was an "effort at a deliberate, barefaced steal" and that the other TVA directors were implicated because they had attempted to negotiate a conciliation agreement with Berry. When the court decided against Berry, Morgan issued a public statement charging his co-directors with dishonesty. When he refused to participate in open hearings conducted by the President, Roosevelt reacted by removing him from office. The resulting investigation, though, proved to be a great disappointment to the scandalmongers. The majority report finally concluded that "Dr. A. E. Morgan's charges of dishonesty . . . are without foundation, not supported by the evidence, and made without due consideration of the available facts." [16]

IV

By the late nineteen thirties, then, in spite of numerous difficulties, a new power policy had taken shape. The Power Trust had been humbled; the holding companies were being compelled to return to financial sanity; and public yardsticks had demonstrated the potentialities of cheap power and volume operations. The power question was by no means solved, but the lines of conflict had been mapped out, and new techniques of regulation had been tested.

Power policy, moreover, had taken a direction that contrasted sharply with legislation for other industries. Especially noticeable was the contrast between it and trans-

[16] Barnes, *Willkie*, 118, 125–48; Harold L. Ickes, *Secret Diary*, II (N.Y.: Simon & Schuster, 1954), 60–61, 130; Pritchett, *TVA*, 64–65, 71–73, 139, 194–211, 247–49; *Congressional Record*, 75 Cong., 1 Sess., LXXXI, 5280–81, 5335, 5341; Joint Committee on TVA, *Investigation*, 59–94, 192–221; and *Report on Investigation of the TVA* (Senate Doc. 56, 76 Cong., 1 Sess., 1939), 237–39; *Removal of a Member of the TVA* (Senate Doc. 155, 75 Cong., 3 Sess., 1938), 7, 17, 77, 96–104; *Alabama Power Co. v. Ickes*, 302 U.S. 464 (1938); *Tenn. Electric Power Co. v. TVA*, 306 U.S. 118 (1939); *Business Week*, Feb. 11, 1939, pp. 14–15; *Congressional Digest*, Aug. 1937, pp. 193–94; Jan. 1938, pp. 3–4, 7–10; President Roosevelt's Press Conferences, Feb. 9, 1937, Roosevelt Papers; NPPC, "History of Bills Relating to Power," Nov. 1, 1937; Cohen to Paul Kellogg, Aug. 10, 1937; Cohen to Stuart Chase, Aug. 16, 1937; Harry Woodring to Ickes, Feb. 15, 1937; PWA PR 68548, Jan. 18, 1937; Drafts of a Bill for Conservation Authorities, Feb. 26, April 23, May 6, 1937, all in Cohen File, NPPC Records.

portation policy. Reform in the first instance was being forwarded by public competition and the injection of new competitive elements to force rates down. Reform in the second was trying to reduce a competitive situation to one approximating regulated monopoly so as to keep rates up. Nor were the two industries so dissimilar as they might appear at first sight. Power, to be sure, was a relatively new industry, railroads a relatively mature one; yet both were essentially monopolistic, both were overcapitalized, and in both a program designed to reduce rates, increase consumption, and stimulate high volume operations would involve a rather drastic simplification of the financial structure. In the power industry such a program was attempted, but in the field of transportation much more solicitude was shown for railroad security holders. Not only were there no public yardsticks and no real attempts to bring about financial simplification, but efforts were directed toward eliminating the competition of newer forms of transportation, the one element that might have forced lower rates. The Power Trust, it seemed, was on a par with Wall Street. For it nothing was too bad, not even a little competition.

For the advocates of decentralization, the New Deal power program was a step in the right direction. In the Holding Company Act they saw the beginning of a battle against bigness and absentee control. In the TVA and other public projects they saw the possibility of decentralizing industry, rehabilitating exploited regions, and promoting a better and more abundant life. In both lines of attack, they saw a way to break the Power Trust and reduce the political and economic strength of the power interests. Yet the implications of the power program for monopoly in general were decidedly limited. The production of electrical power, after all, was essentially a monopolistic operation. Consequently, the ideas of public competition and enforced decentralization could not be pushed to extremes without resulting in gross waste, chronic losses, or the complete substitution of public power, none of which the antitrusters really wanted. There was the possibility, too, that geographic integration might actually promote monopoly by guaranteeing exclusive rights and territories to a given company. Finally, the breakthrough involved was really a special case, one that was limited to an industry that had overreached itself and had become actively hated by a wide variety of people. Such a victory would hardly loom large in any general antitrust program. It, like the battle against the Money Power, was essentially a skirmish on the flanks.[17]

[17] Coyle, *New America*, 221–25; Schlesinger, *Politics of Upheaval*, 379; Paul T. Homan, in *Political Science Quarterly*, June 1936, pp. 163–65; Hutchinson, in *Scribner's*, Oct. 1934, pp. 197–200; *Fortune*, Feb. 1938, pp. 62, 131, 134. Some of the misgivings about the power program are expressed in Ben Gray to FDR, March 20, 1936; Samuel Pettengill to FDR, Aug. 17, 1935; John M. Keynes to FDR, Feb. 1, 1938, all in Roosevelt Papers (OF 1893, 293, PPF 5235).

CHAPTER 18. THE ANTITRUSTERS AND THE TAXING POWER

DURING the early New Deal, as previous chapters have indicated, the neo-Brandeisians had been concerned chiefly with the reform of corporate finance, and in this area, had relied primarily upon regulatory and prohibitory laws, supplemented by such devices as publicity and public competition. A number of them, however, had long felt that proper use of the taxing power would be a "more effective, if cruder" way of dealing with the problem of concentrated economic power. As Brandeis told Alfred Lief, "It is idle to say we are helpless. By taxation bigness can be destroyed." Consequently, almost from the beginning of the New Deal, Felix Frankfurter and his lieutenants had urged the President to make full use of the taxing power.

As early as 1934, too, Tom Corcoran and Benjamin Cohen had drawn up tentative drafts of possible legislation. One of their proposals would strike at "tramp corporations" by levying a special tax on companies that were organized in states where they did not do a substantial proportion of their actual business. A second would encourage simplification by taxing all transactions between corporations under common control, regardless of whether such control was exercised through a holding company, interlocking directorates, or interlocking ownership. A third, the "anti-bigness" bill introduced by Senator Burton K. Wheeler in February 1935, would levy a graduated tax on corporate incomes, starting with a rate of two percent at the three million dollar level and increasing to twenty-five percent on incomes over fifty million dollars. To get around the charge that such a tax would destroy efficiency, the bill would authorize the Federal Trade Commission to study the relation of total resources to efficiency and make recommendations for rate changes so as to encourage the most desirable maximum size in each class of business.[1]

Also, these proposals for a tax on bigness were often coupled with a variety of suggestions for using the taxing power to redistribute wealth and income. By early 1935, for example, Huey Long's share-the-wealth movement was giving Democratic politicians the jitters. Progressives like George Norris, Robert LaFollette, Jr., Gerald Nye, Hiram Johnson, and William Borah were all calling for more steeply graduated income, inheritance, and estate taxes. And Secretary of the Treasury Henry Morgenthau's tax study group, composed of such men as Herman Oliphant, Jacob Viner, George Haas, and Roswell Magill, had come up with a series of recommendations, including steeply graduated inheritance and gift taxes, a steep tax on inter-corporate dividends, corporate income taxes graduated according to size, and a tax on undistributed corporate surpluses.

At first the President tended to regard both the Treasury proposals and those of the Frankfurter group as being politically premature; but by June 1935 his attitude was changing. The Long movement seemed to be gathering momentum, sentiment for economic redistribution was

[1] Alfred Lief, ed., The Brandeis Guide to the Modern World (Boston: Little, Brown, 1941), 20; and Brandeis (N.Y.: Stackpole, 1936), 471–72; Alpheus T. Mason, Brandeis (N.Y.: Viking, 1946), 621–22; Herbert Agar and Allan Tate, eds., Who Owns America? (Boston: Houghton Mifflin, 1936), 11–12, 32–35, 105; Rexford G. Tugwell, in Western Political Quarterly, Sept. 1951, p. 481; Congressional Record, 74 Cong., 1 Sess., LXXIX, 2199–2208; Business Week, March 2, 1935, p. 10; FDR to Henry Morgenthau, Jan. 16, 1935; Tom Corcoran to FDR, Jan. 14, Feb. 4, 1935; Corcoran to Marguerite LeHand, Feb. 4, 1935, with accompanying draft of Wheeler Bill; Norman Hapgood to William Borah, May 30, 1936, all in Roosevelt Papers (OF 1560, PPF 1820, 2278); Drafts of "tramp corporation," "corporate bigness," and "anti-bigness" bills, with supporting memoranda, Cohen File, NPPC Records. In the original version of the Wheeler Bill, a tax was to be levied on each thousand dollars of gross assets, beginning with one dollar on corporations having assets of one million dollars and rising to ten dollars on those having over three hundred million.

intensifying, business opposition was growing, and the Supreme Court had just knocked out the NRA. Under the circumstances, Roosevelt felt, the tax weapon might enable him to recapture the political and economic initiative. Properly used, it might serve the triple function of confounding his business opponents, placating the share-the-wealth clamor, and saving the capitalist system. Accordingly, with the aid of Morgenthau, Frankfurter, and Raymond Moley, he began work on a tax message. The original draft, as it was prepared by the Treasury, reiterated the earlier recommendations and added a proposal to increase surtaxes on incomes above $50,000. Frankfurter strongly endorsed the program; but Moley was appalled, both by its implications and by the President's attitude toward them. "Pat Harrison's going to be so surprised," the President informed him, "he'll have kittens on the spot." Moley was unable to kill the tax message, but he did succeed in persuading Roosevelt that he should narrow the range of graduation in the corporate income tax and delete the proposal to tax corporate surpluses.[2]

II

When the President's tax message reached Congress on June 19, 1935, it contained five major proposals: (1) a federal inheritance tax with a counterbalancing tax on gifts; (2) increased taxes on incomes over one million dollars; (3) a corporate income tax, under which the existing

[2] Roy G. and Gladys C. Blakey, *The Federal Income Tax* (N.Y.: Longmans, Green, 1940), 370–71; Sidney Ratner, *American Taxation* (N.Y.: Norton, 1942), 467–68; Raymond Moley, *After Seven Years* (N.Y.: Harper, 1939), 305–12; Ernest K. Lindley, *Halfway with Roosevelt* (N.Y.: Viking, 1937), 252–53; John M. Blum, *From the Morgenthau Diaries*, 1 (Boston: Houghton Mifflin, 1959), 298–301; Randolph E. Paul, *Taxation for Prosperity* (N.Y.: Bobbs-Merrill, 1947), 43–44; Arthur M. Schlesinger, Jr., *The Politics of Upheaval* (Boston: Houghton Mifflin, 1960), 325–27; *New York Times*, Feb. 16, March 15, 1935; FDR to Morgenthau, March 20, 1935; Herman Oliphant to Morgenthau, Dec. 18, 1934, both in Roosevelt Papers (OF 21, 137).

levy of 13.75 percent would be replaced by graduated rates ranging from 10.75 percent to 16.75 percent; (4) a tax on intercorporate dividends; and (5) a study of methods by which the taxing power might be used to eliminate unnecessary holding companies and discourage unwieldy and unnecessary surpluses. A major effort was to be made, the President indicated, to reverse the trend toward unjust concentration of wealth and economic power. Apparently, the move came as something of a surprise to friend and foe alike. As the message was read, Huey Long stopped, grimaced, raised his eyes, and almost waltzed. When the clerk had finished, he wanted to make a comment. "I just wish to say," he declared, "Amen!"

During the next few days the rumor spread that the message was in reality only a political gesture designed as a sop to the share-the-wealth advocates. To test the President's sincerity, Senator LaFollette, with the backing of other progressives, then proposed to attach a new tax measure to a pending resolution extending the expiration date of existing excise taxes. For a time, it seemed that Roosevelt would go along. On June 24 he summoned congressional leaders to the White House and indicated that he favored quick enactment of the program in the manner suggested by LaFollette. Reluctantly, Senator Pat Harrison and Representative Robert Doughton agreed to make the attempt. Immediately, however, the idea drew a barrage of criticism. Members of the Senate Finance Committee refused to go along without holding hearings; House leaders objected to what they called a "usurpation" of their chamber's constitutional powers; and the business world was furious. Congressional leaders were soon looking for a way out, a way to avoid the necessity of passing a major tax measure in five days. Accordingly, House leaders pledged themselves not to push for hasty adjournment, LaFollette agreed to withdraw his amendments, and Senator Harrison promised that the Senate Finance Committee would report out a tax bill during the present session. The President then cancelled the rush order, and professing innocence, asked reporters why they had ever thought the measure would be passed in such a fashion.[3]

During the hearings that followed, the chief burden of defending the President's proposals fell upon such officials as Robert Jackson of the Treasury Department and Lovell H. Parker, chief of staff of the Joint Committee on Internal Revenue Taxation. Jackson, in particular, stressed the evil effects of concentrated wealth and power, the ability of larger corporations to pay more taxes, and the desirability of encouraging small enterprises if a competitive system were to be preserved. The majority of business spokesmen, on the other hand, argued that the new tax proposals would destroy incentive, penalize efficiency, wipe out the interests of corporate investors, and turn back the economic clock. The New Deal, partly for political advantage, partly for spite, had not only adopted the "Share-the-Wealth" philosophy, but had added "Save-Little-Business," if not "Kill-Big-Business." "I have read all of Justice Brandeis's writings on the subject," declared Robert E. Wood of Sears, Roebuck and Company, "and . . . I am sure no greater fallacy was ever enunciated." [4]

[3] FDR, *Public Papers and Addresses*, IV (N.Y.: Random House, 1938), 270–77; Schlesinger, *Politics of Upheaval*, 327–31; Blakey, *Income Tax*, 366, 369–73; and in AER, Dec. 1935, pp. 673–74; Blum, *Morgenthau Diaries*, 301–3; *Congressional Record*, 74 Cong., 1 Sess., LXXIX, 9657–59; Raymond Clapper, in *Review of Reviews*, Aug. 1935, p. 19; Ashmun Brown, in *American Mercury*, April 1936, p. 392; *New York Times*, June 20–23, 25–27, 1935.

[4] House Ways and Means Committee, *Proposed Taxation of Individual and Corporate Incomes, Inheritances, and Gifts* (74 Cong., 1 Sess., 1935), 15–59, 199–223, 245–75; Senate Finance Committee, *Revenue Act of 1935* (74 Cong., 1 Sess., 1935), 4–30, 37–42, 62–76, 173–207, 210–26; Blakey, in AER, Dec. 1935, pp. 675–76, 681–82; *Business Week*, June 22, 1935, p. 5; July 6, 1935, pp. 7–8; Aug. 10, 1935, pp. 7–8; Edward Hutton and Alfred P. Sloan, Jr., in *Review of Reviews*, Aug. 1935, pp. 20–21, 76; NAM, "Industrial Stockholders Threatened by New Tax Proposals," June 27, 1935; BAPC, Report on the Tax Bill, Aug. 13, 1935; Robert E. Wood to FDR, July 18, 1935, all in Roosevelt Papers (OF 8246, 3Q, PPF 1365).

Apparently impressed by the business arguments, the House Ways and Means Committee tried to substitute an extension of the excess profits tax, but the President refused to go along. "The principle" of the graduated corporate income tax, he insisted, must be established. The result was a compromise, a bill that retained the "principle," but limited the graduation to only two rates, 13.25 percent and 14.25 percent. Also included in the House measure were provisions for increased inheritance and gift taxes, an extension of the excess profits tax, and increased rates on incomes over $50,000. In the Senate there were further changes. There the Senate Finance Committee cut out the proposed inheritance tax and substituted a plan calling for increased personal income and estate taxes, a corporate income tax graduated from 12.5 percent to 15.5 percent and a small tax on intercorporate dividends. After a brief debate, in which LaFollette tried but failed to obtain higher surtax rates, the Senate passed the measure and sent it to conference.

In the conference committee, differences were settled largely in favor of the Senate bill. The final measure resembled the Senate version in that it contained a provision under which corporate income taxes would be graduated from 12.5 percent on incomes of $2,000 to 15 percent on those over $40,000. It also retained the Senate tax on intercorporate dividends, although it lowered the taxable amount from fifteen to ten percent. Finally, it provided for increased surtax rates on all incomes over $50,000, increases in the capital stock and estate taxes, and a change in the form of the excess profits tax from flat to graduated rates. In this form, the bill was approved by both houses, and on August 30 the President added his signature.[5]

[5] Schlesinger, *Politics of Upheaval*, 331–33; Blakey, *Income Tax*, 375–82; and in *AER*, Dec. 1935, pp. 677–86; Ratner, *American Taxation*, 469–71; *Congressional Record*, 74 Cong., 1 Sess., LXXIX, 12418–45, 12499, 12897, 13201–13, 13221–28, 13254, 14484–86, 14627–32, 14644, 14822; 49 *U.S. Statutes* 1014, Public, No. 407, 74 Cong.; Harley L. Lutz, in *AER Supplement*, March 1936, pp.

As eventually passed, the Revenue Act of 1935 was hardly sufficient to effect much change in competitive relationships or bring about much redistribution of wealth, especially when one balances it against such regressive measures as the processing and social security taxes. Nevertheless, the advocates of decentralization regarded the act as an opening wedge. The small tax on intercorporate dividends might someday evolve into a weapon that would eliminate useless and monopolistic holding companies. People like David Coyle regarded the graduated corporation tax as "the most important contribution of the New Deal before 1936." "When the differential can be made severe enough," said Coyle, "there will be results." Justice Brandeis, too, thought that Roosevelt had made a "gallant fight," one that at least seemed to "appreciate fully" the "evils of bigness." [6]

III

The second major tax battle of the New Deal era began in March 1936 with the President's proposal for a tax on undistributed corporate surpluses, an idea that had a long history behind it and over the years had won the support of people with widely divergent views and philosophies. One group of basically conservative supporters, for example, thought of the tax either as a revenue-producing measure or as a means of eliminating the loophole that allowed wealthy individuals to evade their income taxes by leaving the money in corporate surpluses. On these

163–64; Business Week, Aug. 3, 1935, pp. 7–9; Aug. 24, 1935, p. 9; New York Times, July 16, 19–20, 26, Aug. 1, 11, 15–16, 21, 25, 1935; FDR to Morgenthau, July 22, 1935; Memo. re telephone call from Oliphant, Aug. 20, 1935, both in OF 137, Roosevelt Papers.

[6] David C. Coyle, in Agar and Tate, eds., Who Owns America?, 11; Lindley, Halfway with Roosevelt, 254; Ratner, American Taxation, 463, 472; Schlesinger, Politics of Upheaval, 333–34; Blakey, in AER, Dec. 1935, p. 689; Frederick Shelton, in Nation's Business, Oct. 1935, p. 21; Business Week, July 20, 1935, p. 5; Hapgood to FDR, Aug. 3, 11, 1935, PPF 2278, Roosevelt Papers.

grounds, there had been considerable agitation for such a tax during the nineteen twenties. In the immediate post-World War I period the Treasury had recommended it as a substitute for the excess profits tax. In 1924 Senator Andrieus Jones of New Mexico had nearly gotten it through Congress. And in 1935 the conservative arguments for the proposal continued to appeal to such Treasury officials as Jacob Viner and Roswell Magill.

In the liberal camp the tax appealed for somewhat different reasons to planners, spenders, and antitrusters alike. Among the planners, Rex Tugwell had long advocated a tax that would drive corporate surpluses into the open investment market, where the government could supervise their use. Among the spenders, men like Marriner Eccles regarded such a levy as a natural supplement to the spending program, as a device that would force corporations to distribute their surpluses, which in turn would add to consumer purchasing power, reduce excessive savings, and prevent the creation of an invisible banking system outside the regular monetary controls. Among the antitrusters, Robert Jackson and Herman Oliphant argued that the tax would strike a blow against business oligarchy and private monopoly, particularly against the managerial elite that controlled investment decisions, limited investment opportunities, and deprived stockholders of any decision as to how their funds would be used. By democratizing corporate finance, forcing large corporations to compete for their new funds in the money market, and restoring financial control to the stockholders, it would make for greater innovation and more venturesomeness. It would also help to equalize opportunities for proprietors and partnerships, who in the past had been required to pay income taxes on their earnings while corporations could accumulate surpluses free from such burdens.[7]

[7] Blakey, *Income Tax*, 405, 410; Lindley, *Halfway with Roosevelt*, 255–60; Twentieth Century Fund, *Facing the Tax Problem* (N.Y., 1937), 173–74, 464–65, 468–70; Alfred G. Buehler, *The Undis-*

In 1935, in spite of all these arguments, Roosevelt had decided to postpone the consideration of an undistributed profits tax. It seems probable that he would have continued to do so had it not been for two unexpected events in early 1936. One of these was the Supreme Court's decision overthrowing the agricultural processing tax. The other was the passage of the veterans' bonus bill. Both actions created a need for new revenue, and a tax on undistributed surpluses seemed to be the easiest and best way of raising it. A sales tax or a broadening of the income tax base would be politically inexpedient and economically undesirable. A new processing tax, even if it were upheld by the Court, would be regressive in nature. But an undistributed profits tax might be both a political and economic asset. It would repair the budget and stimulate new spending; it would strike chiefly at the opponents of the Administration; and it would actually increase the incomes of thousands of taxpayers by forcing payment of larger corporate dividends.

In any event, on March 3, 1936, the President sent a message to Congress, proposing several major changes in the tax system. First of all, largely on the recommendations of Herman Oliphant, he proposed that the new tax on undistributed profits should be combined with the repeal of existing corporate income, capital stock, and excess profits taxes. Second, he called for a tax that would recover the "windfall" profits of those that had escaped payment of the processing tax. Third, he suggested the temporary re-

tributed Profits Tax (N.Y.: McGraw-Hill, 1937), 8–14, 24; Rexford G. Tugwell, The Industrial Discipline and the Governmental Arts (N.Y.: Columbia U. Press, 1933), 206–7; Marriner S. Eccles, Beckoning Frontiers (N.Y.: Knopf, 1951), 257–60; Blum, Morgenthau Diaries, 306–8; Schlesinger, Politics of Upheaval, 505–7; House Ways and Means Committee, Revenue Act, 1936 (74 Cong., 2 Sess., 1936), 23–24, 658–59; Robert Jackson, in Vital Speeches, April 6, 1936, pp. 431–34; Newsweek, March 14, 1936, p. 11; Thomas Corcoran and Benjamin Cohen, "The Fight against Monopoly," Oct. 1936, Cohen File, NPPC Records; President Roosevelt's Press Conferences, March 3, 1936, Roosevelt Papers.

enactment of a low-rate processing tax. Such a program, he declared, would stop tax leakage, simplify tax procedure, and remove major inequities in the tax system.[8]

A House subcommittee then began constructing a measure based on the President's proposals. By late March it had a suitable bill ready, one that provided for the immediate or gradual elimination of the excess profits, corporate income, and capital stock taxes and the substitution of a new tax on corporate surpluses. The latter, as finally devised, would be levied according to two schedules, one to apply to corporations having less than $10,000 income, the other to those having more. Under the first the rate of graduation would rise to 29.5 percent, under the second to 42.5 percent, and in each case it would depend on the ratio of undistributed net income to adjusted net income. There would also be a tax of eighty percent on "windfall" profits, but no processing tax. On March 30 the House Ways and Means Committee opened hearings on the measure; on April 21 it was reported to the House; and eight days later, after a stiff debate but only minor changes, that chamber gave its approval.

The measure now moved to the Senate Finance Committee, where the Administration seemed somewhat surprised by the volume, unanimity, and intensity of business opposition. Nearly one hundred witnesses appeared, almost all of them in opposition to the measure. Instead of stimulating recovery, the critics argued, such a tax would deplete "rainy day" reserves, accentuate booms and depressions, hamper small firms, and check the development of new business enterprises. It would fall most heavily on the

[8] Buehler, *Undistributed Profits Tax,* 19–23; Blakey, *Income Tax,* 401–2; Eccles, *Beckoning Frontiers,* 256–57; FDR, *Public Papers,* v, 102–7; Ratner, *American Taxation,* 472–73; Schlesinger, *Politics of Upheaval,* 505; Blum, *Morgenthau Diaries,* 301, 305–8; House Ways and Means Committee, *Revenue Act, 1936,* 606–11; Max Lerner, in *Nation,* May 27, 1936, pp. 669–70; *Newsweek,* March 14, 1936, pp. 11–12; Memo. re Tax Program, Feb. 1936, OF 358, Roosevelt Papers.

smaller corporations that were in genuine need of building up surpluses, thereby actually promoting monopoly by making it impossible for any new competitor to grow large enough to challenge existing corporations. It would have other dire effects. It would complicate the tax structure and leave revenue dubious and incalculable. It would create difficulties for corporations desiring to make up a deficit or reduce indebtedness. And it would substitute the judgment of a government bureaucracy for that of business management.

In reply to these criticisms, Administration spokesmen argued that the basic difficulty was too much saving, not too little, that saving for a "rainy day" simply made it rain harder. The proposed tax, they maintained, would not hamper small firms or make expansion impossible. It would simply dissuade management from expanding without the consent of stockholders. Small firms could always secure funds in the capital market or by inducing their stockholders to reinvest the earnings that had been distributed. The latter argument, though, was never very convincing, even to the Administration spokesmen themselves. The House bill, it seemed, would actually decrease the tax load of several large corporations while increasing that of middle-size firms.[9]

[9] Buehler, *Undistributed Profits Tax*, 23–28, 32–36; Blakey, *Income Tax*, 411–16; Schlesinger, *Politics of Upheaval*, 508; Eccles, *Beckoning Frontiers*, 261–62; Blum, *Morgenthau Diaries*, 309–12; House Ways and Means Committee, *Revenue Act, 1936*, 4–13; and *House Report 2475* (74 Cong., 2 Sess., 1936), 5–13; Senate Finance Committee, *Revenue Act, 1936* (74 Cong., 2 Sess., 1936), 29–31, 252–93, 680–82, 890–927, and *passim*; *Congressional Record*, 74 Cong., 2 Sess., LXXX, 5828, 5978–6012, 6079–6136, 6229–6314, 6367; *Congressional Digest*, May 1936, pp. 133, 143; *Business Week*, April 25, 1936, p. 7; Lerner, in *Nation*, May 27, 1936, pp. 670–71; Joseph S. Lawrence, in *Review of Reviews*, May 1936, pp. 40–43; *Nation's Business*, May 1936, pp. 50, 52–53; *Business Week*, May 2, 1936, p. 16; May 9, 1936, p. 48; Jackson, in *Vital Speeches*, April 6, 1936, pp. 431–44; Ernest Draper and Roy Blakey, "The Proposed Revenue Act of 1936," May 7, 1936, OF 962, Roosevelt Papers.

As business criticism mounted, the conservative wing of the Senate Finance Committee took the initiative and threatened to eliminate the President's proposals altogether. Senator Harrison, however, by threatening to withdraw and carry the fight to the Senate floor, persuaded the conservatives to accept a compromise, a measure that retained much of the existing tax structure but added a small levy on undistributed profits. As adopted, it would retain the existing capital stock and excess profits taxes, increase corporate income taxes by a flat three percent, levy a tax on "windfall" profits, place a tax of seven percent on corporate surpluses, and provide for steeper penalty taxes on the retention of corporate earnings in excess of "reasonable" business needs.

In the meantime, the House bill had also produced a growing sense of apprehension within the Administration itself. Jesse Jones argued that revision was necessary to encourage new plant construction. Henry Morgenthau was worried, both about the bill's revenue potential and the possibility that it would handicap small or medium-sized concerns. President Roosevelt himself was willing to take a second look at the measure, particularly after he learned that under its provisions American Telephone and Telegraph would pay no taxes whatsoever, while under existing schedules it paid nearly $30,000,000 a year. It was Marriner Eccles, though, who finally took the initiative in proposing a new formula. The existing corporate income tax, he suggested, should be retained, all corporations having an annual income of less than $15,000 should be exempt from the undistributed profits tax, and the latter should then be levied at graduated rates running from twenty to fifty percent, depending upon the amount of profits distributed. Such changes, Eccles felt, were necessary if the measure was ever to achieve its avowed economic and social objectives. Senators Hugo Black and Robert LaFollette, Jr., however, had little success in selling them to Senator Harrison's Finance Committee; and partly because Morgenthau felt that Eccles' interference was uncalled for, the latter also failed to get much support from the Treasury.

On May 26, in a last effort to salvage something of the original proposal, Roosevelt summoned the members of the Senate Finance Committee to the White House and tried to persuade them to adopt the "Eccles Plan." The committee, however, refused to budge from its original proposal. On June 5 the Senate passed the measure, and little could be salvaged in conference. The House conferees, with strong Presidential backing, did succeed in getting the undistributed profits tax graduated from seven to twenty-seven percent, but the rest of the measure followed the lines laid down by the Senate. It retained the capital stock, excess profits, and corporate income taxes, although the latter was now graduated from eight to fifteen percent. The final outcome, said Marriner Eccles, was "better than nothing, but not very much better." [10]

IV

Although its sponsors had failed to carry out their original intentions, the Revenue Act of 1936 was one of the most bitterly criticized measures ever enacted by the New Deal. Republican orators leveled many a barrage at it during the campaign of 1936, and businessmen later denounced it as

[10] Blakey, *Income Tax*, 417–27; Eccles, *Beckoning Frontiers*, 261–64; Blum, *Morgenthau Diaries*, 310–18; Buehler, *Undistributed Profits Tax*, 28–31, 39–40; Ratner, *American Taxation*, 473–74; Schlesinger, Politics of Upheaval, 508–9; Senate Finance Committee, *Senate Report 2156* (74 Cong., 2 Sess., 1936), 11–27; *Congressional Record*, 74 Cong., 2 Sess., LXXX, 8526–28, 8648–52, 8656–64, 8785–8805, 9041–49, 9052–9110, 10257–71, 10469–76; 49 *U.S. Statutes* 1648, Public, No. 740, 74 Cong., *Business Week*, May 16, 1936, p. 15; May 30, 1936, p. 12; June 27, 1936, pp. 11–12; *Wall Street Journal*, May 16, June 9, 1936; *New York Times*, May 13, 15, 20, 22–23, 27, 29, 1936; Marriner Eccles to FDR, May 11, 27, 1936; Memoranda re Proposals of Senate Finance Committee, House Bill, and the President's Suggestions, June 1, 5, 1936, all in OF 962, Roosevelt Papers.

a primary cause of the recession of 1937. Actually, the measure was probably too moderate and too short-lived to have much effect one way or the other, although there were some indications that it did bear most heavily upon small and medium-sized firms. At least many small businessmen, who might have been expected to support a tax on bigness, believed this to be the case; their associations were just as hostile to the act, if not more so, than the representatives of big business.

In any event, the year 1936 marked the highpoint of the New Deal's efforts to use the taxing power as an instrument of economic and social reform. For a time in 1937, President Roosevelt and Secretary of the Treasury Morgenthau managed to divert congressional interest into a drive against tax evasion, a move that resulted in widely publicized hearings, followed by a new law that closed a number of obvious tax loopholes. After the court fight, however, and particularly after the onset of the new recession, Congress was much more receptive to business arguments. Such arguments stressed the need for repealing or at least modifying the undistributed profits tax. Within the Administration, too, opposition to the tax was growing. Joseph Eastman was convinced that it hindered refinancing of railway improvements. Jesse Jones thought it was a cause of the recession. And Joseph Kennedy, Harry Hopkins, and Bernard Baruch all advocated its immediate repeal.

The President, with the backing of Oliphant and other Treasury officials, still felt that the real solution lay in steeper graduation, coupled with preferential treatment for smaller corporations. But in the light of congressional sentiment, such proposals stood little chance of being adopted. Instead, by 1938, the Senate seemed bent upon the complete destruction of the earlier tax laws and the substitution of a flat corporation tax. The House, with Presidential backing, did manage to salvage a remnant of the undistributed profits tax; but even this remnant, a levy

357

of up to 2.5 percent on the undistributed earnings of corporations with incomes in excess of $25,000 a year, was to expire at the end of 1939. In the process, too, the principle of the graduated corporate income tax was largely abandoned.

In practice, then, the effort to tax bigness never got much beyond the stage of preparatory skirmishing. It might be true, as Justice Brandeis said, that the taxing power offered the most effective way of returning to an economy of small units, but the Administration as a whole was never convinced that it could or should be used in this way. Actually, the tax proposals of 1935 and 1936 seem to have been motivated more by other considerations, by revenue needs, share-the-wealth agitation, and the idea of discouraging corporate savings and increasing purchasing power. The anti-bigness bias in both measures was largely in the nature of rhetoric and window dressing, and the effects of the anti-bigness provisions in practice were largely nominal. The undistributed profits tax, in fact, seemed to work to the disadvantage of small units, and the degree of graduation in the corporate income tax was never sufficient to bring about much readjustment in size. In reality, the advantage given small corporations by the slightly graduated rates was probably less than the advantage lost in 1932 when the principle of exempting the first two to five thousand dollars of corporate income was discarded.

When it came to encouraging decentralization, then, both the graduated corporate income tax and the undistributed profits tax were failures. Neither worked as expected. Other taxes that might have been used against monopoly power were never adopted. There were suggestions, for example, that a tax might be levied so as to encourage rapid turnover, thus offsetting the tendency of industrial monopolies to restrict production and lay off workers. Other reformers thought that the same end might be achieved by a tax on excess capacity and idle plants.

All of these suggestions, however, involved administrative difficulties, and none of them met with much favor within the Roosevelt Administration. Even the excess profits tax of the New Deal era, the levy established by the National Industrial Recovery Act and continued by the Revenue Acts of 1935, 1936, and 1938, was largely a misnomer. It was designed not to tax monopoly profits as such, but to make effective the capital stock tax by preventing companies from declaring too little capital.

Yet, when viewed in retrospect, it seems that the relatively innocuous acts of 1935 and 1936 were about as strong as any that could have been passed at the time. In view of the long, drawn-out struggles to enact them and the emasculation that the original proposals received at the hands of Congress, one might conclude that neither the American people nor their elected representatives had any real desire to destroy large corporate units. The fight for a tax on bigness, the antimonopolists had hoped, was the beginning of a struggle that might effect a breakthrough into the central bastion of concentrated economic power. But as it turned out, the attack never reached much beyond the outer picket lines. It resulted only in a few short-lived "principles," none of which was strong enough to effect much actual reconstruction. Essentially, this struggle too was a skirmish on the flanks.[11]

[11] Blum, *Morgenthau Diaries*, 319–23, 333–37, 440–49; Ratner, *American Taxation*, 474–75, 477–79, 489; Schlesinger, *Politics of Upheaval*, 326–28, 334, 506–7, 509; Lief, ed., *Brandeis Guide*, 20; M. S. Kendrick, *The Undistributed Profits Tax* (Washington: Brookings, 1937), 9–40; Blakey, *Income Tax*, 436–50; Clifford J. Hynning and Gerhard Colm, *Taxation of Corporate Enterprise* (TNEC Monograph 9, 1941), 67–79, 88–89, 116–19; Paul, *Taxation for Prosperity*, 58–61; Arthur Dahlberg et al., *Recovery Plans* (TNEC Monograph 25, 1940), 80–86; 50 *U.S. Statutes* 813, Public, No. 377, 75 Cong.; 52 *U.S. Statutes* 447, Public, No. 554, 75 Cong.; E. S. Duffield, in *Nation's Business*, Aug. 1936, pp. 53–54; *New York Times*, Feb. 3–5, 17, March 1–3, 20, 25, April 8, 14, 23, May 28, 1938; FDR to R. L. Doughton, April 13, 1938, OF 962, Roosevelt Papers.

CHAPTER 19. FURTHER SKIR-
MISHES ON THE ANTITRUST
FRONT, 1934–1937

PRIOR to 1937, as noted previously, the antitrust tradition in the New Deal was represented largely by the
relatively ineffective attempts to use the taxing power, the
simultaneous attack upon such popular enemies as Wall
Street and the Power Trust, and the relatively successful
effort to block the political programs of planners and business rationalizers. If one focused solely on these activities,
however, he would miss the whole story. Most antitrusters
had a broader and more positive program in mind. In some
areas, especially where there was intra-industry conflict or
a long history of past agitation against particularly flagrant
abuses, they were able to generate considerable support for
specific reforms. Even though they were unable to get
much in the way of administrative or legislative action,
their activities did help to shape the content, scope, and
rationale of the antitrust campaign that got underway in
1938.[1]

II

One practice that had long troubled antitrusters was that
of basing-point pricing, the system whereby a manufacturer charged a delivered price calculated by adding the
freight charges from an agreed basing point, regardless of
the actual point from which the product was shipped. Over

[1] For statements of what the antitrusters had in mind, see Leon
Henderson, in *Annals Am. Acad.*, Jan. 1936, pp. 267–69; Frank A.
Fetter, "Big Business and the Preservation of the Competitive
Principle"; Robert Jackson, Addresses, May 28, Sept. 17, 1937, all
in Monopoly File, Borah Papers; Benjamin Cohen, Outline of a
Program to Solve the Problem of Concentration of Economic Power;
Memo. re Points for Inclusion in Revision of Antitrust Laws, both
in Cohen File, NPPC Records.

the years this practice had become strongly entrenched in such industries as steel, cement, lumber, paper, rubber, glass, sugar, and fertilizer, and the efforts to eliminate it had been singularly ineffective. The FTC's 1924 order against the Pittsburgh-plus system in the steel industry had resulted only in the creation of a few new basing points. During the NRA period, much to the dismay of confirmed antitrusters, the government had sanctioned the practice, not only in the steel industry but in a number of others as well. The result, according to the critics, was price uniformity and collusive bidding. Both during and after the NRA, professional antitrusters, supported in general by business groups in the areas that were discriminated against, continued to expound upon the iniquities of the system. In effect, they charged, it eliminated geographical position as a substantial element in competition, produced phantom freight charges and wasteful cross-hauling, and when coupled with price leadership and open-price reporting, virtually eliminated price competition.

One particularly persistent critic was Harold Ickes, the Secretary of the Interior and head of the Public Works Administration. During the NRA period Ickes had tried repeatedly to get the cement companies to submit f.o.b. bids, and when unable to do so, had finally decided to award the contracts to the cement manufacturer farthest removed from the project "on the theory that we would get a little extra railroad employment out of it anyhow." After the NRA, he continued to complain about collusive bidding, which, in his opinion, was often closely connected with basing-point pricing. Between June 1935 and March 1936, he said, his agency had received identical bids no less than 257 times.[2]

[2] Earl Latham, *The Group Basis of Politics* (Ithaca: Cornell U. Press, 1952), 59–65; Fritz Machlup, *The Basing-Point System* (Philadelphia: Blakiston, 1949), 17–21, 61–70, 73–80, 125–36; Frank A. Fetter, *The Masquerade of Monopoly* (N.Y.: Harcourt, Brace, 1931), 118–23, 146–51, 158–63, 221–42; John P. Miller, *Unfair Competition* (Cambridge: Harvard U. Press, 1941), 179–89;

The most widely publicized case of this sort arose in the fall of 1935, when the PWA opened bids for steel sheet piling on three major projects, the Triborough Bridge, the Miami Deep Sea Harbor, and the Morehead Port Terminal. The bids, Ickes discovered, were identical, and they were also approximately twenty percent higher than foreign prices for the same material. Accordingly, since PWA regulations provided for only a fifteen percent differential between foreign and domestic prices, Ickes ordered the pilings from a German steel firm. Almost immediately he found himself in the midst of a political storm. The American Iron and Steel Institute filed a vigorous protest; labor, too, was "up in arms." Consequently, even though the President was convinced that steel prices were excessive, he ordered Ickes to cancel the contract. At the same time, though, he asked the FTC to investigate and try to determine if the identical bids were the result of collusion.[3]

By 1936 the criticisms of Ickes and others had sparked a drive to outlaw the basing-point system, a drive that resulted in an unsuccessful attempt to attach such a provi-

---

FTC, *The Basing Point Problem* (TNEC Monograph 42, 1941), XI, 1–9, 31–63, 91–140; George W. Stocking, *Basing Point Pricing and Regional Development* (Chapel Hill: U. of N.C. Press, 1954), 4–7, 50–59; C. C. Linnenberg, Jr., and D. M. Barbour, *Government Purchasing* (TNEC Monograph 19, 1940), 35–36; Senate Commerce Committee, *To Prevent Uniform Delivered Prices* (74 Cong., 2 Sess., 1936), 6–7, 286–91; *Washington Times*, July 1, 1937; *Fortune*, April 1936, pp. 128–34; Harold Ickes, "Statement on Anti-Basing-Point Act," March 20, 1936, Speeches File, Ickes Papers.

[3] Linnenberg and Barbour, *Government Purchasing*, 36–37; Senate Commerce Committee, *Uniform Delivered Prices*, 296; *New York Times*, Nov. 9, 10, 12–16, 20–22, 27, 1935; FDR to Joseph Kennedy, June 11, 1935; Ickes to Marvin McIntyre, Oct. 26, 1935; Horatio Hacket, Memo. re Contract for Morehead Port Terminal; Stephen Early to FDR, Nov. 2, 1935; Early to McIntyre, Nov. 2, 1935; FDR to Ickes, Nov. 4, 1935; FDR to Ewin L. Davis, Nov. 20, 1935; Davis to FDR, Nov. 22, 1935, all in Roosevelt Papers (OF 342, 466); President Roosevelt's Press Conferences, Nov. 15, 26, 1935, Roosevelt Papers.

sion to the Robinson-Patman Act, the introduction of an anti-basing-point bill by Senator Burton K. Wheeler, and the holding of extensive hearings at which business spokesmen tried their best to answer the critics. The practice, so some of them argued, was really an aid to competition. It permitted a given company to compete for business anywhere in the nation, and this naturally resulted in a "uniform price." It seemed doubtful, however, whether the industrialists themselves really took such arguments seriously. As John Treanor of the Riverside Cement Company admitted, most of them were "sheer bunk and hypocrisy." The "truth" was that in such industries as steel and cement, where standardized products were produced under conditions that necessitated heavy capital investments and huge overhead costs, systematic restraint of competition became an absolute necessity. Failure to restrain it would lead to ruinous price wars. Closely connected with this argument, too, was the contention that any general change to f.o.b. mill-base pricing would result in serious economic disruption. It would cause "untold relocation," heavy losses to investors, and the eventual destruction of small firms that depended upon the "protection" of freight differentials.[4]

Such arguments were apparently sufficient to block the Wheeler bill, but the basing-point issue itself was still far from dead. In the economic journals, Frank A. Fetter continued to denounce both the basing-point practice and its apologists. In Congress, Senator Wheeler continued to sponsor anti-basing-point legislation. And in the Adminis-

[4] James R. Withrow, Jr., in Benjamin Werne, ed., *Business and the Robinson-Patman Law* (N.Y.: Oxford U. Press, 1938), 77–78; FTC, *Basing Point Problem*, 11–30; Machlup, *Basing-Point System*, 92–93, 117–25; Samuel M. Loescher, *Imperfect Collusion in the Cement Industry* (Cambridge: Harvard U. Press, 1959), 84–86; Carroll R. Daugherty et al., *The Economics of the Iron and Steel Industry*, II (N.Y.: McGraw-Hill, 1937), 1095–1106; *Congressional Record*, 74 Cong., 2 Sess., LXXX, 2408; Senate Commerce Committee, *Uniform Delivered Prices*, 1–2, 26, 47, 434–37, 562; *Fortune*, April 1936, p. 136; Robert Duncan, in *Today*, May 2, 1936, p. 16.

tration, George L. Berry reviewed the Wheeler investigation for the President and reported that the abolition of basing-point pricing might be an excellent way of placating antimonopoly sentiment. In any event, it would have a "wholesome effect" on Senators Nye and Borah. By this time, too, the Federal Trade Commission had concluded that the identical bids on steel sheet piling were a direct result of the basing-point system. And after Roosevelt had referred the Commission's report to the Department of Justice, John Dickinson's Antitrust Division did embark upon an extensive investigation of collusive bidding, particularly in such industries as steel, lumber, sugar, and cement. Much of the evidence offered by procurement officers and purchasing officials, however, was so sketchy as to be useless. Accordingly, Dickinson decided that under existing law little could be done. Those who believed that "price rigidity and the practices which promote it" were contrary to the public interest would have to "appeal to Congress for legislative action rather than to the Department of Justice for antitrust proceedings."

Consequently, there was little occasion for surprise when Attorney-General Homer Cummings announced in the spring of 1937 that the steel industry would not be prosecuted. He insisted, however, that this did not mean that the matter should be forgotten. The "type of practices complained of" were characteristic of "many of the basic industries of the country"; and if such problems were to be dealt with adequately, there must be a "restatement" of the antitrust laws. As a first step, he suggested that a committee should be established "to study the Antitrust laws as to their adequacy, their enforcement, and the desirability of amendment, extension, and clarification." [5]

[5] Linnenberg and Barbour, Government Purchasing, 113; FTC, Basing Point Problem, XII, 140; FTC, Annual Report (1936), 30; and Report on Steel Sheet Piling (1936); Frank A. Fetter, in Journal of Political Economy, Oct. 1937, pp. 577–605; Aug. 1938, pp. 568–70; Business Week, June 27, 1936, p. 15; Wall Street Journal, Aug. 25, 1936; Paul W. Ward, in Nation, April 17, 1937, p. 428;

By early 1937, then, the drive against the basing-point system had seemingly made little headway; yet the pattern of complaint and projected action had already been set. Already the high, rigid prices of steel, cement, and other building materials were being blamed for choking off a revival in housing construction; later they would be denounced as a major cause of the recession of 1937. New evidence of collusive bidding had also been amassed. Remedial legislation had been drafted. The Attorney-General had suggested a major investigation. And the FTC, by issuing complaints against the basing-point system in the cast iron soil pipe and cement industries, had begun the long process of winning judicial sanction for its contention that the practice was already illegal. The latter complaint, after some eleven years of hearings and litigation, would finally force a return to f.o.b. mill-base pricing.[6]

III

A second situation about which antitrusters became deeply concerned was the concentration of economic power in the motion picture industry. By the nineteen thirties, eight major companies dominated the field. Together they produced seventy percent of all films, controlled ninety-five percent of all film distribution, owned or controlled some

---

Newsweek, May 8, 1937, pp. 28, 30; George Berry to FDR, June 20, 1936; FDR to Burton Wheeler, June 25, 1936; FDR to Homer Cummings, June 15, 1936; White House PR, June 22, 1936, all in OF 342, Roosevelt Papers; President Roosevelt's Press Conferences, April 27, 1937, Roosevelt Papers; John Dickinson, Address, Dec. 10, 1936, CIC File, NRA Records.
    [6] Latham, Group Basis of Politics, 67–68; Stocking, Basing Point Pricing, 152–53, 159–60; Loescher, Cement Industry, 244–63; Benjamin S. Kirsh and Harold Shapiro, Trade Associations in Law and Business (N.Y.: Central, 1938), 284; Congressional Record, 75 Cong., 1 Sess., LXXXI, 1272; FTC, Annual Report (1937), 45; (1938), 49; FTC v. Cement Institute, 333 U.S. 683 (1948); New York Times, April 3, 28, 29, May 2, 9, 23, Dec. 27, 30, 31, 1937.

sixteen percent of all theatres, including eighty percent of the metropolitan, first-run theatres, and were in a position to dictate terms to the remaining independents. They had forced independent exhibitors, for example, to accept the practices of block-booking and blind-selling, arrangements whereby they offered their entire output on an all-or-none basis. Frequently, too, they could designate playing dates, impose clearance regulations, fix admission prices, and establish zoning restrictions. When independents refused to go along, they were threatened with the "freeze-out," the possibility that the major producer would acquire or build a competing theatre that would have its choice of the best pictures.

Confronted with such tactics, independent exhibitors had long been agitating for remedial action, and by stressing the idea that independent selection would improve moral standards, they had been able to enlist considerable support from women's clubs and local censorship groups. Prior to 1935, however, they had accomplished little. An FTC order against block-booking had been set aside by the courts. Remedial legislation sponsored by Senator Smith W. Brookhart had failed to pass. And the effort to write a prohibition of the practice into the industry's NRA code had resulted only in one minor concession, a provision that allowed exhibitors, under certain circumstances, to reject ten percent of any block.[7]

[7] Morris L. Ernst, *Too Big* (Boston: Little, Brown, 1940), 136–60; Daniel Bertrand et al., *The Motion Picture Industry* (TNEC Monograph 43, 1941), 3–13, 23–27, 30–49, 59–62; Bertrand, *NRA Work Materials 34* (*Motion Picture Industry*), 83–97, 115–26; Mae D. Huettig, *Economic Control of the Motion Picture Industry* (Philadelphia: U. of Penn. Press, 1944), 31–39, 64–95, 116–17; Senate Commerce Committee, *Compulsory Block-Booking and Blind Selling in the Motion-Picture Industry* (74 Cong., 2 Sess., 1936), 14–17, 124; *Congressional Record*, 70 Cong., 1 Sess., LXIX, 544; *Christian Century*, Feb. 1, 1933, p. 140; Sept. 20, 1933, p. 1170; Dec. 20, 1933, pp. 1600–1; May 20, 1934, p. 715; Wilmoth D. Evans, "NRA Code History 124" (Motion Pictures), 14–17, CHF, NRA Records. The eight major companies were generally divided into two groups. The Big Five, Paramount, Loew's, Twentieth Cen-

Following the overthrow of the NRA, the independents and their allies renewed their efforts to outlaw block-booking completely. Thomas Irwin of Columbia University drafted a new bill for the Motion Picture Research Council; Senator Matthew Neely agreed to sponsor it. In the hearings that followed, the measure again won the support of numerous women's clubs, church organizations, and civic groups. Block-booking, so these groups argued, was not only an unfair and monopolistic practice, but also one that compelled the showing of undesirable and immoral pictures. The majors, on the other hand, argued that the practice was a perfectly justifiable one. It was "merely the selling of pictures at wholesale." It had nothing to do with public morals since producers merely produced what the public wanted. Outlawing it would be highly undesirable because it would increase the risks taken by producers, lead to higher admission prices, and make it impossible for a producer to take a chance on an "art" picture. The majors, moreover, could supplement their argument with skillful and effective lobbying. Will Hays, as head of the Motion Picture Producers and Distributors of America, was a man with extensive and valuable political contacts. And once again his organization was able to block the political moves of the independents.[8]

---

tury-Fox, Warner Brothers, and Radio-Keith-Orpheum, had interests in all three branches of the industry. The three satellites, Universal, Columbia, and United Artists, were limited to the fields of production and distribution.

[8] Kenneth G. Crawford, *The Pressure Boys* (N.Y.: Messner, 1939), 90–96, 104–5; Donald C. Blaisdell, *Economic Power and Political Pressures* (TNEC Monograph 26, 1941), 182–83; Huettig, *Motion Picture Industry*, 117–19; Allied States Association of Motion Picture Exhibitors, *Compulsory Block Booking and Blind Selling of Motion Pictures* (1935), 13–14, 20–21; *Congressional Record*, 74 Cong., 1 Sess., LXXIX, 8746; Senate Commerce Committee, *Compulsory Block-Booking*, 1–13, 19, 25–33, 80–83, 103–31; and *Anti "Block-Booking" and "Blind Selling" in the Leasing of Motion Picture Films* (76 Cong., 1 Sess., 1939), 12–13; *Newsweek*, March 7, 1936, p. 30.

The Seventy-fourth Congress, then, failed to act on the Neely bill. Yet again the pattern of complaint and projected action had been established. Remedial legislation had been drafted and support enlisted behind it. The Department of Justice was showing increased interest in the situation. And both independent exhibitors and antitrust officials were rapidly becoming convinced that the only real solution lay in the complete divorcement of production and exhibition, either by a special law or by antitrust action. In view of all the agitation, it was virtually certain that once the antitrust campaign got underway, the motion picture industry would become one of the major objects of reform.[9]

IV

A third abuse about which antitrusters had become increasingly concerned was the use of patent laws to create and perpetuate monopolistic strongholds. Such laws, it seemed, offered the favored concern every opportunity to dig in, to fortify its position, seize the channels of distribution, and barricade the trade against any newcomer. Once entrenched, a firm could use the law to hold and expand its position. It could threaten complicated infringement suits in which the odds naturally favored the party with the greatest financial staying power. It could hem in a basic process by acquisition of patents covering all possible improvements, especially since improvement had become more and more a matter of conscious design on the part of captive inventors. And if the circumstances warranted, it could use such devices as patent pools and cross-

[9] Blaisdell, *Economic Power*, 183; Attorney-General, *Annual Report* (1936), 29; *Congressional Record*, 75 Cong., 1 Sess., LXXXI, 67; *Newsweek*, March 7, 1936, p. 30; *Business Week*, Feb. 19, 1938, pp. 22, 24; *New York Times*, July 21, 24, 1938; June 11, 1939; Will Hays to FDR, Thurs. Night (early 1938), PPF 1945, Roosevelt Papers.

licensing agreements to limit the business to a favored few.[10]

The situation, as the antitrusters saw it, called for remedial action; and during the nineteen thirties, numerous reforms were being suggested. In 1935 the Science Advisory Board recommended a number of procedural changes, including publication of all patent applications, creation of a single court of patent appeals, and the appointment of technical advisers to juries hearing patent cases. Some critics, too, suggested changes in current classification procedures, changes, in particular, that would limit the classes of inventions patentable, eliminate design patents, or differentiate between basic and improvement patents. Others proposed that patent pools, restrictive patent contracts, and cross-licensing agreements be outlawed or that the number and character of assignable patents be strictly limited. Still others advocated some type of compulsory licensing or some system of graduated taxes that would increase with each year the patent remained in force. From still other quarters came suggestions for measuring the life of a patent from the date of application instead of the date of issuance, for simplification of the interference procedure, for the provision of counsel to indigent patentees, and for the abolition of renewals, reissues, and disclaimers.

Prior to 1938, however, only two bills received more than passing attention. The first of these, the Sirovich bill that became the subject of extensive hearings in 1935, would require that patent pooling arrangements be registered with the Commissioner of Patents, who could then request FTC action against those that were not in the

[10] Kirsh and Shapiro, *Trade Associations*, 235–36; Leverett S. Lyon et al., *Government and Economic Life*, 1 (Washington: Brookings, 1939), 132–45; Walton Hamilton et al., *Patents and Free Enterprise* (TNEC Monograph 31, 1941), 45–49, 145–63; Floyd L. Vaughan, *The United States Patent System* (Norman: U. of Okla. Press, 1956), 215–26, 261–85; Joseph Barkin, in *Law and Contemporary Problems*, Winter 1940, pp. 75–77; "Patent Reform," in Exec. Secretary's File, TNEC Records.

public interest. The second, sponsored by Senator Mc-Adoo, would establish a single court of patent appeals, a proposal that had behind it a long history of previous agitation. In the end, though, neither bill generated enough enthusiasm to get through Congress, and both encountered stiff opposition from businessmen and patent lawyers, many of whom seemed firmly convinced that any major changes in the existing laws would destroy the American system.[11]

Nevertheless, the pattern of complaint and projected action had once again been established. Robert Jackson and other antitrusters were convinced that patent law revision should be a vital part of any antitrust program. The Department of Justice had filed a test case against the Ethyl Gasoline Corporation, charging that the requirement of a fixed differential between regular and ethyl gasoline was a misuse of patents to stabilize prices. Congressmen like William McFarlane and Lawrence Connery were already thinking in terms of a compulsory licensing system. Again it was not surprising that patent abuses should play a key role in subsequent antitrust activities.[12]

[11] Lyon et al., *Government and Economic Life*, I, 145–50; Harry A. Toulmin, *Patents and the Public Interest* (N.Y.: Harper, 1939), 75–77, 101–24; *Congressional Record*, 74 Cong., 1 Sess., LXXIX, 46, 137, 534, 860, 1202; 75 Cong., 1 Sess., LXXXI, 36, 111; House Patent Committee, *Pooling of Patents* (74 Cong., 1 Sess., 1935), 1–2; Senate Patent Committee, *Court of Patent Appeals* (75 Cong., 1 Sess., 1937), 1–4, 47, 55–56; *Business Week*, Oct. 26, 1935, p. 30; Dec. 28, 1935, p. 21; Herman Oliphant to Henry Morgenthau, Dec. 18, 1934, OF 137, Roosevelt Papers; Thomas Blaisdell to Willard Thorp, Sept. 1, 1934, Blaisdell File, NRPB Records.

[12] CCH, *The Federal Antitrust Laws* (N.Y., 1952), 175; Hamilton et al., *Patents*, 83–85; House Patent Committee, *Compulsory Licensing of Patents* (75 Cong., 3 Sess., 1938), 1–5, 11, 16, 40; TNEC, *Preliminary Report* (Senate Doc. 95, 76 Cong., 1 Sess., 1939), 14–22; Barkin, in *Law and Contemporary Problems*, Winter 1940, pp. 79–81; Mortimer Feur, in *Temple U. Law Quarterly*, Feb. 1940, pp. 1–15; Buel W. Patch, in *Editorial Research Reports*, June 6, 1938, pp. 346–48; *Ethyl Gasoline Corp. v. U.S.*, 309 U.S. 436 (1940); *Newsweek*, Dec. 5, 1938, p. 34; William McFarlane to FDR, Feb. 16, 1938, OF 808, Roosevelt Papers.

V

Another group of measures that had long troubled anti-trusters was the lax incorporation laws adopted by a number of the state legislatures. Almost any veteran antitruster, in fact, could recite how this "competition in laxity" had produced giant "tramp" corporations, great sprawling empires with more power than the states that created them. Consequently, it was not surprising that the nineteen thirties should witness a revival of the ancient proposals for federal licensing and federal charters of incorporation. The appeal of the idea, moreover, was not confined to antitrusters. It enjoyed some support from economic planners, like Rex Tugwell, who saw it as a way to implement a program of positive regulation. It also attracted labor representatives, like Charlton Ogburn, general counsel for the American Federation of Labor, who hoped that federal licensing could be used to maintain labor standards.

The licensing provisions of the National Industrial Recovery Act, although the President had failed to invoke them, had given some encouragement to the proponents of federal charters. During the NRA period, a committee on federal incorporation, headed by Harold Stephens of the Department of Justice, had carried on an extensive investigation of the idea. Then, following the demise of the NRA, the proposal became associated primarily with the measures sponsored by Senators William Borah and Joseph C. O'Mahoney. At first, these attracted little attention, but by the end of 1937 the two senators had combined their earlier proposals into a joint bill that became the subject of hearings and widespread public discussion in 1938. Under its provisions, corporations engaged in interstate commerce would be licensed by the FTC, and in order to secure such licenses, they would have to meet certain federal standards. They could not employ child labor, discriminate against women workers, or ob-

371

struct the organization of their employees. They would be required to maintain their chief place of business in the state in which they were organized. And they must observe all antitrust laws, eliminate all non-voting stock, and refrain from practices that were designed to inflate their capital structures or rob their stockholders. Failure to live up to these standards would result in revocation of a corporation's license, without which it could not do business.

The FTC seemed to think that Borah and O'Mahoney were on the right track, but its representatives, like some of Roosevelt's other advisers, felt that the scheme in its present form was too cumbersome and too rigid. Any licensing agency, they thought, should have a greater degree of discretion and flexibility. Some observers felt that such sentiments were partially responsible for the monopoly investigation in 1938, that it was designed in part to sidetrack the rigid Borah-O'Mahoney bill. Once O'Mahoney had been chosen to head the inquiry, however, it was practically certain that the idea of federal charters would be fully explored and would find its way into the final recommendations.[13]

[13] Noel Kaho, *An Analysis of Monopoly* (Washington, 1938), 11–16; Rexford G. Tugwell, *The Industrial Discipline and the Governmental Arts* (N.Y.: Columbia U. Press, 1933), 201–2; William Z. Ripley, *Main Street and Wall Street* (Boston: Little, Brown, 1927), 18–35; Louis Loss, *Securities Regulation* (Boston: Little, Brown, 1951), 58–61; Rudolph L. Weissman, *Small Business and Venture Capital* (N.Y.: Harper, 1945), 100–7; David Lynch, *The Concentration of Economic Power* (N.Y.: Columbia U. Press, 1946), 27–28; Arthur M. Schlesinger, Jr., *The Coming of the New Deal* (Boston: Houghton Mifflin, 1959), 99, 108–9; James J. Robbins, in *Tulane Law Review*, Feb. 1939, pp. 217–23; William Hard, in *Harper's*, April 1936, p. 580; Herbert Harris, in *Today*, Jan. 9, 1937, pp. 6–7, 26–28; *Newsweek*, Jan. 31, 1938, p. 8; July 18, 1938, p. 32; *Congressional Record*, 74 Cong., 1 Sess., LXXIX, 254, 12452, 12551–57; 75 Cong., 1 Sess., LXXXI, 65, 178–79; 2 Sess., LXXXII, 494–98; 3 Sess., LXXXIII, 2446–49; Senate Judiciary Committee, *Federal Licensing of Corporations* (75 Cong., 1 Sess., 1937), 1–25, 80–81; and *Federal Licensing of Corporations* (75 Cong., 3 Sess., 1938), 351–59; TNEC, *Final Report and Recommendations* (Senate Doc. 35, 77 Cong., 1 Sess., 1941), 24–29; Homer Cummings to FDR, Nov. 24, Dec. 13, 1933; Jan. 26, July 19, 1934; Robert

VI

Another weapon available to antimonopolists was the traditional one of antitrust prosecution. Yet prior to 1937 they had failed to get much action. The Antitrust Division had confined its activities largely to what one observer called "peanut cases," to disputes that "would have been handled by local courts if the Federal Government had not been pleased to relieve them of the unpleasantness of local disputes." Four suits, for example, grew out of design disputes in the women's apparel trade; eight related to racketeering in the trucking industry; three were concerned with intimidation in the New York fur trade; three dealt with local price-fixing activities in the fishery trade; and others related to such issues as ice distribution in Kansas City, the stabilization activities of the cloth-sponging industry, and coercion of theatre operators in St. Louis. A few cases, to be sure, did deal with national problems, but only three were of any real significance. One, the case of the *United States v. Mather*, struck at the practice of interlocking directorates in the steel industry. A second, that of the *United States v. Republic Steel Corporation*, attempted without success to prevent a merger of the Corrigan, McKinney Steel Company with Republic Steel. And a third forced the Columbia Gas and Electric system to divest itself of interest in the Panhandle Eastern Pipeline.[14]

Healy, "Federal Incorporation or Licensing of Corporations Engaged in Interstate or Foreign Commerce," Dec. 12, 1934; FDR to Cummings, July 11, 1935; Joseph O'Mahoney to FDR, Jan. 2, 1937; Charlton Ogburn to FDR, Dec. 30, 1936; March 3, 1937, all in Roosevelt Papers (OF 10, 1132, PPF 3794); Willis Ballinger to O'Mahoney, Jan. 27, 1938; O'Mahoney to Arthur Himbert, Feb. 16, 1938, both in Federal Incorporation File, O'Mahoney Papers.

[14] Attorney-General, *Annual Report* (1934), 17–18, 23–24; (1935), 20–26; (1936), 24–29; H. E. Miles, in Senate Commerce Committee, *Uniform Delivered Prices*, 697–702; CCH, *Antitrust Laws*, 163–73; *Business Week*, May 11, 1935, pp. 9–10; Cummings to FDR, Feb. 6, 1936; Justice Dept. PR, March 6, 1935, both in OF 10, Roosevelt Papers.

In 1937, however, under the leadership of Robert Jackson, the Antitrust Division did begin to concentrate on a number of test cases in significant industries, particularly in areas where intra-industry conflict had produced a demand for prosecution. Among the most widely publicized of these actions were the so-called Madison Oil cases, stemming from long-standing complaints on the part of independent jobbers in the petroleum industry. Prosecution resulted in a bitter trial in Madison, Wisconsin, a contest marked by harsh expressions on both sides of the table. Eventually, in early 1938, the jury convicted sixteen corporations and thirty individuals of a conspiracy to rig prices by means of a secret buying pool. Each major company, it developed, had selected or been assigned an independent refiner, humorously referred to as a "dancing partner," whose surplus gasoline it was to purchase and keep off the market. The defendants, of course, were to appeal the decision, but the attempt to force the petroleum industry into a more competitive pattern was off to a good start.

Much of the publicity given to the Madison Oil cases was due to charges that the government was acting inconsistently and in bad faith. Under the NRA, the Petroleum Administration had tacitly encouraged, although it had not openly sanctioned, the very practices for which the oil companies were now being prosecuted. Accordingly, the defendants argued that they were simply carrying out the principles of the NRA, just as numerous Administration spokesmen had urged them to do, and to prosecute them for doing so was "an unjust, unwarranted, and very technical move." It was like the small boy who was "spanked by mamma for doing something papa told him to do." The government, however, maintained that the invalidation of the NRA restored the antitrust laws to full force. "There seems to have been an impression in the country that only a part of N.R.A. was unconstitutional," said Robert Jackson, "that the part they did not like was unconstitutional, but they could still use those parts they did like." And with this view, the jury apparently agreed.[15]

A second major case associated with Jackson's tenure was that designed to break up the Aluminum Company of America, long regarded as the outstanding example of a private monopoly. In 1937, however, this case seemed to make little progress. On April 29, six days after the government filed its suit in New York, the company filed a countersuit in Pennsylvania, seeking an injunction against prosecution of the New York case on the ground that the parties, issues, subject matter, and relief sought were all substantially the same as those covered by an old consent decree of 1912. The district court granted the injunction, but in September a special three-judge expediting court reversed the decision. The company then appealed to the Supreme Court, which sustained the expediting court. Not until December 1937, then, was the government free to proceed with the New York suit, and the trial itself did not begin until June 1938.

A third major case was that relating to automobile financing, an industry with a long history of agitation and complaint on the part of automobile dealers and independent finance companies. This case, too, had a rather inauspicious beginning. Following the launching of a grand jury investigation in 1937, the government, at the behest of the independent finance companies, opened negotiations with the major automobile companies for an acceptable consent decree. News of the resulting conferences soon reached Judge Ferdinand Geiger, under whose direction the grand jury had been proceeding. Geiger regarded

[15] Attorney-General, *Annual Report* (1937), 35, 41–42, 46–48; (1938), 54, 307–10; Senate Judiciary Committee, *Nomination of Robert H. Jackson* (75 Cong., 3 Sess., 1938), 36–37, 43–44; *U.S. v. Socony-Vacuum Oil Co.*, 310 U.S. 150 (1940); *Time*, Oct. 18, 1937, p. 63; Jan. 31, 1938, p. 51; J. J. O'Connell, "Madison Oil Cases," Special Studies File, TNEC Records; John F. O'Ryan to Marvin McIntyre, Aug. 13, 1937; O'Ryan to Robert Jackson, June 23, 1937; O'Ryan to FDR, April 19, 1937, all in PPF 1948, Roosevelt Papers.

them as evidence of bad faith on the part of the government, whereupon he proceeded to dismiss the jury. The consent decree negotiations then fell through, and it was not until May 1938 that a new grand jury could be impaneled.

Most of the other cases instituted by Jackson resembled the "peanut cases" of the earlier period, but one of them was sufficiently significant to attract some attention. This, as noted previously, was the Ethyl Gasoline case, the forerunner of the later drive against patent restraints. Thus by early 1938 the foundations for the expansion of antitrust activities had been laid. Four major cases were already in process, and there were growing indications that the government would soon move into other areas.[16]

VII

In other respects as well, the antimonopoly campaign of 1938 and 1939 was closely related to the activities of the earlier period. The later concern with railroad reorganization and transportation abuses, for example, seems to have grown, partially, from the voluminous railroad financing investigations of a committee headed by Senator Wheeler, investigations that ran from December 1936 to April 1938 and eventually resulted in the publication of some twenty-nine volumes of testimony. Even Vice-President John Garner thought that the inquiry had thrown "a great white light on the concentration of wealth" and had demonstrated the need for action. Similarly, the later drive against abuses in the foods industries was a logical

[16] Attorney-General, *Annual Report* (1937), 46–48; (1938), 306; Senate Judiciary Committee, *Nomination of Jackson*, 70–72, 75–82; House Judiciary Committee, *Official Conduct of Judge Ferdinand A. Geiger* (75 Cong., 3 Sess., 1938), 3–6, 120–26; CCH, *Antitrust Laws*, 175–79; Harold Reuschlein, in *U. of Penn. Law Review*, March 1939, pp. 536–40; James Wechsler, in *Nation*, Oct. 8, 1938, pp. 346–47; *New York Times*, Dec. 7, 1937; March 13, 1938; *Business Week*, May 28, 1938, pp. 13–14.

outgrowth of the FTC's massive investigation of the so-called "food trust." As part of its Agricultural Income Inquiry, beginning in the fall of 1935, the Commission had compiled some eight typewritten volumes on the monopolistic practices in the dairy, flour-milling, bakery, meat-packing, and other food industries. In this field, as one commentator noted, it had been "shouting monopoly for many months" and could "furnish the Administration with a long list of names of the bad boys of American business." [17]

For a long period, too, the FTC had been adding its voice to the demands for antitrust law revision, particularly in regard to two major loopholes. In the first place, it felt, there should be an amendment to the Federal Trade Commission Act that would provide direct protection to the public. It should not be necessary to show that a fraudulent practice was injurious to a competitor. And in the second place, there should be a provision against mergers that substantially lessened competition. Businessmen should not be allowed to evade the Clayton Act by substituting the merger for the holding company. Both of these proposals won strong support during the antitrust campaign of 1938 and 1939, and both of them were eventually adopted.[18]

[17] Senate Commerce Committee, *Investigation of Railroads, Holding Companies, Affiliated Companies, and Related Matters* (74 Cong., 1 Sess., 1936–38), 1–2, and *passim*; and *Railroad Reorganization Act of 1939* (76 Cong., 1 Sess., 1939), 69–70; Charles A. Beard, in *New Republic*, Jan. 20, 1937, pp. 350–53; Harold L. Ickes, *Secret Diary*, II (N.Y.: Simon & Schuster, 1954), 62; Norman Cousins, in *Current History*, Feb. 1938, pp. 26–30; FTC, *Report on Agricultural Income Inquiry* (1938); *Business Week*, Nov. 4, 1939, p. 19; Nov. 30, 1940, p. 15.

[18] FTC, *Annual Report* (1935), 15–16; (1937), 15; (1938), 19; *Congressional Record*, 74 Cong., 2 Sess., LXXX, 6436–37; Senate Commerce Committee, *To Amend the FTC Act* (74 Cong., 2 Sess., 1936), 5–34; Joseph W. Burns, *A Study of the Antitrust Laws* (N.Y.: Central, 1958), 69, 252–55. The first loophole was closed by the Wheeler-Lea Act in 1938, the second by the Celler-Kefauver Act in 1950.

In several areas, then, the New Deal's antimonopoly campaign was foreshadowed by the agitation and activities of the earlier years. What actually happened, it would seem, was not the substitution of one set of policies for another, but a shift in emphasis between two sets of policies that had existed side by side throughout the entire period. Thus, even during the early period, the New Deal had its antitrust aspects. Within the NRA the market restorers fought for policy changes and code revisions. Outside the organization the neo-Brandeisians worked for financial reforms, tax revision, the break-up of holding companies, and the provision of cheap electrical power. Alongside these major activities there were a variety of skirmishes, attacks on the monopolistic aspects of the steel, cement, petroleum, aluminum, and movie industries, on such practices as basing-point pricing, collusive bidding, and block-booking, on patent law abuses and lax corporation laws, and on industrial policies that tended to rigidify the price structure. Such attacks might accomplish little, but they were not without significance. On one hand, they served to placate antimonopoly sentiment and make the proper obeisance to antitrust ideals. On the other, they served to formulate and advance a positive program, to define objectives, suggest methods, educate and enlist support, and lay the groundwork for later action.

Gradually, too, the antimonopolists had acquired a greater voice in New Deal councils. Tom Corcoran had emerged as the President's chief speechwriter and handyman. Benjamin Cohen had become the New Deal's legislative draftsman par excellence. Robert Jackson had taken over the Antitrust Division. And men like William Douglas, Corwin Edwards, Leon Henderson, and Herman Oliphant had all emerged in influential positions. Prior to 1937, circumstances had seemed to be against them. But now the tide was turning, and their advocacy of an antitrust program was facilitated by a rare conjuncture of other factors, by the onset of a new recession, the break with organized business, and the growing conviction that monopoly was a major cause of depressions. The result was an economic and political situation to which their ideals and program seemed admirably suited. The attempt to put that program into practice, to turn the ideal of decentralization into something approaching reality, was one of the central themes of latter-day New Deal policy.[19]

[19] Raymond Moley, *After Seven Years* (N.Y.: Harper, 1939), 275–81, 333–34, 344–49; Rexford G. Tugwell, *The Democratic Roosevelt* (Garden City: Doubleday, 1957), 414–16, 420–21; Lyon et al., *Government and Economic Life*, 75–79, 145–50, 302–3; Arthur M. Schlesinger, Jr., *The Politics of Upheaval* (Boston: Houghton Mifflin, 1960), 132, 222–36, 307, 328, 385–98, 576–79; and *Coming of New Deal*, 58, 128–35, 232, 368, 444–45; Joseph Alsop and Robert Kintner, in *Saturday Evening Post*, Oct. 29, 1938, pp. 77–79; Nov. 12, 1938, pp. 8–9, 102, 104–5, 108–9, 112; William H. Hale, in *Common Sense*, May 1938, pp. 10–12; June 1938, pp. 13–17; July 1938, pp. 16–20.

PART IV

NEW DEAL POLICY AND THE RECESSION OF 1937

Business enterprise needs new vitality and the flexibility that comes from the diversified efforts, independent judgments and vibrant energies of thousands upon thousands of independent business men.—*Franklin D. Roosevelt*

I would very much favor making it a completely legal thing to do, for them to meet around a table to find out what the demands are, what the purchasing power is, what the inventories are, with the help of the Government.—*Franklin D. Roosevelt*

CHAPTER 20. THE RECESSION
AND THE SEARCH FOR A POLICY

I N the nation's capital the year 1937 dawned amid an atmosphere of buoyancy and confidence. Stocks were strong, commodity prices were rising, wages were up, profits were high, and unemployment was shrinking. At last, it seemed, prosperity was "just around the corner." Beneath the outward optimism, however, a number of New Dealers were expressing fear that the boom could not last. Leon Henderson, for example, had become convinced that rising prices, particularly in the more monopolistic industries, were threatening the whole balance of forces necessary for recovery. In late March he sent the President his famous "Boom and Bust" memorandum, predicting that failure to solve the price problem would result in a major recession before the year was over. Nor was Henderson alone in his concern about the future. Henry Wallace and his advisers in the Department of Agriculture were again calling for a great cooperative effort to correct present imbalances and shift the nation's emphasis from scarcity to expansion. Marriner Eccles felt there was a "grave danger" that "monopolistically organized industries" and "skilled trades" would "capitalize on the scarcity factor to secure excessive wage and price advantages." Hugh Johnson admitted that his NRA copper cartel was "now operating very adversely to the public interest." And others thought that the recent decisions to reduce relief expenditures and raise reserve requirements were decidedly premature.[1]

[1] John M. Blum, *From the Morgenthau Diaries*, I (Boston: Houghton Mifflin, 1959), 369–71; Marriner S. Eccles, *Beckoning Frontiers* (N.Y.: Knopf, 1951), 288–99; David Lynch, *The Concentration of Economic Power* (N.Y.: Columbia U. Press, 1946), 18–19; Paul W. Ward, in *Nation*, March 6, 1937, pp. 258–59; April 17, 1937, p. 427; Joseph Alsop and Robert Kintner, in *Saturday Evening Post*, Nov. 12, 1938, pp. 108–9; *Newsweek*, March

In his press conference on April 2, 1937, the President also expressed fear that some prices were entirely too high, especially in such industries as copper and steel. Because of this, he declared, the government intended to spend more on consumer items and less on such things as "steel bridges and great permanent structures that use certain materials, the prices of which are going up and up and up." His concern, however, seemed to be relatively short-lived. As the speculative boom leveled off and prices stabilized, the dire predictions of the spring were apparently forgotten. By late summer, governmental spending activities were being rapidly abandoned; a balanced budget appeared in prospect; and even Leon Henderson was predicting "a new burst of vigor in recovery." [2]

Nevertheless, the agitation of early 1937 did leave a residue of concern about monopolistically controlled prices. Following his April press conference, the President established several "study groups" to consider such things as the high costs of housing materials, the excessive price of steel, and the general rise in the cost of living, all of which, he felt, were destroying consumer purchasing power. There

27, 1937, pp. 7–8; Leon Henderson to Benjamin Cohen, Feb. 22, 1937; Henderson, "Recovery and Recession," March 20, 1937, both in Cohen File, NPPC Records: Henderson to Harry Hopkins, March 1937, Relief Plans File, Hopkins Papers; Charles Eliot, Memo. re Conference with Secretary of Agriculture, Feb. 15, 1937; Henry Wallace to Frederic Delano, Feb. 17, 1937, both in Industrial Committee Minutes—CCF, NRPB Records; Arthur M. Lamport, "Recovery and Recession"; Henderson, "Boom and Bust," March 29, 1937; Eccles, "The Rise of Prices and the Problem of Maintaining an Orderly Revival," March 11, 1937; Hugh Johnson to FDR, Feb. 9, 1937; Hopkins to FDR, March 31, 1937, all in Roosevelt Papers (PPF 1820, Recovery File—PSF, OF 401, WPA File—OF).

[2] Sumner Slichter, in *Review of Economic Statistics*, Aug. 1938, pp. 98–100; Ward, in *Nation*, April 17, 1937, pp. 427–28; *Time*, April 12, 1937, pp. 15, 77; *New York Times*, April 3, May 1, July 1, Aug. 5, 6, 16, 20, 26, 1937; President Roosevelt's Press Conferences, April 2, 1937, Roosevelt Papers; Henderson to Hopkins, Aug. 31, 1937, Relief Plans File, Hopkins Papers.

were indications, too, that he was planning an antitrust campaign for the not too distant future and was now weighing the political implications of such a move. As early as September 1937, he indicated to Ickes that he was ready to join forces with Senator Borah on the monopoly issue. Later, on his western trip, he discussed the matter with Borah himself and hinted that antimonopoly legislation was on the way, something that the senator regarded as the best news in "many, many a political day." Still later, following his return to Washington, he authorized Robert Jackson to investigate the "anti-monopoly laws" and directed the FTC to investigate the "marked increase in the cost of living . . . attributable in part to monopolistic practices and other unwholesome methods of competition."

In view of such developments, it seems possible that even without a recession much more attention might have been given to the monopoly issue. Conceivably, there might have been a monopoly investigation and a revival of antitrust prosecution even without the breakdown of late 1937 and early 1938. The latter event, however, greatly facilitated the development of such a program. It was the added element that made some sort of action imperative, the element needed for the antimonopolists to win the ear of the President and draw the whole problem to public attention. In a sense, the crisis of 1937 and 1938 was to bring them and their philosophy to the fore, much as the crisis of 1933 had advanced the views of their rivals.[3]

[3] Lynch, *Economic Power*, 10, 14–17; Harold L. Ickes, *Secret Diary*, II (N.Y.: Simon & Schuster, 1954), 214, 232; Alsop and Kintner, in *Saturday Evening Post*, Nov. 12, 1938, p. 109; Whaley-Eaton Service, *American Letter*, May 8, 1937; *Business Week*, July 31, 1937, pp. 17–18; *Fortune*, Feb. 1938, pp. 165–66, 168; *Washington Post*, Oct. 22, 1937; Isador Lubin to Marvin McIntyre, July 12, 1937; FDR to Christian Peoples, Aug. 2, 1937; FDR to Robert Jackson, Oct. 22, 1937; Huston Thompson to FDR, Sept. 7, 1937; FDR to William Ayres, Nov. 16, 1937; Ayres to FDR, Sept. 15, Nov. 20, 1937, all in Roosevelt Papers (OF 15-c, 342, 277, 100);

In spite of the earlier warnings, the recession of 1937 seemed to surprise New Dealers and businessmen alike. Even as the economic indices turned downward, there was a widespread feeling that a serious recession was impossible. "The general rule," said the monthly letter of the National City Bank, "is that depression is preceded by credit stringency and excessive activity in capital investment and construction. . . . It would be something novel to go into a second severe depression before getting completely out of the first." And other business and governmental spokesmen echoed the same general sentiments. The country, they thought, was simply experiencing a "leveling-off process," a "corrective" dip, a "period of readjustment." Business conditions, said Secretary of Commerce Daniel Roper, were still fundamentally sound, and the economy would soon begin to expand again.

Subsequent developments, however, were to make a hollow mockery out of such prophecies. On October 19, Black Tuesday, stock prices took a drastic dip, and in the weeks that followed other economic indices turned sharply downward. The Federal Reserve Board's index of industrial production fell from 119 in August 1937 to 80 by April 1938. The New York Times index of business activity dropped from 111 to 75. And during the same general period, from September 1937 to June 1938, durable goods production declined over fifty percent, profits seventy-eight percent, payrolls thirty-five percent, and manufacturing employment twenty-three percent. In terms of the

President Roosevelt's Press Conferences, July 13, 1937, Roosevelt Papers; Leon Henderson and Charles Merriam, "Emerging Problems," July 26, 1937; Delano to FDR, Nov. 15, 1937; Merriam to Henry Dennison, July 30, 1937, all in NRPB Records (Advisory Committee Minutes—CCF, Housing File—CCF, Industrial Section File—CCF).

rapidity of decline, the new recession was one of the most severe in American economic history.[4]

Tracing the economic decline, though, was a good deal easier than explaining it. As might be expected, the latter process produced sharp disagreements, many of which have persisted to the present. One group of theories stressed the decline in business investment and offered various explanations as to why this decline had occurred. Some blamed it on the general depression psychology, some on the rising costs of labor and raw materials, some on restrictive financial and monetary policies, and some on a shortage of available capital. Others, more critical of the New Deal, attributed the whole setback to governmental policies, especially such policies as the encouragement of labor, the undistributed profits tax, government competition with private enterprise, and the failure to balance the budget.

A second group of theories stressed the decline in consumer purchasing power, although again there was considerable disagreement as to why this decline had occurred. According to one view, and the one that seems most valid to me, the crucial factors were the withdrawal of governmental spending and the collapse of consumer credit in the summer of 1937. The spending had never really been enough to get a recovery cycle started, and once the government withdrew, the economy promptly collapsed again. Opposed to this view, however, was one that laid much less stress on fiscal policy, much more on the effects of monopolistically controlled prices. Arbitrary price increases, so the argument ran, had siphoned off all the

[4] Douglas A. Hayes, *Business Confidence and Business Activity* (Ann Arbor: U. of Mich. Press, 1951), 10–11, 14–15, 21; Kenneth D. Roose, in *Journal of Political Economy*, June 1948, p. 241; Emerson Axe, in *Annalist*, Oct. 22, 1937, pp. 658–59; Max Lerner, in *Nation*, Oct. 30, 1937, pp. 468–70; *Newsweek*, Nov. 1, 1937, pp. 7–9; *New York Times*, Oct. 4–9, 13, 15–17, 19, 20, Nov. 14, 1937; Jan. 3, May 29, June 26, 1938.

gains to wealthy savers. These people had failed to find profitable investment outlets, and the result was a new failure of purchasing power. Yet instead of lowering prices, businessmen had again reacted by laying off workers, reducing output, and postponing investments, a process that cut purchasing power that much more and made the recession worse.[5]

Disagreement about the causes of the recession led naturally to the proposal of widely divergent remedies. Nor was it surprising that each group tended to regard the recession as confirmation of what it had been saying all along. Many businessmen, for instance, seemed to regard it as a Heaven-sent opportunity to junk the New Deal. Numerous business speeches in late 1937 were built around the theme that recovery would soon get under way again if the government would only "lift the fog" on what lay ahead and remove the "shackles" imposed by restrictive legislation. Republican politicians, too, lost little time in blaming the whole state of affairs on the New Deal. The President, they declared, was "solely responsible," and anyone with a grain of economic sense would deplore "the tragic results of the government-made Roosevelt depression, brought about by economic fallacies, attacks on business, destructive taxation, squandering the people's money, and administration by confusion."

The first reaction of Administration leaders was to issue "Hooverish statements," minimizing the slump; but before long, it became apparent that they were badly divided over

[5] Eccles, *Beckoning Frontiers*, 294–95; Hayes, *Business Confidence*, 118–26; Melvin D. Brockie, in *Economic Journal*, June 1950, pp. 292–309; Roose, in *Journal of Political Economy*, June 1948, pp. 244–46; Alexander Sachs, in *Annalist*, Jan. 14, 1938, pp. 35–36; George Soule, Alvin Hansen, and Arthur Gayer, in *New Republic*, Feb. 2, 1938, pp. 377–84, 388–93; Ralph W. Robey, in *Newsweek*, Dec. 27, 1937, pp. 35–36; Slichter, in *Review of Economic Statistics*, Aug. 1938, pp. 97–110; Henderson to Cohen, Dec. 20, 1937, Cohen File, NPPC Records; Henderson, "What Has Happened to Recovery?" Jan. 1, 1938, Blaisdell File, NRPB Records; BAC, "Underlying Causes of the Recession," Jan. 20, 1938, OF 3-Q, Roosevelt Papers.

the proper course to follow. The conservatives, men like Jesse Jones, Daniel Roper, Henry Morgenthau, and Joseph Kennedy, wanted to conciliate business by balancing the budget, revising the tax laws, and declaring a recess on reform. The antimonopolists and spenders, however, had different ideas, and for a time, the President seemed inclined to listen to them. Again, he seemed to think, business interests were ganging up on him. When Morgenthau called him on the night of November 3, he became "very excited and disagreeable and quoted at great length a man he described as a 'wise old bird' who had said that business was deliberately causing the depression in order to hold a pistol to his head and force a retreat from the New Deal." At the Cabinet meeting the next day, he was still "greatly disturbed" and expounded at length on the theory that big money interests were in an "unconscious conspiracy" to force the hand of the Administration. Morgenthau and Jim Farley argued that he should reasure business, but he seemed highly skeptical about such a policy. Harold Ickes, for one, did not think it would do a bit of good. As the session ended, he wrote out a memo and handed it to Roosevelt. "This looks to me like the same kind of fight that Jackson made against the United States Bank except that big capital is occupying at this time the role of the bank." "That's right," said the President.

For the antimopolists and spenders, for men like Ickes, Henderson, Jackson, Corcoran, and Cohen, the theory that capital was on a sitdown strike was soon to become the official version of the recession. For some, this was probably mere political convenience, but for others it represented a conviction that some sort of conspiracy did exist. On November 27, Leon Henderson wrote a long memorandum in which he argued that a number of large banks and corporations were "acting in concert" in regard to their buying activities, shut downs, and credit policies. There was, he thought, a definite "identity of interest" among those responsible for the recession, although he admitted in a concluding sentence that he might be thinking too much about Andrew Jackson. In any event, he felt, the theory of a loss of business confidence was so much nonsense. There had been a high degree of confidence in July and August, even though the undistributed profits tax and all the other New Deal measures were in effect. The real culprit was the "outrageous price increases," which had strangled the housing boomlet and brought a new failure of purchasing power; the need now was for a resumption of spending, coupled with a broad drive against price rigidity and monopolistic practices.[6]

III

In the late fall of 1937 the struggle for the Presidential ear continued. On November 10, in a speech that had been "checked and double-checked" by the President himself, Henry Morgenthau promised the National Academy of Political Science that the Administration would make a strong effort to balance the budget and revise inequitable taxes. In spite of his sincerity, though, a highly unreceptive audience openly tittered and hooted at his promises. The whole experience, said Herman Oliphant, proved the utter "hopelessness" of trying to work with business leaders. The other antimonopolists thought so too, and they were now making a determined effort to win the President to their point of view. On November 8 Harry Hopkins ar-

[6] Ickes, *Diary*, II, 223–24, 229, 240–42; James A. Farley, *Jim Farley's Story* (N.Y.: McGraw-Hill, 1948), 101–7; Blum, *Morgenthau Diaries*, I, 381, 390–93; Alsop and Kintner, in *Saturday Evening Post*, Nov. 12, 1938, p. 109; Henry Morgenthau, Jr., in *Collier's*, Oct. 4, 1947, p. 21; *Fortune*, Feb. 1938, p. 59; March 1938, pp. 75, 128, 132; *New York Times*, Oct. 7–9, 20, 23–24, Nov. 13, 16, 18–19, Dec. 3–5, 8–10, 17, 1937; Daniel Roper to FDR, Nov. 20, 1937, OF 172, Roosevelt Papers; Henderson to Hopkins, Nov. 27, 1937, Cohen File, NPPC Records; Henderson to Hopkins, Nov. 1937, Relief Plans File, Hopkins Papers; NRC, "Emerging Industrio-Governmental Problems," Nov. 9, 1937, Presidential Correspondence File—CCF, NRPB Records; Robert Jackson to Thurman Arnold, Dec. 31, 1937, Box 37, Arnold Papers.

ranged a Presidential interview for Leon Henderson, Isador Lubin, and Lauchlin Currie, and the three economists presented the President with a trenchant memorandum arguing that the slump was "directly traceable to an upsurge in costs and prices." In late November, Ickes, Jackson, and Hopkins accompanied the President on a fishing trip to Florida, discussed the political situation with him, and tried again to impress him with the dangers inherent in a policy of conciliating business.

The President, however, was still allowing matters to drift. His opening message to the special session of Congress on November 15 said little about spending or antitrust action, and the housing message on November 29 was almost equally disappointing to the antimonopolists. It asked only for a revised law that would reduce the expense of financing new building. Congress, moreover, was in an increasingly rebellious mood, one that led it to concentrate on tax revision, shelf the wages-and-hours bill, and ignore most of the President's recommendations. When the special session ended, Roosevelt jokingly remarked that it had failed to vote anything except mileage expenses for its members.[7]

To New Dealers of the Jackson-Corcoran-Cohen persuasion, the President's indecision seemed not only exasperating but dangerous. Accordingly, in early December, they decided to do something on their own, to take the risk themselves and leave the President free to repudiate them if need be. Jackson was groomed for the platform part;

[7] James M. Burns, *Roosevelt* (N.Y.: Harcourt, Brace, 1956), 321–23; Blum, *Morgenthau Diaries*, 394–97; Eccles, *Beckoning Frontiers*, 303–4; Ickes, *Diary*, II, 258, 260–63; Morgenthau, in *Collier's*, Oct. 4, 1947, p. 21; *Congressional Record*, 75 Cong., 2 Sess., LXXXII, 5–7, 418–20; *Congressional Digest*, Jan. 1938, pp. 33–36; *New York Times*, Nov. 9, 11, 16, 29–30, Dec. 2, 4–5, 16, 18–22, 1937; Isador Lubin, Leon Henderson, and Lauchlin Currie, "Causes of the Recession," Nov. 1937, Recession File, Hopkins Papers; NRC, "Emerging Industrio-Governmental Problems," Nov. 9, 1937; Currie to Blaisdell, Dec. 16, 1937, both in NRPB Records (Presidential Correspondence —CCF, Blaisdell File).

Corcoran and Cohen cooperated in drafting the speeches; and Lubin and Henderson supplied the economic data. The first efforts came in mid-December, when Jackson spoke before the Farm Bureau Federation in Chicago and a consumers' organization in New York. "I do not believe," he declared, "that we can have a stable economic structure that is half monopoly and half free competition. Either we must get rid of monopoly pegged prices or we must find controls which will peg other prices in relation to them." And he, for one, did not want the government engaged in the price-fixing business.

It was not until late December, though, that Jackson really began to attract public attention. On December 26 he delivered a major address over the Mutual Broadcasting System. Three days later, on December 29, he spoke before the American Political Science Association in Philadelphia. In both speeches, he minced few words. The monopolists, he declared, had "simply priced themselves out of the market" and "into a slump." They had tried to "skim all the cream off recovery" and then screen their operation by accusing the Administration and calling a "general strike" against the government. Actually, the "only just criticism" of the New Deal was that it had failed to act vigorously enough. It had set out "a breakfast for the canary and let the cat steal it." [8]

In the meantime, Corcoran and Cohen had enlisted the aid of Harold Ickes, and the latter had discovered a convenient text in Ferdinand Lundberg's *America's Sixty Families*, a book whose thesis could be summed up in its first sentence: "The United States is owned and dominated

[8] Louis W. Koenig, *The Invisible Presidency* (N.Y.: Holt, Rinehart & Winston, 1960), 281; Alsop and Kintner, in *Saturday Evening Post*, Nov. 12, 1938, pp. 109, 112; *Fortune*, March 1938, p. 78; *New York Times*, Dec. 12, 14, 27, 30, 1937; Henderson to Cohen, Dec. 18, 20, 1937, with accompanying charts and memoranda, Cohen File, NPPC Records; Robert Jackson, Addresses, Dec. 11, 13, 1937, Monopoly File, Borah Papers; Jackson, Addresses, Dec. 26, 29, 1937, Barrows File, NRPB Records.

today by a hierarchy of its sixty richest families, buttressed by no more than ninety families of lesser wealth." Ickes no doubt knew that Lundberg had indulged in gross exaggerations, but the general thesis could be used with telling effect. In a major speech over the NBC network on December 30, he called upon Americans to engage in a battle to the finish against the "Sixty Families," the "plutocrats" who were directly responsible for the recession. It was these people who had jacked up prices, hoarded their money, held down wages, and then demanded the liquidation of the New Deal. And unless the American people called their bluff, they would end up by creating a "Big Business Fascist America."

At last the antimonopolists had got something started. Headlines burst forth gratifyingly; editors deplored this new effort to find a "scapegoat"; and from the business community came screams of pained indignation. "There has been a great stirring of the animals," noted Ickes, "and this isn't likely to subside for several days." In Congress, on the other hand, there were many expressions of approval, particularly from the old-line progressives. It seems probable, too, that the speeches struck a respondent chord in the general populace. Jackson claimed that the letters he received could be classified by the kind of paper on which they were written. Those on tablet paper in lead pencil expressed warm approval, while those on engraved stationery were bitter denunciations.[9]

Since the press had no inkling that Roosevelt was not

[9] Ickes, *Diary*, II, 266, 282–84; Ferdinand Lundberg, *America's Sixty Families* (N.Y.: Citadel, 1937), 3; Alsop and Kintner, in *Saturday Evening Post*, Nov. 12, 1938, p. 112; Marquis Childs, in *Forum*, March 1940, p. 153; *New York Times*, Dec. 28, 30–31, 1937; Jan. 2, 1938; *Chicago Tribune*, Jan. 1, 5, 1938; *New Republic*, Jan. 5, 1938, pp. 239–40; *Nation*, Jan. 8, 1938, pp. 31–32; *Portland Express*, Dec. 31, 1937; *Boston Transcript*, Dec. 31, 1937; *Kansas City Star*, Dec. 31, 1937; *San Francisco Chronicle*, Dec. 31, 1937; *Washington News*, Dec. 31, 1937; Ickes, Addresses, Dec. 8, 30, 1937; Thomas Corcoran to Ickes, Dec. 20, 1937; Ickes to Lundberg, Feb. 1, 1938, all in Speeches File, Ickes Papers.

behind the speeches, there was a good deal of speculation concerning his intentions. Some thought he was planning an open declaration of war against monopolies, some that he was paving the way for new regulatory or planning legislation, and some that he was motivated chiefly by a desire to drive down prices, particularly the prices of building materials. Others held that the Administration was merely trying to create a scapegoat, to get the drop on businessmen that were grumbling about the "Roosevelt depression." Still others ascribed it all to politics. Jackson, they said, was being groomed for the governorship of New York. Nor did the speechmakers themselves know with any degree of certainty how the President might react. "I don't know how far he will go," Ickes confided to his diary, "but I hope that he won't let us down entirely."

Roosevelt's actions during the next few days only added to the confusion. Antimonopoly action, he insisted, was necessary. Yet his State of the Union Message on January 3, 1938, proved to be amazingly mild. In the words of the *San Francisco Chronicle*, those who had expected him to "out-Jackson the Jacksons and out-Ickes the Ickes found themselves let down badly." Then, at his press conference on January 4, he loosed a trial balloon of an entirely different sort. The recession, he seemed to be saying, was due to a lack of planning, particularly in the automobile and steel industries. He went on to discuss a scheme of planned production, under which business leaders might gather around the conference table with government representatives to determine production policies and prevent overproduction. Such a scheme, he emphasized, would not mean a revival of the NRA, but critics of the proposal could see little difference.[10]

[10] Ickes, *Diary*, II, 284–86; Lynch, *Economic Power*, 22; Koenig, *Invisible Presidency*, 282; Alsop and Kintner, in *Saturday Evening Post*, Nov. 12, 1938, p. 112; *New Republic*, Jan. 19, 1938, pp. 308–9; *New York Times*, Dec. 28, 31, 1937, Jan. 1–2, 4–5, 1938; *Newsweek*, Jan. 10, 1938, p. 10; *Fortune*, March 1938, pp. 75, 78, 136; Dorothy Thompson, in *Washington Star*, Jan. 7, 1938; David

In the meantime, in spite of the President's reluctance to sanction their approach, the antimonopolists continued their campaign. On January 1 Leon Henderson came to the support of Jackson and Ickes with a further explanation of how monopoly prices had produced the recession. On January 6 Jackson returned to the fray in a debate with Wendell Willkie. And two days later, at the Jackson Day celebrations, Ickes loosed another blast at the "Sixty Families." Such speeches, the antimonopolists seemed to feel, might commit the Administration to an antitrust program; and in any event, they would lift the curse of the recession from the New Deal and shift the blame to its enemies.[11]

IV

The antimonopolists, moreover, were not the only ones who were trying to explain the setback and prescribe a remedy. As the recession deepened, business planners and trade association executives felt that competition had again become "excessive" and that business leaders should again be called upon to lead a new cooperative recovery effort. Men like Benjamin Javits and Fred Kent revived their proposals for a business commonwealth. Bernard Baruch wanted a new War Industries Board. And Donald Richberg argued that the solution lay in a revision of the antitrust laws and the establishment of a "cooperative" program, one that would eliminate "unfair trade prac-

Lawrence, in *Boston Transcript*, Jan. 7, 1938; Alsop and Kintner, in *Washington Star*, Jan. 4, 12, 1938; Walter Lippmann, in *Cleveland Plain Dealer*, Jan. 6, 1938; Whaley-Eaton Service, *American Letter*, Jan. 1, 1938; *St. Louis Post-Dispatch*, Jan. 4, 1938; *San Francisco Chronicle*, Jan. 4, 1938; President Roosevelt's Press Conferences, Dec. 31, 1937; Jan. 4, 1938, Roosevelt Papers.

[11] Henderson, Address, Jan. 1, 1938, Blaisdell File, NRPB Records; Jackson, Address, Jan. 6, 1938, Barrows File, NRPB Records; Ickes, Address, Jan. 8, 1938, Speeches File, Ickes Papers; *New York Times*, Jan. 9, 1938; *Washington Post*, Jan. 2, 1938; Childs, in *Forum*, March 1940, p. 153.

tices," coordinate business operations, "iron out the peaks and valleys of . . . periodic booms and depressions," and enable business management to fulfill its "obligations to the general welfare." It was Richberg, too, who seemed to bear the brunt of answering the antitrusters. "The true side of the New Deal," he told the President, was represented by its policies in regard to agriculture, labor, bituminous coal, and the NRA, not by the philosophy of the "fanatic trust busters." And the need now was for "greater cooperation within industry and between industry and the government," not for intensified enforcement of the antitrust laws.

The Richberg approach, of course, attracted less support in 1937 than it had in 1933. The sense of crisis was less acute; and both businessmen and government officials, remembering the experiences of the NRA, were suspicious of new cooperative ventures. Yet businessmen still wanted relief from the antitrust laws; and within the Administration, the Department of Commerce and its Business Advisory Council still offered a refuge for the business planners. In cooperation with the Council, for example, Blackwell Smith had worked out a plan for a new agency that could sanction desirable cooperative agreements, and for a time it seemed that the President might endorse such a proposal. Once again, it appeared, he was drawing upon his past experiences with the War Industries Board, the American Construction Council of the nineteen twenties, and the planning activities of the NRA; and once again, as illustrated by his press conference on January 4, he was toying with the idea of business planning under governmental supervision.[12]

Speculation about a new cooperative scheme increased

[12] Daniel R. Fusfeld, *The Economic Thought of Franklin D. Roosevelt and the Origins of the New Deal* (N.Y.: Columbia U. Press, 1956), 101–8, 252–53; *Fortune*, Feb. 1938, pp. 61, 150, 152, 162, 165–66, 168; *New Republic*, Nov. 24, 1937, p. 74; Jan. 19, 1938, p. 308; Benjamin Javits to Stephen Early, Nov. 23, 1937, and accompanying memo. of Oct. 28, 1937; Javits to FDR, Jan. 13, 1938; Bernard Baruch to FDR, Dec. 30, 1937; Baruch to Marguerite

in mid-January, when the President held a series of conferences with business leaders. On January 11 Richberg arranged a conference with such outspoken business critics as Ernest T. Weir, Lewis Brown, Colby Chester, and Alfred P. Sloan. Three days later Adolf Berle and Rexford Tugwell ushered in another group of business and labor leaders. During the following week, Roosevelt held two additional conferences, one with the Business Advisory Council, the second with representatives of the automobile industry. At all of these meetings, there was talk of cooperation, planning, economic councils, and the need for greater business stability; but the businessmen remained wary of any proposal that would transfer power to government officials.

A lighter note was added to the proceedings when a conference of small businessmen, sponsored by Secretary Roper, met in Washington on February 2. During the two-day session a noisy minority took over, and amid cries of "throw him out" and forcible ejections, the delegates fought each other for control of the speakers' platform. Eventually, though, the conference did adopt a series of resolutions denouncing New Deal reforms and asking for tax relief, government economy, and special loans. When a reporter asked the President whether he expected to hold other small business conferences, Roosevelt replied with a gust of laughter. "I do not know," he said. "Of course, they might ask for another one."

In this whole trend of events, the antimonopolists could

LeHand, Jan. 7, 1938; Fred Kent to FDR, Dec. 10, 1937; May 2, 1938; Richberg to LeHand, Dec. 29, 1937, with accompanying memoranda; Blackwell Smith to McIntyre, Jan. 14, 1938; Javits to Jackson, Dec. 29, 1937; Richberg, Addresses, Jan. 26, March 3, May 19, 1938; Richberg to FDR, April 23, 1938; Report of BAC Committee on Business Legislation, Jan. 6, 1938; Roper to FDR, Jan. 17, 1938, all in Roosevelt Papers (PPF 3577, 88, 744, 1820, 2697, OF 10, 1961, 277, 3Q); President Roosevelt's Press Conferences, Nov. 23, 1937; Jan. 4, 1938, Roosevelt Papers; Blackwell Smith, "Federal Regulation of Industry," Nov. 11, 1937; W. L. Batt to Blaisdell, Nov. 24, 1937; Ernest Draper to Walter White, Nov. 20, 1937, all in Blaisdell File, NRPB Records.

see little that looked encouraging. "The President, after letting Jackson and me stick our necks out with our anti-monopoly speeches, is pulling petals off the daisy with representatives of big business," grumbled Ickes. He was somewhat consoled, however, when the President remarked during a Cabinet meeting, "Do you know that this confercence would not have been possible if it had not been for the speeches of Bob Jackson and Harold Ickes? Prior to the speeches these businessmen refused even to come in to talk to me. After the speeches they were only too glad to come in." The majority of the Cabinet members, noted Ickes, felt that the President should be conciliatory toward business, but some did agree that the speeches had driven "the herd into the corral where the President could pat their necks and tell them all they had to do was to be good." [13]

V

By early 1938 antitrusters, budget-balancers, spenders, and business planners were all bidding for the Presidential ear. Nor did the solutions offered by these groups exhaust the alternatives from which the President might choose. There was, for example, a renewed interest in centralized governmental planning and in such proposals as Mordecai Ezekiel's Industrial Expansion Plan and the Voorhis-Allen bill that was based upon it. Ezekiel himself was promoting a series of conferences between government economists and liberal congressmen. Henry Wallace was talking about the need for balanced production, an "ever normal" warehouse, and renewed cooperation between economic interest

[13] Ickes, *Diary*, II, 295, 326; *Newsweek*, Jan. 24, 1938, pp. 11–12; Feb. 14, 1938, pp. 11–12; *New York Times*, Jan. 12–15, 20, 22, 27, Feb. 3–5, 1938; Alsop and Kintner, in *Washington Star*, Jan. 24, 1938; McIntyre to Alfred Sloan et al., Jan. 10, 1938; Sloan to FDR, Feb. 10, 1938, with accompanying memo.; Draper to McIntyre, Jan. 20, 1938; Thomas Lamont to FDR, Feb. 16, 1938, all in Roosevelt Papers (OF 172, 3Q, PPF 70); President Roosevelt's Press Conferences, Jan. 21, Feb. 4, 1938, Roosevelt Papers.

groups. The Industrial Section of the National Resources Committee was pushing a similar approach. Actually, it argued, there were two possible alternatives. One was a reflationary program, based primarily upon a resumption of public spending. The other was "concerted expansion of industrial production, under programs jointly developed with industry and labor, and enforced by Federal sanctions." The latter program, it felt, if carefully sold to the public, could be put into action "within a few months." Over a period of two years, it could produce "almost as much expansion" as a five billion dollar spending program. Under it, the chances would be much greater "that the higher level of production could be maintained without subsequent recession." [14]

The influence of the planners was also clearly apparent in the President's press conference of February 18. Ostensibly, the four-page memorandum that he read to newsmen was the work of an interdepartmental price committee headed by Henry Morgenthau. Actually, it was largely written by Gardiner Means, with the whole emphasis upon reflating the flexible price areas rather than bringing down rigid prices. One reporter asked the President if he proposed to do anything about the latter problem. "Now you are asking about the industries that are more

[14] Joseph Alsop and Robert Kintner, *Men around the President* (N.Y.: Doubleday, Doran, 1939), 138–41; Herbert Harris, in *Survey Graphic*, April 1938, pp. 227–32; *New York Times*, Nov. 15, Dec. 26, 1937; Jan. 4, 9, 1938; NRC, "Industry Regulation," April 1938; and "Where Are We?" April 9, 1938; Jerry Voorhis to FDR, May 6, 1938; Wallace to FDR, Dec. 22, 1937; March 24, Aug. 8, 1938, all in Roosevelt Papers (OF 1092, 172, PPF 1820); Mordecai Ezekiel to Blaisdell, April 15, 1938, with accompanying Memoranda of Feb. 10 and March 15, 1938; NRC, "What to Do If March 1938 Resembles March 1933," Dec. 20, 1937, both in Blaisdell File, NRPB Records. The NRC proposals described in the text were the ones being discussed in late 1937 and early 1938. In April 1938 the NRC's Industrial Section also recommended the creation of a Federal Industrial Board to conduct business conferences and devise production and marketing programs. Such a board, it felt, might also investigate and make recommendations in regard to uniform bidding, concentration of control, and monopolistic abuses.

monopolistic," said Roosevelt. "We hope so but are not ready to shoot on it." Another correspondent suggested that if inflexible prices were reduced so as to increase sales, production could then be expanded to full capacity. "No, no," the President replied. "There is such a thing as increasing production to the point where the country cannot swallow it—get indigestion." [15]

By the end of February, observers who were trying to predict the course of Administration policy were plainly baffled. The business conferences seemed to indicate that some program of planned cooperation was in the offing; yet these very indications were interspersed with a series of overtures to the antitrust camp. The President was still expressing concern about the steel monopoly, the high price of building materials, and the evils of corporate pyramiding.[16] He was asking the FTC for more information about monopolistic practices and corporate organization.[17]

[15] Blum, *Morgenthau Diaries*, 410–11; *New York Times*, Feb. 19–20, 1938; President Roosevelt's Press Conferences, Feb. 18, 1938, Roosevelt Papers; White House PR, Feb. 18, 1938; Charles Eliot, Memo. re White House Conference, March 1, 1938, both in NRPB Records (Advisory Committee Minutes—CCF, Presidential Correspondence—CCF).

[16] Stanley High, in *Saturday Evening Post*, April 9, 1938, pp. 110, 112–13; *Newsweek*, Jan. 24, 1938, pp. 11–12; Feb. 7, 1838, pp. 9–10; *Fortune*, March 1938, p. 75; Blum, *Morgenthau Diaries*, 412; President Roosevelt's Press Conferences, Jan. 14, 25, 1938, Roosevelt Papers; FDR to Jackson, March 8, 1938, with accompanying memoranda; Charles Edison to FDR, Jan. 13, 1938, both in OF 342, Roosevelt Papers.

[17] In April 1938 the Commission filed a report on "monopolistic practices and other unwholesome methods of competition," the result of the investigation requested back in November 1937. The report described price-raising activities in some forty-three industries and dealt at considerable length with the steel, oil, and cement industries. In view of the pending cases against the cement and petroleum companies, however, the Commission decided not to make the report public. See FTC, "Report on Monopolistic Practices and Other Unwholesome Methods of Competition," 1–4, 13–35, and *passim*; FDR to Garland Ferguson, Jan. 25, 1938; Ferguson to FDR, Jan. 31, 1938; FDR to the FTC, March 22, 1938; Robert Freer to FDR, May 11, 1938, all in Roosevelt Papers (OF 100, 277).

And, much to the dismay of Richberg and the business planners, he was discussing the problem with Senator Borah and giving the impression that he and Borah were essentially in agreement.[18]

In the Treasury, where Morgenthau seemed to think that an antimonopoly approach would take the President's mind off the arguments of the spenders, Herman Oliphant was pushing a series of antitrust activities. The procurement division had begun a new study of collusive bidding; plans were being devised to check or eliminate bank holding companies; and Oliphant had succeeded in selling the President a scheme under which the Treasury would take over the bankrupt Genessee Valley Gas Company, reorganize it, and prove to the public that a properly financed utility corporation could operate profitably. The Treasury had also taken the lead in pushing an interdepartmental investigation of the cement industry, which had resulted in concrete recommendations that were put into effect in March 1938. Under the new regulations, all governmental purchasing of cement would be concentrated in the Treasury's procurement division; bidders would be required to quote f.o.b. mill-base prices and to certify that there had been no collusion, either among themselves or among subcontractors; and the successful bidders would have to sell to all government contractors at the price quoted to the government.

Under the circumstances, it was difficult to tell just where the New Deal was headed. Before long, some critics were referring to the moves of the Administration as the great "shell game." The shells, so the insinuation ran, were the usual three in number and went currently by the names of "antimonopoly," "voluntary cooperation between business and government," and "collectivism." Presumably, there was a pea called "ultimate Administration

[18] *Newsweek*, Feb. 7, 1938, p. 9; William Borah to FDR, Jan. 29, 1938, Monopoly File, Borah Papers; Richberg to FDR, April 23, 1938, OF 277, Roosevelt Papers.

policy," but so fast did the game move that it could not be discovered by either the "Right" or the "Left" under any of the shells.[19]

VI

Keener observers, however, soon realized that a major policy struggle was taking place, a debate somewhat reminiscent of the one between Theodore Roosevelt and Wilson in 1912. In the press, Richberg and Jackson became symbols for the two opposing views. Richberg stood essentially for a policy of business-government cooperation, under which the government would aid businessmen in planning and coordinating their future activities. Jackson, on the other hand, thoroughly distrusted the idea of business cooperation, with or without governmental supervision. The regulated, he felt, too often became the regulators, and production could not be planned except at the expense of monopolistic abuse, economic stagnation, and violent fluctuations in the employment level. Monopolistic practices must be prevented and broken up, not fostered and sanctioned.

Summed up in the speeches of these two men was one of the central dilemmas of the New Deal. It was trying, on one hand, to check deflationary forces and achieve a greater degree of economic security, goals that seemed to call for the organization of industrial aggregates whose economics could not fail to be monopolistic. Yet at the same time, it was trying to preserve the traditions of individualism, competition, private property, flexibility, and dynamic change. Once the difficulty of resolving such a conflict became apparent, there was a growing disposition

[19] Blum, *Morgenthau Diaries*, 406–9, 413–14, 427–28; Paul Anderson, in *Nation*, Feb. 5, 1938, p. 147; *Fortune*, March 1938, p. 75; Arthur Krock, in *New York Times*, Jan. 19, 1938; Wayne Taylor to FDR, March 29, 1938; Committee on Cement, Recommendations, March 21, 1938, both in Roosevelt Papers (OF 21, 21-Y); Morgenthau to FDR, May 20, 1938, Box 1, Arnold Papers.

not to resolve it, a tendency to postpone decisions and pass the buck to some investigating commission. As the New Republic put it, trustbusting was "futile," business planning was "dangerous," and government management was impossible without a "long period of study, political preparation and legal conflict." Under the circumstances, it seemed, an investigation would offer the most harmless way of dealing with the issue. Those who advocated a definite approach could use such an inquiry as a sounding board for their ideas. Those who were satisfied with the status quo could use it as a way to block or postpone any action. And those who did not pretend to know the answer might hope that a full-scale study would provide one.

By early 1938 an approach of this sort seemed more and more likely. Once again the country was faced with a serious economic crisis. Once again this crisis had sharpened both the traditional bias against big business and the demand for stabilization, security, and economic planning. Once again a three-cornered policy conflict had developed, reminiscent of the days of the NRA. But this was not 1933. Behind the leaders of 1938 lay the unhappy experiences of the the NRA, with its conflicts, disillusionments, and disappointments. Consequently, the result was not likely to be another NRA-type of concoction, blending all three approaches into one inconsistent and incongruous whole. It was likely to be no action at all, an evasion of the whole issue by tucking it away in a governmental investigation, which in all probability would end by expressing the same conflicting views with which it had started.[20]

[20] National Industrial Conference Board, A Practical Program for the Coordination of Government, Labor, and Management (1938), 79–80; Donald Richberg, in Proceedings of the Academy of Political Science, May 1938, pp. 35–42; Dwight MacDonald, in American Scholar, Summer 1939, pp. 302–3; Myron W. Watkins, in Yale Review, Dec. 1938, pp. 324–28, 336–38; Walter Millis, in Virginia Quarterly Review, July 1938, pp. 360–63; Marquis Childs, in Nation, Jan. 29, 1938, p. 119; Newsweek, Jan. 10, 1938, p. 5; Jan. 17, 1938, p. 44; New York Times, Jan. 27, 29, Feb. 20, 23, March 4, 1938; New Republic, Jan. 19, 1938, pp. 295–96; Fortune, Feb. 1938, pp. 58, 150, 152, 162, 165–66, 168.

CHAPTER 21. THE MONOPOLY INQUIRY AND THE SPENDING PROGRAM

W HEN great moral issues arise, when deep-seated policy conflicts cannot be resolved, when practical necessities run against the ingrained traditions of a people, wrote Thurman Arnold in 1937, the inclination is to submit the troublesome problem to an "oracle," to an expert commission, which studies the question and often ends by representing the same internal conflict that led to its creation. Arnold had in mind the Wickersham Commission. In 1937 he could not yet predict that he himself would be sitting on what was probably the greatest example of this phenomenon during the dismal decade.

By 1938 the debate over the monopoly problem was approaching the status described by Arnold. Caught in the throes of a new depression, torn by conflicting counsels, placed on the defensive before the country, the Roosevelt Administration sought a way out. Yet what was that way to be? Should industry be atomized and concentrated economic power dispersed? Should it be organized and rationalized so that the businessmen themselves might engage in economic planning? Or would it be necessary to transfer economic power to the state or to non-business groups? And did any of these alternatives offer a real solution? Was it really possible to preserve American ideals, the traditions of democracy, flexibility, competition, economic opportunity, and individual initiative, without renouncing the goal of economic security or sacrificing the advantages of integration, order, mass production, and large-scale organization?

Perhaps there was no real answer. Perhaps, as one observer concluded, the whole problem grew out of deep-seated promptings of human nature, which were perpetually at odds with each other. No one seemed to know, or at least few could agree. In a situation of this type it was only natural that men should resort to an expert commission. Perhaps, in the course of piling up a mountain of facts, the point of resolution might emerge. Perhaps, as some men hoped, an investigation might show conclusively that their particular solution was the correct one. Perhaps, if the problem were postponed long enough, it would disappear of its own accord.[1]

In any event, the idea of an investigation was soon attracting support in a variety of quarters. As early as December 1935, Leon Henderson and Theodore Kreps had proposed a "broad inquiry into the present status of competition"; Henderson had reiterated the proposal in 1936; and once the recession of 1937 set in, he strongly favored a "careful but complete Congressional hearing." "I keep insisting on a wide survey . . . ," he told John Chamberlain, "because (1) I believe it would indicate many rigid areas which could be unfrozen by compulsion to market competition, because (2) I would like to see the alternative to competition derived from wide survey." Mordecai Ezekiel, too, felt that a select investigating committee would be helpful, both in educating the public and in preventing "price-controlling industries from again raising prices and checking recovery." From consumer spokesmen and organizations came similar arguments and recommendations. While in Congress, men like James Shanley, Martin Dies, and Maury Maverick were introducing measures to establish investigating committees. Even the business groups seemed willing to go along. Attorney-General Homer Cummings had again recommended a broad study of the antitrust laws; and Cummings' proposal had re-

[1] Thurman W. Arnold, *The Folklore of Capitalism* (New Haven: Yale U. Press, 1937), 152–55; Myron W. Watkins, in *Yale Review*, Dec. 1938, pp. 323–28, 336–39; *Fortune*, Feb. 1938, p. 58; Francis Downing, in *Commonweal*, Jan. 6, 1939, pp. 287–88; *Business Week*, Dec. 24, 1938, pp. 22–25; Victor S. Yarros, in *Christian Century*, July 13, 1938, pp. 869–70.

ceived the endorsement of the Business Advisory Council and various other business organizations.

Increasingly, then, it appeared that the agitation against monopoly would result in nothing more than an investigation. Men of widely divergent views—antimonopolists, economic planners, proponents of business rationalization, and advocates of compensatory spending—could all agree that an investigation might do some good. And even if it did not, it could not do much harm. Congress, noted Mark Sullivan, would do nothing "momentous." It would simply refer the whole problem to a study group. That would take time, and it would not discover much that had not already been discovered by previous commissions.[2]

II

While the antitrust debate moved in the direction of a large-scale investigation, many of the antimonopolists were advocating increased federal spending. Some of them, like Leon Henderson and Tom Corcoran, had worked out a rationale that regarded spending and trustbusting as complementary rather than alternative programs. For one thing, said Henderson, full employment and sustained

[2] Homer Cummings, *The Unsolved Problem of Monopoly* (1937), 8; Leon Henderson, in *Annals Am. Acad.*, Jan. 1936, p. 267; *Congressional Record*, 75 Cong., 2 Sess., LXXXII, 1128; 75 Cong., 3 Sess., LXXXIII, 74, 1323; Willard L. Thorp, in *Dun's Review*, Aug. 1938, p. 24; Mark Sullivan, in *Washington Star*, Jan. 1938, clipping in Ickes Scrapbook, XIX, Ickes Papers; *Newsweek*, Nov. 29, 1937, p. 7; Jan. 10, 1938, p. 5; *New York Times*, Jan. 4, 7, Feb. 25, 1938; Leon Henderson and Theodore Kreps, "On the Necessity for a Broad Inquiry into the Present Status of Competition," Dec. 30, 1935; Mordecai Ezekiel, "Outline of a Reserve Program to Create and Maintain Recovery," Feb. 10, 1938, both in Blaisdell File, NRPB Records; Donald Montgomery to Benjamin Cohen, March 14, 1938, with accompanying memoranda, Cohen File, NPPC Records; Henderson to John Chamberlain, Jan. 29, 1938, Relief Plans File, Hopkins Papers; Report of BAC Committee on Business Legislation, Jan. 6, 1938, OF 3Q, Roosevelt Papers.

production were dependent upon both a balance in prices and a balance between savings and investment. While the former could be achieved by dislodging monopolistic controls, the latter would require governmental investment to offset the decline in private investment. Antitrust action would also add to the effectiveness of spending by breaking down restrictions on production and economic expansion. At the same time, spending would facilitate antitrust action by arresting deflationary forces and thus reducing the demand for cartelization.

The spending issue, moreover, was one upon which most of the so-called "liberals" could agree. Here the anti-trusters could join forces with the Keynesians, men like Lauchlin Currie and Marriner Eccles. A number of the planners had also accepted the idea of compensatory investment. Even in conservative circles, a spending program was not likely to encounter the intense opposition that would have met any genuine effort to restore competition or deprive businessmen of their decision-making power. It did have to overcome a certain reverence for a balanced budget, but in essence, it was designed to make the system work by applying an outside stimulus, not by reshaping the power structure or rearranging the internal machinery.[3]

In early 1938, though, the budget-balancers were still firmly entrenched, and it took three months of deepening depression to dislodge them. There were, to be sure, some concessions to the spending view. The RFC, for example, resumed its lending activities, the Treasury reversed its sterilization policies, the President requested an additional $250 million for relief, and special committees were set

[3] James M. Burns, *Roosevelt* (N.Y.: Harcourt, Brace, 1956), 325, 331–35; Lawrence R. Klein, *The Keynesian Revolution* (N.Y.: Macmillan, 1947), 166–68; Joseph Alsop and Robert Kintner, in *Saturday Evening Post*, Nov. 19, 1938, pp. 14–15; Henderson to Harry Hopkins, Nov. 27, 1937, Cohen File, NPPC Records; Henderson to Chamberlain, Jan. 29, 1938; Henderson and Beardsley Ruml to Hopkins, March 1938; Aubrey Williams to Hopkins, Jan. 1938, all in Hopkins Papers (Relief Plans File, Correspondence File).

up to study the possibilities of relaxing bank examination rules, providing loans to small business, and subsidizing the railroads. Yet none of these measures gave much promise of providing the "great gobs" of purchasing power that were needed. And the President, far from accepting the spending ideology, was still expressing hope that he could balance the budget.[4]

Not until late March did worsening economic conditions give the spenders a chance to convert the President. But once the chance appeared, they were quick to take advantage of it. Harry Hopkins, who had recently undergone a serious operation and had been convalescing in Florida, arrived in Atlanta to confer with Aubrey Williams, Leon Henderson, and Beardsley Ruml. Then, primed with arguments and memoranda, he proceeded to Warm Springs, Georgia, to discuss the situation with the President. The outlook, Hopkins indicated, was grim. Prices were badly out of line, purchasing power had to come from somewhere, and there was little likelihood of any large increase in private spending. It was doubtful, moreover, whether recovery could ever come along "orthodox" lines. Henderson and Ruml were now arguing that American capitalism had been sustained from the beginning by federal intervention, by such expedients as the public land grants, wartime spending, protective tariffs, and deficit financing. If this were true, it seemed obvious that the government would have to intervene again. By April 2, while Morgenthau was at Sea Island, Georgia, working on a program that he hoped would eventually

[4] Harold L. Ickes, Secret Diary, II (N.Y.: Simon & Schuster, 1954), 317; John M. Blum, From the Morgenthau Diaries, I (Boston: Houghton Mifflin, 1959), 400–1, 405–6, 411, 415–16, 428, 431; Alsop and Kintner, in Saturday Evening Post, Nov. 19, 1938, pp. 15, 85; Henderson to Hopkins, Oct. 12, 1937, Relief Plans File, Hopkins Papers; NRC, "Where Are We?" March 18, 1938, Blaisdell File, NRPB Records; RFC to all banks, Feb. 26, 1938; FDR to Walter Splawn, Feb. 1, 1938; Wayne Taylor to FDR, April 4, 1938; William O. Douglas to FDR, March 26, 1938, all in Roosevelt Papers (OF 643, 5, 706, 1060).

balance the budget, Hopkins had succeeded in convincing the President that a resumption of spending was necessary. "He was completely stampeded," said Morgenthau. "They stampeded him like cattle." [5]

During the same period, too, Corcoran and Cohen had met in Charleston and prepared a fresh prospectus for the antimonopoly drive. Cohen then flew to Atlanta to meet Jackson, and together they boarded the returning Presidential train. Renewed spending, they argued, must be accompanied by a program designed to restore competition, and the President did seem willing to go ahead with plans for a special study of the monopoly problem. A further indication of what might be in store for the future came on April 8, when Hopkins testified before the Senate's Special Committee to Investigate Unemployment and Relief. The recession, Hopkins told the committee, was due to a failure of purchasing power, brought on primarily by monopolistic activities and unwarranted price increases. The solution, he felt, lay in the adoption and application of "two large principles." One was "government contribution to purchasing power." The other was the stimulation of competition "on a scale that we have not known for many years." This, after all, was the "democratic method," the method under which the industrial pattern would be determined through the "voluntary actions of individual consumers," not by "the judgement or caprice of a few monopolists." [6]

[5] Burns, Roosevelt, 327–28; Marriner Eccles, Beckoning Frontiers (N.Y.: Knopf, 1951), 310–11; Blum, Morgenthau Diaries, 417, 421; Robert E. Sherwood, Roosevelt and Hopkins (N.Y.: Harper, 1948), 93; Henry Morgenthau, Jr., in Collier's, Oct. 4, 1947, pp. 45, 48; Henderson to Hopkins, March 23, 1938; Henderson and Ruml to Hopkins, March 1938, both in Relief Plans File, Hopkins Papers; Advisory Committee Minutes, April 23, 1938, CCF, NRPB Records.

[6] Special Senate Committee, Unemployment and Relief (75 Cong., 3 Sess., 1938), 1338–39, 1352–54; Alsop and Kintner, in Saturday Evening Post, Nov. 19, 1938, p. 86; Business Week, Oct. 8, 1938, pp. 18, 20; New York Times, April 3, 9, 1938; James Roosevelt to Marvin McIntyre, March 30, 1938, OF 10F, Roosevelt Papers.

While the press speculated about future policies, the details of the new spending program were hammered out within the Administration. When the President outlined his plans to Morgenthau on April 10, the latter was crestfallen. Two days later, when Hopkins discussed the spending program in detail, he realized that his dreams of a balanced budget were being thoroughly demolished. As a last effort, he tried to substitute desterilization of $1,400,-000,000 in gold and liberalization of Federal Reserve lending powers. When this was simply added to the Hopkins program, he threatened to resign. "He won't," remarked John Garner. "His father wouldn't let him."

When the President sent his spending message to Congress on April 14, it became clear that the Hopkins group had won. The message called for spending or lending over three billion dollars in the next few months for relief, public works, housing, and aid to state and local governments. In addition, $1,400,000,000 in idle gold would be desterilized, and the reserve requirements of Federal Reserve Banks would be lowered. In a companion fireside chat, delivered on the night of April 14, the President told the American people that the government was stepping in to "take up the slack." A long congressional debate followed; but when the Recovery-Relief bill became law in mid-June, it was clearly in line with the President's recommendations.[7]

III

The antimonopolists still doubted that spending would be enough, but without a long period of political preparation,

[7] Blum, *Morgenthau Diaries*, 420–25; *Congressional Record*, 75 Cong., 3 Sess., LXXXIII, 5381–84, Appendix, 1501–4; 52 *U.S. Statutes* 809, Public Res., No. 122, 75 Cong.; Alsop and Kintner, in *Saturday Evening Post*, Nov. 19, 1938, p. 86; Morgenthau, in *Collier's*, Oct. 4, 1947, pp. 48–49; Bascom N. Timmons, *ibid.*, Feb. 21, 1948, p. 49; *Newsweek*, April 18, 1938, pp. 11–12; June 27, 1938, pp. 7–9; *New York Times*, April 13, 15, June 22, 1938.

the chances of getting anything more seemed decidedly slim. The best that could be hoped for, it appeared, was a massive investigation of the monopoly problem, one that might generate enough steam for a breakthrough at a later date. After all, the securities and utility holding company laws had been preceded by similar investigations.

Accordingly, interested parties were soon plying the President with suggestions. Wright Patman, for example, hoped that the inquiry would tackle the "feudalistic chain store system." Herman Oliphant wanted a careful reexamination of court rulings, patent measures, bank holding companies, corporation laws, and tariff and financial policies. And Thurman Arnold, the newly appointed head of the Antitrust Division, felt that the antitrust laws should be revised so that the government could strike at market domination, regardless of how the power over prices had been acquired and regardless of motive or intent. "If, through the application of the Antitrust Laws . . . , we can restore price competition," said Arnold, "we will have gone a long way toward solving one of the major problems of the recession."

Some of Roosevelt's advisers, however, were still worried about the effect of an antimonopoly message on business confidence. Henry Wallace was urging a policy of caution. He had "no illusions" about the attitude of businessmen, he told the President, but still these men controlled "the bulk of the flow of private capital," and at the "present juncture" it was "absolutely necessary to induce that flow." Secretary Roper agreed. On April 26, after sixteen leading businessmen had indicated their willingness to cooperate, he urged that they be called into conference to draft a recovery program. And Homer Cummings, while willing to go along with a "searching investigation," wanted it to emphasize the broad problem rather than specific changes. In view of such sentiments, congressional leaders were expressing doubt that there would even be a message on the subject. The monopoly issue, concluded *Newsweek*, was "about dead," and the message, if sent at all, would not be "very fiery." [8]

The President, though, had decided that a message was necessary; and eventually, the document was completed and sent to Congress on April 29. The country, said Roosevelt, was suffering from a "concentration of private power without equal in history." The American economy was becoming a "concealed cartel system." And this "disappearance of price competition" was "one of the primary causes of our present difficulties." To deal with the situation, he recommended, Congress should appropriate more money for antitrust enforcement; it should pass legislation to control bank holding companies; and it should provide a sum of $500,000 for a "thorough study of the concentration of economic power," a study that would include such items as antitrust procedure, the merger movement, financial controls, trade association activities, patent laws, tax revision, and the feasibility of a Bureau of Industrial Economics.

Reaction to the President's proposals reflected the general belief that they were relatively innocuous. Had he proposed any serious action, there might have been, in Ickes' words, "a great stirring of the animals," but as it was, almost everyone could agree to an investigation. Conservatives congratulated the President on his "reasoned temper." And Senator Borah showed considerable insight when he predicted that the investigation would probably "string along and finally reach the dust of the upper shelf

[8] David Lynch, *The Concentration of Economic Power* (N.Y.: Columbia U. Press, 1946), 54; *Newsweek*, April 18, 1938, p. 9; *New York Times*, March 11, April 27–29, 1938; Thomas G. Corcoran to E. W. Hawley, March 25, 1957, author's files; Wallace to FDR, March 24, 1938; John Hanes to James Roosevelt, April 26, 1938, both in Roosevelt Papers (PPF 1820, 385); Wright Patman to FDR, April 24, 1938; Herman Oliphant, Draft of Antitrust Message, March 26, 1938; Arnold to Cummings, April 13, 1938; Cummings to FDR, April 21, 1938, all in OF 277, Roosevelt Papers.

in the form of ten or twenty volumes which few will ever consult." [9]

In Congress most of the debate centered about the question of legislative versus executive control, not the desirability of the investigation itself. Only a few arch-conservatives, like Robert Rich of Pennsylvania, thought it was "time to stop a lot of this foolishness." In his message, Roosevelt had made no mention of congressional participation, an omission that was immediately seized upon by Senator Joseph O'Mahoney, who quickly emerged as the leading sponsor of the proposed investigation.[10] Congress, he felt, should play the major role. Accordingly, on May 5, he introduced a resolution calling for a committee made up of four congressmen and three members from the Administration. The Administration countered by proposing a separate congressional committee, to be assisted by a temporary commission from the executive agencies; but the only concession O'Mahoney would make was to broaden his resolution to provide for a committee of eleven, three from the Senate, three from the House, and one each from the SEC, the FTC, and the Departments of Justice, Labor, and the Treasury.

As it turned out, the O'Mahoney resolution formed the basis of the Temporary National Economic Committee,

[9] Ickes, *Diary*, II, 284; *Congressional Record*, 75 Cong., 3 Sess., LXXXIII, 5992–96; *Newsweek*, May 9, 1938, pp. 10–12; *New York Times*, April 30, May 1, 1938; Thorp, in *Dun's Review*, Aug. 1938, p. 24.

[10] There was some speculation at the time that the monopoly investigation was designed to block the Borah-O'Mahoney bill. Yet it seems doubtful that this was really the case. Some of Roosevelt's advisers did feel that the bill's provisions were cumbersome and unworkable, but few conceded it any serious chance of passage, at least not in its existing form. See *Congressional Record*, 75 Cong., 3 Sess., LXXXIII, 5995, 8338–40, 8595–96, 9336–41; *Newsweek*, Jan. 31, 1938, p. 8; Lynch, *Economic Power*, 27–28; Joseph O'Mahoney to Arthur Himbert, Feb. 16, 1938; Congressional Intelligence, Inc., *Trends*, March 5, 1938, both in Federal Incorporation File, O'Mahoney Papers.

but not without some changes. A Senate subcommittee began by replacing the Departments of Labor and the Treasury with the Department of Commerce, a move that was admittedly designed to placate business sentiment. Later, however, the full Senate committee restored membership to the Treasury Department, and still later, on the Senate floor, an amendment sponsored by Senator Barkley granted representation to the Department of Labor. In its final form, then, the resolution provided for a twelve-man committee, with membership evenly balanced between Congress and the Administration. On June 9, after efforts to limit the President's power over the agency's funds had been defeated, the measure passed the Senate. On June 14, only five days later, the House gave its approval, and on June 16 the President added his signature.[11]

IV

There remained the question of membership. Roosevelt suggested to Vice-President Garner that he appoint Senators Logan, Neely, and Borah. Borah, he felt, should be made to serve, since this was "his pet hobby." Garner agreed that Borah was a logical choice, but under the circumstances, he could hardly deny a place to O'Mahoney, the sponsor of the resolution; and he felt that the third position should go to the chairman of the Senate Judiciary Committee, Henry F. Ashurst of Arizona. When Ashurst declined, Senator William King of Utah, as the ranking member of the committee, became the next logical choice. King, unlike Borah and O'Mahoney, had long been a staunch defender of the status quo, and following his ap-

[11] *Congressional Record*, 75 Cong., 3 Sess., LXXXIII, 6261, 8338–40, 8497–506, 8588–96, 9336–41, 9545; *New York Times*, May 6, June 4, 7, 1938; Noel Kaho, *An Analysis of Monopoly* (Washington, 1938), 9; 52 *U.S. Statutes* 705, Public Res., No. 113, 75 Cong.; Drafts of TNEC Resolution, May 18, 19, 1938, OF 3322, Roosevelt Papers; Drafts of TNEC Resolution; S. J. Res. 291, May 5, 1938, Cohen File, NPPC Records.

pointment, he seemed bent upon proving that the monopoly problem did not really exist. "There have been studies made and books written dealing with corporations," he told his secretary, Max Kimball, "and some of them have shown their importance and the great contributions they have made." From these he wanted "copious extracts."

In the meantime, the Speaker of the House had named three members from that body. Appointed were Hatton W. Sumners of Texas, an old-line Southern Democrat with years of political experience behind him, B. Carrol Reece of Tennessee, a former economics professor regarded as a conservative but independent Republican, and Edward C. Eicher of Iowa, a liberal lawyer billed as a "one hundred percent New Dealer." The remaining members, of course, came from the Administration, and when the appointments were announced, it was clear that the antimonopolists had secured a majority of the positions. Thurman Arnold was named to represent the Justice Department, Herman Oliphant the Treasury Department, Isador Lubin the Labor Department, and William Douglas the Securities and Exchange Commission. Garland Ferguson of the Federal Trade Commission was also an exponent of the trustbusting view. And Leon Henderson, long one of the key figures in the antimonopoly drive, became executive secretary. Only Richard Patterson of the Department of Commerce was regarded as unsympathetic with the antitrust orientation.[12]

It would be a mistake, though, to assume that the

[12] FDR to John Garner, June 14, 1938, in Elliott Roosevelt, ed., *F.D.R.: His Personal Letters*, II (N.Y.: Duell, Sloan & Pearce, 1950), 792; Lynch, *Economic Power*, 35–47; *Congressional Record*, 75 Cong., 3 Sess., LXXXIII, 9545–46, 9720; Oliver McKee, Jr., in *Commonweal*, Nov. 4, 1938, pp. 35–36; Dwight MacDonald, in *American Scholar*, Summer 1939, pp. 302–8; *Newsweek*, July 4, 1938; *Fortune*, Nov. 1938, pp. 136, 139; *Business Week*, July 2, 1938, pp. 15–17; William King to Max Kimball, July 26, 1938; C. M. Hester to Oliphant, July 11, 1938, both in Adm. Correspondence File, TNEC Records.

antitrusters had completely vanquished their opponents. When one considered the divergent views of the committee's key personnel, not only its official members but its alternate members and research directors as well,[13] it became apparent that the TNEC was a house divided and subdivided along the same general lines that had split the Administration and Congress. The views of Jerome Frank, for example, who served as an alternate member from the SEC, shaded off into some type of national economic planning. The representatives of the Department of Commerce seemed bent upon defending the idea of industrial self-government. Senator O'Mahoney appeared to be chiefly interested in his pet project of federal incorporation. Christian Peoples, the alternate for the Treasury Department, was concerned much more with fair prices than with competitive ones. And men like King, Reece, and Sumners could see no real need for doing anything at all. Even the so-called antitrusters could not really agree among themselves. Some, like Senator Borah and the FTC representatives, tended to stress a classic anti-bigness doctrine with emphasis on the preservation of the small businessman. Others, like Arnold, Henderson, and Lubin, tended to be more managerial in their approach, to emphasize the consumer more than the small businessman, recovery more than decentralization. The antitrust laws, so the latter group felt, should be used as a weapon against price rigidity, a club that could be used to discipline prices, restore price balance, and pave the way for greater expansion.[14]

[13] The Administration alternates included Wendell Berge (Justice), Jerome Frank (SEC), Ewin L. Davis (FTC), A. F. Hinrichs (Labor), Robert Nathan (Commerce), and Christian J. Peoples (Treasury). The research directors were Willard Thorp (Commerce), Hugh Cox (Justice), Willis J. Ballinger (FTC), Thomas Blaisdell (SEC), J. J. O'Connell (Treasury), and Ayrness Joy (Labor). TNEC, *Investigation of Concentration of Economic Power*, Pt. 1 (1939), 1; McKee, in *Commonweal*, Nov. 4, 1938, p. 36.

[14] Lynch, *Economic Power*, 36–49; Thurman Arnold, *The Bottlenecks of Business* (N.Y.: Reynal & Hitchcock, 1940), 10–14, 122–

In view of these divergent attitudes, outside observers were offering all sorts of theories as to what the TNEC might do and which approach it might take. Some, for example, saw the agency as a foreruner of a comprehensive antimonopoly program, some as the first step toward "socializing industry," some as a way to document the spending thesis, and some as a method of promoting industrial self-government, resurrecting the NRA, and educating businessmen to follow their long-range interests. Others felt that it was designed primarily to provide a political scapegoat for the "failure" of the New Deal. Still others held that it was closely connected with the Borah-O'Mahoney bill, although there was considerable disagreement as to whether it was designed to promote the bill or to sidetrack it. Actually, it was doubtful that the committee could ever agree on any specific solution to the monopoly problem. Raymond Moley probably came about as close to the truth as anyone when he noted that the TNEC was the "final expression of Roosevelt's personal indecision, an inquiry that would relieve the President from the nagging of his subordinates, put off the adoption of a definite program, and free his mind for consideration of other matters." [15]

Because of the confusion about the ultimate objectives of the investigation, businessmen were also uncertain as to

31, 271–78; MacDonald, in *American Scholar*, Summer 1939, pp. 302–4; Edwin George, in *Dun's Review*, Sept. 1938, pp. 8–18; *Fortune*, Nov. 1938, pp. 139–40; Willis J. Ballinger, Statement, Feb. 28, 1939; J. J. O'Connell, "Government Purchasing Study," Oct. 29, 1938, both in TNEC Records (Statements Submitted File, Special Studies File); Henderson to Chamberlain, Jan. 29, 1938; O'Mahoney to FDR, June 19, 1939, both in Hopkins Papers (Relief Plans File, Secretary of Commerce File).

[15] Lynch, *Economic Power*, 27–28; Raymond Moley, *After Seven Years* (N.Y.: Harper, 1939), 376; John T. Flynn, in *New Republic*, Oct. 26, 1938, p. 333; *New York Times*, June 10, 1938; *Newsweek*, July 4, 1938, p. 8; May 29, 1939, p. 38; *Nation*, July 16, 1938, p. 60; Dec. 10, 1938, pp. 613–14; *Commercial and Financial Chronicle*, July 23, 1938, pp. 481–83.

just what attitude they should take. At first, they tended to regard it as a "witch hunt," aimed at "bludgeoning industry for the greater glory of the New Deal." But a number of factors soon softened this attitude. For one thing, Senator O'Mahoney kept insisting that the inquiry was an economic "study," not a political inquisition. It began by postponing any hearings until after the election; and once the hearings got underway, there was little disposition to harass business, indulge in publicity stunts, or rule out business defenses. A series of informal meetings and "shirt-sleeve dinners," sponsored by such pro-business officials as John Hanes of the SEC, Prentiss Coonley of the Business Advisory Council, and Richard Patterson of the Department of Commerce, helped too in fostering cooperation between business leaders and New Dealers. Some observers attached considerable significance to the lowering of steel prices after Edward Stettinius of the United States Steel Corporation had a long discussion with Corcoran, Arnold, and Frank.

By the time the hearings began, moreover, the President was moving rapidly toward a policy of conciliating business, a policy that eventually led him to abandon further domestic reforms, make peace with conservative Democrats, and concentrate on rearmament and foreign policy. For a time, immediately following the creation of the TNEC, he did consider another antimonopoly message, one that would warn the price fixers that persistence in their activities would force the President to use "emergency measures." His more cautious advisers, however, counselled against it; the proposed speech was never delivered; and soon the upturn in the economy, the political reverses, and the increased concern with foreign affairs had all combined to emphasize the desirability of a rapprochement with business. Consequently, businessmen gradually moved to a position of reluctant cooperation, one that regarded the inquiry as an opportunity to develop the business side of the debate and improve business relations with the public.

Many business groups, in fact, prepared for the hearings in a thorough and meticulous fashion, mustering every matter of data, spending hundreds of thousands of dollars, and hiring batteries of statisticians, economists, and other specialists.[16]

In late 1938 the Temporary National Economic Committee opened its full-dress study of the economy. Just what the outcome would be was anybody's guess, but in all probability the committee would end by representing the same split in opinion that was responsible for its creation. The investigation, after all, was essentially an escape mechanism, a way to deal with a fundamental policy conflict that could not be resolved. The scene of controversy was simply shifted from administrative bureaus and congressional halls to the committee hearings in the hope that somehow, by writing down all the facts, an answer might emerge. Any real stimulus to expansion, it seemed, would come from government spending, not from any major effort at structural reform or enforced competition.

[16] Broadus Mitchell, *Depression Decade* (N.Y.: Rinehart, 1947), 369-70; Lynch, *Economic Power*, 54, 62-63, 66-67; *Congressional Record*, 76 Cong., 1 Sess., LXXXIV, 74-77; MacDonald, in *American Scholar*, Summer 1939, pp. 296-97, 301-2; Blackwell Smith, in *Dun's Review*, May 1939, pp. 8-9; *Business Week*, July 2, 1938, pp. 13-15; *Newsweek*, July 4, 1938, pp. 8-9; Dec. 5, 1938, p. 34; *Fortune*, Nov. 1938, p. 140; *New York Times*, May 7, June 22, 25, 1938; *Washington Post*, June 22, 1938; Joseph Alsop and Robert Kintner, in *Washington Star*, June 22, July 30, 1938; TNEC Minutes, Oct. 13, 1938, TNEC Records; TNEC Minutes, April 5, 1939, Box 1, Arnold Papers; Draft of Proposed Speech on the Monopoly Issue, with accompanying memoranda, June 1938; Wallace to FDR, June 1938, both in PPF 1820, Roosevelt Papers.

CHAPTER 22. THURMAN ARNOLD
AND THE REVIVAL OF
ANTITRUST PROSECUTION

I N March 1938, when Thurman Arnold left Yale Law School to become the new head of the Antitrust Division, the debate over the monopoly issue was in full swing. In the words of Walter Millis, "the old, scholastic conundrum of 1912" was again occupying the center of public attention, and the position of the President was as uncertain as was the future course of New Deal policy. Arnold had scarcely begun his tenure, moreover, when the President sent his monopoly message to Congress and the whole issue was tucked away in a governmental investigation. "The customers," said Millis, "were left with the sudden feeling that the battle they had been witnessing was only a sham battle after all." [1]

For Arnold, however, the battle was not a sham one. Unlike Robert Jackson, whose major efforts had gone into the campaign for investigation and revision, the new antitrust chief felt that the existing laws could be used to much greater advantage. Their ineffectiveness in the past had been due to the lack of money and personnel, to the reliance on a "corporal's guard" and the tendency of Americans to be content with moralizing and preaching rather than concrete action. This, he thought, could be changed. Given the organization and a constructive use of antitrust procedure toward the achievement of definite goals, the Antitrust Division could be "a most effective instrument" in creating "independent business structures" capable of operating at full capacity.

Accordingly, while the TNEC searched for an appropriate policy, the Antitrust Division was acting as if it had

[1] Walter Millis, in *Virginia Quarterly Review*, July 1938, pp. 358–63; *New York Times*, Feb. 20, March 13, 1938.

already found one. Policy, Arnold insisted, should be formulated by direct action. Clarification should come through enforcement. Under his direction, the Division was soon showing signs of new life. Its staff increased; new appropriations flowed from Congress; new procedures were perfected; and before long it had embarked upon the most intensive antitrust campaign in American history.[2]

II

Nevertheless, it seemed odd to many observers that the author of a savage satire on the antitrust laws should now be placed in charge of enforcing them, that this irreverent, witty professor, who had once described the monopoly statutes as "popular moral gestures" characterized by "economic meaninglessness," should suddenly become the ardent champion of their vigorous enforcement. In his *Folklore of Capitalism*, a widely acclaimed satire in the best Veblenian tradition, Arnold had concluded that there was about as much chance of breaking up large business combinations as there was of doing away with automobiles and going back to horses. Yet this dream of returning to the past, when exploited by men "like Senator Borah," had prevented the development of practical regulation. Every scheme of direct control had broken to pieces on the "protective rock of the antitrust laws."

One would suppose from such passages that Arnold was closer ideologically to Donald Richberg than to Robert Jackson. Yet here he was, less than a year after his book was published, asking for increased appropriations so he

[2] Thurman Arnold, *The Bottlenecks of Business* (N.Y.: Reynal & Hitchcock, 1940), 98–99, 211; in *New York Times*, Aug. 21, 1938; and in *Vital Speeches*, July 1, 1938, pp. 567–68; March 1, 1939, p. 292; Attorney-General, *Annual Report* (1937), 40–42; (1938), 56–61, 66; Robert H. Jackson, in *U.S. Law Review*, Oct. 1937, p. 575; Jackson and Edward Dumbould, in *U. of Penn. Law Review*, Jan. 1938, pp. 231–42, 255–56; Karl A. Boedecker, "Critical Appraisal of the Antitrust Policy of the United States Government from 1933 to 1945," Ph.D. Dissertation, U. of Wis. (1947), 301.

could carry out the same "futile" process of antitrust prosecution. "How," the pundits wanted to know, "can a man who so ridiculed the antitrust laws be placed in charge of their enforcement? What are we coming to when a court jester is made minister?" Even for the loquacious Arnold, noted for his ability to talk his way out of all sorts of situations, this inconsistency took some tall explaining. At the hearings on his nomination, Senator Borah wanted to know if he really believed in the antitrust laws; and when Arnold said he did, Borah confessed that he had been misled. "I think you ought to revise that chapter on trusts," he said, "because it will lead to a great deal of embarrassment."

Arnold admitted that had he foreseen the possibility of heading the Antitrust Division, he might not have written the book the way he did. But he did not think there was any real inconsistency anyway. People had simply misinterpreted his book. They had construed it "as an attack on the antitrust laws," while actually it was nothing of the kind. "Suppose," he explained, "that I would write a book on the pathology of teeth . . . and then suppose my critics would say, 'This man is attacking teeth—he does not show up this beautiful characteristic, he does not say much about the good that the teeth do, and he offers us no substitute.'" This, he thought, was the type of criticism he was getting on his book. Obviously, as presently administered, the antitrust laws were imperfect; yet it would be "fatal" not to do the utmost that one could with them since they were the only instrument available. Borah was apparently convinced of Arnold's sincerity, but as the hearings ended, he added a further warning. "I do not want you to draw indictments," he told Arnold, "on the theory that these corporations will be made bigger and more dangerous by prosecution."

Some people, however, still had difficulty in understanding Arnold's apparent metamorphosis from cynical critic to militant trustbuster. Others found it difficult to understand the man at all. In an age of colorful personalities he took a back seat to no one. A large man, somewhat paunchy, generally attired in a disheveled costume, and given to incessant talking in a loud voice, the new antitrust chief was at first regarded as something of a joke, another Marx brother who had strayed into the government by mistake. He "looks like a small town storekeeper and talks like a native Rabelais," said Joseph Alsop. There was little doubt that his capacity for reducing the most sacred economic and moral beliefs to witty absurdities was irritating to businessmen and old-line politicians alike. The effect on the sensibilities of conservatives reminded Raymond Moley of his boyhood days, when his playmates had inserted wooden wedges under the clapboards of the house, tied strings to the wedges, rubbed the strings with resin, and then twanged away to the great discomfort of the occupants of the house. Thorstein Veblen, said Moley, had been the greatest of the "economic jongleurs"; Arnold was the latest.

In spite of all his non-conformity, though, and in spite of his sly ridicule of the capitalist system, Arnold was apparently an intense believer in a competitive economy and in the idea that such an economy had never had a real chance. Prior to 1938 he had worked closely with William O. Douglas and Robert Jackson as a special consultant. His appointment as head of the Antitrust Division when Jackson became Solicitor General was widely regarded as a victory for the antimonopolists. And once in power, he was determined to do something about the monopoly problem, to build the organization that might be effective where economic preaching had failed.

There was evidence, too, that Arnold was never much worried about the appearance of inconsistency. Duty, he pointed out, often overrode inner convictions. As mayor of Laramie, Wyoming, he had been a convinced wet on the prohibition issue, yet he had given the city the driest administration in its history. Besides, any workable philosophy was "necessarily a maze of contradictions so hung together that the contradictions are either not apparent or else are reconciled by a mystical ritual." In his *Symbols of Government* and to a lesser extent in *Folklore of Capitalism*, in what were widely regarded as anti-democratic passages, Arnold had spoken of how beautifully the social scientists could govern if only they would learn to manipulate the symbols. Could it be that he was now setting out to teach them? [3]

III

Whatever Arnold's real motivation may have been, he had soon worked out a convincing rationale to justify his activities. Like Leon Henderson and other exponents of the administered price thesis, he drew a picture of two economic worlds, one made up of organized industry, the other of small businessmen, farmers, and economic individualists; and it did no good for the government to provide the competitive world with purchasing power so long as the monopolists were allowed to control prices and siphon away the government's contribution. Sustained production could come only with the removal of economic "bottlenecks" and the subjection of business decisions to the full

[3] Thurman Arnold, *The Folklore of Capitalism* (New Haven: Yale U. Press, 1937), 96, 215–17; Senate Judiciary Committee, *Nomination of Thurman W. Arnold* (75 Cong., 3 Sess., 1938), 3–5, 11; House Appropriations Committee, *Second Deficiency Appropriations Bill for 1938* (75 Cong., 3 Sess., 1938), 856–59; Fred Rodell, in *New Republic*, June 22, 1938, pp. 177–78; *Current Biography* (1940), 28; Joseph Alsop and Robert Kintner, in *Saturday Evening Post*, Aug. 12, 1939, pp. 5–6, 30, 33; and in *Washington Star*, March 9, 1938; *Time*, Jan. 3, 1938, p. 11; *New York Times*, Dec. 21, 22, 1937; Raymond Moley, in *Newsweek*, Feb. 28, 1938, p. 44; Max Rheinstein and Albert Levi, in *Ethics*, Jan. 1939, pp. 212–17; April 1941, pp. 320–24; Edson Blair, in *Barron's*, Feb. 17, 1941, p. 4; *Philadelphia Bulletin*, March 12, 1938; Arnold to William E. Borah, March 16, 1938; Memo. summarizing Arnold's governmental experience, Jan. 19, 1939; Arnold to Edward Levi, Dec. 11, 1937, all in Arnold Papers (Boxes 36, 37, 47).

play of market forces. Once restored, competition would have to be safeguarded. The rationalizers, to be sure, seemed to think that in the "warm and easy atmosphere of non-competitive business, wise and kindly managers" would grow "like mushrooms in hot-houses." Yet all past experience demonstrated that private industrialists were capable of little beyond the pursuit of short-run profits. If left to themselves, they would organize against free competition. This would result in increasing statism. Eventually, there would be a resort to fascism, to the German system, where the economy had become so rigid that it could not function without a head, a *fuehrer* to order the workers to work and the mills to produce.

Nor did Arnold have much sympathy with those who would sanction monopoly and regulate it in the public interest. Such people, to be sure, were always "rising in meeting," claiming that the Sherman Act was outmoded, and proposing some "neatly-planned administrative tribunal." Yet such special tribunals rarely worked. The FTC, for example, had never overcome the "deep seated attitude against trusting administrative tribunals with power except in very narrow fields." And the NRA had never worked because any attempt to use the conference table as a general substitute for competition inevitably degenerated into a "political caucus, with each group desperately log-rolling to protect its own interests." Only in a few special areas, like agriculture, coal production, or the textile industry, was there justification for a certain amount of limited planning; and even in these areas, it would work only if it were thrown against a broad background of free enterprise.[4]

[4] Arnold, *Bottlenecks*, 9–19, 91–100, 103–6, 111–15, 117–18, 121–22, 286–97; and *Democracy and Free Enterprise* (Norman: U. of Okla. Press, 1942), 45–46, 53–57; Arnold, in *Law and Contemporary Problems*, Winter 1940, pp. 5–7; in *Vital Speeches*, March 1, 1939, pp. 290–92; and in *Common Sense*, July 1939, pp. 3–6; Attorney-General, *Annual Report* (1938), 54–55; *New York Times*, Aug. 20, 1938; Arnold, in *New York Herald Tribune*, Jan.

The Sherman Act, moreover, possessed advantages that many critics overlooked. Here was a measure that was already available, one that was on the books, ready for use, and not merely a theoretical proposal that would require years of political battle before it could be translated into law. It was also one that was deeply rooted in American traditions, one that over the years had acquired the strength of a moral precept and therefore enjoyed "unquestioned public acceptance." Any revision of the law, to be sure, was extremely difficult. Even the slightest change was usually treated something like "an amendment to a prayer book." Yet this difficulty was no excuse for inaction, since in practice the very clumsiness of the law, the repeated judicial delays that were inherent in present procedure, often worked to the advantage of enforcement officials. The pendency of a criminal proceeding put such a hazard on the continuance of the practice that the defendants invariably stopped their illegal activities. Even an acquittal made the defendants "draw a breath of relief and resolve never to undergo such an expensive hazard again." [5]

11, 1942; Arnold to Evans Clark, July 13, 1942; Arnold to George O. Totten, Oct. 27, 1939; Arnold to William Allen White, Sept. 9, 1943; Arnold, Address, Aug. 19, 1938, all in Arnold Papers (Boxes 7, 14.1, 14.2, 20); Arnold to Cummings, April 13, 1938, OF 277, Roosevelt Papers.

[5] Arnold, *Bottlenecks*, 91–106, 208–10, 271–74; and in *Vital Speeches*, July 1, 1938, p. 567; Arnold, Address, Oct. 1, 1938, Book 47, Arnold Papers. It has been suggested that Arnold's emphasis upon using existing laws was purposely designed to stave off rigid, inflexible legislation of the type of the Borah-O'Mahoney bill. The theory generally advanced here is that the President was not really interested in doing much about monopolies, but that he had to give the appearance of doing something in order to retain political support and to recapture the initiative from such men as Borah and O'Mahoney. Accordingly, Jackson, a man interested in extensive legislative revision, was promoted to the office of Solicitor General, and the Antitrust Division was placed in charge of a man like Arnold, who was willing to use existing laws and develop a rationale that regarded them as sufficient. This whole interpretation, however, is a tortured one, and the author has found no real reason for doubting

Arnold believed, too, that an antitrust campaign could win broad popular support. Independent businessmen should welcome an effort to broaden economic opportunities and eliminate unfair, collusive, and coercive practices. Farmers should be interested in removing the unwarranted exactions of middlemen and increasing consumer purchasing power. Above all, he felt, consumers had finally begun to wake up and take a new interest in prices and price disparities. As he saw it, public concern over monopolistic practices was in the same stage of development, comparatively speaking, as the concern over the marketing of securities had been in 1933. People had first become aroused, then demanded an investigation, and then supported vigorous controls against financial abuses. Following the recession of 1937, he hoped, the nation had again become aroused, had set up the TNEC, and would now support a vigorous campaign against monopolistic practices, particularly when it realized that antitrust enforcement could bring more and cheaper products, that it could affect "the price of pork chops, bread, spectacles, drugs, and plumbing."

To illustrate the role that the Antitrust Division might play, Arnold often compared its activities to those of a traffic officer. Violation of the antitrust laws, he noted, was something like the crime of speeding through a red light. It was highly dangerous to society, yet the offender did not feel that he was involved in a crime of moral turpitude. And in each case, the remedy was similar. Antitrust officials, like traffic policemen, must first spell out and publicize the rules of the road. They must then engage in arrests and prosecutions for their deterrent effect. Finally, they must maintain a constantly vigilant organization to police the highways of commerce. Yet they should realize

---

the sincerity of either Arnold or the President. Nor was the Borah-O'Mahoney bill ever that close to passage. A poll of the Senate in March 1938 showed only nine definitely favorable, thirteen probably favorable, and nineteen favorable with strong reservations. See Congressional Intelligence, Inc., *Trends*, March 5, 1938.

that their job was to facilitate traffic, not halt it or operate it. If an industry could show that efficiency demanded some kind of concerted action, it might get a "green light" from the Department of Justice.

The whole emphasis, moreover, should be upon protecting consumers and increasing consumer purchasing power, not upon making little ones out of big ones. Unlike the Brandeisians, Arnold never seemed greatly concerned about the mere possession of economic power or the social evils of bigness per se. Monopolistic controls, he thought, were bad. They led to economic breakdown, popular exasperation, and a desperate resort to increased statism. But large organizations, as long as they were efficient and passed along the savings to consumers, were desirable. The whole controversy over size, he kept insisting, was "meaningless." To argue that small units were better than large units was "on a par with saying that Milton is more poetical than the pig is fat." It all depended upon the particular situation, upon the purposes to which the units were put. And the Antitrust Division would stand ready to deal with each situation on a case-by-case, industry-by-industry basis, one that would apply a practical test of efficiency and consumer welfare to each particular set of circumstances.[6]

IV

While Arnold was developing a convincing rationale, he was also moving toward a "more constructive" use of antitrust procedure. One innovation was the greater emphasis placed upon the evaluation of prospective cases, upon

[6] Arnold, *Bottlenecks*, 3–4, 10–19, 122–27, 131, 262–67, 274–78; in *New York Times*, Aug. 21, 1938; in *Vital Speeches*, July 1, 1938, pp. 568–69; and in *Common Sense*, July 1939, pp. 5–6; Attorney-General, *Annual Report* (1938), p. 318; (1939), 38, 44; *Business Week*, March 5, 1939, p. 14; Arnold, Addresses, Oct. 24, Dec. 11, 1940; June 13, 1941; Arnold to Clark, July 13, 1942, all in Arnold Papers (Books 49, 50, Boxes 1, 7).

weighing complaints against each other, applying a "rule of reason," deciding when efficient organization and orderly marketing became arbitrary price control, and selecting those areas that would involve the greatest public interest and result in the greatest gains for consumers. Under his direction, Arnold promised, there would be less preaching and more action, and the latter would be directed along rational lines toward well-defined goals.

A second major innovation was in the use that Arnold planned to make of consent decrees. The government, he said, should file both criminal and civil suits, the first as a deterrent, the second for constructive restoration of competitive conditions. Then, if the "enlightened business leadership" in the industry concerned wished to eliminate the conditions that had led to illegal practices and if their plan went farther in the public interest than any criminal penalty could go, the scheme might be incorporated in a consent decree and the Department of Justice might suggest to the court that prosecution be dropped. Such decrees, though, must differ considerably from those issued in the past. They must give substantial advantages to the public; they must not be regarded as pardons for past violations; and to insure compliance, they must be subject to re-examination and must give the government access to corporate books.

To Arnold's critics the whole procedure seemed like legalized blackmail, a way that he could impose his own arbitrary business regulation. But Arnold argued otherwise. Any criminal law, he said, might be used coercively, and the fact that the government brought its actions publicly before an "impartial judicial tribunal" removed the danger of arbitrary regulation. Litigation, in fact, was the only real way to apply general provisions to concrete problems and thus reveal the strengths and weaknesses of the existing laws. Real clarification could come only through enforcement. Consequently, a law suit should be regarded less as an attack on business and more as "the beginning of cooperation between the courts, the legislature, the Department of Justice, and the industry to achieve a common end," that end being an effective and well understood body of law. Arnold was willing, moreover, to minimize the use of criminal actions. If business firms entered into a cooperative plan openly and after informing the Department of Justice, they might experiment without fear of criminal penalty. And if Congress would legalize civil suits with civil penalties, he would prefer using them.

There was a further safeguard, too, in the public statements that the Antitrust Division began issuing in May 1938, statements that explained the conditions in the industry being prosecuted, the reasons for each important action, and the economic results expected. Such pronouncements, said Arnold, would not only help businessmen to understand the law, but would also develop a whole body of departmental precedents, thus aiding in the formulation and maintenance of a consistent antitrust policy.

Nor were these the only new procedures. Another major innovation was the art of massing antitrust proceedings into an industry-wide program. The idea here, as Arnold explained it to Joseph Alsop, was "to hit hard, hit everyone and hit them all at once." In the construction industry, for instance, any effective prosecution would require simultaneous action against materials manufacturers, contractors, and the various other groups contributing to the end product. Only by a shock treatment of this sort, by mass investigations and mass indictments, was it possible to bring down the cost of housing. It would also involve prosecution of labor as well as business combines, particularly when the unions were using their power to support fixed prices, compel the hiring of useless labor, or prevent the use of better materials and methods.[7]

[7] Attorney-General, *Annual Report* (1938), 56–57, 59–66, 305, 318; Antitrust Division, *Public Statement*, Nov. 20, 1939; Arnold, *Bottlenecks*, 37–45, 123, 141–42, 144–49, 151–63, 184–86, 191–92, 241–53; in *Yale Law Journal*, June 1938, pp. 1299–1300; and in *Vital Speeches*, July 1, 1938, pp. 568–70; Arnold, Edward P. Hodges,

Under Arnold's direction, then, one might expect a broader and more purposeful use of antitrust proceedings. Yet the implementation of this whole pattern of policy would depend, in the last analysis, upon securing adequate appropriations and competent personnel. As Arnold himself put it, if anything of permanent value were to be accomplished, there must be, first of all, an adequate prosecuting group sufficient to break up the organizations imposing restraints, and secondly, a field force assigned permanently in each state to hear complaints, preserve past gains, and keep in close contact with the local situation and local consumer groups. Once started, to be sure, the whole process might have a cumulative effect. It might create a demand for the enforcement of local antitrust laws, so that after the initial shock, a small supervisory organization might be sufficient. But the federal government would certainly need a relatively large organization to get the ball rolling.

Accordingly, Arnold set out to dramatize the issues, "manipulate the symbols," and enlist popular support. His use of public statements, criminal indictments, and mass investigations was part of the dramatizing process. The appeal to the revered traditions of the Sherman Act was another part. The colorful language in which he outlined his program was still another. In speech after speech he took his case to the public and spelled out the policies that he hoped to implement. At the same time, he was trying to persuade Congress to carry out the President's recommendation and provide a special $200,000 deficiency appropriation for the Antitrust Division. Past ineffectiveness, he told a House subcommittee, was due chiefly to

and Fowler Hamilton, in *Law and Contemporary Problems*, Winter 1940, pp. 13–14, 17–19, 90–99; Alsop and Kintner, in *Saturday Evening Post*, Aug. 12, 1939, p. 7; Corwin Edwards, in *Political Science Quarterly*, Sept. 1943, pp. 342–50; Fayette Dow, "Antitrust Law Enforcement Policies," March 1939, pp. 10–18, MR&D, NRA Records; Justice Dept. PR, May 18, 1938; Arnold, Statement before TNEC, July 7, 1939; and Address, Jan. 27, 1940; Arnold to Frank Knox, July 6, 1939, all in Arnold Papers (Books 40, 46, 49, Box 44).

lack of funds, and an extra $200,000 would at least be a start toward developing an effective organization.[8]

Congress apparently agreed. It voted the money requested, and, with an immediate increase of $200,000 and a promise of more in the future, Arnold set about building and revamping his organization to meet the task ahead. By the end of 1938 his professional staff had grown from 58 to over a hundred; the total personnel of his division had nearly doubled; and new sections had been created to handle complaints, consent decrees, and economic investigation. Gradually, too, he gathered about him a group of dedicated assistants, men like Corwin Edwards, George Comer, Leo Tierney, and Wendell Berge. Berge, in particular, was widely regarded as the "intellectual spark plug" behind Arnold's dramatic showmanship. As chief assistant in charge of recruiting and training, he was soon scouring the colleges, government bureaus, and law firms for young, energetic talent. Once recruited, the new staff members were subjected to intensive instruction in psychological devices, business structures, grand jury investigations, and the proper methods of building a case. The end product was a competent and effective organization, one in which morale was high and there was a new sense of purpose and mission. Such an organization, it was hoped, might turn the antitrust laws into more than "popular gestures." [9]

[8] Arnold, *Bottlenecks*, 202–6; House Appropriations Committee, *Second Deficiency Appropriation Bill for 1938*, 856–59; Edwards, in *Political Science Quarterly*, 341–43; *New York Times*, April 29–30, May 19, June 16, Aug. 20, 1938; *Business Week*, May 7, 1938, pp. 13–14; Justice Dept. PR, May 18, 1938; Arnold, Addresses, April 28, June 15, Aug. 19, Sept. 3, Oct. 26, 1938, all in Arnold Papers (Books 40, 47).

[9] Arnold, *Bottlenecks*, IX–XI, 276–77; Justice Dept., *Register* (1938), 2–5; (1942), 2; Attorney-General, *Annual Report* (1941), 64; Lester Velie, in *Saturday Evening Post*, Sept. 2, 1944, p. 75; *Fortune*, Aug. 1944, p. 137; *Newsweek*, March 20, 1939, p. 53; Biographical Sketches of Wendell Berge and Corwin Edwards, Adm. Correspondence File, TNEC Records; Arnold to James A. McLaughlin, April 3, 1939, Box 11, Arnold Papers.

V

The first actions came naturally in those cases that Arnold had inherited from Jackson, namely, in the Madison Oil cases and those involving the aluminum trust, the Ethyl Gasoline Corporation, and automobile financing. In most of these areas, however, progress was discouragingly slow in 1938. In both the aluminum and Ethyl cases, there were repeated delays and prolonged trial proceedings. In the Madison Oil cases, the government suffered a severe setback when Judge Patrick Stone granted new trials to eighteen of the defendants and dismissed all charges against eleven others.

Only in the automobile cases did the Antitrust Division score something of a breakthrough. Under the terms of a consent decree negotiated with Ford and Chrysler in November 1938, the two automobile manufacturers agreed that they would no longer require their dealers to do business exclusively with any given finance company. They agreed also to the setting up of an informal finance code, containing rules in regard to insurance, extension charges, reinstatement fees, misrepresentation, and other trade practices. And they agreed that in the future any service, facility, or privilege offered to one finance company must be made available to all others on substantially similar terms. No longer could they recommend or advertise a particular company, although they might still recommend a particular plan of financing. If adequately enforced, the Department of Justice felt, the decree would go a long way toward restoring the vitality of independent finance companies, although any permanent effects would depend upon the outcome of the case against General Motors. If the government lost this case, the restraints imposed upon Ford and Chrysler would have to be lifted.[10]

[10] CCH, *The Federal Antitrust Laws*, 170–73; Attorney-General, *Annual Report* (1938), 306–10, 328–34; Antitrust Division, *Public*

To Arnold's critics the auto-finance decree was a leading example of unjustified coercion and legalized blackmail; and they were particularly critical of his assertion that the limitations on advertising abuses might become an important precedent for dealing with the "mis-use of advertising power" elsewhere. "Mr. Arnold's point," said Raymond Moley, "seems to be that competition becomes unfair if one party has a well-known trade name whereas a competitor has no such well-known name." Moley could see no reason why this should not apply to the "academic funnyman" himself. "When he says something now his statement carries the name of Assistant Attorney General of the United States, whereas such competitors as Eddie Cantor or Bugs Baer are denied that advantage. Is this fair?"

Somewhat taken aback by all the controversy he had stirred up, Arnold finally wrote the associate editor of *Advertising and Selling* that it was all a misunderstanding. The Department of Justice, he noted, had no jurisdiction

---

Statements, May 25, Aug. 28, 1938; *U.S. v. Socony-Vacuum Oil Co.*, 310 U.S. 150; Harold G. Reuschlein, in *U. of Penn. Law Review*, March 1939, pp. 539–40; Harold F. Birnbaum, in *Washington U. Law Quarterly*, June 1939, pp. 530–41, 547–48, 555–57; Milton Katz, in *Harvard Law Review*, Jan. 1940, pp. 434–38; Maxwell S. Isenbergh and Seymour J. Rubin, *ibid.*, pp. 396–401; *Time*, June 6, 1938, p. 48; Nov. 21, 1938, p. 55; July 3, 1939, p. 49; *Newsweek*, Aug. 1, 1938, p. 34; *New York Times*, Aug. 28, 1938; Justice Dept. PR, Nov. 15, 1938, Book 40, Arnold Papers. For those unfamiliar with the auto-finance industry, a word of explanation may be in order. It was common practice for a finance company to pay for new cars and acquire the titles from the manufacturer. The company then delivered the cars to the dealer under a lien instrument, usually a trust receipt, and the dealer agreed to pay the amount advanced at a named date or upon sale. If the dealer then sold on the installment plan, the general practice was for him to sell the retail obligation to a finance company and use a part of the proceeds to pay for his original advance. The difference represented his gross profit. If the automobile was repossessed, the dealer agreed to repurchase it from the company for the amount of the unpaid balance; and for assuming this risk, the dealer also frequently received a portion of the finance charge.

over advertising and no intention of trying to regulate it. His whole position, in fact, had been misinterpreted. He had no desire to eliminate advertising in general. What he opposed was the coercive use of advertising, just as he opposed other types of private coercion. Used to stimulate consumption and inform customers, advertising was desirable, but no firm should be allowed to create a nationwide demand and then use this power to coerce dealers, restrain competition, and control distributive patterns.[11]

In the meantime, Arnold was also making headlines with a series of new cases. On July 7, 1938, he announced that a grand jury in Chicago would investigate the numerous restraints in the dairy industry, an area long characterized by economic "bottlenecks" and fixed profit margins. During the next four months the jury took some three million words of testimony from over three hundred witnesses, and in the end, noted one observer, it "treed the biggest monopoly catch since the oil industry went on trial in Madison." In November it returned two indictments (U.S. v. Borden and U.S. v. National Dairy Products), not only against the leading milk distributors but also against farmers' cooperatives, union leaders, and a number of city officials. The first charged a conspiracy to control prices, prevent the entry of independent distributors, and obstruct the channels of trade, a charge that ran the gamut from price-fixing to the use of arson, flogging, and stench bombings. The second charged a conspiracy to obstruct the installation of counter freezers in the ice cream industry. It seemed that the campaign to aid the consumer was at last striking pay dirt. As a result of the

[11] Katz, in Harvard Law Review, Jan. 1940, pp. 438–40, 445–47; New York Times, Nov. 13, 1938; Business Week, Nov. 19, 1938, p. 55; Nov. 26, 1938, p. 44; Raymond Moley, in Newsweek, Nov. 28, 1938, p. 44; Time, Nov. 21, 1938, p. 55; Nov. 28, 1938, p. 53; Arnold, in Printer's Ink, Oct. 17, 1941, pp. 14–15, 62, 65–66; Justice Dept. PR's, Nov. 7, 16, 1938; Arnold to John B. Long, Sept. 6, 1941; Arnold, Address, Oct. 24, 1940, all in Arnold Papers (Books 40, 43, 49).

investigation, Arnold claimed, the price of milk had already fallen from thirteen cents a quart to nine cents.[12]

By this time, too, Arnold had moved on to the motion picture industry, where independent exhibitors were still complaining about such practices as block-booking, blind selling, and the "freeze-out." On July 20, 1938, he filed a petition in equity (*U.S. v. Paramount Pictures*) charging the eight major producers, their subsidiaries, and 133 individuals with unfair and coercive practices and asking for the complete divorcement of producer from exhibitor interests. The movie suit, however, was not accompanied by a criminal prosecution. Instead, there was an unprecedented apology and explanation, in which Arnold claimed that the suit should be regarded as an effort to cooperate with the industry toward a common solution. "The Government," said *Time*, "took the manner of a family dentist remarking, as he starts extracting a sore tooth from a small boy's jaw, 'I am sorry if this hurts, but it can't be helped and you'll feel better when it's out.' " It was not surprising, then, that Arnold was soon conferring with movie executives and discussing a possible consent decree. Yet he still insisted that the producers divest themselves of their interests in the field of exhibition. But since this was the one thing they refused to consider, the negotiations seemed to offer little prospect of agreement.[13]

[12] CCH, *Antitrust Laws*, 177–83; Arnold, *Bottlenecks*, 192–95; *Business Week*, July 16, 1938, pp. 15–16; Nov. 5, 1938, p. 38; Nov. 19, 1938, p. 40; *Time*, Nov. 28, 1938, p. 53; Julius Cohen, in *Cornell Law Quarterly*, Dec. 1938, pp. 85–95; Attorney-General, *Annual Report* (1938), 310–16; (1939), 40; Justice Dept. PR's, July 7, Nov. 15, 1938, Book 40, Arnold Papers; Frederic C. Howe, "Final Report on the Milk and Dairy Industry," June 15, 1940, Adm. Correspondence File, TNEC Records.

[13] CCH, *Antitrust Laws*, 177; Daniel Bertrand et al., *The Motion Picture Industry* (TNEC Monograph 43, 1941), 23–49, 73–74; Attorney-General, *Annual Report* (1938), 317–22; *New York Times*, July 21, 24–25, Aug. 7, Sept. 30, Oct. 23, 1938; *Business Week*, July 30, 1938, pp. 17–18; *Newsweek*, Aug. 1, 1938, p. 18; *Time*, Aug. 1, 1938, p. 37; Justice Dept. PR's, July 20, 1938; Aug. 17, 1939, Books 40–41, Arnold Papers; Twentieth Century-Fox PR, June 29, 1938, OF 73, Roosevelt Papers.

Still another highly publicized move came in August 1938, when Arnold announced that a grand jury would investigate the American Medical Association and try to prevent it from crushing such "illuminating experiments" as the Group Health Association, an organization through which the employees of the Home Owners' Loan Corporation were attempting to provide themselves with prepaid medical care. The AMA, it seemed, was trying to eliminate this step toward "socialized medicine" by threatening the expulsion of its doctors and excluding them from Washington hospitals, and according to Arnold, this constituted a clear violation of the Sherman Act. In December the grand jury did return an indictment against the AMA, the Medical Society of the District of Columbia, and a number of individual physicians. Yet it was obvious that the physicians were going to fight the case to the hilt. Arnold, they charged, wanted to "socialize" the medical profession, and they argued strongly that their practice was a "learned profession," not a "trade" that was subject to the antitrust laws.[14]

Few activities, of course, aroused as much publicity as the prosecution of the American Medical Association. Yet by the end of 1938 it was apparent that Arnold was transforming the whole scope and function of antitrust policy. The present offensive, noted one observer, constituted a "heavier drive against monopolistic practices . . . than the country has seen in two decades"; there was "every indication" that it would "increase in force and scope in the next year." Already Arnold had more than doubled his professional staff and was now asking for a budget of $1,530,000 for the coming year. A number of highly publicized cases were pending, and others would soon be filed.

[14] CCH, *Antitrust Laws*, 182–83; Attorney-General, *Annual Report* (1938), 323–28; *U.S. v. American Medical Assoc.* (Cr. No. 63221, Dec. 20, 1938), Book 29, Arnold Papers; *New York Times*, Dec. 21, 25, 1938; *Business Week*, Aug. 6, 1938, p. 36; Arnold to Rolla D. Campbell, Feb. 10, 1943; Justice Dept. PR, Aug. 1, 1938, both in Arnold Papers (Box 7, Book 29).

Already, for example, investigations were underway or being scheduled in such areas as housing, fertilizer, tobacco, shoe machinery, automobile tires, and newsprint.

In fact, as Arnold reviewed his efforts, he was certain that he was on the right track. At last the law was being clarified through actual enforcement in specific industrial areas. New solutions, like the one in the automobile financing case, were being developed. Independent businessmen were showing a new willingness to bring their complaints to the Department of Justice. Unsolved problems were being sent to Congress for appropriate action. And gains were being registered for the American consumer. Eventually, he hoped, there would be a "new respect for the antitrust laws" and a new awareness of the concrete benefits that could be derived from vigorous enforcement.[15]

[15] Attorney-General, *Annual Report* (1938), 63, 67; (1939), 37–42; Arnold, in *Oregon Law Review*, Dec. 1939, p. 25; *New York Times*, Nov. 13, 1938; Jan. 2, 1939; *Newsweek*, Nov. 28, 1938, p. 42; April 3, 1939, p. 45; Justice Dept. PR's, Oct. 19, Nov. 4, Dec. 21, 1938, Book 40, Arnold Papers.

CHAPTER 23. THE ARNOLD
PROGRAM IN PRACTICE

ANYONE that chanced to drop into the offices of the Antitrust Division in the fall of 1938 would almost certainly have noticed the change. No longer could the Division be described as the "graveyard of the Justice Department." No longer was it merely a "corporal's guard" tucked away in the intricacies of a governmental department. A dynamic and colorful leader had taken over. New policies had been enunciated, new men added, and new objectives set forth. At last, it seemed, the antitrust laws were to be treated as more than statutory symbols. And in the wake of these changes came a new atmosphere, a new sense of purpose, optimism, and great expectations. The change, noted Tom Blaisdell, was "like a fresh breeze blowing in the hot afternoon." [1]

For a time, it seemed that these expectations might be fulfilled. In 1939 came the first of Arnold's industry-wide investigations, the long-heralded drive against the building and construction industry. To break the "log jam" and secure "economic results in housing," the Antitrust Division divided the nation into ten districts; investigators poured into each, and by the end of the year grand juries were sitting in eleven major cities and tolling off a long list of indictments. Eventually, the drive produced some ninety-nine criminal actions and twenty-two civil suits, a shock treatment that, according to Arnold's estimates, had saved consumers over $300,000,000 in building costs. "Hot stuff," said David Coyle, "and in the right order." [2]

[1] Walton Hamilton and Irene Till, *Antitrust in Action* (TNEC Monograph 16, 1941), 23; *Business Week*, May 28, 1938, pp. 13–14; Drew Pearson and Robert Allen, in *San Francisco Chronicle*, Nov. 24, 1937; Thomas Blaisdell to Paul Homan, Dec. 3, 1938, Blaisdell File, NRPB Records.

[2] Thurman Arnold, *The Bottlenecks of Business* (N.Y.: Reynal & Hitchcock, 1940), 196–97; Attorney-General, *Annual Report* (1940),

The year 1939 also brought a number of other significant actions. In February Arnold announced the filing of a civil suit charging eighteen major tire manufacturers with collusive bidding and claiming that the government was entitled to triple damages. In March he announced the beginning of a major investigation in the fertilizer industry. And in the months that followed, the Antitrust Division delved into the activities of management engineering firms and started new grand jury investigations in the petroleum, newsprint, billboard, and typewriter industries. Late in the year, too, came the beginning of major drives against transportation restrictions and patent abuses. In October the government filed a civil suit against the Association of American Railroads, charging it with unfair discrimination against motor carriers, and in December it filed a key patent case in the glassware machinery and glass container industry, a field in which the practices of the Hartford-Empire Company had formed one of the central themes of the TNEC investigation.[3]

The period after 1939 lies outside the scope of this study. By 1940 the Roosevelt Administration was much more interested in foreign policy and rearmament than in economic reform. Yet the antitrust campaign did not come to an abrupt halt. On the contrary, appropriations and the size of Arnold's professional staff continued to grow. During the period from 1939 through 1941 the Antitrust Divi-

54; Antitrust Division, *Public Statement*, Nov. 25, 1940; Corwin Edwards, in *Political Science Quarterly*, Sept. 1943, pp. 345–46; and in *Journal of Land and Public Utility Economics*, Nov. 1939, pp. 456–57; *Business Week*, July 15, 1939, p. 14; Jan. 6, 1940, pp. 15–16; Justice Dept. PR's, Oct. 3, 6, 1939; Feb. 24, March 11, 29, June 28, 1940; Jan. 7, 1941; Arnold, Statements before TNEC, July 7, 1939; June 14, 1940; and Address, Sept. 20, 1940; David C. Coyle to Arnold, July 15, 1939, all in Arnold Papers (Books 41–43, 46, 49, Box 22).

[3] Antitrust Division, *Public Statements*, Feb. 20, March 1, April 20, May 1, 17, 24, June 12, 27, July 28, Oct. 25, Dec. 11, 1939; *Business Week*, Dec. 16, 1939, pp. 18, 20; Justice Dept. PR's, Feb. 20 through Dec. 11, 1939, Book 41, Arnold Papers.

sion filed no less than 180 cases. And when Arnold left office in 1943, he could claim credit for nearly half of all proceedings instigated under the Sherman Act. Some of these actions, moreover, were of major importance. There were large-scale, coordinated drives, against patent abuses, transportation restrictions, and the restraints surrounding the processing and sale of foods. At the same time, the tobacco, drug, school supplies, fire insurance, and music publishing industries were all having their troubles with the Department of Justice.[4]

For a time, in fact, Arnold kept insisting that the antitrust laws were of greater importance now than ever before, that they could be used to prevent wartime profiteering and the abuse of the war controls, to protect consumers, farmers, and independent businessmen, and to break down restrictive arrangements and stimulate greater production. In practice the Antitrust Division could become a vital defense agency. It was already showing that many of the shortages and "production bottlenecks" in such key industries as magnesium, optical instruments, synthetic rubber, and chemicals were due to an "economic fifth column," to the cartel agreements and patent arrangements between such German firms as Krupp and I. G. Farben and such American giants as Du Pont, General Electric, and Standard Oil. And in the future, it should be used even more intensively to prevent any further "economic sabotage of defense industries by foreign powers." For a time, Arnold seemed to be carrying the public with him. As the

[4] CCH, *The Federal Antitrust Laws* (N.Y., 1949), 195–298; Antitrust Division, *Public Statements*, July 12, 24, Sept. 16, 30, Nov. 25, 1940; Edwards, in *Political Science Quarterly*, Sept. 1943, pp. 339, 342–45, 348–50; House Select Committee on Small Business, *Antitrust Law Enforcement* (House Report 3236, 81 Cong., 2 Sess., 1951), 50–51; Attorney-General, *Annual Report* (1940), 52; (1941), 63–64; *Business Week*, Nov. 30, 1940, p. 15; Dec. 28, 1940, p. 17; Justice Dept. PR's, March 11, 1940 through Jan. 26, 1943; George Comer to Arnold, July 20, 1942; Arnold, Memo. re Transportation Plans, Sept. 28, 1942, all in Arnold Papers (Books 42–45, Folders 6–7, Box 1.

"funeral orations" over antitrust enforcement grew louder and more insistent, noted *Time*, he proceeded to dance the aging Sherman Act "away from its grave, through the tombstones, almost out of the cemetery gate."

In the end, however, the antitrust campaign became a casualty of the war effort. The conduct of a war, so it was argued, called for a carefully planned, highly controlled, and well-coordinated economy. Accordingly, as this new system was established, the center of influence shifted from the antimonopolists to the business-oriented directors of the new defense agencies, to such men as Donald Nelson, Edward R. Stettinius, and William Knudsen. As John T. Flynn put it, "most of the old NRA gang" moved back into power, this time under "the banner of national defense." These men took an increasingly dim view of Arnold's so-called "national-defense cases." In the opinion of Donald Nelson, for example, these "systematic and unrestrained attacks" amounted to "unremitting interference" and "cumulative harassment," and they were making it impossible for him to obtain the services of able and seasoned industrial officials. Gradually, then, Arnold was forced to yield. The War Production Board received power to grant immunity from antitrust action to such activities as were requisite for the prosecution of the war. The Antitrust Division called off its investigations of the steel, shipbuilding, and aircraft industries and postponed major suits in the petroleum, electrical manufacturing, chemical, and plumbing industries. As a final concession, the Department of Justice agreed to shelve the attack on transportation restraints and rate-making conferences after the proposed cases there had run into stiff opposition from the Interstate Commerce Commission and the defense agencies.

By January 1943 Arnold had come to the conclusion that the public was tiring of his personality and tactics, and that under the circumstances, he could no longer accomplish much in the way of antitrust enforcement. Consequently, when the President offered to appoint him to the Circuit

Court of Appeals, he promptly submitted his resignation and withdrew from the scene of conflict, kicked upstairs, so his critics said, for obstructing the war effort. His successors promised to carry on a vigorous enforcement policy, but the drama of the Arnold days was gone. The "golden age" of antitrust law enforcement, already sadly tarnished and corroded, had come to an end.[5]

II

Even if there had been no war, however, it seems doubtful that the antitrust campaign could ever have developed into the massive program envisioned by Arnold and his supporters. By the end of 1939 critics were already making much of the seeming inconsistency of New Deal policies, and antitrust prosecution was already running into stiff opposition, particularly from those with a vested interest in the status quo or in the anticompetitive programs of the earlier New Deal. The oil industry, for example, thought it odd and unjust that the "cooperative activities" of 1933 should now be prosecuted as "criminal collusion." Farmers' cooperatives and milk distributors argued that the Capper-Volstead and Agricultural Adjustment acts exempted them

[5] Harold L. Ickes, *Secret Diary* (N.Y.: Simon & Schuster, 1954), II, 716; III, 5, 76, 181–82, 212, 393, 397, 529–30, 591; Broadus Mitchell, *Depression Decade* (N.Y.: Rinehart, 1947), 369, 372–81; Attorney-General, *Annual Report* (1940), 57; (1941), 58–61; (1943), 14; John T. Flynn, in *New Republic*, Oct. 28, 1940, p. 585; Arnold, *ibid.*, May 19, 1941, pp. 686–90; and in *Oregon Law Review*, Dec. 1939, pp. 22, 29; *Time*, Sept. 9, 1940, pp. 69, 72–73; Feb. 22, 1943, p. 18; *Business Week*, Sept. 14, 1940, p. 15; *Fortune*, Aug. 1944, p. 139; *New York Times*, Aug. 10, 1940; Justice Dept. PR's, Aug. 1, Sept. 14, 30, 1940; April 29, May 31, July 16, Aug. 4, Sept. 2, Dec. 23, 1941; April 25, June 11, 15, 25, July 29, 30, Oct. 1, 1942; Jan. 4, Feb. 10, 1943; Arnold, Addresses, Sept. 13, 29, 1939; June 15, 1940; June 13, Sept. 19, Oct. 10, 1941; Arnold, Policy Memo. of Dec. 23, 1941; Joseph Barkin to Arnold, Feb. 3, 1942; Arnold to Attorney-General, Jan. 8, 1941; Aug. 14, Sept. 9, 1942; Arnold to David Lilienthal, May 12, 1943; Memo. by R. B. Hummel, Feb. 22, 1944, all in Arnold Papers (Books 42–45, 48–50, Folders 4, 7, Boxes 7, 13); FDR to Arnold, Jan. 8, 1943, PPF 8319, Roosevelt Papers.

from all workings of the antitrust laws. Labor unions, convinced that words as sinister as "monopoly" and "conspiracy" were never meant to apply to them, claimed a blanket exemption under the Clayton, Norris-LaGuardia, and Wagner acts. In retail distribution, there was the obstacle presented by the fair trade and unfair practices acts. In fact, there was scarcely a day that passed, noted George Comer, but someone in his office filed the standard complaint: "Good night, you prosecute us for doing what the NRA prosecuted us for not doing."

Criticism was also growing on other grounds. By subjecting business leaders to "humiliation and injury," declared Donald Richberg, the Department of Justice was destroying business confidence, retarding recovery, and hampering "industrial efficiency and stability." In effect, it was using the consent decree and the threat of criminal prosecution to reorganize industry according to its own economic theories, to terrorize honorable men into surrendering their rights and accepting a system of arbitrary regulation. And it was doing all this at the same time that it was urging business to cooperate with the TNEC. "Is this supposed to be reassuring?" asked Raymond Moley. "Does it help a school-boy to concentrate on his studies . . . when he knows that his mother is reorganizing his room at home—throwing out such fishing tackle, marbles, slingshots and baseballs as she considers unnecessary?"

Most conservative critics, however, did not advocate outright repeal or suspension of the antitrust laws, at least not openly and in public. The fault, they insisted, lay not in the principles of the Sherman Act, but rather in their application, in such things as the uncertainty of the law, the use of arbitrary procedures, and the faulty selection of cases. Underlying the criticism was a tendency to place ideals and reality in separate compartments, to feel that antitrust belonged in one world, the actualities of business conduct in another. As Arnold himself pointed out, most businessmen were "enthusiastically in favor of anti-monop-

oly policy in general and against it in particular cases."
They were the most vociferous critics of the new enforcement program; yet they also supplied most of the complaints against monopolistic practices.[6]

Consequently, most of the criticism of the competitive
ideal itself came from the so-called "liberal" camp, from
leftist economic planners who regarded Arnold as an unconscious ally of the private monopolists, as a sort of "liberal outlander," who was still talking about a competitive
economy in a world headed toward controls, planning, and
regulation. The failure of trustbusting since 1890, they
argued, showed that it ran counter to all the natural trends
of the business system, that any real solution to the economic problem called for a "more realistic approach," for
some measure that would facilitate "cooperation among
government, business and labor with a view to getting
production on a high level." The trustbusters, said the
historian Charles A. Beard, were "just whistling in the
wind." They were "prolonging the dangerous tensions in
American society"; they were "unwittingly the foes of getting our economic machine in full motion"; and they were
"destined to defeat besides." If all we could do was "snap
at the heels of big business," while our economic machine
ran at "about 50 percent of efficiency" and ten to twelve
million people sank into "the degradation of permanent
unemployment," then we might as well quit and "go to
whistling, not in the wind, but in the graveyard."

[6] Arnold, *Bottlenecks*, 156–58, 186–89; Hamilton and Till, *Antitrust*, 3–4; Attorney-General, *Annual Report* (1939), 42–43; Walton
Hamilton, in *New Republic*, April 15, 1940, p. 494; John T. Flynn,
ibid., Jan. 8, 1940, p. 52; Arnold, in *Proceedings of the Academy
of Political Science*, Jan. 1939, p. 113; *Business Week*, June 18,
1938, p. 48; Nov. 26, 1938, p. 44; Feb. 25, 1939, p. 16; March 25,
1939, p. 68; *New York Times*, Aug. 21, 1938; Raymond Moley, in
Newsweek, Dec. 19, 1938, p. 48; Burnham Carter, in *American
Mercury*, April 1941, pp. 427–31; Edward H. Gardner, in *Printer's
Ink*, Oct. 17, 1941, pp. 84–85; *Fortune*, Aug. 1944, pp. 136–37;
George Comer, "Rationalization vs. Competition"; Frank Knox to
Arnold, Oct. 20, 1939; Arnold to Knox, Dec. 18, 1939, all in Arnold
Papers (Folder 6, Box 44).

A number of labor spokesmen, too, particularly those from the American Federation of Labor, agreed that Arnold must be an arch reactionary, a "self-inflated theoretician" with the mistaken notion that the Sherman Act was a panacea for everything. Under his tutelage, "the shades of the Debs case, the Danbury Hatters case, the Duplex case, and other labor-crushing decisions," cases which labor hoped had been interred by the New Deal, were now being revived to provide a "judicial barrier" against labor's development. Once again, a campaign was underway to "send men to prison because they have organized for raises." "The world certainly moves fast," said Arnold. At Yale, during the Remington Rand strikes, he was a "radical" because he insisted that "a labor union ought to be uncurbed by Federal law for as long as they pursued the legitimate objects of a union." Now, he told Reed Powell, in exactly the same position, he was a "labor baiter." Nor could he ever fully comprehend the defection of much of his liberal support over the labor issue. As he complained to Freda Kirchway of the Nation, "The Herald-Tribune praises us for our labor prosecution and condemns us when we prosecute the doctors for doing exactly the same thing. . . . You praise us for going after the doctors and condemn us for going after the labor unions." The trouble with liberals, he thought, was that they were "unable to see any individuals." All they could see was slogans and unions and labor movements and collective regimentation.[7]

[7] Charles A. Beard and George H. E. Smith, The Old Deal and the New (N.Y.: Macmillan, 1940), 150–51; Nation, March 18, 1939, p. 309; April 15, 1939, p. 421; Dec. 2, 1939, p. 597; Sept. 14, 1940, pp. 220–21; Edson Blair, in Barron's, Feb. 17, 1941, p. 4; Business Week, March 25, 1939, p. 15; Beard, in New Republic, Sept. 21, 1938, p. 184; Louis Goldberg, Matthew Woll, and Joseph Padway, in American Federationist, March 1940, p. 264; June 1941, pp. 18–19; April 1942, p. 20; Richard Boyer, in Friday, May 17, 1940, p. 28; Arnold to Reed Powell, Feb. 21, April 19, 1941; Charles A. Beard to New Republic, May 17, 1939; Arnold to Freda Kirchway, Dec. 14, 1939, all in Arnold Papers (Boxes 13, 44, 46).

In view of the mounting criticism and opposition, it seems doubtful that the Antitrust Division could ever have developed and retained enough political support for a really large-scale, long-range enforcement effort. Arnold, to be sure, claimed that there was more "consistent pressure" for the enforcement of the Sherman Act than ever before, pressure that came "from independent business men and consumers all over the country." Yet in all probability, his claims were exaggerated. Paul Homan, in his study of antitrust policy published in 1939, concluded that there existed no strong political groups pressing for more stringent enforcement, while there were strong groups opposing it, both in labor and business circles. And Walton Hamilton, in a study conducted for the TNEC, concluded that the cause of Antitrust lacked the "massed support which causes congressional purse strings to loosen." The pressure groups were not interested, and the hope that massed support might come from a broad and vigorous consumers' movement seemed doomed to disappointment. Most Americans, with exceptions limited to particular areas and times, tended to remain producer conscious, to show much more interest in bettering their lot as producers than in any gains they might achieve in the role of consumers. Some groups might seize upon the antitrust laws as effective weapons against their rivals or competitors. Yet the whole trend of events seemed to point not toward a greater diffusion of economic power, but to the creation of new and offsetting power concentrates.

Actually, it appears, the bulk of Arnold's support came not from any uprising of consumers, but from smaller businessmen or dissatisfied business groups unable to compete successfully with their larger rivals, from such groups as the American Finance Conference in the auto-finance industry, the National Oil Marketers' Association in the petroleum industry, and the Allied States Association of Motion Picture Exhibitors in the movie industry. What political constituency he had consisted chiefly of dissident business groups, and typically, the cases that enjoyed the strongest political support were those designed to protect and preserve small competitors, not those that would enhance consumer purchasing power. Arnold argued that there was no real conflict here, that the interests of independent business groups and consumers were usually identical. But his statements to this effect were generally unconvincing. In a number of areas, he did face a considerable dilemma. If he pushed the cases backed by small business interests, he ran the risk of rewarding inefficiency, discouraging innovation, and forcing consumers to pay higher prices. Yet if he concentrated exclusively on consumer welfare, he ran the risk of alienating his main source of political support.

Several cases illustrated the dilemma. On one hand, was an action like the auto-finance case, one that had the strong support of the smaller finance companies, but also one that seemed likely to result in higher finance charges. In this area, as a number of critics pointed out, restraint of competition among finance companies had lowered charges to the consumer, not raised them, and it was difficult to see how consumers would benefit from an order restraining the manufacturers from recommending particular low-rate companies or requiring their dealers to patronize such companies. On the other hand were cases like those in retail distribution, an area in which most of the restraints on trade were obviously the work of the "little fellow." Here Arnold tried to break up collusion and prevent the abuse of fair trade legislation in the food, drug, liquor, and publishing industries. Yet in doing so, he alienated the political champions of small business and incurred the wrath of the vociferous lobbies maintained by the retail druggists, independent grocers, and other small merchants. A Brandeisian like Morris Ernst, for instance, thought that Arnold's action in the publishing trade was "perfectly absurd." [8]

[8] Hamilton and Till, *Antitrust*, 25, 37–38; Attorney-General, *Annual Report* (1939), 54; (1940), 56; Joseph C. Palamountain, Jr.,

In retrospect, it appears unlikely that Arnold had or could win the support of any strong political pressure group. His program had originated largely in the belief among an influential group within the Administration that lack of competition was a major cause of depression and unemployment. It gained strength temporarily from the political repercussions inherent in the recession of 1937, from a group in Congress that had long been shouting about the trusts, and from independent business groups, who saw in the antitrust program a chance to better their competitive position. Once interest in sticky versus flexible prices began to wane, the vitality of the movement seems to have rested almost entirely upon Arnold's aggressive leadership and the simple fact that his agency brought in more money in fines than it spent. Denunciations of "monopoly" and "big business" might be popular, but when it came to implementing the antitrust laws in particular cases, the enforcer was apparently destined to make more enemies than friends.[9]

III

Even if Arnold had been able to develop strong political support, however, it seems doubtful that he could ever have accomplished what he had in mind. He might praise the Sherman Act, but when all was said and done, the pro-

---

The Politics of Distribution (Cambridge: Harvard U. Press, 1955), 114–16; Paul T. Homan, in *QJE*, Nov. 1939, pp. 73–102; Wendell Berge, in *Michigan Law Review*, Feb. 1940, p. 465; Edward P. Hodges, in *Law and Contemporary Problems*, Winter 1940, p. 90; *Time*, June 6, 1938, p. 48; Aug. 1, 1938, p. 37; *Business Week*, May 28, 1938, p. 14; July 20, 1940, p. 44; Feb. 22, 1941, p. 35; April 26, 1941, pp. 45–46; Morris Ernst to FDR, April 26, 1938, PPF 2697, Roosevelt Papers; Justice Dept. PR's, Nov. 1, 4, Dec. 19, 1941; Feb. 6, March 12, 1942; Corwin Edwards to Arnold, Feb. 10, 1941; Arnold, Statement before TNEC, Feb. 12, 1941, all in Arnold Papers (Books 41–44, 46).

[9] Hamilton and Till, *Antitrust*, 25–26, 37; Attorney-General, *Annual Report* (1940), 54; *Business Week*, May 28, 1938, pp. 13–14; Dec. 24, 1938, p. 22; Mary J. Bowman, in *AER*, May 1951, p. 17; Theodore O. Yntema, in *Journal of Political Economy*, Dec. 1941, pp. 844–46.

longed delays, legal technicalities, and judicial conservatism inherent in court procedure made antitrust prosecution a clumsy weapon for promoting economic expansion or ironing out the business cycle. At best, economic reconstruction became a lengthy and tedious task. Even when the government could win victories in court, it had trouble translating them into economic victories. The whole emphasis, after all, was upon legal proofs, not upon economic values or economic analysis, and it was difficult to find any legal formula that would transform a monopolistic industry into a competitive one. The government, noted one observer, had "won many a lawsuit but lost many a case."

Arnold had hoped that the consent decree might be used to fill the gap between legal victory and economic results. Yet in practice the device was far from an unqualified success. It, too, was a product of litigation and legal harassment, not of economic analysis, and once written, it was inflexible and difficult to police. Although contempt actions might be brought, the likelihood that they would be, once the Division moved its personnel and interests to another spot along the industrial front, was slight indeed. It was apparent, moreover, that the mere injunction of monopolistic practices did little to dissipate monopoly power, that the enjoining of certain behavior patterns rarely affected the industrial structure that lay behind them. Real reform, it appeared, would require dissolution or divestiture, and as a practical matter, the courts were extremely reluctant to break up a going concern, particularly when workers and innocent investors might be adversely affected and when any gains for the consuming public were at best problematical. Judges, in fact, would almost never agree to outright trustbusting unless there had been particularly flagrant abuses or unless it could be carried out painlessly in such a manner that no one got hurt. And dissolution of the latter sort was hardly worth having. The mere fact that no one was getting hurt meant either that the monopoly power of the combine had not been greatly disturbed or that it had been negligible to begin with.[10]

In a number of instances, the outcome of the actions begun in the late nineteen thirties illustrated the limitations inherent in antitrust prosecution. After thirteen years of litigation, for example, the Aluminum Company of America remained essentially intact. The fact that it no longer enjoyed a complete monopoly was due mostly to wartime expansion, not to antitrust action. The numerous cases in the construction industry also failed to have much permanent effect. And the criminal convictions in the petroleum and tobacco industries, while they did result in new judicial strictures against price-fixing and tacit collusion, did little to alter market structures.

In only two cases, in fact, did the government succeed in bringing about structural changes. In the Pullman case (U.S. v. Pullman Co.) it finally succeeded in divorcing the manufacture of sleeping cars from the provision of sleeping-car services, and in the Paramount case (U.S. v. Paramount Pictures) it eventually forced the motion picture producers to withdraw from the exhibition end of the industry. Neither case, however, constituted a clear-cut victory for the consuming public. In the former, the mere transfer of sleeping-car services from one company to another in a monopolistic industry subject to federal regulation could hardly produce much in the way of greater competition, better service, or cheaper fares. And the effects of the latter were obscured by the impact of television. The movie industry was undoubtedly less centralized and more competitive than it had been in the past, but whether the antitrust action had much to do with it was debatable, and few would argue seriously that the case had done much to pro-

[10] House Small Business Committee, *Antitrust Law Enforcement*, 62–64, 77; Hamilton and Till, *Antitrust*, 32–34, 77–78, 92–93; and in *Washington U. Law Quarterly*, Dec. 1940, pp. 7, 22–23; Donald Dewey, *Monopoly in Economics and Law* (Chicago: Rand McNally, 1959), 246–54, 308–309; J. J. O'Connell, "The Consent Decree," Special Studies File, TNEC Records.

vide cheaper entertainment, improve the quality of films, or raise the moral standards of the industry.[11]

Restoration of competition was even more difficult, too, when other statutes and agencies continued to foster monopolistic arrangements and grant broad exemptions from the antitrust laws. Arnold early concluded that the fair trade and unfair sales acts should be repealed, that the goals embodied in such measures were in direct conflict with those embodied in the Sherman Act. He was also strongly critical of current patent procedures, the trends in transportation policy, and the protective aspects of regulatory commissions. And he was particularly perturbed about the Supreme Court's decision in 1941 that labor unions were almost completely exempt from the antitrust laws. In effect, he declared, the decision meant that "the imposition of useless and unnecessary work was a legitimate objective under the Federal law." The only remedy, he felt, was to change the law, to write a new statute that would bring unions back under the jurisdiction of the Sherman Act.[12]

Even with favorable legislation and sympathetic courts, however, it would have been extremely difficult, if not im-

[11] George W. Stocking and Myron W. Watkins, *Monopoly and Free Enterprise* (N.Y.: 20th Century Fund, 1951), 284–304; William F. Hellmuth, in Walter Adams, ed., *The Structure of Industry* (N.Y.: Macmillan, 1954), 383–92; Dewey, *Monopoly*, 163, 236–47, 257–63; *U.S. v. Socony-Vacuum Oil Co.*, 310 U.S. 150 (1940); *U.S. v. Paramount Pictures*, 334 U.S. 131 (1948); *U.S. v. Pullman Co.*, 330 U.S. 806 (1947); *U.S. v. Aluminum Co. of America*, 148 F (2d) 416 (1945); *American Tobacco Co. v. U.S.*, 328 U.S. 781 (1946); CCH, *Antitrust Laws*, 170–83; House Small Business Committee, *Antitrust Law Enforcement*, 62–64, 77; Walter Adams, in *AER*, Dec. 1951, pp. 915–22.

[12] Attorney-General, *Annual Report* (1938), 62; (1941), 62; *Business Week*, Feb. 22, 1941, pp. 35–36; Arnold, in *Reader's Digest*, June 1941, pp. 136–40; and in *Atlantic Monthly*, July 1942, pp. 14–20; Arnold, Statements before TNEC, Feb. 12, 13, 1941; Arnold to Elsa Maxwell, Dec. 22, 1943; Arnold to Reed Powell, April 19, 1941; Arnold to Francis Biddle, March 25, 1942; Arnold to Edward A. Evans, Feb. 17, 1941; Arnold, "The Right to Transport," all in Arnold Papers (Book 46, Boxes 1, 7, 13, 18, 44, Folder 4).

possible, to restore anything approaching the automatic economy of the competitive model. And even if an atomistic economy devoid of monopoly power could be created, it was by no means certain that it would function in the way that Arnold and his supporters seemed to think that it would. A number of economists, in fact, have questioned the basic underlying assumptions of the administered price thesis. They have argued that there is no direct connection between the degree of concentration or monopoly power in an industry and the flexibility of its prices, that price rigidity is more closely related to rigid costs, industrial custom, and the nature of the product than it is to market structure. Others have doubted that perfect price flexibility, even if it could be achieved, would be desirable. In practice it might make for a highly unstable system, one in which large changes would result from small causes. A small increase in the money supply, for example, might start a one-way movement of prices that could sweep through the economy like wildfire, and a small decline in demand might generate a vicious downward cycle, one in which expectations of future decline would lead consumers to postpone purchases while producers liquidated inventories and postponed investment. If such were the case, attempts to achieve the goal envisioned by the antitrusters might do far more harm than good.[13]

IV

As a countercyclical weapon, then, or as a means of stimulating economic expansion, Arnold's antitrust campaign

[13] Dewey, *Monopoly*, 73; Mark S. Massel, *Competition and Monopoly* (Washington: Brookings, 1962), 29, 252–53; Richard Ruggles, in National Bureau of Economic Research, *Business Concentration and Price Policy* (1955), 486–89; Alfred C. Neal, *Industrial Concentration and Price Inflexibility* (Washington: Am. Council on Public Affairs, 1942), 121–34, 144–45, 156–66; Don Patinkin, in AER, Sept. 1948, pp. 557–64; Jules Bachman, in *QJE*, May 1940, pp. 474–89.

could only be adjudged a failure. Even if it had not been derailed by the war, it was too cumbersome, too rigid, and too slow. It stood little chance of ever developing the necessary political constituency, winning the necessary congressional support, securing the necessary legislative changes, and persuading the courts to make the necessary alterations in basic market structures. Even if all these things could have been achieved, there was no guarantee that price rigidities would disappear, or if they would, that price flexibility would bring the economic utopia envisioned by the antitrusters. As official trustbuster, wrote one critic, Arnold was "trying something not much less arduous or improbable than Davy Crockett's famous feat of thawing the frozen axis of the earth with warm bear's grease."

This is not to say, however, that the antitrust campaign was all wasted effort. There were certain elements of strength in the Arnold approach, elements that went beyond the mere fulminations of a typical Western trustbuster. Basically, he was using the old trustbusting slogans and procedures to fashion and support new instruments of industrial control, and so long as the objectives were limited and took into account the economic and political realities of the situation, these instruments could be effective. The Antitrust Division could and did discourage outright price collusion, break up some loose combinations, make businessmen more cautious about what they attempted, and punish particularly flagrant offenders whose practices violated common standards of fairness and decency. It could and did help dissatisfied business groups to improve their competitive position and reduce or restrain the market power of their rivals. And it did pave the way for the post-war antitrust activities and a broader and more liberal interpretation of existing statutes.

Yet all of these things failed to alter the fundamental structure of the business system or the basic patterns of business behavior. Wherever the antitrusters really threatened to break up going concerns, dislodge vested interests, reduce economic security, or interfere with vital planning activities, they soon found that they were up against almost insuperable political, judicial, and technical barriers, that as a practical matter, they stood little chance of ever reshaping the economy in the image of the competitive model.[14]

Consequently, it was not surprising that the antitrust campaign did little to bring recovery. Like centralized planning or government-sponsored cartelization, it could operate only in limited areas or under special circumstances; and even if its assumptions about the desirability of flexible prices were correct, it could do little to implement them. On the contrary, the areas in which it could develop the necessary support for effective action, those in which it had the strong backing of public opinion or the strong support of a relatively powerful but dissatisfied business group, usually bore little relation to the areas where action was needed. Recovery, when it came, would be due primarily to government spending, coupled perhaps with the stabilizing activities of the new farm and labor measures passed in 1938. This, after all, was the easiest solution, the one that followed the line of least resistance, and when spending on public works and social benefits proved insufficient or politically impossible, armament spending would come to the rescue.

[14] Edwards, in *Political Science Quarterly*, Sept. 1943, pp. 340–41, 353–55; Edward Mason and Paul T. Homan, in AEA, *Readings in the Social Control of Industry* (Philadelphia: Blakiston, 1942), 217–25, 256–57; David Lasser, *Private Monopoly* (N.Y.: Harper, 1945), 231–34; Dewey, *Monopoly*, 236–44, 246–53, 302–10; Dexter M. Keezer, "An Inquiry into the Effectiveness of Federal Antitrust Laws," Box 10, Arnold Papers; Alsop and Kintner, in *Saturday Evening Post*, Aug. 12, 1939, p. 5.

CHAPTER 24. THE CONTINUED DEBATE

WHILE the antitrust campaign was getting underway in late 1938 and stepping up its activities in 1939, the Temporary National Economic Committee was conducting a massive study of the business system, and among New Deal advisers and officials the debate over economic policy continued. One group still held that the best way to achieve full employment and the good society was through some type of economic planning, some system of centralized controls and regulations under which organized economic groups could cooperate with each other and expand over-all production. A second group was still intent upon restoring flexible prices and getting back to an automatic economy in which competition would be the real regulator. And a third group, relying more and more on the Keynesian analysis, argued that the easiest and most effective way of dealing with unemployment was through a program of public investment, that further tampering with the price-wage structure was unnecessary and unwise. Eventually, of course, the coming of the war and the return of prosperity would take much of the steam out of the debate, but in the late nineteen thirties this was not yet the case.

In June 1938, when a group of Administration advisers and economists gathered at the Blaisdell farm near Leesburg, Virginia, they soon became involved in a long rambling discussion of government policy. The chief issue, noted one of the participants, was "whether Government effort should be primarily to restore competition or to set up a regulation of business decisions." The majority, led by such men as Mordecai Ezekiel and Gardiner Means, favored the regulatory approach. Large parts of the economy, they argued, were necessarily non-competitive. Even the most vigorous antitrust programs would fall far short of creating the automatic economic mechanisms necessary to insure full use of resources. Besides, an antitrust approach was likely to alienate the labor unions and thus destroy the political base of the New Deal. These views, however, were sharply countered by a few members of the group, particularly by men like Leon Henderson and Corwin Edwards, who had previously been associated with the NRA. Any "broad program of regulation," they maintained, was impossible because of "the lack of essential knowledge, the lack of a sufficient informed and disinterested personnel, and the likelihood that, as in NRA and in British experiments with industrial control, the regulated industries would come to dominate their regulators."

Some of the participants also tried to bridge the gap between the two points of view. Some noted, for example, that there were degrees of monopolistic abuse, and that even where a policy of enforcing competition was not wholly successful, it might eliminate some of the worst evils. Others argued that the remedy should depend upon the type of monopoly under consideration. For monopoly power resulting from economic and technological progress, regulation was probably the only answer; but for monopolies growing out of the desire for market control or out of financial manipulation, there was much more justification for trustbusting. Besides, noted Corwin Edwards, there were obvious practical limits to both approaches. The possibilities of genuine regulation in the public interest, as opposed to mere acquiescence in private interest-group planning, were definitely limited by the lack of political support and by the inadequacy of information and personnel. A policy of restoring competition, on the other hand, would be limited by the difficulty of enforcement and by the disruptive and deflationary effects that were likely to accompany the break-up of going concerns. Both approaches, then, would have to be economized; once this was realized, Edwards thought, much of the heat would go out of the controversy. Both groups could agree that the further development of private monopoly must be prevented; in dealing with existing monopolies, they might adopt a case-by-case approach, one that would use either regulation or dissolution, depending upon whichever seemed most sound under the circumstances.[1]

In all probability, too, Edwards was essentially right. If the policy makers could have agreed upon a common goal, if they could have agreed, for example, that the objective was the most efficient and most productive system possible and that any action conducive to this end was desirable, then tests of efficiency and productivity could probably have been devised and careful and detailed studies of the economy would probably have revealed that different areas and different circumstances called for the use of different methods. In some industries and under some conditions, enforced competition might yield the largest output of goods at the lowest possible cost. In other areas or under other conditions, it might be necessary to resort to government ownership, regulated monopolies, government-supervised cartels, or government competition with private enterprise. As a matter of fact, though, the problem could not be solved so easily. Not everyone would agree that the most efficient society was necessarily the good society, and even among those who would agree that efficiency was a desirable goal, there were many who would insist that the attainment of it must be compatible with other goals, with the retention of democratic institutions, the decentralization of power, the preservation of small competitors, the advancement of economic freedom and opportunity,

[1] Gardiner Means and Thomas Blaisdell, Summaries of Discussion at Blaisdell Farm, June 5, 1938; Mordecai Ezekiel to Blaisdell, June 14, 1938; Corwin Edwards to Blaisdell, June 17, 1938, all in NRPB Records (Advisory Committee Minutes—CCF, Meetings File—CCF); Edwards to Leon Henderson, April 22, 1939, Cohen File, NPPC Records. Present at the meeting described were Frederic Delano, Charles Merriam, Beardsley Ruml, Henry Dennison, Gardiner Means, Lauchlin Currie, Mordecai Ezekiel, Harry Dexter White, Leon Henderson, Lewis Bean, Corwin Edwards, Benjamin Cohen, Jerome Frank, Charles Eliot, Harold Merrill, and Thomas Blaisdell.

the protection of public health and safety, the achievement of economic balance and full employment, the observance of common standards of decency and fair play, the attainment of a reasonable level of security and stability, or the furtherance of national security.

Because of the conflicting goals, then, and the tendency to confuse goals with methods or to elevate the latter above the former, the policy makers found that it was extremely difficult to reach a common basis of agreement. Actually the problem was one that would not yield readily to the techniques of scientific research. It was not a matter for which any amount of statistics and factual data would provide a clear-cut and indisputable answer. At its core it was a matter of philosophical values and moral judgments, and while the case-by-case approach might look good on paper, it was difficult to apply because the decisions in individual cases would call into play the same value judgments that lay beyond the original battle of principles. Men like Thurman Arnold might praise the doctors for effecting practical cures without engaging in metaphysical arguments, but it never seemed to occur to them that doctors were in substantial agreement on the nature of a healthy individual and the ills that they undertook to cure. The same could not be said about the attitude of the American people toward the problem of monopoly.[2]

In view of these ambivalent attitudes and the difficulty of doing much of anything about the existing economic structure, the spending solution became increasingly attractive. And by 1939 the views of the outright Keynesians, of economists like Lauchlin Currie and Alvin Hansen, did seem to carry greater weight in Administration councils. These men were arguing now that the debate over mo-

[2] See Mark S. Massel, *Competition and Monopoly* (Washington: Brookings, 1962), 15–41; Max Rheinstein, in *Ethics*, Jan. 1939, p. 217; AEA, *Readings in the Social Control of Industry* (Philadelphia: Blakiston, 1942), 239.

nopoly and administered prices was largely meaningless or at least irrelevant to the problem of stimulating economic recovery. The real difficulty, they insisted, stemmed from the low level of investment. Economic maturity and the resulting decline in private investment opportunities had caused a decline in income and hence in effective demand. This in turn had produced the price dispersion, and consequently, any tinkering with the price-cost structure was like "tampering with the thermometer to change the temperature." Even if prices had been perfectly flexible, there would still have been a decline in purchasing power, and any attempt now to chase rigid prices down to the level of flexible prices was likely to make matters worse since it would lead to a further curtailment of investment, a new decline in income, and a fresh price disparity. It would be far better to concentrate upon stimulating investment and stepping up public expenditures.[3]

II

It was only natural, too, that these conflicting counsels should be reflected in the deliberations of the Temporary National Economic Committee and that planners, antitrusters, and spenders should all attempt to influence the actions of the agency, the questions it should ask, and the content of its studies. An early version of the planning orientation, for example, was that set forth by Adolf Berle in a widely publicized memorandum in July 1938. At the request of Jerome Frank and Thurman Arnold, Berle undertook to discuss the lines of inquiry that the TNEC might pursue and the pitfalls it should avoid. It should begin, he thought, with the development of ade-

[3] Alvin Hansen, "Price Flexibility and Full Employment of Resources," Jan. 6, 1939; Lauchlin Currie to Gardiner Means, Nov. 28, 1938; Mordecai Ezekiel to Thomas Blaisdell, June 14, 1938, all in NRPB Records (Structure of Economy File—CCF, Meetings File —CCF); Currie, "Full Employment," March 18, 1940, OF 264, Roosevelt Papers.

quate criteria of judgment, and he hoped that these would emphasize the effective functioning of the economy, not some theoretical notion concerning monopoly and competition. The agency, to be more specific, should not assume that all monopoly was bad, that cartels were necessarily harmful, that small business was necessarily competitive or necessarily humane, or that big business necessarily grew by predatory tactics, and it should realize that there were immense practical difficulties in the way of applying the theory of an "elastic price." One could not "gamble with the economic safety of a large district simply in the hope that the expansion of inventory will lead to a lower price, which in turn will lead to expansion."

The opposite position, that of the antitrusters, was set forth by Herman Oliphant during a heated dispute over the methods to be used in studying monopolistic practices. In drawing up the questionnaires for the study of governmental purchasing and collusive bidding, Admiral Christian Peoples of the Treasury's procurement division stressed the fairness of prices in relation to profits and costs, an approach that was promptly challenged by Oliphant and his subordinates. The very idea, they felt, was based on a glaring "misconception," both of the "fundamental policy and purpose" of the study and of the "fundamental precept of our competitive system." There could be no "fair price," except a "price determined by competition." And wherever it appeared that prices were monopolistically controlled, the actual price at which the goods were offered was immaterial.

The Justice Department, too, supported the position taken by Oliphant. Hugh Cox, director of the Department of Justice studies, was asked to follow out the "idea that the cold fish eye of a technician cast upon H.O.'s two memoranda and the Admiral's memorandum would show that the Admiral's memorandum is spinach"; and Cox obliged with a critique of the Admiral and his staff. "Some chapter and verse," he declared, "will illustrate the double

461

fact that (a) the preparers of the memorandum are ignorant; and (b) they are ignorant of their ignorance." In
no event, he maintained, was it consistent with present
policy "to ascertain the magnitude of profits accruing on
past contracts predicated upon identical bids." It would
not only result in a waste of time and money, but would
also violate "the traditional American policy, and the
policy of the Committee, that if competitors fix prices by
agreement, the agreement is illegal no matter what *profits*
or *losses* result from such an agreement." Eventually, the
Oliphant view prevailed. The purchasing study was restricted primarily to the incidence of identical bidding. But
there were still those who felt that it might have accomplished much more.[4]

Similar conflicts also persisted once the TNEC hearings
got underway. The spenders relied upon the testimony
of such men as Alvin Hansen and Mordecai Ezekiel to
establish a case for continued governmental investment,
but such testimony failed to convince Senator O'Mahoney
and the more conservative members of the Committee. In
reality, O'Mahoney told the President, deficit financing
was the same sort of thing the monopolist did when he
issued watered stock based upon future expectations. On
the matter of patent law revision, too, there was considerable debate, particularly between the business-oriented
representatives of the Department of Commerce and the
more confirmed antitrusters of the Department of Justice.
Nor was there much agreement on revision of the anti-

[4] David Lynch, *The Concentration of Economic Power* (N.Y.:
Columbia U. Press, 1946), 56–57; Myron W. Watkins, in *Yale
Review*, Dec. 1938, pp. 324–28, 336–39; Adolf A. Berle, Jr., to
Stephen Early, July 15, 1938, OF 3322, Roosevelt Papers; *Berle
Memorandum of July 12, 1938*; Govt. Purchasing Questionnaire,
Sept. 10, 1935; J. J. O'Connell, Jr., "Government Purchasing Study,"
Oct. 24, 29, 1938; Hugh Cox to O'Connell Oct. 22, 1938; O'Con-
nell to Herman Oliphant, Oct. 11, 1938; Oliphant to Morgenthau,
Oct. 17, 1938; Oliphant to Christian J. Peoples, Oct. 14, 1938;
Report on Govt. Purchasing, June 30, 1939, all in TNEC Records
(Statements Submitted File, Special Studies File).

trust laws themselves. Men like Jerome Frank and Willard Thorp still supported the idea of a special agency with discretionary power to approve and encourage cooperative business agreements, but to the FTC and the Antitrust Division, such plans were anathema. The whole approach, declared Thurman Arnold, was like asking an umpire to rule in advance of a play whether or not the runner was out. The real need, he felt, was for stronger antitrust laws, and some of Arnold's associates would add such things as graduated taxes, limits on size, and drastic simplification of complicated corporate structures. Admittedly, said Benjamin Cohen, "atomization" in the literal sense was impossible and undesirable, but there was "quite a difference between imperfect competition among a dozen or more units and a monopoly exercised by one or two." [5]

Even the administered price thesis, which in the beginning was widely accepted by both the planners and antitrusters, came in for increased criticism from TNEC economists and staff members. And in the monographs dealing with it, there was a marked tendency to cast doubt upon the basic underlying assumptions. The one written by Saul Nelson and Walter Keim, for example, noted that the problem of price changes was a highly complex one, that such things as custom, the nature of the product, and differences in elasticity of demand sometimes played a far

[5] Lynch, *Economic Power*, 315–16, 319–21, 335–36; TNEC, *Investigation of Concentration of Economic Power*, Pt. 9, 3495–3520; and *Preliminary Report* (Senate Doc. 95, 76 Cong., 1 Sess., 1939), 14–16; *New York Times*, Dec. 3, 1938; Edward S. Mason, chairman, "Round Table on Preserving Competition vs. Regulating Monopoly," *AER Supplement*, xxx (March 1940), 213–18; Joseph O'Mahoney to FDR, June 19, 1939, Secretary of Commerce File, Hopkins Papers; Testimony of Alvin Hansen, May 16, 1939; Recommendations of Thurman Arnold, Feb. 12, 1941, both in Statements Submitted File, TNEC Records; Arnold, Patent Recommendations, May 2, 1939; Milton Handler, "Revision of Antitrust Laws"; Milton Katz to Arnold, Sept. 8, 1938; Benjamin Cohen, Outline of a Program to Solve the Problem of Concentration of Economic Power; and Memo. re Revision of Antitrust Laws; Cohen to Henderson, June 12, 1939, all in Cohen File, NPPC Records.

greater role in price rigidity than did the possession of monopoly power, and that often there was little correlation between production curtailment and rigid prices. "It is unlikely," the authors concluded, "that uniform flexibility of prices, even if it were attainable, would itself turn the tide of depression and bring about recovery." The same general view, in an even more emphatic form, was apparent in the monograph written by Willard Thorp and Walter Crowder. "Products produced under conditions of high concentration," they concluded, "show about the same changes in quantity and in price over periods of recovery and recession that are shown by products with low concentration." Divergent quantity behavior appeared to be more closely tied to "the varying economic characteristics of the products themselves" than to differences in competitive conditions.[6]

In a sense, too, these internal conflicts and divided counsels helped to shape the final nature of the TNEC's report. In the beginning the agency had hopes of finding some magic formula that would cure the nation's ills to the satisfaction of everyone, something that, in the words of David Lynch, "would alter none of our basic institutions, affront few of our vested interest groups, change little in the organization and pattern of economic society, yet at the same time adjust its most far-reaching dislocations and solve its most fundamental problems." When it came time to write the final report, however, the mountain of facts had failed to produce any magic formula, and the policy conflict with which the Committee had begun was still unresolved. Each faction continued to view the problem from the standpoint of its own value judgments and to stick with its own ideas concerning the origins of mo-

[6] Saul Nelson and Walter G. Keim, *Price Behavior and Business Policy* (TNEC Monograph 1, 1940), XXI, 11–20, 40–43, 51; Willard L. Thorp and Walter F. Crowder, *The Structure of Industry* (TNEC Monograph 27, 1941), 411–12; Summary of Testimony on Price Behavior and Business Policy, Hearings File, TNEC Records.

nopoly, the extent and effects of it, and the remedial action that should be taken. The result was a report as timid as it was unoriginal. About all that a majority of the Committee could agree upon were some minor changes in the antitrust laws and minor reforms in patent procedures, and few of these were ever implemented.[7]

III

The TNEC, moreover, was not the only scene of conflict. Similar debates about the nature, effects, and desirability of policies affecting competition were taking place within and between other agencies, and there, too, it was difficult to arrive at any general consensus. By 1939 a particularly heated controversy had developed over the desirability of reviving or strengthening competition in the transportation industries. On one side were the antitrusters, men like Benjamin Cohen and Thurman Arnold, who were thoroughly disenchanted with the whole noncompetitive approach of transportation policies. The railroads, they charged, were using the law to protect and shield themselves from the competition of newer, better, and cheaper methods of transportation, and it was time now to un-

---

[7] Lynch, *Economic Power*, 338–53, 362–65, 371–77; TNEC, *Final Report and Recommendations* (Senate Doc. 35, 77 Cong., 1 Sess., 1941), 24–40. About all that resulted in the way of legislation was some minor revision of the patent laws growing out of the preliminary report in 1939. These changes reduced the period during which an inventor might make public use of inventions before filing application for a patent, simplified interference practices, and abolished renewal applications. It might be possible, too, to relate the Anti-Merger Act of 1950 or some of the activities of the Antitrust Division, the FTC, and the SEC to the recommendations and hearings of the TNEC. See Lynch, *op. cit.*, 354–59, 373; David D. Martin, *Mergers and the Clayton Act* (Berkeley: U. of Calif. Press, 1959), 221–26; TNEC, *Preliminary Report*, 14–16; TNEC PR, Aug. 2, 1939, Statements Submitted File, TNEC Records; Bob Black, "Digest Showing Direct and Indirect Results and Benefits of TNEC Hearings and Investigations," Aug. 15, 1940, TNEC File, O'Mahoney Papers.

leash these competitive forces, to remove the restrictions on entry and rate-cutting, break up private rate-making bureaus and conferences, stimulate technological progress, restore flexible rates, and expand the volume of traffic. Most transportation and regulatory officials, however, were still insisting that there was too much competition, not too little, that there was still too much waste motion, too much duplication of facilities, too much conflict between rival groups. The answer, as it was set forth in numerous articles, reports, and speeches, was a program that would lead to more consolidation, better coordination, stricter controls, and bigger subsidies.[8]

A second major controversy, also in progress in the late nineteen thirties, concerned the desirability of providing special aid to small business. Once again the champions of the little businessman were arguing that bigness itself was an evil and that the preservation of a competitive system necessarily required the preservation of small competitors. They were particularly interested now in providing small businessmen with better credit facilities and easier access to capital, and by 1939 they had set forth a wide variety of proposals, ranging from special banks and investment companies to loan insurance and government guaranteed mortgages. Except for a limited extension of the RFC's lending powers, however, the plans came to nothing. In the Department of Commerce, in particular, several key officials were convinced that such measures were unwise and that most of the complaints from small businessmen were really unjustified. No reasonable person,

[8] NRPB, *Transportation and National Policy* (1942), 281–82; William N. Leonard, *Railroad Consolidation under the Transportation Act of 1920* (N.Y.: Columbia U. Press, 1946), 244–50; Leslie Craven, in *Atlantic Monthly*, Dec. 1938, pp. 767–76; *Current History*, March 1938, pp. 27–30; Feb. 1939, p. 52; *Fortune*, Aug. 1939, pp. 82–84, 86–88, 90; Truman C. Bigham, in *Southern Economic Journal*, July 1941, pp. 2, 20–21; Thurman Arnold, "The Right to Transport," Folder 4, Arnold Papers; Benjamin Cohen, Outline of a Program to Solve the Problem of Concentration of Economic Power, Cohen Files, NPPC Records.

they argued, would consider the typical applicant for small business loans a promising risk. In any event, the Administration should not encourage any further squandering of capital in mercantile, service, or distributive fields, areas that were already overbuilt and suffering from excessive competition.[9]

There were sharp debates, too, both within the government and among academic economists, about the validity and usefulness of the administered price thesis. As noted previously, the antitrusters had made extensive use of the thesis in 1937 and 1938. It had played a prominent role in the agitation leading up to the creation of the TNEC and the revival of antitrust prosecution, and President Roosevelt himself had accepted and used it in his monopoly message. By 1939, however, a growing number of officials and economists, particularly those of a more conservative political orientation, were questioning the basic underlying assumptions about the relationship between monopoly, rigid prices, and depression. Inflexible prices, they argued, were due not so much to monopoly power or economic concentration as they were to such factors as rigid costs, inelastic demand, durability of the product, long-term contractual arrangements, use of published price lists, habit, and custom. After a study of price changes during each major depression since 1837, Rufus Tucker concluded that prices were actually less flexible a hundred years ago than they were at present. The recent discovery of rigid prices by certain economists and politicians was in his opinion "no more important and no less ridiculous

[9] Rudolph L. Weissman, *Small Business and Venture Capital* (N.Y.: Harper, 1945), 54–55, 68–72, 74–78, 88–94; Harmon Zeigler, *The Politics of Small Business* (Washington: Public Affairs Press, 1961), 87–89; Marshall D. Ketchum, in *Journal of Business*, July 1944, pp. 164, 169–71; Grosvenor Jones, "Loans to Small Business," March 27, 1939; Cohen to Stuart Guthrie, May 1, 1939, with accompanying memo. and draft of bill; Jerome Frank to Harry Hopkins, June 9, 1939; Willard Thorp to E. J. Noble, May 15, 1939; Guthrie to Cohen, May 5, 1939; E. E. Anderson to Guthrie, May 4, 1939, all in Secretary of Commerce File, Hopkins Papers.

than the discovery by Moliere's bourgeois gentilhomme that he had been speaking prose all his life."

Men like Tucker also denied that there was any necessary connection between price rigidity and curtailment of production. In many areas of the economy, particularly in the capital goods industries, changes in the outlook for profits produced marked variations in demand, and hence in production. And since price was only a secondary consideration in the development of these variations, it followed that output could never be stabilized by changes in price. "We know at any rate," said Edwin George, "that locomotives will never be sold like wheat. They will never go down a couple of hundred dollars in price on a dull day when no orders are received. Nobody expects it including the critics."

Defenders of the business system doubted, moreover, that there was much correlation between industries in which competition was of the old-fashioned price variety and those that were best serving the public interest. Price cutting, after all, might lead to a shrinkage of markets, since customers would refrain from buying while prices were going down or were expected to go down, and even if price competition was declining, there were still other forces that could be relied upon to protect consumers and provide the mainsprings of economic progress. There was still a good deal of competition, for example, between industries and in such areas as salesmanship, research, the improvement of quality, the provision of services, and the development of substitutes.[10]

[10] Alfred C. Neal, *Industrial Concentration and Price Inflexibility* (Washington: Am. Council on Public Affairs, 1942), 23–24, 29–37; Rufus S. Tucker, in *AER*, March 1938, pp. 41–54; and in *Annalist*, Feb. 4, 1938, pp. 195–96; Edward S. Mason, in *Review of Economic Statistics*, May 1938, pp. 53–64; Jules Bachman, in *QJE*, May 1940, pp. 474–89; Edwin G. Nourse, in *Nation's Business*, Sept. 1938, pp. 17–19; Edwin George, in *Dun's Review*, Nov. 1938, pp. 24–27; Sumner H. Slichter, in *Review of Economic Statistics*, Aug. 1938, pp. 100–10; Raymond Moley and Ralph W. Robey, in *Newsweek*,

From a second angle, too, came the arguments of the economic planners, arguments that still defended the administered price thesis, but denied that antitrust action would provide an effective remedy. Even if rigid prices had existed in the past, so the argument ran, their effects had not been nearly so disruptive as they were at present. The old economy, aside from agricultural markets, had been largely a priceless economy of self-sufficient family units. The new was a highly complex and interdependent mechanism in which the relative importance of rigidly priced products had greatly increased. It might also be conceded that price rigidity was associated with certain characteristics of the product, with its closesess to the ultimate user, its durability, and the degree to which it was differentiated from other products; but this did not rule out the explanation of administrative control. The market tended to narrow as a product approached its final stage and became more highly differentiated. It involved fewer and fewer producers, and the opportunity for administrative control was therefore enhanced. Yet this control could not be rooted out by even the most stringent of trustbusting campaigns, and its disruptive effects could not be overcome on any permanent basis by reliance upon government spending. At bottom, the problem of the level of economic activity was a problem in industrial policy-making; until the making of such policy was lodged in the hands of those interested in increased output at lower prices, full recovery and sustained expansion were not likely to be achieved.[11]

May 8, 1937, p. 44; Dec. 27, 1937, pp. 35–36; Jan. 3, 1938, pp. 37–38; Jan. 10, 1938, p. 44.

[11] Gardiner Means, *The Structure of the American Economy* (NRC, 1939), 129–45; Mordecai Ezekiel, *Jobs for All through Industrial Expansion* (N.Y.: Knopf, 1939), 232–35; Ralph C. Wood, in *AER*, Dec. 1938, pp. 663–73; Alan Sweezy, "Notes on Industrial Policy," July 15, 1938; Means, "Possibilities and Limitations of Antitrust Policy," July 1938, both in Cohen File, NPPC Records; Means, Summary of Meeting of the Advisory Committee, June 5, 1938, Advisory Committee Minutes—CCF, NRPB Records.

Finally, from still another angle, came the arguments of the Keynesians, of men who felt that both the antitrusters and planners were unduly concerned about price policy and price relationships. Recovery, they argued, should be built around a program of public investment, coupled with measures to increase the propensity to consume and reduce the propensity to save. Within this framework measures designed to break up or regulate monopolies might be useful. They might create new investment opportunities, make for a better distribution of income, and prevent arbitrary price increases. But alone, they provided no adequate solution. If carried to extremes, they could create disinvestment and become distinctly harmful. In the long run, noted Lauchlin Currie, antitrust action might maintain sufficient flexibility to insure that technological gains would be passed on to the consumer, but from the point of view of curing depressions, it was "probably hopeless" to depend upon readjustments in price.[12]

The New Dealers, then, failed to arrive at any real consensus about the origins and nature of economic concentration, the effects of it, or the methods of dealing with it. In 1939, in fact, they seemed to be even more divided than they had been in 1933. Perhaps, as some commentators insisted, they were wrestling with a problem for which there was no real solution, at least in terms of satisfying all the groups, interests, and attitudes involved.[13] In any event, the only solution that the Roosevelt Administration ever discovered was essentially a political rather than an eco-

[12] Richard V. Gilbert et al., *An Economic Program for American Democracy* (N.Y.: Vanguard, 1938), 31–40, 45, 74–79; Alvin H. Hansen, *Full Recovery or Stagnation* (N.Y.: Norton, 1938), 270–89; Don D. Humphrey, in *Journal of Political Economy*, Oct. 1937, pp. 658–61; Alvin Hansen, "Price Flexibility and Full Employment of Resources," Jan. 6, 1939; Lauchlin Currie to Means, Nov. 28, 1938; Mordecai Ezekiel to Thomas Blaisdell, June 14, 1938, all in NRPB Records (Structure of Economy File—CCF, Meetings File—CCF); Currie, "Full Employment," March 18, 1940, OF 264, Roosevelt Papers.

[13] See Watkins, in *Yale Review*, Dec. 1938, pp. 323–24, 336.

nomic one. It made the necessary concessions, both to the competitive ideal and the demands for planning, security, and rationalization. It shied away from drastic institutional reform and came to rely primarily on the spending solution. And it remained a house divided, one in which conflicting ideologies, divergent goals, and different sets of values continued to produce heated debates and inconsistent policies.

CONCLUSION. THE NEW DEAL
AND THE PROBLEM
OF MONOPOLY:
RETROSPECT AND PROSPECT

Two souls dwell in the bosom of this Administration," wrote Dorothy Thompson in 1938, "as indeed, they do in the bosom of the American people. The one loves the Abundant Life, as expressed in the cheap and plentiful products of large-scale mass production and distribution. . . . The other soul yearns for former simplicities, for decentralization, for the interests of the 'little man,' revolts against high-pressure salesmanship, denounces 'monopoly' and 'economic empires,' and seeks means of breaking them up." "Our Administration," she continued, "manages a remarkable . . . stunt of being . . . in favor of organizing and regulating the Economic Empires to greater and greater efficiency, and of breaking them up as a tribute to perennial American populist feeling." [1]

Dorothy Thompson was a persistent critic of the Roosevelt Administration; yet her remarks did show considerable insight into the dilemma that confronted New Dealers, and indeed, the dilemma that confronted industrial America. The problem of reconciling liberty and order, individualism and collective organization, was admittedly an ancient one, but the creation of a highly integrated industrial system in a land that had long cherished its liberal, democratic, and individualistic traditions presented the problem in a peculiarly acute form. Both the American people and their political leaders tended to view modern industrialism with mingled feelings of pride and regret. On one hand, they tended to associate large business units and economic organization with abundance, progress, and a rising standard of living. On the other, they associated

[1] Dorothy Thompson, in *New York Herald Tribune*, Jan. 24, 1938.

them with a wide variety of economic abuses, which, because of past ideals and past standards, they felt to be injurious to society. Also, deep in their hearts, they retained a soft spot for the "little fellow." In moments of introspection, they looked upon the immense concentrations of economic power that they had created and accused them of destroying the good life, of destroying the independent businessman and the satisfactions that came from owning one's own business and working for oneself, of reducing Americans to a race of clerks and machine tenders, of creating an impersonal, mechanized world that destroyed man as an individual.[2]

The search in twentieth-century America, then, was for some solution that would reconcile the practical necessity with the individualistic ideal, some arrangement that would preserve the industrial order, necessarily based upon a high degree of collective organization, and yet would preserve America's democratic heritage at the same time. Americans wanted a stable, efficient industrial system, one that turned out a large quantity of material goods, insured full employment, and provided a relatively high degree of economic security. Yet at the same time they wanted a system as free as possible from centralized direction, one in which economic power was dispersed and economic opportunity was really open, one that preserved the dignity of the individual and adjusted itself automatically to market forces. And they were unwilling to renounce the hope of achieving both. In spite of periodic hurricanes of anti-big-business sentiment, they refused to follow the prophets that would destroy their industrial system and return to former simplicities. Nor did they pay much attention to those that would sacrifice democratic ideals and liberal traditions in order to create a more orderly and more

[2] See Arthur R. Burns, in AER, June 1949, pp. 691–95; Burton R. Fisher and Stephen B. Withey, *Big Business as the People See It* (Ann Arbor: U. of Mich. Press, 1951), 21–22, 34–38; Rexford G. Tugwell, in *Western Political Quarterly*, Sept. 1950, pp. 392–400.

rational system, one that promised greater security, greater stability, and possibly even greater material benefits.

There were times, of course, when this dilemma was virtually forgotten. During periods of economic prosperity, when Americans were imbued with a psychological sense of well-being and satiated with a steady outflow of material benefits, it was hard to convince them that their industrial organization was seriously out of step with their ideals. During such periods, the majority rallied to the support of the business system; so long as it continued to operate at a high level, they saw no need for any major reforms. So long as the competitive ideal was embodied in statutes and industrial and political leaders paid lip service to it, there was a general willingness to leave it at that. If there were troubled consciences left, these could be soothed by clothing collective organizations in the attributes of rugged individuals and by the assurances of economic experts that anything short of pure monopoly was "competition" and therefore assured the benefits that were supposed to flow from competition.

In a time of economic adversity, however, Americans became painfully aware of the gap between ideal and reality. Paradoxically, this awareness produced two conflicting and contradictory reactions. Some pointed to the gap, to the failure of business organizations to live by the competitive creed, and concluded that it was the cause of the economic debacle, that the breakdown of the industrial machine was the inevitable consequence of its failure to conform to competitive standards. Others pointed to the same gap and concluded that the ideal itself was at fault, that it had prevented the organization and conscious direction of a rational system that would provide stability and security. On one hand, the presence of depression conditions seemed to intensify anti-big-business sentiment and generate new demands for antitrust crusades. On the other, it inspired demands for planning, rationalization, and the creation of economic organizations that could weather deflationary forces. The first general effect grew directly out of the loss of confidence in business leadership, the conviction that industrial leaders had sinned against the economic creed, and the determination that they should be allowed to sin no more. The second grew out of the black fear of economic death, the urgent desire to stem the deflationary tide, and the mounting conviction that a policy of laissez-faire or real implementation of the competitive ideal would result in economic disaster.

During such a period, moreover, it would seem practically inevitable that the policy-making apparatus of a democracy should register both streams of sentiment. Regardless of their logical inconsistency, the two streams were so intermixed in the ideology of the average man that any administration, if it wished to retain political power, had to make concessions to both. It must move to check the deflationary spiral, to provide some sort of central direction, and to salvage economic groups through the erection of cartels and economic controls. Yet while it was doing this, it must make a proper show of maintaining competitive ideals. Its actions must be justified by an appeal to competitive traditions, by showing that they were designed to save the underdog, or if this was impossible, by an appeal to other arguments and other traditions that for the moment justified making an exception. Nor could antitrust action ever be much more than a matter of performing the proper rituals and manipulating the proper symbols. It might attack unusually privileged and widely hated groups, break up a few loose combinations, and set forth a general program that was presumably designed to make the competitive ideal a reality. But the limit of the program would, of necessity, be that point at which changes in business practice or business structures would cause serious economic dislocation. It could not risk the disruption of going concerns or a further shrinkage in employment and production, and it would not subject men to the logical working out of deflationary trends. To do so would amount to political suicide.

To condemn these policies for their inconsistency was to miss the point. From an economic standpoint, condemnation might very well be to the point. They were inconsistent. One line of action tended to cancel the other, with the result that little was accomplished. Yet from the political standpoint, this very inconsistency, so long as the dilemma persisted, was the safest method of retaining political power. President Roosevelt, it seems, never suffered politically from his reluctance to choose between planning and antitrust action. His mixed emotions so closely reflected the popular mind that they were a political asset rather than a liability.[3]

II

That New Deal policy was inconsistent, then, should occasion little surprise. Such inconsistency, in fact, was readily apparent in the National Industrial Recovery Act, the first major effort to deal with the problems of industrial organization. When Roosevelt took office in 1933, the depression had reached its most acute stage. Almost every economic group was crying for salvation through political means, for some sort of rationalization and planning, although they might differ as to just who was to do the planning and the type and amount of it that would be required. Pro-business planners, drawing upon the trade association ideology of the nineteen twenties and the precedent of the War Industries Board, envisioned a semi-cartelized business commonwealth in which industrial leaders would plan and the state would enforce the deci-

---

[3] See Adolf A. Berle, Jr., in *Virginia Quarterly Review*, Summer 1938, pp. 324–33; K. E. Boulding, in *QJE*, Aug. 1945, pp. 524, 529–42; Arthur M. Schlesinger, Jr., *The Politics of Upheaval* (Boston: Houghton Mifflin, 1960), 650–54.

sions. Other men, convinced that there was already too much planning by businessmen, hoped to create an order in which other economic groups would participate in the policy-making process. Even under these circumstances, however, the resulting legislation had to be clothed in competitive symbols. Proponents of the NRA advanced the theory that it would help small businessmen and industrial laborers by protecting them from predatory practices and monopolistic abuses. The devices used to erect monopolistic controls became "codes of fair competition." And each such device contained the proper incantation against monopoly.

Consequently, the NRA was not a single program with a single objective, but rather a series of programs with a series of objectives, some of which were in direct conflict with each other. In effect, the National Industrial Recovery Act provided a phraseology that could be used to urge almost any approach to the problem of economic organization and an administrative machine that each of the conflicting economic and ideological groups might possibly use for their own ends. Under the circumstances, a bitter clash over basic policies was probably inevitable.

For a short period these inconsistencies were glossed over by the summer boomlet of 1933 and by a massive propaganda campaign appealing to wartime precedents and attempting to create a new set of cooperative symbols. As the propaganda wore off, however, and the economic indices turned downward again, the inconsistencies inherent in the program moved to the forefront of the picture. In the code-writing process, organized business had emerged as the dominant economic group, and once this became apparent, criticism of the NRA began to mount. Agrarians, convinced that rising industrial prices were canceling out any gains from the farm program, demanded that businessmen live up to the competitive faith. Labor spokesmen, bitterly disillusioned when the program failed to guarantee union recognition and collective bargaining, charged that the Administration had sold out to management. Small businessmen, certain that the new code authorities were only devices to increase the power of their larger rivals, raised the ancient cry of monopolistic exploitation. Anti-trusters, convinced that the talk about strengthening competition was sheer hypocrisy, demanded that this disastrous trust-building program come to a halt. Economic planners, alienated by a process in which the businessmen did the planning, charged that the government was only sanctioning private monopolistic arrangements. And the American public, disillusioned with rising prices and the failure of the program to bring economic recovery, listened to the criticisms and demanded that its competitive ideals be made good.

The rising tide of public resentment greatly strengthened the hand of those that viewed the NRA primarily as a device for raising the plane of competition and securing social justice for labor. Picking up support from discontented groups, from other governmental agencies, and from such investigations as that conducted by Clarence Darrow's National Recovery Review Board, this group within the NRA had soon launched a campaign to bring about a reorientation in policy. By June 1934 it had obtained a formal written policy embodying its views, one that committed the NRA to the competitive ideal, renounced the use of price and production controls, and promised to subject the code authorities to strict public supervision. By this time, however, most of the major codes had been written, and the market restorers were never able to apply their policy to codes already approved. The chief effect of their efforts to do so was to antagonize businessmen and to complicate the difficulties of enforcing code provisions that were out of line with announced policy.

The result was a deadlock that persisted for the remainder of the agency's life. Putting the announced policy into effect would have meant, in all probability, the complete alienation of business support and the collapse of the whole structure. Yet accepting and enforcing the codes for what they were would have resulted, again in all probability, in an outraged public and congressional opinion that would have swept away the whole edifice. Thus the NRA tended to reflect the whole dilemma confronting the New Deal. Admittedly, declared policy was inconsistent with practice. Admittedly, the NRA was accomplishing little. Yet from a political standpoint, if the agency were to continue at all, a deadlock of this sort seemed to be the only solution. If the Supreme Court had not taken a hand in the matter, the probable outcome would have been either the abolition of the agency or a continuation of the deadlock.

The practical effect of the NRA, then, was to allow the erection, extension, and fortification of private monopolistic arrangements, particularly for groups that already possessed a fairly high degree of integration and monopoly power. Once these arrangements had been approved and vested interests had developed, the Administration found it difficult to deal with them. It could not move against them without alienating powerful interest groups, producing new economic dislocations, and running the risk of setting off the whole process of deflation again. Yet, because of the competitive ideal, it could not lend much support to the arrangements or provide much in the way of public supervision. Only in areas where other arguments, other ideals, and political pressure justified making an exception, in such areas as agriculture, natural resources, transportation, and to a certain extent labor, could the government lend its open support and direction.

Moreover, the policy dilemma, coupled with the sheer complexity of the undertaking, made it impossible to provide much central direction. There was little planning of a broad, general nature, either by businessmen or by the state; there was merely the half-hearted acceptance of a series of legalized, but generally uncoordinated, monopolistic combinations. The result was not over-all direction, but a type of partial, piecemeal, pressure-group planning, a type of planning designed by specific economic groups to balance production with consumption regardless of the dislocations produced elsewhere in the economy.

III

There were, certainly, proposals for other types of planning. But under the circumstances, they were and remained politically unfeasible, both during the NRA period and after. The idea of a government-supported business commonwealth still persisted, and a few men still felt that if the NRA had really applied it, the depression would have been over. Yet in the political context of the time, the idea was thoroughly unrealistic. For one thing, there was the growing gap between businessmen and New Dealers, the conviction of one side that cooperation would lead to bureaucratic socialism, of the other that it would lead to fascism or economic oppression. Even if this quarrel had not existed, the Administration could not have secured a program that ran directly counter to the anti-big-business sentiment of the time. The monopolistic implications in such a program were too obvious, and there was little that could be done to disguise them. Most industrial leaders recognized the situation, and the majority of them came to the conclusion that a political program of this sort was no longer necessary. With the crisis past and the deflationary process checked, private controls and such governmental aids as tariffs, subsidies, and loans would be sufficient.

The idea of national economic planning also persisted. A number of New Dealers continued to advocate the transfer of monopoly power from businessmen to the state or to other organized economic groups. Each major economic group, they argued, should be organized and allowed to participate in the formulation of a central plan, one that would result in expanded production, increased employment, a more equitable distribution, and a better balance of prices. Yet this idea, too, was thoroughly impractical when judged in terms of existing political realities. It ran counter to competitive and individualistic traditions. It threatened important vested interests. It largely ignored the complexities of the planning process or the tendency of regulated interests to dominate their regulators. And it was regarded by the majority of Americans as being overly radical, socialistic, and un-American.

Consequently, the planning of the New Deal was essentially single-industry planning, partial, piecemeal, and opportunistic, planning that could circumvent the competitive ideal or could be based on other ideals that justified making an exception. After the NRA experience, organized business groups found it increasingly difficult to devise these justifications. Some business leaders, to be sure, continued to talk about a public agency with power to waive the antitrust laws and sanction private controls. Yet few of them were willing to accept government participation in the planning process, and few were willing to come before the public with proposals that were immediately vulnerable to charges of monopoly. It was preferable, they felt, to let the whole issue lie quiet, to rely upon unauthorized private controls, and to hope that these would be little disturbed by antitrust action. Only a few peculiarly depressed groups, like the cotton textile industry, continued to agitate for government-supported cartels, and most of these groups lacked the cohesion, power, and alternative symbols that would have been necessary to put their programs through.

In some areas, however, especially in areas where alternative symbols were present and where private controls had broken down or proven impractical, it was possible to secure a type of partial planning. Agriculture was able to avoid most of the agitation against monopoly, and while retaining to a large extent its individualistic operations, to find ways of using the state to fix prices, plan production, and regularize markets. Its ability to do so was attributable in part to the political power of the farmers, but it was also due to manipulation of certain symbols that effectively masked the monopolistic implications in the program. The ideal of the yeoman farmer—honest, independent, and morally upright—still had a strong appeal in America, and to many Americans it justified the salvation of farming as a "way of life," even at the cost of subsidies and the violation of competitive standards. Agriculture, moreover, was supposed to be the basic industry, the activity that supported all others. The country, so it was said, could not be prosperous unless its farmers were prosperous. Finally, there was the conservation argument, the great concern over conservation of the soil, which served to justify some degree of public planning and some type of production control.

Similar justifications were sometimes possible for other areas of the economy. Monopolistic arrangements in certain food-processing industries could be camouflaged as an essential part of the farm program. Departures from competitive standards in such natural resource industries as bituminous coal and crude oil production could be justified on the grounds of conservation. Public controls and economic cartelization in the fields of transportation and communication could be justified on the ground that these were "natural monopolies" in which the public had a vital interest. And in the distributive trades, it was possible to turn anti-big-business sentiment against the mass distributors, to brand them as "monopolies," and to obtain a series of essentially anti-competitive measures on the theory that they were designed to preserve competition by preserving small competitors. The small merchant, however, was never able to dodge the agitation against monopoly to the same extent that the farmer did. The supports granted him were weak to begin with, and to obtain them he had to make concessions to the competitive ideal, concessions that robbed his measures of much of their intended effectiveness.

In some ways, too, the Roosevelt Administration helped to create monopoly power for labor. Under the New Deal program, the government proceeded to absorb surplus labor and prescribe minimum labor standards; more important, it encouraged labor organization to the extent that it maintained a friendly attitude, required employer recognition of unions, and restrained certain practices that had been used to break unions in the past. For a time, the appeals to social justice, humanitarianism, and anti-big-business sentiment overrode the appeal of business spokesmen and classical economists to the competitive ideal and individualistic traditions. The doctrine that labor was not a commodity, that men who had worked and produced and kept their obligations to society were entitled to be taken care of, was widely accepted. Along with it went a growing belief that labor unions were necessary to maintain purchasing power and counterbalance big business. Consequently, even the New Dealers of an antitrust persuasion generally made a place in their program for social legislation and labor organization.

The general effect of this whole line of New Deal policy might be summed up in the word counterorganization, that is, the creation of monopoly power in areas previously unorganized. One can only conclude, however, that this did not happen according to any preconceived plan. Nor did it necessarily promote economic expansion or raise consumer purchasing power. Public support of monopolistic arrangements occurred in a piecemeal, haphazard fashion, in response to pressure from specific economic groups and as opportunities presented themselves. Since consumer organizations were weak and efforts to aid consumers made little progress, the benefits went primarily to producer groups interested in restricting production and raising prices. In the distributive trades, the efforts to help small merchants tended, insofar as they were successful, to impede technological changes, hamper mass distributors, and reduce consumer purchasing power. In the natural resource and transportation industries, most of the new legislation was designed to restrict production, reduce competition, and protect invested capital. And in the labor and agricultural fields, the strengthening of market controls was often at the expense of consumers and in conjunction with business groups. The whole tendency of interest-group planning, in fact, was toward the promotion of economic scarcity. Each group, it seemed, was trying to secure a larger piece from a pie that was steadily dwindling in size.

From an economic standpoint, then, the partial planning of the post-NRA type made little sense, and most economists, be they antitrusters, planners, or devotees of laissez-faire, felt that such an approach was doing more harm than good. It was understandable only in a political context, and as a political solution, it did possess obvious elements of strength. It retained the antitrust laws and avoided any direct attack upon the competitive ideal or competitive mythology. Yet by appealing to other goals and alternative ideals and by using these to justify special and presumably exceptional departures from competitive standards, it could make the necessary concessions to pressure groups interested in reducing competition and erecting government-sponsored cartels.[4] Such a program might be logically inconsistent and economically harmful. Perhaps, as one critic suggested at the time, it combined the worst features of both worlds, "an impairment of the efficiency of the competitive system without the compensating benefits of rationalized collective action."[5] But politi-

[4] See Paul T. Homan, in AEA, *Readings in the Social Control of Industry* (Philadelphia: Blakiston, 1942), 242–46, 252–54; and in *Political Science Quarterly*, June 1936, pp. 169–72, 178–84; Berle, in *Virginia Quarterly Review*, Summer 1938, pp. 330–31; Ernest Griffith, *Impasse of Democracy* (N.Y.: Harrison-Hilton, 1939), 231.

[5] Homan, in *Political Science Quarterly*, June 1936, p. 181.

cally it was a going concern, and efforts to achieve theoretical consistency met with little success.

Perhaps the greatest defect in these limited planning measures was their tendency toward restriction, their failure to provide any incentive for expansion when an expanding economy was the crying need of the time. The easiest way to counteract this tendency, it seemed, was through government expenditures and deficit financing; in practice, this was essentially the path that the New Deal took. By 1938 Roosevelt seemed willing to accept the Keynesian arguments for a permanent spending program, and eventually, when war demands necessitated pump-priming on a gigantic scale, the spending solution worked. It overcame the restrictive tendencies in the economy, restored full employment, and brought rapid economic expansion. Drastic institutional reform, it seemed, was unnecessary. Limited, piecemeal, pressure-group planning could continue, and the spending weapon could be relied upon to stimulate expansion and maintain economic balance.

IV

One major stream of New Deal policy, then, ran toward partial planning. Yet this stream was shaped and altered, at least in a negative sense, by its encounters with the anti-trust tradition and the competitive ideal. In a time when Americans distrusted business leadership and blamed big business for the prevailing economic misery, it was only natural that an antitrust approach should have wide political appeal. Concessions had to be made to it, and these concessions meant that planning had to be limited, piece-meal, and disguised. There could be no over-all program of centralized controls. There could be no government-sponsored business commonwealth. And there could be only a minimum of government participation in the planning process.

485

In and of itself, however, the antitrust approach did not offer a politically workable alternative. The antitrusters might set forth their own vision of the good society. They might blame the depression upon the departure from competitive standards and suggest measures to make industrial organization correspond more closely to the competitive model. But they could never ignore or explain away the deflationary and disruptive implications of their program. Nor could they enlist much support from the important political and economic pressure groups. Consequently, the antitrust approach, like that of planning, had to be applied on a limited basis. Action could be taken only in special or exceptional areas, against unusually privileged groups that were actively hated and particularly vulnerable, in fields where one business group was fighting another, in cases where no one would get hurt, or against practices that violated common standards of decency and fairness.

This was particularly true during the period prior to 1938. The power trust, for example, was a special demon in the progressive faith, one that was actively hated by large numbers of people and one that had not only violated competitive standards but had also outraged accepted canons of honesty and tampered with democratic political ideals. For such an institution, nothing was too bad, not even a little competition; and the resulting battle, limited though its gains might be, did provide a suitable outlet for popular antitrust feeling. Much the same was also true of the other antitrust activities. Financial reform provided another outlet for antitrust sentiment, although its practical results were little more than regulation for the promotion of honesty and facilitation of the governmental spending program. The attacks upon such practices as collusive bidding, basing-point pricing, and block-booking benefited from a long history of past agitation. And the suits in the petroleum and auto-finance industries had the support of discontented business groups. The result of such activities, however, could hardly be more than marginal. When the antitrusters reached for real weapons, when they tried, for example, to use the taxing power or make drastic changes in corporate law, they found that any thorough-going program was simply not within the realm of political possibilities.

Under the circumstances, it appeared, neither planning nor antitrust action could be applied in a thorough-going fashion. Neither approach could completely eclipse the other. Yet the political climate and situation did change; and, as a result of these changes, policy vacillated between the two extremes. One period might see more emphasis on planning, the next on antitrust action, and considerable changes might also take place in the nature, content, and scope of each program.

Superficially, the crisis of 1937 was much like that of 1933. Again there were new demands for antitrust action, and again these demands were blended with new proposals for planning, rationalization, and monopolistic controls. In some respects, too, the results were similar. There was more partial planning in unorganized areas, and eventually, this was accompanied by a resumption of large-scale federal spending. The big difference was in the greater emphasis on an antitrust approach, which could be attributed primarily to the difference in political circumstances. The alienation of the business community, memories of NRA experiences, and the growing influence of antimonopolists in the Roosevelt Administration made it difficult to work out any new scheme of business-government cooperation. These same factors, coupled with the direct appeal of New Dealers to the competitive ideal, made it difficult for business groups to secure public sanction for monopolistic arrangements. The political repercussions of the recession, the fact that the new setback had occurred while the New Deal was in power, made it necessary to appeal directly to anti-big-business sentiment and to use the administered price thesis to explain why the recession had occurred and why the New Deal had failed to achieve sustained recovery.

Under the circumstances, the initiative passed to the antitrusters, and larger concessions had to be made to their point of view.

One such concession was the creation of the Temporary National Economic Committee. Yet this was not so much a victory for the antitrusters as it was a way of avoiding the issue, a means of minimizing the policy conflict within the Administration and postponing any final decision. Essentially, the TNEC was a harmless device that could be used by each group to urge a specific line of action or no action at all. Antimonopolists hoped that it would generate the political sentiment necessary for a major breakthrough against concentrated economic power, but these hopes were never realized. In practice, the investigation became largely an ineffective duplicate of the frustrating debate that produced it, and by the time its report was filed, the circumstances had changed. Most of the steam had gone out of the monopoly issue, and antitrust sentiment was being replaced by war-induced patriotism.

The second major concession to antimonopoly sentiment was Thurman Arnold's revival of antitrust prosecutions, a program that presumably was designed to restore a competitive system, one in which prices were flexible and competition would provide the incentive for expansion. Actually, the underlying assumptions behind such a program were of doubtful validity. Price flexibility, even if attainable, might do more harm than good. The Arnold approach had definite limitations, even assuming that the underlying theories were sound. It could and did break up a number of loose combinations; it could and did disrupt monopolistic arrangements that were no necessary part of modern industrialism. It could and, in some cases, did succeed in convincing businessmen that they should adopt practices that corresponded a bit more closely to the competitive model. But it made no real effort to rearrange the underlying industrial structure itself, no real attempt to dislodge vested interests, disrupt controls that were actual checks against deflation, or break up going concerns. And since the practices and policies complained of would appear in many cases to be the outgrowth of this underlying structure, the Arnold program had little success in achieving its avowed goals.

Even within these limits, moreover, Arnold's antitrust campaign ran into all sorts of difficulties. Often the combinations that he sought to break up were the very ones that the earlier New Deal had fostered. Often, even though the arrangements involved bore little relation to actual production, their sponsors claimed that they did, that their disruption would set the process of deflation in motion again and impair industrial efficiency. Arnold claimed that his activities enjoyed great popular support, and as a symbol and generality they probably did. But when they moved against specific arrangements, it was a different story. There they succeeded in alienating one political pressure group after another. Then, with the coming of the war, opposition became stronger than ever. As antitrust sentiment was replaced by wartime patriotism, it seemed indeed that the disruption of private controls would reduce efficiency and impair the war effort. Consequently, the Arnold program gradually faded from the scene.

It is doubtful, then, that the innovations of 1938 should be regarded as a basic reversal in economic policy. What actually happened was not the substitution of one set of policies for another, but rather a shift in emphasis between two sets of policies that had existed side by side throughout the entire period. Policies that attacked monopoly and those that fostered it, policies that reflected the underlying dilemma of industrial America, had long been inextricably intertwined in American history, and this basic inconsistency persisted in an acute form during the nineteen thirties. Policy might and did vacillate between the two extremes; but because of the limitations of the American political structure and of American economic ideology, it was virtually impossible for one set of policies to displace the other. The New Deal reform movement was forced to adjust to this basic fact. The practical outcome was an economy characterized by private controls, partial planning, compensatory governmental spending, and occasional gestures toward the competitive ideal.

V

In conclusion one might ask whether the experiences of the New Dealers have any relevance for the problems of today, and for various reasons he might doubt that they do. After all, the setting has changed. The concern with business power, mass unemployment, and rigid prices has given way to concern over inflation, labor power, and the price-wage spiral. In the increasingly affluent society of the organization man, there is less criticism of big business, less agitation for government-supported cartels, and less awareness of the gap between economic reality and the competitive ideal. Some economists, in fact, argue that the gap has largely disappeared. They claim that the process of economic concentration has been reversed, that technological innovation has stimulated a "revival of competition," and that any realistic definition of workable competition should include a variety of behavior patterns that economists in the nineteen thirties would have regarded as monopolistic.[6] Others disagree about the prevalence of competition, but maintain that the concentrations of economic power involved in big business, big labor,

[6] See M. A. Adelman, in *Review of Economic Statistics*, Nov. 1951, pp. 293–96; Clair Wilcox and Shorey Peterson, in *AER*, May 1950, pp. 67–73; March 1957, pp. 60–78; Joseph A. Schumpeter, *Capitalism, Socialism, and Democracy*. (N.Y.: Harper, 1942), 81–86; A. D. H. Kaplan, *Big Enterprise in a Competitive System* (Washington: Brookings, 1954), 231–48; Sumner H. Slichter, *The American Economy* (N.Y.: Knopf, 1950), 13–19; John M. Clark, *Competition as a Dynamic Process* (Washington: Brookings, 1961), 2–18, 465–90; *Fortune*, June 1952, pp. 98–99, 186, 188, 190, 192, 194, 197.

big agriculture, and big government are not so bad after all. For example, they argue that the power is being used wisely, that one power concentrate tends to offset the other, or that excessive power can be checked by public opinion. Democracy, they seem to think, is still possible in an organizational system, and concentrated power can be used to liberate as well as oppress.[7]

The concern with monopoly as a major cause of economic depression has also faded from the scene. The majority of economists seem to doubt that there is much connection between concentration and rigid prices or that price flexibility, even if it could be attained, would insure full employment and sustained prosperity. In any event, they seem convinced that tampering with the price-wage structure is one of the most difficult and least desirable ways of controlling the business cycle. Consequently, most current discussions of countercyclical programs tend to revolve about the use of fiscal and monetary policies rather than central planning or antitrust action. The return of prosperity, however, has had less effect on the older indictment of monopoly. The fear of centralized economic power has not completely vanished. The older charges that monopoly is unfair, wasteful, uneconomic, and injurious to consumer welfare are still repeated. A number of economists, politicians, and scholars are still concerned about the gap between ideal and reality, about the continued growth of collectivization, planning, and administrative

[7] See John K. Galbraith, *American Capitalism* (Boston: Houghton Mifflin, 1952), 118–39; David E. Lilienthal, *Big Business* (N.Y.: Harper, 1952), 26–28, 47–57, 137–61, 198–201; Dexter M. Keezer, et al., *New Forces in American Business* (N.Y.: McGraw-Hill, 1959), 152–55; Oswald Knauth, *Managerial Enterprise* (N.Y.: Norton, 1948), 206–13; Adolf A. Berle, Jr., *The 20th Century Capitalist Revolution* (N.Y.: Harcourt, Brace, 1954), 43–60, 180–88; and in Thurman Arnold et al., *Future of Democratic Capitalism* (Philadelphia, 1950), 57–62; Bruce R. Morris, *Problems of American Economic Growth* (N.Y.: Oxford U. Press, 1961), 91–96, 154–55, 159–61, 223, 229–32, 246–49.

491

controls in a land that professes to believe in free markets and economic individualism.[8]

Those concerned with the problem, moreover, are still puzzled by the ambivalence of the attitudes involved and the inconsistency and irrationality of policies relating to competition and monopoly. The deep respect for efficiency, they point out, is counterbalanced by sympathy for the "little fellow" and concern about the political and economic power that giant successful enterprises can wield. The belief in free competition is offset by substantial support for tariff barriers, private controls, and limitations on the entry of new entrepreneurs in a number of industries and trades. The desire for competitive incentives is tempered by a strong drive for economic security, for protection against such hazards as unemployment, declining incomes, shrinking markets, and price wars. And the general tradition in favor of a free market economy is combined with an amazing array of exceptions, with a wide range of activities designed to insulate economic groups from the rigors of market rivalry. Current policy, it seems, like that of the New Deal era, is still a maze of conflicting crosscurrents, and so long as the intellectual heritage remains and conflicting goals persist, it seems doubtful that any set of simple, consistent policies can be drawn up and implemented.[9]

[8] See National Bureau of Economic Research, *Business Concentration and Price Policy* (Princeton: Princeton U. Press, 1955), 450–89; and *Policies to Combat Depression* (1956), 3–22, 60–74; Walter Adams and Horace Gray, *Monopoly in America.* (N.Y.: Macmillan, 1955), 1–24, 173–78; T. K. Quinn, *Giant Business* (N.Y.: Exposition, 1953), 9–12, 300–1, 310–13; Henry A. Wells, *Monopoly and Social Control* (Washington: Public Affairs Press, 1952), VII, 2–7, 101–14; Knauth, *Managerial Enterprise*, 23–24, 203–13; A. D. Neale, *The Antitrust Laws of the U.S.A.* (Cambridge: Cambridge U. Press, 1960), 419–24; Donald Dewey, *Monopoly in Economics and Law* (Chicago: Rand McNally, 1959), 70–81; George W. Stocking, *Workable Competition and Antitrust Policy* (Nashville: Vanderbilt U. Press, 1961), 2–17, 408–28; Ben W. Lewis, in *AER*, June 1949, pp. 703–9.

[9] See Mark S. Massel, *Competition and Monopoly* (Washington: Brookings, 1962), 16–20, 317–19.

In some respects, then, the problems with which current policy-makers must deal are comparable to those facing the New Dealers. If the experiences of the nineteen thirties have any relevance at all, it is in illustrating the limitations of logical analysis, the pitfalls inherent in broad theoretical approaches, the difficulty of agreeing upon policy goals, and the necessity of making due allowances for the intellectual heritage, current trends of opinion, and the realities of pressure-group politics. The margin within which innovations could be made was considerably broader during the nineteen thirties than at present; yet the New Dealers were never able to agree upon a clear-cut program or to impose any rational and consistent pattern. The planners discovered that centralized, over-all planning was not really feasible, that because of political, practical, legal, and ideological considerations, any attempt to apply such an approach quickly degenerated into a type of single-industry, pressure-group planning that brought few of the benefits presumably associated with rationalized collective action. The antitrusters, too, discovered that their approach had to be economized, that it could be applied only on a limited basis or in special areas and special cases. The attempts to combine the two approaches, to work out pragmatic tests and choose between regulation and antitrust action on a case-by-case, industry-by-industry basis, ended typically in the same clash of values that lay behind the original battle of principles.

It seems doubtful, moreover, that research, investigation, and logical analysis can ever resolve this clash of values. In any event, decades of debate, coupled with massive investigations like that conducted by the TNEC, have failed to produce any general consensus about the causes of business concentration and combination, their results and effects, and the proper methods of dealing with them. Barring a revolution or drastic changes in techniques, attitudes, values, and institutions, it seems likely that policy in this area will remain confused and contradictory, that programs designed to combat monopoly will still be intermingled with those designed to promote it.

This is not to say, of course, that research and analysis are useless. Within limits they can be of great aid to the policy-maker. They can help to define the issues, identify points of pressure, and clarify national objectives. They can evaluate existing programs in terms of these goals and provide evidence as to the nature, feasibility, and relative effectiveness of the various methods whereby they might be attained. And they can acquaint the policy-maker with the range of alternatives at his disposal and the probable consequences of choosing any one of them.[10] This study, it is hoped, will contribute something in all of these areas, and further inquiries into particular periods, problems, or developments can contribute a good deal more. Yet such studies are unlikely to resolve the underlying policy dilemma. They are unlikely to come up with any line of policy that will be acceptable to all and that will really reconcile the conflicting goals, attitudes, and values that Americans have inherited from the past.

Consequently, the conflict in American ideology and American economic policy seems likely to continue. The gap between ideal and reality, particularly if the economy should falter, will continue to generate demands for economic reorganization and reform. Yet the possibilities for planning and rationalization will still be limited by the popular belief in free markets, and those for antitrust action by the realities of large-scale economies, vested interests, and pressure-group politics. The relative strength of the conflicting forces and ideologies may change, and new debates concerning the location, use, and control of power may develop; but so long as the competitive ideal and democratic heritage continue to mean anything, the dilemma itself seems likely to persist. And the problem of monopoly, in its broadest aspects, will remain unsolved.

[10] *Ibid.*, 40–41, 83–84, 108–22, 325–27, 337–39.

INDEX

495

Perkins, George, 8, 11

Perkins, Frances, Secretary of Labor, and the thirty-hour week, 22; and the NRA, 25, 28; and consumer councils, 76; on small business, 83; heads Cabinet Committee on Prices, 95; and Hugh Johnson

Petroleum Administration, 73, 214, 374

Petroleum Administrative Board, 214–15

petroleum industry, see oil industry

"pineboards," advent of, 248

Pittsburgh-plus system, 361

Plan Age, 171

planning, see economic planning

plumbing fixtures industry, 115, 442

Podell, David, 24, 41–42

Polakov, Walter, 170–71

Policy Board (NRA), 65–66, 98

Policy Group (NRA), 98–99, 99n, 100n

Powell, Reed, 446

power industry, see electrical power industry

power policy, trends in, 341–42; nature and implications of, 341–43

power pooling, idea of, 338, 338n; conference on, 338; and the Morgan-Lilienthal feud, 339

Power Trust, agitation against, 16, 324, 326–28, 330–31, 333, 486; and the antitrusters, 324–43; rise of, 325–26; abuses of, 326–27, 330; investigation of, 326–27, 327n; reforms affecting, 328–29, 335–36; and the TVA, 328, 337–338; lobbying of, 332, 334–35; humbled, 341; compared to Money Power, 342–43

premiums, control of under NRA, 60, 63, 99n, 100n, 103, 108

President's Reemployment Agreement, 53–55

price-filing plans, see open-price systems

Price Hearing of 1934, 79–81, 85

Price Hearing of 1935, 111

price fixing, and the Borah Amendment, 30–31; business support for, 30, 40–41, 58, 93, 109–111; under NRA codes, 57–59, 58n, 72–73, 75–76, 80–82, 87–88, 92–94, 96, 109, 111, 114–17, 137–38, 206, 213–14, 213n, 214n, 255; NRA policy on, 63–64, 85–88, 94–96, 99–101, 103, 108–113, 137; and the debate over NRA extension, 123, 126; post-NRA schemes of, 149–50, 164–65, 180, 181n, 183; and the FTC, 161; through private arrangements, 166–68, 400n, 435; in agriculture, 191–94, 273; and labor, 198; in "sick" industries and trades, 206–211, 213–14, 213n, 214n, 218–19, 233–35, 238–39, 242, 244, 254–60, 263–64, 273–75; and the recession of 1937, 387–88, 390, 391–93, 395, 409, 411–12; and the courts, 451. *See also* administered price thesis, price policy, and cartelization

price policy, under NRA, 63–64, 85–88, 94–96, 99–101, 103, 108–113, 137; subsequent concern with, 177, 383–84, 399–400; and the goal of price flexibility, 453. *See also* price fixing and administered price thesis

printing industry, 80

production controls, and the NRA, 60–61, 64, 72–73, 75–